THE REALITIES BEHIND DIPLOMACY

PAUL KENNEDY is J. Richardson Dilworth Professor and Director of International Security Studies at Yale University. He is also Co-Director, with Bruce Russett, of the Secretariat to the Independent Working Group on the Future of the United Nations, an international commission which is producing a report for the Secretary-General entitled, 'The United Nations in its Second Half-Century'. He also coordinates the Olin Foundation Fellowship Program in Military and Strategic History, the Bradley Foundation annual lecture series and conferences on military and diplomatic history, the Bradley Foundation Scholarships in Diplomatic and International History and the Smith Richardson Foundation Program on the *Historical Roots of Contemporary International and Regional Issues*. With Professor Bruce Russett he co-chairs the MacArthur Foundation Program on *Peace and International Cooperation*. In addition to teaching an undergraduate course (*Global Security Issues, Old and New*) and, with Bruce Russett, a graduate course (*International Security Studies: Historical and Political Science Approaches*) on the history of international security, he has begun to research a new book on the history of the United Nations. He continues to deliver numerous lectures worldwide, including a presentation to the Bruno Kreisky Forum in Vienna, and has received several honorary degrees in the past year. He is on the advisory boards of numerous journals and institutions.

Paul Kennedy's other books include *The Rise and Fall of British Naval Mastery* (1976; 2nd edn, Fontana Press, 1992), *The Rise of Anglo-German Antagonism 1860–1914* (1980), *Strategy and Diplomacy 1870–1945* (Fontana Press, 1984), *The Rise and Fall of the Great Powers* (Fontana Press, 1989) and *Preparing for the Twenty-First Century* (Fontana Press, 1994).

Paul Kennedy

The Realities Behind Diplomacy:

Background Influences on British External Policy, 1865–1980

FontanaPress
An Imprint of HarperCollins*Publishers*

Fontana Press
An Imprint of HarperCollins*Publishers*
77–85 Fulham Palace Road,
Hammersmith, London W6 8JB

Published by Fontana Press 1985
9 8 7 6

First published by
Fontana 1981

Set in Lasercomp Times

Printed in Great Britain by
HarperCollinsManufacturing Glasgow

To Matthew –
who distracted
and delighted

Contents

Foreword

Since this book is intended as an experiment, I should make clear at the outset what it is (and is *not*) supposed to be. Its chief purpose is to provide a brief analysis of the various forces which have influenced the external policy of Great Britain over the past century. It is not intended, therefore, as a rival to those standard narrative works upon British foreign policy by Bourne, Lowe and Dockrill, Hayes, and Medlicott;* if anything, it should be viewed as complementary to them, analysing the background influences to which they make reference but, understandably in a chronological treatment, have little space to dwell upon. This present work assumes a certain familiarity with the chief events and personalities in British and international affairs since the death of Palmerston. It does not, for example, provide details of the various clauses of the Locarno Treaty or give a day-by-day account of the Suez crisis, since such facts are described elsewhere; but it *does* try to suggest what the Locarno Treaty meant, and what the implications of Suez were.

A book upon 'background influences' could in theory be purely thematic and analytical, dispensing with a chronolo-

* K. Bourne, *The Foreign Policy of Victorian England 1830–1902* (Oxford, 1970); C. J. Lowe, *The Reluctant Imperialists: British Foreign Policy 1878–1902*, 2 vols. (London, 1967); C. J. Lowe and M. L. Dockrill, *The Mirage of Power: British Foreign Policy 1902–1922*, 3 vols. (London, 1972); P. Hayes, *The Twentieth Century 1880–1939* (Modern British Foreign Policy: London,1978); W. N. Medlicott, *British Foreign Policy since Versailles 1919–1963* (London, 1968).

gical format altogether. Although at first tempted to adopt
such a structure, I concluded that it might not be so suitable
in a work intended for an audience of undergraduate and
graduate students, and general readers and fellow-
academics who wish to familiarize themselves with the
results of the vast outpouring of new books and articles upon
British external policy. In any case, some of the 'background
influences' which existed at the beginning of this story
disappeared during the course of it, and newer pressures and
forces came upon the scene. For these reasons, I have divided
the book into four main chronological sections, each
containing a basically thematic chapter ('Structures and
Attitudes'), linked with another chapter which narrates the
chief alterations in external policy ('Debates and Policies').
Of course, it is impossible to provide a complete separation
between the *analytical* and the *chronological* in any history
book, and a certain amount of overlap exists in what follows
here. Since the present structure is simply a device, an
experiment, to cater for the book's various purposes, I would
be interested to learn from readers whether they believe it has
succeeded.

Like any attempted synthesis, the present work represents
a pillaging of the researches and ideas of a large number of
historians of Britain's recent past. I have attempted to keep
notes to a minimum, providing them only for a direct
quotation or a set of statistics, or to support a comment
which may be controversial or at least not the accepted
wisdom. Because this is not a scholarly monograph, I have
also resisted the temptation to offer detailed references to the
many writings of recent German historians, whose analyses
of the 'background influences' on British external policy are
among the most thought-provoking of all. But I hope that
German scholars such as Wolf Gruner, Klaus Hildebrand,
Gunther Hollenberg, Reinhard Meyers, Gottfried Niedhart,
Gustav Schmidt, Rainer Tamchina and Bernd-Jürgen
Wendt will take some satisfaction at seeing how much this
work has benefited from their investigations.

In a book of compressed analysis and narrative, I have often fallen back upon such terms of historical shorthand as 'London', 'Whitehall', 'Washington' and so on; they are, of course, to be understood as meaning 'the leading decision-makers in the government (in London)', and not to imply that those places were either individuals or monolithic structures.

Some early work for this book was done during my pleasant year at the Institute for Advanced Study, Princeton, but the greater part was written after returning to my home University of East Anglia; both institutions, and especially their libraries, gave valuable assistance. I am also grateful to Bob Woodings and Helen Fraser, successive editors at Fontana, for encouraging me in this venture; and to my agent, Bruce Hunter, for his advice and support. Mrs Vera Durrell and Mrs Ann Cook typed the manuscript with efficiency and speed. Seven people were good enough to be drawn away from their own work to read and comment upon the first draft: Michael Balfour, Eric Homberger, James Jones, Geoffrey Searle, Iain Smith, Zara Steiner and my wife Cath. They eliminated most of my mixed metaphors and other infelicities of style, and improved my argument with many additional points; but I alone am responsible for the final version.

The book is dedicated to my youngest son, who still wonders what his father does in his study and who tries so often to tempt him from it.

PAUL M. KENNEDY
Norwich, March 1980

I
The Diplomacy of Imperialism, 1865–1914

1. Structures and Attitudes

The Setting

In the mid-nineteenth century, a small group of islands lying off the north-west coast of Europe constituted the leading nation in world affairs. Just why and how it had become so is not the subject of this book, although some brief explanations will be provided below. But that it was so *is* of vital importance to the present study, for Britain's unique position and the British people's consciousness of their country's global leadership conditioned the formulation of external policy. Those who took an active part in that policy did not operate, as did their contemporaries in Sweden or Argentina, at a relatively local level: they acted as the establishment of a country which controlled around one-fifth of the world's land surface and had interests in much of the remainder, which was the leading maritime nation and which was, in industrial and commercial terms, in a class of its own. Because it occupied such a major role in world politics, and continued to loom large during the greater part of the period covered in this book, what it did – or did not do – was clearly important. By the same token, why it pursued certain policies and not others is also important. The following is an exploration of the whys, with intermittent attention paid to what was done and how it was done.

The reason for the pre-eminence of the British Isles – and not, say, Japan or Jamaica or Formosa – in world affairs around 1865 was largely a result of geopolitics, technology and social structure. The 'rise of the West' in general had been the consequence of economic change, shifting trade patterns, a ferment of new ideas, the creation of certain well-organized nation states, and a remarkable series of breakthroughs in the construction of the gunned, long-range sailing ship which had given European adventurers the power to reach out and dominate overseas peoples. Once the benefits of gaining control of precious metals, spices and other goods had become widely appreciated, merchants, landowners and monarchs themselves began to move in; and, when this struggle for economic advantage brought with it the existing rivalries between the courts and the religions of Europe, the role of the state in the quest for empire became ever more prominent. Because such endemic conflicts possessed both a European and a non-European aspect, countries with land frontiers such as Spain, France and even the Netherlands were only able to concentrate a portion of their resources and attention upon the wider world: England, by contrast, was not only well placed to take advantage of the changing pattern of international trade but was protected by its insularity from the danger of overland attack. A powerful fleet, provided one existed, could be simultaneously a guarantee against invasion *and* an instrument for the domination of the shipping lanes.[1] Being thus immune from invasion from an early date, the English had been able to establish a (relatively) ordered society with a predictable legal system enforced from a strong centre into the localities. This in turn offered a framework for the rise of the middle classes, for it made sense to trade, to save and to invest; in other words, the accumulated wealth of the past was preserved, not pillaged. Political stability and security were the foundations of economic enterprise, surplus capital, the credit and banking system, and many of those other attributes which have been identified as prerequisites for commercial and industrial growth.

It is the political and social structure of early modern England which also explains the decision of its élites to support overseas expansion. The country suffered from a few of the geographical and domestic handicaps which restrained their putative rivals for world power. The cultural reservations which held back the Chinese Empire just as it was poised to develop its early ventures across the oceans[2] did not exist in the British Isles. Nor did that social disdain for 'mere trade' which characterized most of the politically dominant French nobility affect their English equivalents. Instead, aristocrats and gentry joined with city merchants in financing overseas trading companies and in ensuring that the government provided the necessary martial support to keep foreign rivals at bay. In this respect the English Revolution was of key importance, for, whatever its origins, it brought to prominence social forces eager to boost the nation's foreign trade and naval might – a yearning which was not subdued after the return of the monarchy. The Glorious Revolution of 1688 not only seemed to produce a British synthesis of Dutch commercial flair with the French respect for national power, but it also led to a political settlement which was soon exhibiting 'adamantine strength'. Civil war was a thing of the past, and there existed 'a sense of common identity in those who wielded economic, social and political power', especially over the necessity of preserving and enhancing Britain's place in the world.[3] Both in the mercantilist theory and in the practice of successive British governments, the economic arm and the fighting arm of the country were now mutually supporting organs of a grand strategy predicated upon commercial expansion, colonial exploitation, domestic stability and insular security.

Although the very term 'grand strategy' suggests a continuity and coherence in external policy which in fact many British statesmen did not live up to, the overall pattern of the nation's rise to world power during the eighteenth century is impressive. In the seven great conflicts which took place between 1689 and 1815, the French, Dutch and Spaniards saw their economies weakened, their colonial empires reduced and their naval power eradicated, whereas the British – apart from the exceptional circumstances of

1776–83 – went from strength to strength. 'The result of this century of intermittent warfare was the greatest victory ever achieved by any state: the virtual monopoly among European powers of overseas colonies, and the virtual monopoly of world-wide naval power.'[4] The whole movement was one of alternating cause and effect. The navy's decisive victories gave its merchants the lion's share in maritime trade, which itself helped to stimulate the Industrial Revolution; yet this in turn was to sustain the country's continuing growth, making it into a new sort of state – the only real world power. Industrialization not only furthered the British ascendancy in commerce and finance and shipping, but also underpinned its naval supremacy with a previously unheard-of economic potential.

Economic Pre-eminence, and Decline

Between 1815 and 1865 British predominance in the fields of industry and commerce was further enhanced. In mid-century, the country produced about two-thirds of the world's coal, about half its iron, five-sevenths of its steel, two-fifths of its hardware and about half its commercial cotton cloth. Indeed, by that stage 'over 40 per cent of the entire world output of traded manufactured goods [was] produced within the country'. Moreover, 36 per cent of the total exports of all other countries went to Britain in the 1840s, making it by far the largest market for raw materials the world had ever known.[5] In consequence, foreign trade, or, better, transoceanic trade, largely centred around the 'first industrial nation', over 92 per cent of the imports of which (measured by volume) consisted of raw materials and foodstuffs in 1854–7, while 85 per cent of its visible exports were finished goods. 'The several quarters of the globe [are] our willing tributaries,' exulted the economist W. S. Jevons in 1865, as he detailed the way his country had brought various overseas regions into a global system of commercial exchange.[6]

By that date, however, Britain had probably reached its true zenith as a world power and may be imagined like some ball or shell at the height of its trajectory before it begins its slow, steady descent. This new development – the relative decline of Great Britain as an economic power – is perhaps the most critical conditioning element in the formulation of the country's external policy over the past hundred years, and it will be a major aspect of this present study. It did not, admittedly, determine all decisions all the time. Nonetheless, every British government, whether Conservative, Liberal or, later, Labour, undoubtedly was affected by this factor in the implementation of its diplomacy.

In the final three or four decades of the nineteenth century, Britain's position as an industrial power of the first order declined rapidly as other nations overtook it in various fields of manufacturing and technology. Established British industries such as coal, textiles and ironware increased their output in absolute terms, but their relative share of world production steadily diminished; and in the newer and increasingly more important industries such as steel, chemicals, machine-tools and electrical goods, Britain soon lost what early lead it possessed. Industrial production, which had been growing at an annual rate of about 4 per cent in the period 1820 to 1840 and about 3 per cent between 1840 and 1870, became more sluggish; between 1875 and 1894 it grew at just over $1\frac{1}{2}$ per cent annually, far less than that of the country's chief rivals. This loss of industrial supremacy was soon felt in the cut-throat competition for customers. British exports were forced, first of all, out of their favourable position in European and North American markets, while those countries themselves industrialized, often behind high tariff barriers; then out of certain colonial markets, where other powers competed both commercially and, in further imitation of British habits, by establishing their own colonies and placing tariffs around them; and, finally, British industry found itself weakened by an ever-rising flood of imported foreign manufactures into the unprotected home market. The latter fact was the clearest sign of all that its industry was becoming inefficient and uncompetitive, for it could not be explained away by reference to unfair foreign protectionism.

The slowing-down of British productivity and decrease in competitiveness in the later nineteenth century has been one of the most hotly debated issues in economic history.[7] It involves such complex matters as national character, generational differences, the social ethos and the educational structure as well as more specific economic reasons like low investment, out-of-date plant, bad labour relations, poor salesmanship and the rest. Quite apart from disagreement about which one, if any, of these causes is the most important, there has also been a lengthy dispute between the 'pessimists' who focus attention upon the failures of British industry, and the 'optimists' who point to certain brighter aspects such as new industries and areas of growth. Little of this need concern the student of external policy, for he must pay attention to the *relative* picture; and even if one accepted the 'optimists'' viewpoint that some sectors of the economy were doing well, the blunt fact remains that the country as a whole was steadily losing ground. Whereas in 1870 the United Kingdom still contained 32 per cent of the world's manufacturing capacity, this was down to 15 per cent by 1910; and while its share of world trade was 25 per cent in 1870, by 1913 this had shrunk to 14 per cent. Given the close connection between industrial wealth and military-political power, these were ominous trends.

In a certain sense this decline had always been probable, for the country's economic rise and then its post-1815 period of ascendancy had rested upon a unique concatenation of very favourable circumstances. It was not to be expected that other countries would remain permanently retarded by the deleterious effects of those eighteenth-century wars, or would be constantly weakened by internal conflicts. It was still less to be expected that Britain would remain eternally the only or even the greatest industrialized nation; when others, with larger populations and more resources, took the same path, a relative decline was inevitable. As Professor Mathias has put it, 'When half a continent starts to develop, then it can produce more than a small island.'[8] In some ways Britain itself made decisive contributions to this process, both by building railways in foreign countries which would enable their industrial and agricultural products to be transported and thus to rival its own, and by establishing and developing those foreign industries with repeated financial injections while tending to invest proportionately less in British industry. Thus, the Industrial Revolution itself was not of unqualified advantage to Britain when measured in the long term. While the arrival of steam power, of the factory system, railways, and later electricity, enabled the British to overcome natural, physical obstacles to higher productivity, and therefore increased the country's wealth and strength, such inventions were soon to help the United States, Germany and Russia even more, because the natural, physical obstacles to the development of *their* landlocked potentials were much greater. What industrialization did was to equalize countries' chances to exploit their indigenous resources and, over time, to take away some of the advantages hitherto enjoyed by small, peripheral, maritime-cum-commercial states such as Britain and the Netherlands, giving them instead to the great land-based powers.

Perhaps this can all be put another way. Given that, to a very large degree, the early British industrial lead was a happy accident, conditioned by geography and certain broad economic and technological trends rather than by native virtues, the only possible way in which this lead could have been preserved against nations with superior populations and resources was by keeping ahead technically – as Britain still does, even today, against India, China and Indonesia. But this technical advantage could only be preserved by constant research and training, which the country's educational structure did not provide. It would also have needed a high rate of replacing obsolescent plant; yet in fact the proportion of Gross National Product invested *inside* Britain fell behind that of its competitors. With these possibilities closed, the long-term eclipse was inevitable. From about the time of Palmerston's death (1865), Britain – and the extensive colonial and commercial network it sustained – came under ever-increasing pressure at various levels in consequence of the swifter growth of American, German, Russian and, later, Japanese power.

If this is the basic long-term trend, it is important to emphasize that the loss of primacy did not immediately affect all sectors of the British economy. The shipbuilding industry, for example, benefited from the steady expansion of global commerce, as did shipping itself. So, too, did the various services of the City of London, which were, literally, 'cosmopolitan' in their activities since they aspired to be bankers, insurers, investors and commodity-dealers to the whole world. The growth in the economies and trade of other countries in the second half of the nineteenth century meant even more business for the City, and the massive rise in earnings from such 'invisible' services more than compensated for the otherwise alarming increase in the balance-of-payment deficit on 'visible' trade. To put it crudely, while many British industries were suffering from greater foreign competition, the City of London was in its heyday in the decades before 1914, funding and arranging and insuring and shipping – and thus profiting from the growth in – the trade of *foreign* countries. Not surprisingly, this important sector of the economy could not share in the alarmism shown elsewhere in the country, and strongly opposed all efforts to reintroduce protective tariffs and other tools of the enclosed and combative world of mercantilism.

Quite apart from such vested interests which were *not* suffering decline, it would be wrong to suggest that economic crisis was at hand almost before the 1860s were over: it is only with the benefit of hindsight that one can point to the mid-century decades as the zenith of Britain's relative position in the world economy. Very few statesmen shared the apprehensions of the *Annual Register,* which in 1867 precisely warned that if the British neglected 'the arena of industry and commerce' then the country would be lost, 'not perhaps to the extent of being conquered and reduced to a province, but undoubtedly to the extent of having to give up the lead, and ceasing to be a first-rate power.'[9] Even the coming of the so-called Great Depression in the 1870s did not shake the ingrained attitudes of the political nation. All Liberals and most Conservatives clung to the belief that free trade was best; and, even if more calculating Tories like Lord Randolph Churchill watched the 'Fair Trade' agitation with interest, he soon concluded that protectionism was an electoral loser. Too many sectors of the economy were wedded to a global market, and foreign countries which returned to high tariffs were generally regarded by politicians and newspaper editors as flying in the face of nature's laws. Only in the years around the turn of the century, when the evidence of Britain's decline was much more visible, did the alarmist calls return. Even then, this was always a *sectoral* agitation (e.g. by parts of the iron and steel industry), resisted by other sectors; and the campaign for protection and other forms of state assistance was often muted by an uplift in the trade cycle. Finally, it is always to be remembered that the political decision-makers and their senior advisers in Whitehall did not usually concern themselves in any intimate way with economic trends, frequently manifesting an aristocratic scorn for businessmen.

Nevertheless, if all this delayed a proper recognition of the extent and seriousness of Britain's growing loss of industrial leadership, there gradually emerged an uneasiness, in business circles and among Conservative politicians and intellectuals, that the older *laissez-faire* recipes were no longer proving so efficacious. Such anxiety did not always derive from concern about the competitiveness of British industry *per se*; indeed, in most cases it was triggered off by feelings of shock and dismay at political challenges, such as the acquisition of colonies by other powers, or the heightened pace of warship-building by foreign rivals. These threats reinforced the concern felt about Britain's future in global affairs and, as some commentators argued, could not be divorced from the economic trends. The fact was, as the famous editor of the *Observer*, J. L. Garvin, pointed out, that power was relative, and that such power ultimately depended upon a nation's resources and industrial efficiency. If, therefore, the period 1870–1910 saw a twofold British superiority over Germany in annual steel output gradually change to a situation where the Germans produced more than twice as much as the British, then it was not surprising that Britain should come under pressure from Germany in the field of power-politics as well. Older-fashioned Liberals might scorn this line of reasoning and argue that the nation's wealth was steadily increasing in absolute terms; but, as time went on, there were more and more Britons who wondered with Garvin, 'Will the Empire which is celebrating one centenary of Trafalgar survive for the next?'[10]

The diplomatic implications of Britain's changing economic position throughout the nineteenth century were well understood by most of its statesmen. In becoming the centre of a global exchange system based upon free trade, it had willingly abandoned its previously successful mercantilist habits – in the calculation, to be sure, that while other nations would have to follow suit the country with a head-start had most to gain from the ending of tariffs and trade monopolies. And even if other countries did not share the conviction of Richard Cobden, the leader of radical Liberalism, that free trade was 'the great panacea', they did for a while reduce their tariffs. Yet while this produced enormous economic benefits, it also meant that Britain, more than any other country, was a 'hostage' to the international commercial boom. Any disruption of trade caused by political uncertainties or, worse still, by war, affected its economy more than those of its protectionist neighbours. Arms races, too, were frowned upon, not only because they might lead to conflict but because they diverted resources from what Liberal economists termed 'productive' to 'unproductive' ends. Obviously, a small-scale colonial war was less worrying in this respect, because it did not derange the peacetime market economy; but if it did escalate, like the second Boer War (which eventually cost ten times the sum originally foreseen), then the government was bitterly attacked for the deleterious consequences. This attitude did not alter even when Britain was being overtaken by the United States and Germany industrially, for if anything its growing preponderance in 'invisible' trade tied the British economy even more firmly to international peace and prosperity. The alarm of the City at the Venezuela crisis of 1895, and at the prospect of an Anglo-German war after 1905, offered ample testimony of this concern.

This was not, moreover, a stance adopted by Liberals and bankers alone. In 1864 Disraeli had insisted that his party was 'interested in the tranquillity and prosperity of the world, the normal condition of which is peace'; four decades later, another Conservative Prime Minister, Balfour, could assure the King that 'the interest of this country is now and always – Peace'.[11] Quite apart from any altruistic horror at the slaughter which a great-power conflict would bring, such expressions were motivated by an awareness of the decline of trade, ruination of credit and material losses which would accompany war, and of the possible civil unrest which might follow. This did *not* mean that British governments would choose peace at any price but – unlike the militaristic élites of certain other countries – they did know that war was bad for business and that the essence of diplomacy was to secure British interests without recourse to a large-scale conflict.

Imperial Pressures and Imperial Sentiment

The spread of industrialization was the most important influence upon international politics in the second half of the nineteenth century simply because it altered the global balance in so many ways. Nations long dormant, though potentially powerful because of their populations and resources, had been galvanized by the impact of technology and industrial organization, and those revolutions were to have important strategical consequences. In the western hemisphere the United States assumed a more and more dominating position, its economic activities and political influence permeating the Caribbean and Latin America, and its traders beginning to challenge Britain's commercial monopoly. Slightly later, Japan began to pull ahead of its neighbours in the Far East and to extend its control there. The newly united German Empire, boosted by an amazingly swift industrial growth, was steadily changing the old balance of power in Europe. Finally, industrialization was not only enabling Russia to take the first real steps to develop its immense resources, but strategic railway construction was giving it a means of applying direct military pressure upon China and India. All these changes implied at least some diminution of Britain's influence on the areas concerned.

The same was true in consequence of the scramble for colonies which occurred in the final quarter of the nineteenth century. Previously, the British had had to contend with spasmodic challenges from the French. Now, a world-wide demand for fresh markets and sources of raw materials, a rise in nationalism and changes in the balance of power, a 'yellow press' catering for the first time to a mass readership, internal challenges to the political *status quo*, the spread of Darwinistic notions – perhaps all consequences or associates of the Industrial Revolution – had helped to push many more powers into a frantic search for overseas possessions. The result was that Britain's comfortable and extensive 'informal influence' in Africa and Asia, which had given the mid-Victorians the benefits of empire without its burdens, virtually disappeared: either it had to be made formal or it would be annexed by others. The whole experience was an unpleasant one for most British statesmen. Although both Whig and Tory ministers ensured that London took a larger share of colonial real-estate than anyone else – given Britain's head-start, this was hardly surprising – once again the real position was one of relative decline. Informal control of most of the tropics was exchanged for formal control of one quarter of it. Many a continental cartoonist of this time enjoyed portraying a breathless and bewildered John Bull, burdened by the fruits of his earlier colonial greed, being now outdistanced by nimbler rivals.

This loss of a near-monopoly in overseas and imperial affairs affected the British in various ways. Strategists were alarmed at the acquisition by foreign powers of territories next to their own or of bases along the world's shipping routes, for example, Bizerta, Dakar, Diego Suarez, Manila and Hawaii. Protestant missionary societies felt unable to turn the other cheek when their operations were terminated in Madagascar and the Pacific, and threatened in Nyasaland and Uganda. Most important of all, probably, was the concern expressed by business circles, for the foreign annexation of colonies brought with it in many cases the imposition of metropolitan tariffs. How could British traders continue to operate in West Africa, it was asked, if their goods were to be discriminated against by the French; or in Manchuria if it was ever enclosed by the colossal Russian tariff? Moreover, these threats were occurring just after many British industrialists, having suffered in European and American markets from the return of protectionism, had concluded that they must find new outlets in the tropics. Not surprisingly, therefore, British chambers of commerce by the 1880s and 1890s were to be found demanding ever more governmental support to preserve overseas markets – in contrast to their casual and *laissez-faire* attitude in earlier decades.[12]

Mingled with this defensiveness and unease, however, was an increasing display of imperial pride and bravado. Much of the latter was no doubt a nervous reaction, concealed in patriotic assertiveness. On the other hand, if rival powers were so keen to emulate Britain's Empire, this must indicate how prized a possession that must be. This indeed was the message articulated by a number of political commentators and intellectuals such as Froude, Ruskin, Dilke and Seeley, who detected a potential 'Greater Britain' lurking beneath the structure of the ramshackle and often neglected Empire. Seeley, whose book *The Expansion of England* (1884) was probably the most influential of all these tracts, pointed to the immense changes which 'steam and electricity' were bringing to the United States and Russia, against whose consolidated resources the British would be unable to compete unless they drew upon the white settlers living in the self-governing colonies. Extrapolating from economic and population trends, these writers (and the politicians who joined them to campaign for 'imperial federation') argued on the one hand that the days of the traditional European powers were drawing to a close; and on the other, that Britain could escape their fate by merging with Canada, Australia, New Zealand (and later, the Union of South Africa) into a trans-global but organic power unit. If this was seen, especially in its Chamberlainite form, as a positive and creative policy, it was still obviously underlaid by that world-political *Angst* which Kipling's turn-of-the-century poems captured so well. One later authority, in fact, has suggested that the attention paid by the British to their Empire from 1870 to 1970 was essentially an attempt to stave off that decline to which all the indices of world power pointed.[13]

Whatever its long-term meaning, this attention certainly

implied a newer warmth of reference to the colonies than in the days when they were regarded, if not completely as 'millstones', then as considerable burdens upon the British taxpayer. Instead of the *laissez-faire* belief that the self-governing colonies would drop away like ripe fruit from the tree, there was now talk of integration, of tighter ties, of closer co-operation. All this, it may be noted, flew in the face of another trend which was working to Britain's disadvantage: the growing nationalism, and pride in the freedom achieved, of the colonists themselves. Few, if any, colonial statesmen wanted to be merged into an Imperial Cabinet; and even fewer of their constituents wished to lose their fiscal autonomy, or to shoulder a heavy tax burden for imperial defence. Even the rhetoric and symbolism of unity was a touchy issue for Canadian leaders, who had to contend with the deep suspicions of their French-speaking countrymen. Nevertheless, the self-governing colonies were not totally impervious to the imperial idea, perceiving certain points in its favour: that they might obtain improved naval and military protection in an increasingly dangerous world, that they might better influence Whitehall's diplomacy towards those powers now establishing colonies on Australasian doorsteps, that they might even gain some form of preference for the goods they despatched to the home market. From 1887 onwards, therefore, the metropolitan authority and its self-governing dependencies (soon to be termed Dominions) engaged in a series of Colonial and Imperial conferences in order to explore means of improving consultation, decision-making, defence and trade.

While the results of such endeavours in the years before 1914 were mixed – some advances, some disappointments for the federationists – two general consequences were detectable. One was the heightened awareness of the Empire in the British public mind, and especially of its potential benefits to the homeland, a consideration perhaps best seen in the eulogistic commentaries upon the presence of colonial troops at the 1887 and 1897 Jubilee celebrations, and in the fond Boer War illustrations of the British lion surrounded by its breed of healthy young cubs. The second was rather more unsettling, at least to the traditionalists: namely, the growing regard which the British government now had to pay to Dominion sentiment, something which had scarcely existed in Palmerston's day. Rosebery no doubt exaggerated when he claimed: 'Our foreign policy has become a colonial policy, and it is in reality dictated much more from the extremities of the Empire than from London itself.'[14] Nevertheless, the federationists in Britain accepted that there could be no collective imperial policy without consultation, and even those politicians and officials who were less imbued with the new doctrines recognized that certain aspects of their external policy now required prior soundings with the 'sub-imperialists' of Wellington, Sydney, Ottawa, Cape Town and Simla. Although foreign statesmen such as Bismarck refused to regard, say, Queensland as an independent entity when colonial disputes arose in the Pacific, Whitehall could not afford to be so dismissive.

Defence Problems and Armaments Expenditure

The most remarkable feature of the post-1815 *Pax-Britannica* was its cheapness. Apart from several short-lived 'scare' periods, the naval budget during the early and middle parts of Victoria's reign averaged around £7 million to £8 million *per annum* – a reasonable insurance policy for a position of unmatched global pre-eminence. The army tended to be rather more expensive (in 1870 it cost £13.4 million as opposed to £9.8 million for the navy), but even in that year the total defence budget worked out at 14s. 9d. per head of the British population.[15] This successful imperialism and world influence on the cheap was due, of course, to the fact that outside Europe Britain largely operated in a power-political vacuum: after all, what other nation wished to rival London's influence along the Argentine or East African coastline in the 1850s? Only in Europe itself, where armies were the ultimate arbiters of international disputes, was British power limited; but since Foreign Secretaries such as Canning and Palmerston had no desire to intervene militarily on the continent and possessed the gift of knowing where their fleets might be exploited and where not, such limitations upon British influence were usually cloaked. When they were exposed, as in the Crimean War or in the mistaken attempt of Palmerston and Russell to interfere in the Schleswig-Holstein affair in 1864, the country's leaders drew the conclusion that their interventions in Europe should be even more restricted. 'We are fish,' Salisbury often remarked. Provided the continental balance was maintained, the British could remain offshore islanders.

The ending of this power-political vacuum in the non-European world obviously upset Palmerston's heirs. The first and best-known of the new developments was the rise of various naval challenges. Not content with pressing the British in the industrial field, and of jostling them in the scramble for tropical territories, foreign rivals were now seeking to dispute command of the sea. The first naval scare of the late-Victorian period occurred in 1884–5, provoked by the *Pall Mall Gazette*'s revelations: 'The Truth about the Navy.' Thereafter, the alarms rarely ceased. For two decades, the French and Russian navies (especially when united by alliance) posed the greatest danger and seemed to make untenable the Royal Navy's traditional hold upon the Mediterranean. In the background were arising even more formidable naval challengers – the Americans in the western hemisphere, the Japanese in the Far East, the Germans nearer home. The Royal Navy kept ahead of any individual foreign fleet, but it was now more difficult to preserve its supremacy over the next two largest navies combined and quite impossible to be a match for all these new naval powers. A surrender of local naval mastery in certain regions was the inevitable result.

Possibly even more disturbing – since a combination of all the other maritime nations against Britain was hardly feasible – was the geopolitical shift against sea power itself, at least in the classical form it had occupied since the coming of the oceanic sailing-ship. The 'Columbian era' inaugurated by those early Iberian adventures had given the west European maritime states an influence in world affairs out of all proportion to their actual size and population: now, with industrialization, with railways, with investment, with new agricultural and mining techniques, the power-balance was inexorably shifting towards the vast continent-wide nations such as Russia, the United States, perhaps Imperial Germany. This, at least, was the opinion of the famous geopolitician Sir Halford Mackinder when he delivered his classic lecture 'The Geographical Pivot of History' early in 1904, and there was already by then sufficient evidence to suggest that, in its broad outline, his diagnosis was correct.[16] How could a small island compete in the long run with these modern Leviathans? How could the traditional maritime weapon of the blockade prevail against virtually self-sufficient nations such as Russia and the United States? How, even if the Royal Navy managed to preserve command of the seas, could the small British army hold Canada along its 3000-mile border with its southern neighbour, or check the creeping landward advance of Czarist imperialism across Asia? The latter, indeed, was the danger most evident to the late-Victorians, since the Orenburg-Tashkent and trans-Siberian railways posed threats to India and China respectively which no fleet of battleships could counter.

Some of these slow-maturing problems were insoluble by British means alone. Others could be solved by diplomacy, that is, by discreet withdrawals, by tacit concessions, by regional *ententes*. Taken together, as is done here, these various aspects of British world policy suggest that the country's military capabilities were being outdistanced by its obligations; not without justification did Joseph Chamberlain refer to the 'weary Titan, staggering under the too-vast orb of its fate'. In actual fact, as will be shown in the narrative chapters following, these problems were *not* taken together but simply dealt with, in the pragmatic British manner, as they arose; and only slowly did some of the politicians begin to sense the cumulative effect.

The more immediate response, predictably enough, lay in the field of military spending. As a reaction to pressure upon the Empire and, even more, to naval challenges, the defence budget spiralled ever upwards, to the dismay of successive Prime Ministers and Chancellors of the Exchequer:

	Naval budget (£ million)	Army budget (£ million)
1870	9·8	13·4
1880	10·2	15·0
1890–1	14·1	17·6
1900–1	29·5	91·7 (incl. Boer War)
1910–11	40·3	27·4

The chief reason for this horrifying escalation in costs was not inflation, but that weapons were becoming more complex, and also rapidly obsolescent – another side-effect of the new technology. A ninety-gun warship of the mid-century could cost as little as £100,000; the 'Majestic' class battleships of 1893–5 cost around £1 million each; the 'Queen Elizabeth' class battleships of 1912–13 cost around £2.5 million each. The higher the cost of armaments, the greater would be the number of countries which would ultimately be forced to abandon the race, at least on a great-power scale. And although all Britons, from Cobden himself to the most enthusiastic navalist, felt that the Royal Navy should stay supreme, the question was one which would ultimately be answered by resources, not sentiment.

To repeat: all the above remarks about the decline of Britain's economic, colonial and strategic superiority are extrapolations of long-term trends. The country's resources, especially its accumulated overseas holdings, were enormous up to 1914; its diplomatic flexibility offered a good prospect against a global disaster from an overwhelming foreign coalition; and this decline was relative, not absolute. Non-Britons were as likely to notice the country's strengths as its weaknesses. Voices at home who called *Finis Britanniae* were usually regarded as alarmists, if not cranks. Tennyson's gloomy forecast in his poem 'Locksley Hall Sixty Years After' (1886) – composed in a mood completely different from the confident 'Locksley Hall' of 1838 – was firmly rebutted by a Gladstone still sure that the signs of political and social progress outnumbered the indications of decay. The inevitability of decline was not self-evident to him, nor to Disraeli and Salisbury, nor even to many of Asquith's colleagues. Since these were the men who actually directed British external policy in response to events abroad (and pressures at home), it is now appropriate to consider the political structure in which they operated.

The Political Establishment and the Parties

Mid-century Britain occupied a special position not only in a global economic and strategical sense but also by virtue of its internal political arrangements. The country was an ancient monarchy, although the powers of the crown were checked by parliament. It was governed by a land-owning aristocracy, although an increasing amount of influence was wielded by the professional and commercial middle classes. The electoral franchise was selective and small, but there existed the possibility of its gradual extension. Workers and middle-class radicals often pressed for reforms, but their deference, coupled with various forms of social control, and a preference for non-revolutionary solutions, ensured a basic political stability. The 'English ideology', if it can be called such, adroitly fused Liberal progressivism with a Conservative respect for law and order and 'good form'; just as in the Anglican Church, extremes were eschewed, and commonsense and compromise prevailed. As the newspaper *True Briton* put it, 'On the Continent of Europe, Reform is Revolution. In England, Reform is Reason.'[17]

Although Britain was the so-called 'workshop of the world', there was no doubt that landed wealth still played the crucial role in British Politics; the influence of the Cecils, Russells, Derbys and Cavendishes was testimony enough to that, as was the unconcealed scramble by businessmen to acquire a country house. Nevertheless, the old order had compromised with the new, taking greater account of the country's commercial interests – in which, after all, many an aristocratic family had a stake. In 1865, about 52 per cent of MPs were merchants, industrialists and men of finance (whereas only 8 per cent of the members of the 1871 *Reichstag* came from such circles). This practice of integrating the middle classes into the political system had a long tradition, going back to the Glorious Revolution in some respects; and the 1832 Reform Act was to a large extent simply an attempt to update that tradition in the light of economic and social developments over the preceding half-century. Much more radical was the consideration by politicians of extending the franchise to certain social groupings *below* the middle class. In 1865, the opening-date for this particular study, that possibility had become a reality with the death of Palmerston, who in his final years had successfully stalemated all moves at parliamentary reform. By 1867, the deed had been done; and in 1884 a further enlargement of the franchise occurred. Even then, Britain was by no means *democratic,* but its establishment could boast a record of regular constitutional adjustments.

There are two ways of interpreting this pattern. The first would represent it as the steady working-out of the natural and progressive laws of society. An attachment to liberty, a belief in progress and being on the 'right side of history', and a widely held assumption in the irrefutability of the laws of political economy, formed the ideological aspect of this stance; and the self-evident growth of prosperity the material aspect. The recipe for their own success, these Victorians believed, was to let men be free. The whole age, Gladstone later recalled, was 'a history of emancipation – that is of enabling man to do his work of emancipation, political, economical, social, moral, intellectual.'[18] Of course, liberty alone was not enough, but it was the basis for all improvement; and it was quite proper, therefore, that when the upper ranks of the working classes had given evidence of their moral worth and political maturity, they also should be allowed to enter the political Pale and be giving voting rights.

A second view would suggest that this rhetoric about emancipation and progress actually concealed well-calculated efforts to preserve the *essential* interests of the higher orders. All that was happening was that the establishment was adjusting, in its usual pragmatic way, to certain pressures; but, far from capitulating before such pressures, it was ensuring that it would not be hurt by them. Provided the actual running of the country was left in traditional hands and there was no attempt to redefine the proper aims of politics, there was little objection to a cautious widening of the franchise. The latter, in fact, was a useful means of strengthening the base of the social order, and thus a far better way of preserving the real constitution than a policy of repression and reaction. As the great Whig journal, the *Edinburgh Review*, put it, the Liberals con-stituted the natural governing party precisely because theirs was a policy of 'true conservatism – the *via media* of improvement without destruction and progress without revolution'.[19] These had been the sentiments of Palmerston, too, in his earlier and more liberal phase, when he had denounced the stupidity of Metternichean reaction:

No doubt there are many who want Revolution and they should be opposed; but the more people they are opposed by, the less likely they are to succeed. *Divide et Impera* should be the Maxim of Government in these times. Separate by reasonable concessions the moderate from the exaggerated, content the former by fair concessions and get them to assist in resisting the insatiable demands of the latter. This is the *only* way to govern nowadays.[20]

While the historical consensus inclines to this latter interpretation of mid- to late-nineteenth-century British politics, the result is perhaps not so important for our purposes. Whether one holds that the country's leaders were happily bringing the lower orders into the body politic, or instead believes that these were essentially conservative rather than libertarian measures, the fact is that the arbiters of policy remained a very small group. 'High politics', in the view of some historians, was conducted by about fifty, or perhaps one hundred individuals. Gladstone, now viewed as one of the most successful operators of this system, once referred to 'the upper ten thousand', but there he was obviously thinking of all those who might have an *influence* upon policy. Even so, it was still a small part of the population – the great aristocratic families of Britain, the middle-range gentry, members of parliament, senior officials of state, successful businessmen, editors of serious newspapers and journals, religious leaders, university dons. Within this variety of professions, they were a reasonably homogeneous group, the majority of the members of which had been moulded into cultural uniformity by those celebrated institutions, the public schools and the ancient universities.

The ideological and (in part) occupational differences which did exist inside this national establishment were recognized in the activities of the two great political parties of the age, the Liberals and the Conservatives. Of the two, the Liberal Party appeared the more successful in the 1860s.

At its head was a coterie of Whig aristocrats, owners of vast tracts of land and dispensers of enormous political patronage; they were, in most of the ways which mattered, the real rulers of Britain, small in numbers but dominating successive Liberal cabinets. They existed in an uneasy political alliance with an articulate group of radicals and intellectuals (John Bright, John Stuart Mill and so on) on the 'left' flank of the parliamentary party and, through them, gained the support of Nonconformity and of industrialists in the Midlands and the North. Through them, too, they could secure the sympathies of the provincial press, which was overwhelmingly Liberal in hue. Moreover, the radical wing, together with certain of the more unorthodox Whigs (Gladstone above all) were seeking fresh sources of electoral support from the skilled artisan class. All this implied that the party was a heterogeneous social organization or, as one scholar terms it, 'a coalition of convenience, not the instrument of a creed'.[21] Its leadership had to pay attention to radical wishes on some issues, while the non-aristocratic components were willing to defer to the Whigs because they hoped that through them their own interests would be fostered. On this tacit compromise, the bargain was struck.

The Conservative Party, too, was becoming a conglomerate, mainly because that arch-politician, Disraeli, recognized that only by discovering additional areas of voting strength could the Liberal monopoly of power be broken. Free of ideological baggage, he laid stress upon the tactical handling of political problems. From the late 1860s onwards, therefore, he was in his element, bidding for the newly enfranchised working-class vote with his appeal to the idea of 'Tory Democracy' yet simultaneously reassuring the middle classes that the party was a safe home for those retreating from Gladstonian 'radicalism' – and capping all this with the assertion that the country required the leadership of its traditional 'aristocratic settlement'. This ingenuity doubtless gave British Conservatism a larger electoral base than before, but it involved a constant guidance from above in order to paper over the cracks between the various social groupings which were brought under this Disraelian panoply. The task was made easier by an improved national party organization, and by the Conservatives' insistence that extensions to the franchise were accompanied by redrawings of electoral boundaries and the redistribution of seats in order to preserve their own interests; and it was also aided, as time went on, by the expansion of suburbia, which provided borough seats to add to those held in the counties.[22]

The composition of the two major parties had implications, as may be imagined, for the country's foreign policy. All Liberals paid lip-service to the movement's prevailing tenets: free trade; distaste for the reactionary regimes of eastern Europe, and corresponding support for the idea of national self-determination in Greece, Italy, Poland, the German states and elsewhere; avoidance of entangling alliances with another European power; lack of enthusiasm for colonial expansion; and a general preference, subject to the need to preserve British maritime supremacy, for arms reductions and the settlement of international quarrels by arbitration and compromise rather than war. Yet whereas the religious dissenters, the skilled artisans, and the 'Manchester men' who followed Cobden and Bright were enthusiastic upholders of this ideology, the Whigs were altogether more cautious. Being less moved by ideals than by practical considerations, and aware of the dangers which might attend a policy of interference and innovation abroad, Whig ministers and diplomats tended towards policies of 'stabilization', worried about too-drastic cuts in the Royal Navy's budget, and were less willing to believe that the foreigner held the same enlightened views as the average Englishman. Despite this fundamental difference of attitude, however, the party was rarely divided over foreign policy in the first decade after 1865: the post-Palmerstonian policy of recoil from Europe by his Whig successors following the

Schleswig-Holstein affair fitted in nicely with the well-known desires of the radicals for peace, retrenchment and reform. Only later, during the 'Bulgarian Horrors' agitation of 1876 and especially during the second Gladstone administration (1880–5), was the fissure to re-emerge.

For many years, the foreign-policy stance of the Conservatives had been cautious, non-interventionist and, under the influence of the Fourteenth Earl of Derby (and even more his son, Lord Stanley) in full accord with the ideas of the Manchester school. Since a policy of national assertiveness had been pre-empted by Palmerston, it was deemed best that the Conservatives should present themselves as the party of sobriety and peace. Although Disraeli had originally subscribed to such views, he soon perceived the advantages of a change of course. Since the Liberals had left the patriotic mantle of Palmerston lying on the gound, he would pick it up and use it, thus emphasizing the differences between the 'national' policy of the Tories and the 'weak' and 'appeasing' stance of Gladstone which could only lead to England's humiliation. Such a rallying-cry, scholars have pointed out, was also a means of preserving party unity and his own position:

> Disraeli's purchase of the Suez Canal shares, his belligerent attitude towards Russia in 1878, and his 'forward' policies in Afghanistan and South Africa in 1879, were not just the result of his own interests and prejudices and misapprehensions. They were also, in a sense, an attempt to escape from the internal contradictions of Conservative domestic policy in the seventies by a brilliant display abroad.[23]

Although Conservative propaganda emphasized the need for a 'strong' external policy, the party was not otherwise committed to a set of principles like that which burdened their political opponents. Instead, there developed a pragmatic, flexible *Realpolitik*, well suited to a power needing to preserve its world position and only occasionally disrupted by fits of Disraelian enthusiasm. With Salisbury's coming to power, even those spasmodic aberrations disappeared and there was a heightened awareness that external policy had to be formulated within a global context. All this implied that the Conservatives' views of foreign nations were not dictated in advance, but were moved primarily by their assessment of whether or not those nations would be a threat to Britain's world interests.

The Impact of Labour

As the years went by, the respective positions of the two parties and their policies both in domestic *and* in external affairs were affected by the growth of a working-class electorate and, more distantly, by the possibility of a large working-class political party. Given the steady industrialization of the country, the occasional extensions of the franchise, the elimination of corrupt practices for 'controlling' votes, the vast expansion of primary education, and the signs of an increasing public concern about 'the condition of England', the rising political influence of Labour was scarcely surprising. The 'social question', as it was also euphemistically termed, had always been there, in Elizabeth I's reign or in the time of the Chartists; it had lurked, incipiently, behind the parliamentary reform agitation of the 1860s. Near the end of the nineteenth century, however, it has been claimed that 'the scale of the cumulative demands for economic, social and political reform . . . was of a size sufficient to distinguish the period qualitatively from previous eras of reformist agitation . . .'[24] Discussions on the distribution of voting power were being joined by discussions on the distribution of wealth. More ominously, so the established classes felt, these were debates in which the lower orders insisted upon having their own voice heard.

Viewed in the longer perspective, this change had come about surprisingly swiftly, within the average lifetime. In mid-Victorian Britain, there had been little pressure for political organization and representation at Westminster for the working classes, even among the skilled artisans; and, in general, the craft unions tended to give their support to the 'left' wing of the Liberal Party, although they could be occasionally seduced by Disraelian propositions. The first real sign of change came with the rise in trade-union membership itself: $1\frac{1}{2}$ million in 1892, $2\frac{1}{2}$ million in 1909, 4 million in 1913. The sheer strength of these organizations, whether in the élite trades or in the 'new' unions, was amply demonstrated by some of the more spectacular strikes of this period, such as the 1889 dockers' strike, the 1893 miners' strike, and the great wave of unrest in 1911–12. To a large extent, the creation of a formal political party to ensure the implementation of the aims of the workers was an outgrowth of this, even though it also fused with other strands of British radicalism. The Labour Representation Committee, formed in 1900, already had thirty seats in the Commons by 1906 (or fifty-three, if one counted miners' representatives, 'Lib-Labs' and others). Was this not evidence that, despite the still-restricted franchise, the political balance was beginning to reflect the social balance as between classes, and that the end of the old oligarchical order was in sight?

Given their preoccupation with 'non-class' issues such as Ireland and Church disestablishment, it was not at all clear how swiftly or how successfully the two major parties, as the political centres of the oligarchical order, would adjust to this trend. In the 1860s, the Liberals had confidently assumed that the prevailing economic and social forces would operate ever more in their favour; twenty years later, this appeared much less certain. The Cabinet, and the party as a whole, had in any case suffered from repeated feuds during the early 1880s, as that earlier 'coalition of convenience' disagreed over land reform, Egypt, dis-establishment, the size of the franchise and redistribution; and, above all else, over Ireland, where Gladstone's conversion to Home Rule provided the catalyst for a party revolt which had long been possible. The loss of the Whigs was by then not such a great blow to the party, but the break by Chamberlain himself and much of his Midlands caucus was more serious; and the rightward shift of middle-class businessmen, clerks, intellectuals and many in the professions was the most serious of all. What segments remained of the Liberal Party during its post-1886 period of demise were frequently no more unified, and neither Gladstone nor his successor Rosebery was really capable of forming the movement afresh. Temporarily dominated by its Non-conformist elements, the party was in some danger of losing touch with the working classes.

Yet, although electorally weak, the Liberals were also producing at this time a ferment of ideas about the proper aims of politics, much of which was to benefit them in the future when their opponents stumbled. These policy debates did not, on the whole, lead to a greater degree of uniformity than had existed in the 1860s but, rather, to a reconstruction of sub-groups within the party. The 'Gladstonian' Liberals remained, attached to the older causes of disestablishment, non-Church schools, temperance and *laissez-faire* finance, on which issues they could at least garner votes in Wales, Scotland and certain industrial regions. The 'New' Liberals, by far the most exciting group intellectually, were redefining the party's aims so as to favour economic and social 'freedoms' as well as constitutional liberties, to permit the collective good to override the claims of the individual, and to justify progressive taxation for redistributive purposes. By such means it was hoped to win the political allegiance of the working classes. This calculation was threatened, however, by the activities of a third group, the Liberal Imperialists, who were not especially strong in numbers but (like their Whig forebears) influential where it mattered, in the Cabinet. These, too, agreed that the days of the 'night watchman' state were over and, believing in the cause of national efficiency, supported various schemes of social reform; but they were also heirs of the Whigs in that, unlike the two other segments of the party, they were deeply concerned to preserve Britain's diplomatic obligations, imperial commitments and military strength. While this ensured a certain continuity of Tory habits in foreign policy, it also meant that the 'left' and 'right' wings of the Liberal Party frequently disagreed over external issues, although never to the point of splitting the movement. It also meant, of course, that the New Liberals could never fully effect that combination of low armaments, diplomatic isolation and social reform which they felt the party needed if it was to keep the allegiance of the masses.

The Liberal decline after 1886 was naturally of great advantage to the Conservatives: they not only gained the tactical adherence of the Whigs under Devonshire and the 'industrial' radicals under Chamberlain, but could pose as a party of stability and maturity as compared with their faction-ridden opponents. Moreover, social and demographic trends now appeared to aid the party. Redistribution of seats, and the more static and deferential nature of rural society, kept the county constituencies in Tory hands; the increase in white-collar workers, and the growth of suburbia, allowed the party to win a large share of the city and 'commuter' seats; working-class deference and regional anti-Catholicism, together with the appeal and organization of Chamberlain, brought many parts of the Midlands and Lancashire into the Conservative-Unionist fold. Nevertheless, in becoming 'the party of government', the Conservatives also suffered – like the Liberals a decade or two earlier – the consequences of heterogeneity. It was extremely difficult to satisfy traditional supporters in the counties and the Church, *and* the newer business interests, *and* the working-class Conservatives, *and* the white-collar vote. Like Disraeli himself, of course, his successors could appeal to patriotic instincts, and to solidarity against the internal and external forces of disintegration, to smother the differences. In the 1895 and 1900 general elections, this appeal worked well; in 1906, however, it fell on its face. By that time, the Unionists had made too many mistakes in power and were suffering from their own internal fissures.

The Tory 'split' early in the century was interesting because it was due both to internal *and* to external factors, and therefore could not be papered over by appeals to unite behind the flag. Although Chamberlain's decision to campaign for tariff reform in 1903 marks the beginnings of this divide officially, there were signs of unrest before then. By the 1890s, the long-term trend of Britain's relative decline as a great power had become obvious to many in the party, and could no longer be ascribed to Liberal incompetence alone. What was needed, the critics felt, was a thorough overhaul of Britain's foreign and defence policies, changes in the decision-making structure, and a reconsideration of the ancient prejudices against conscription, protectionism, high armaments and alliances. All this, patently, would not be provided by the slow-moving Salisbury or the philosophical Balfour. The defeats and revelations of incompetence in the Boer War were in a long line of recent shocks to national pride, but they were sufficiently large to propel the 'new' Tories openly to push for reforms.

The point was, that these reforms were not only to be in the domain of military matters and diplomacy, but in domestic affairs as well. The spread of socialist ideas and the rise of the Labour Party was as alarming to these newer Conservatives as it was to the traditional-minded; but people such as Chamberlain, Leo Amery, Alfred Milner, J. L. Garvin and others believed that this challenge should be met by positive means, by offering imperialism *and* social reform. The 'physical deterioration' of the British people, the vile condition of the inner cities and the poverty of the countryside, were problems from which the state should no longer hold back: *laissez-faire* had little appeal to these so-called 'social imperialists' desperate to save the nation before it was too late. They offered instead a whole package of policies, based chiefly upon the reintroduction of tariffs. This, it was claimed, would protect British industry, assist employment, provide fresh finds for pensions and battle-ships, and tighten imperial ties. A twofold aim lay behind this programme: on the one hand, it was hoped to attract the working classes and thus strike a blow at the Labour Party *and* at the New Liberals who were making their own rival bid for that vote; on the other, to turn back that ominous decline in British industry and British power which neither traditional Conservatives nor any of the Liberals seemed able to prevent. The intensity of feeling shown by Chamberlain's followers gave a harsher, less tolerant tone to Edwardian politics, which manifested itself in the agitations against the 'German peril', internal 'traitors' and Irish 'rebels'. On various occasions, these right-wingers embar-rassed their own party leaders; and, ironically, helped to keep the Liberal Party together since the radicals and Nonconformists in it dared not split with the Liberal Imperialists just to let the much more dangerous Tories get back into office. This was even more important after the 1910 crisis, not only because the right had shown itself to be so extreme but also because the December 1910 election left Conservatives and Liberals with an equal number of seats (272 each), thus making the threat of a Tory-Liberal Imperialist coalition more practicable than before.

This all meant that the two or three decades before 1914 witnessed an increasingly heated debate upon the proper ends and priorities of national policy, this debate being provoked *both* by the rise of Labour *and* by the rise of external challenges. It was, moreover, not a debate on which the different aspects of policy could be dealt with separately. The arms race impinged upon government finance, and that upon taxation, and that upon social policy and the domestic-political constellation; the 'social question', in its turn, could also affect government spending and taxation, and have impacts upon external policy; the furious quarrels about tariffs, or about direct *versus* indirect taxation, were immediately related to the naval race, social reforms, the 'threat' to capital, and so on. Armaments policy and foreign policy and taxation policy and social policy all hung together. In consequence, the attitudes of, say, the New Liberals or the Tariff Reformers towards Germany in the years before 1914 cannot be properly understood without a knowledge of these other issues: to see foreign affairs lifted out of this larger context is artificial and misleading.

The budgetry result of this long-running debate shows that late-Victorian and Edwardian Britain decided to have both imperialist and social reform policies – the Liberal Imperialists pulling the rest of their party towards a big navy and concern for the European balance, and the Chamberlainite wing of the Unionists pushing towards social, educational and other domestic reforms. Consequently, the mid-century financial assumptions laid down in Mill's *Principles of Political Economy* were steadily abandoned in favour of increased expenditure and increased taxation. During the 1860s, the annual average of total government spending was around £65 million; by the eve of the First World War, it was around £200 million. If the 1914–15 estimates allowed a colossal £51 million for the Royal Navy, it also allotted £57 million for education, old-age pensions, national health insurance and other civil needs. Equally remarkable was the altering patterns of taxation, for it was no longer practicable to expect the traditional indirect taxes of customs, excise, stamp duties etc. to provide sufficient revenue. Instead, direct taxes (income tax, super-tax, death duties) were relied upon, and provided 58 per cent of total revenue by the eve of war.[25] It was scarcely surprising, therefore, that politicians and journalists heatedly debated the respective merits of battleships *versus* pensions, or tariffs *versus* super-tax; scarcely surprising, either, that Liberal calls for a foreign policy of 'understanding and goodwill', or Tory appeals to 'the Power, Glory and Welfare of Great Britain and her Empire', had implications which went far beyond the well-phrased diplomatic messages which were daily despatched from the Foreign Office to other capitals.

Exactly how and when party-political disputes influenced the course of British external policy will be discussed in the following chapters. It should not be assumed, however, that it simply involved a one-way causal process, with domestic developments constantly affecting governmental diplomacy. The actual dynamics were rather more complicated than that. In the first place, there were many aspects of foreign policy where the matters at stake were so distant (e.g., border disputes in West Africa, or the disposal of certain Pacific island groups, or quarrels within the Danube River administration) that ministers and their officials could formulate a policy without much regard to party politics: the agitated debates about franchise reform and Home Rule in the early-to-mid-1880s, or about the 'rise of Labour' in the 1900s, certainly did not influence *all* British diplomacy *all* of the time. Secondly, the causal process was two-way, that is, there was an interaction between domestic trends and external events, the latter having a momentum of their own and often considerably affecting the former. Without the massacre of the Bulgarians, after all, Gladstone and Disraeli could not have manoeuvred against each other in 1876; without a rising German battlefleet, there would have been far less of a domestic quarrel about naval expenditure and taxation in 1909–10. Because developments abroad had their own meaning and momentum, the defence and foreign policy 'experts' in Whitehall often felt that they were to be understood – and dealt with – on their own terms, and deplored the fact that they became entangled in domestic politics. Imperialists, too, frequently argued that defence and diplomacy should be removed from the internal political domain. Curiously (though understandably), from the other side of the political spectrum committed social reformers wished to be rid of the distractions caused by foreign affairs.

All such aspirations were a delusion. In theory, it might have been preferable to disconnect, say, the Boer War from the 'Khaki' election, or social policy from armaments; in practice, such a separation was impossible.

The Press and Public Opinion

The attention paid by governments to franchise enlargement and domestic social reform was an indication of their growing awareness that they required a much larger body of support to sustain and 'legitimize' their rule than had been thought necessary earlier. Statesmen disagreed about just how widely the 'political nation' should be extended and what forms of opinion should be recognized, but most of them would have agreed with the Whig Foreign Secretary, Clarendon, when he wrote in 1869 that 'Governments no more than individuals can afford nowadays to despise public opinion . . .'[26] How precisely one measured that 'public' opinion was, of course, a key problem of politics, because each party felt bound to claim that its stance attracted popular support. Before the Gallup polls and other more sophisticated forms of measuring opinion were introduced, the press was regarded – rightly or wrongly – as the chief indicator, apart from the ballot box itself. Journalists, observed Carlyle, had now become the true kings and clergy. Although exaggerated, this respect for newspapers and journals seemed in part justified by their circulation figures, which in the case of most popular papers rose from tens of thousands to hundreds of thousands in the 1860s; but in the main it derived from the conviction of the early and mid-Victorians that the press was yet another manifestation of the new, progressive, liberating forces at work in modern society. As the *Westminster Review* immodestly put it, 'newspapers . . . are the best and surest civilizers of a country', a regular fountain of intellectual light.[27] To understand this widespread regard for the journalist and the editor, it is also important to recall that the press became 'popular' only in the 1850s and 1860s – because of the new printing technology, the repeal of stamp duties, and the expansion of the railways and stock exchanges.

Perhaps this influence was further exaggerated because of the press's very intimacy with the political world. A large amount of newspaper space was given over to comments and information upon events of the day, and parliamentary debates were reported in full. No party felt that it could survive without its own press organs, and statesmen such as Palmerston and Disraeli made persistent efforts to influence the editors they knew. In addition, the monthly and quarterly journals frequently published articles by politicians or other members of the national élite, and this was regarded by many as a superior form of disputation than a crowded debate in the Commons. This last point is only fully comprehensible, however, when it is recalled that the growth of the press *coincided* with the widening of the franchise. This in turn had caused politicians to feel that they needed more than the support of their backbenchers; and the newspapers, after all, offered a daily commentary upon politics to the wider constituency. Finally, just as franchise enlargement increased the potential influence of the press, so it simultaneously was forcing the parties to create efficient national organizations and tighter control over the individual MP. The newspaper rose as the backbencher fell – or so it seemed. It was to be some time, in fact, before politicians gained a sense of the limitations as well as the influence of the 'fourth estate'.

The political press of mid-century Britain was overwhelmingly Liberal. This was due, in part, to the Liberal ascendancy in London and the Home Counties, which provided the readership for such best-selling and pro-Liberal papers as the *Daily Telegraph, Daily News, Daily Chronicle* and *Pall Mall Gazette;* but even more important was the

Liberal domination of the provincial press, in the North, the Midlands, the South-west and elsewhere. Most of the Sunday newspapers (with their even bigger sales) were Liberal, as was the great majority of the weeklies, monthlies and quarterlies – the *Westminster*, the *Edinburgh*, the *Fortnightly*, the *Spectator* and the *Economist*. Against this, the Tories could field only the *Standard* (for the London area), the aristocratic *Morning Post*, reviews like *Blackwood's*, the *Quarterly Review* and the *Saturday Review*, and a smaller number of provincial papers. Finally, there were various organs which proclaimed themselves 'independent', the most famous of which was *The Times* – although for a long time it had tended to follow Palmerston. These affiliations should not be taken too strictly, however, and (as in the Commons) the 'party line' was a rather blurred one: individual owners and editors cherished their independence even while lending their support to one party or the other. Moreover, a study of press opinions provides perhaps the most massive confirmation of all that 'Liberalism' in this period meant much more than the Liberal Party itself: tenets about *laissez-faire*, freedom of speech, parliamentary government, tolerance of opposition and free trade were the property of a part of public opinion much larger than that which voted for Russell or Gladstone.

The views of the British press upon foreign affairs tended to reflect – and in many cases helped to create – those put forward by the political parties. A decidedly radical paper in the provinces would offer regular denunciations of the ractionary regimes of Europe, and plead the cause of liberty and free trade. Whig journals would offer a much more muted version of this ideology. Stalwart Tory papers like the *Morning Post* and *Quarterly Review* would display their regard for the established order, whether in the Austrian Empire or in the American South. Virtually all organs assumed the superiority of English institutions; those favouring Cobdenite doctrines lectured their own and foreign governments on their failure to follow the

Manchester philosophy, while most other papers vigorously upheld what they believed to be 'national interests'. The press was not, on the whole, an aid to good relations between Britain and its neighbours. The sneering descriptions of European nations, and the powerful assaults upon such 'threats' to the Empire as Czarist Russia or 'public nuisances' as Napoleon III, frequently embarrassed the Foreign Office, which had some difficulty in convincing fellow-governments that it could not control the press. *The Times,* because of its great reputation, was a particular problem in this respect, but the various attempts (from the Queen downwards) to get it to alter its tone usually met with little success. Its hectoring articles, or the contemporaneous *Punch* cartoons of pretentious 'Froggies', eccentric German professors, and malevolent Russian bears, were the dark side of the generally held assumption that one Englishman was the equal of at least several foreigners. The steady pricking of that assumption in the decades following did not make the tone any more charitable.

The great 'duel' between Disraeli and Gladstone over external (and, of course, internal) policies in the 1870s, and the many diplomatic problems encountered by the second Gladstone administration in the early 1880s, made the political divisions within the press much clearer: one either praised the Grand Old Man's Christian diplomacy, or denounced his lack of realism; inveighed against Disraelian bluster and imperialism, or urged him on in his 'courageous' and 'patriotic' actions. Partly in consequence of this polarization, newspaper attitudes towards specific foreign countries also emerged more distinctly. France, since 1871 a democratic republic, was warmly regarded by most Liberals, many of whom also desired to improve relations with Russia, the 'protector' of the Balkan peoples against Turkish misrule; Bismarckian Germany and its ally, Austria-Hungary, were not so well regarded although religious, cultural and dynastic ties with Britain sometimes muted this Liberal suspicion of Prussian militarism. Tory views were generally the reverse of this: France and Russia, threatening British interests in Asia, Africa and also, by the 1880s, on the high seas, were viewed with deep suspicion, while the Triple Alliance was seen as a force for peace and stability, deterring Russia from a sortie against Constantinople and paralysing the French lust for expansion in the Mediterranean.

The 1880s also witnessed a shift in the political balance of the British press to the Liberals' disadvantage. This was chiefly caused by the Home Rule issue although it was clear that many owners and editors, like others in the professional and intellectual classes, had already been disturbed by Gladstone's policies prior to 1886. *The Times, Daily Telegraph, Spectator, Punch* and many lesser journals now gave their support to a 'unionist' policy over Ireland and to an even firmer line in foreign and imperial affairs. Newer developments also hit Liberalism's previous dominance in the newspaper world. The rise of suburbia and the white-collar workforce strengthened Conservatism in the London area, and aided the rightward shift of the political press in the capital; and the improvement in rail communications allowed the London dailies to reach the provinces by breakfast-time and challenge the Liberal regional papers. Moreover, the existing London dailies were joined in the following decade by the *Daily Mail* and then the *Daily Express,* which (now selling over a million copies each day) loudly trumpeted the glories of the British Empire, the need for unchallenged naval supremacy, the dangers posed by the Boers, the Russians, later the Germans, the Fenians and other foes. Once again, it was difficult for contemporaries to get a full measure of the impact of the 'new journalism' which Alfred Harmsworth had introduced; only after the 1906 election did it become evident that the circulation figures of the political press were not always a good guide to the voting public's inclinations. Before then, the trend alarmed Liberals and also many traditional Conservatives. 'You would be astonished,' James Bryce reported to an

American friend during the Boer War, 'remembering the England of forty years ago, to see the England of today, intoxicated with militarism, blinded by arrogance, indifferent to truth and justice . . . We have had a formidable lesson of the power which the press and financial groups can exert.'[28] This was not, incidentally, a source of complete satisfaction to the Conservative leadership since it was in the 'jingo' press above all that Imperialists and Tariff Reformers were also to attack what they considered to be Balfour's effete conduct of military, colonial and diplomatic affairs.

While the press occasionally *did* influence governmental policy, historians should not assume that it was always of overwhelming import. Public opinion was a factor in foreign-policy-making, but it was rarely the case that statesmen and permanent officials became the helpless puppets of the press. Party leaders could usually count upon the support of those newspapers which shared the same beliefs and economic interests as themselves; and abuse by the rival party's press was usually of no concern. For example, although Unionist papers launched bitter attacks upon the Liberal governments of Campbell-Bannerman and Asquith, the latter's policies were defended by an array of papers which, although not rivalling the *Daily Mail* in sales terms, easily surpassed it in intellectual argument – C. P. Scott's *Manchester Guardian*, J. A. Spender's *Westminster Gazette*, W. H. Hurst's *Economist*, A. L. Gardiner's *Daily News* and H. W. Massingham's *Nation*. It was only if these friendly papers showed unease that the government needed to be worried. Furthermore, individuals as masterful as Disraeli and Lloyd George could exploit 'public' opinion for their own ends, by influencing editors or making open appeals for the people's support. The *vox populi* could also be used, negatively, as an excuse for avoiding an unwelcome policy – as when Salisbury (who usually scorned newspaper opinion) turned aside German approaches for an alliance by declaring that such a step would be unpopular.

Perhaps the real significance of the press lay not so much

in its impact upon official policy but in its ability to worsen the political atmosphere. Even in the mid-nineteenth century, as noted above, the tone of many papers towards foreign states was xenophobic and arrogant, qualities which could easily be transmitted to a susceptible readership. In the age of imperialism and the various pre-1914 international crises and 'scares', this tone became stiffer. Bitter denunciations of a 'traitorous' Liberal government, venomous attacks upon Irish Home Rulers, alarmist stories about German invasion plans, demands for conscription and enormous battlefleets, all indicated an intolerance and a nervousness which had been much less general fifty years earlier. The average Briton, Harmsworth once claimed, liked a 'good hate'; now, with the aid of the *Daily Mail,* he could have one every day.

One further aspect of this apparent rise in public chauvinism deserves note: the creation of organizations and pressure groups which agitated for particular patriotic causes. The existence of pressure groups in British politics was certainly not new, but earlier bodies had nearly always been 'progressive' in their purposes – the anti-slavery and aborigine protection societies, the anti-Corn Law League, and constitutional reform associations. Those of late-Victorian and Edwardian Britain tended to be much more consolidationist, protective and conservative. This 'proliferation of bodies devoted to the eradication of surmised national weaknesses', as one scholar describes them,[29] can only be understood in the context of Britain's relative decline as a great power. The Navy League (1894) and its right-wing breakaway organization, the Imperial Maritime League (1907), constantly claimed that British maritime supremacy was slipping away. The National Service League (1902), arising out of the Boer War humiliations, pressed for military service by 'every able-bodied white man in the Empire' and agitated about the country's vulnerability to invasion. The Tariff Reform League (1903), painting a frightening picture of the 'deindustrialization' and demise of Britain, called for a firm tariff policy against foreign commercial rivals. Each of these bodies endeavoured to penetrate parliament (especially, of course, through the Unionist Party) and to influence the government of the day. If they were checked in the latter aspiration by the pre-war Liberal administration, this does not mean that they were without influence upon public opinion. The patriotic leagues spent a great deal of their time in producing pamphlets and house journals, challenging candidates at elections, persuading editors to feature their campaigns and – last but not least – indoctrinating British youth through visits to schools, patriotic speeches at prize-day, 'junior' navy leagues, emphasizing physical fitness, and so on.

It would not do to exaggerate the importance of this 'Edwardian militarism'. Most of the arch-patriots complained of the lethargy and indifference of their own Conservative Party leaders, and of course felt that they were making no headway against the Liberal government. As has been pointed out, the greatest pressures upon Grey to change his foreign policy came from the left, not the right.[30] Nevertheless, the growth of radical nationalism did have some impact. It certainly led to a rightward shift among Tory MPs, and that in turn enhanced the tactical position of the Liberal Imperialists within the government – as could be seen in the 1914 crisis. Furthermore, this alarmism was deeply symbolic, for it was, surely, a characteristic response to evidence of decline. As such, it represented a marked change from those happier days when the British public believed that the country had reached unchallengeable heights of world influence; when Kingsley could write, in 1851:

> The spinning jenny and the railroad, Cunard's liners and the electric telegraph, are to me . . . signs that we are, on some points at least, in harmony with the universe; that there is a mighty spirit working among us . . . the Ordering and Creating God.[31]

It would be surprising if the disappearance of this sort of cosmic confidence a half-century later had no impact upon external policy. One might argue – with a fair amount of evidence – that this change of mood produced a more widespread feeling of *Angst,* an excessive suspicion of perceived foreign rivals, a desire to escape from 'isolation', and a concomitant wish to stay close to whatever friends or *entente* partners one had secured. Such sentiments were not shared by all Britons, perhaps not by most Britons. But they do seem to have existed where it counted – in the Unionist Party, among the Liberal Imperialists, within the ministries of state, along much of Fleet Street: in other words, among a high proportion of the 'upper ten thousand'.

Government Institutions and the 'Official Mind'

The chief reason why it is wise to be cautious towards claims about the influence of the press and organized pressure groups is that the decision-making process did preserve, through its structure and its ingrained prejudices, a considerable degree of autonomy from outside pressures. It has been suggested, indeed, that the 'Official Mind' of government had an existence and force of its own; it was able to 'assemble and weigh all the factors' in a deliberate and calculated fashion, 'partly insulated from pressures at home, and remote from reality in overseas situations'; and it was 'consciously above and outside' the day-to-day political and economic processes. Government ministers, briefed by their permanent officials, did sit down in Cabinet and seek to arrive at a common policy on, say, Egypt or China; in doing this, they 'registered and balanced all the contingencies', taking into account such factors as press opinion, but also business interests and backbench pressures – yet they were not overawed by any one influence, and also paid great attention to the flow of reports from 'the man on the spot'.[32]

This image of an aloof – almost autonomous – governmental process derives in part from the nature of the Foreign Office itself. Foreign Secretaries were always aristocrats (until Grey in 1905), and all were experienced and senior politicians. Although someone like Salisbury disagreed strongly with, say, Derby or Granville over aspects of foreign policy, they possessed a similarity of style which tended to disguise such differences: all exhibited an essential pragmatism, a habit of understatement, and a feigned nonchalance which make their correspondence a delight to read. These qualities were clearly regarded as proper to aristocratic demeanour, as much shaped by public-school and university attitudes as by innate inclinations, so uniform was the end result. A cool, detached view of politics, a global perspective, a distaste for mere trade, for the *nouveaux riches* and for foreign governments which did not follow the gentlemanly code, all this occasionally gives the reader of diplomatic despatches a sense that their authors were *in* but not *of* this world. As with proconsuls of Empire like Cromer and Curzon, there was something 'Roman' in their habit of authority and conviction that they knew best, and it was perhaps no coincidence that they had usually received a classical education.

The bureaucratic structure in which the Foreign Secretaries operated could only confirm this habit. The permanent officials, headed by the Under-Secretary, had received the same public-school and university education and were often distantly related to Cabinet ministers (this was even more the case with senior members of the diplomatic corps). Their social exclusiveness undoubtedly affected their attitude to the world outside. Conservative in the bureaucratic practices, generally 'Whiggish' in their views on foreign affairs, conscious of their expertise and knowledge of private information, the Foreign Office staff regarded with some disdain and occasional apprehension the outbursts of public sentiment, the probings of backbench

MPs, and the inflated language of pamphleteers and leader-writers. With rare exceptions such as Sir Eyre Crowe, they paid little attention to economic matters and claimed to have no interest in trade; diplomacy should, if possible, be kept separate from business matters – a prejudice only slowly abandoned under a barrage of press attacks upon the government's failure to protect and support British enterprise abroad in the face of unscrupulous foreign tactics. Since the only economics book prospective diplomats were likely to have read before entry into the service was Adam Smith's *The Wealth of Nations,* this wish to keep the two spheres separated is understandable. Only if an economic action had some ulterior political or strategical purpose – such as giving state support to British financiers in Turkey, Persia and China so as to preserve Whitehall's 'informal influence' in the face of rival powers – did the Foreign Office show much interest.[33] Thus detached from business, parliament and the press, these permanent officials do at first sight appear to justify the claim that they were free from domestic pressures and could conduct diplomacy with a single-minded regard for *die grosse Politik.*

Before and during the First World War, the role of the Foreign Office staff was a matter of some controversy: radical journalists and politicians claimed that, far from being the neutral advisers and executors of the elected government's wishes, these officials had sought to influence and even to direct policy contrary to the wishes of the Liberal Cabinet and party. Grey, it was hinted, had been captured by his clerks and led into an anti-German policy. There were, indeed, some grounds for this allegation. From Palmerston's time to Salisbury's, the officials had well understood that their task was to execute the Foreign Secretary's (and Cabinet's) orders and to provide answers to requests for information. After the turn of the century, this situation altered, partly because of changes in the structure of the Office hierarchy and its functions, and partly because of the sheer increase in telegrams and letters which forced the delegation of some duties. It was also caused, however, by the rise of a distinct group of officials and diplomats – Charles Hardinge, Francis Bertie, Arthur Nicolson, Eyre Crowe, Louis Mallett – who had a strong mistrust of Germany and consequently of those Liberals who favoured a more friendly policy towards Germany together with social change at home. No doubt the opinions of his staff did sharpen Grey's perception of German designs; but it would not nowadays be accepted that his officials 'made policy' or compelled the Liberal government to follow a course to which it was opposed. The day-to-day management of affairs was in the Foreign Office's hands; the really big decisions were not.[34]

The reason for this was that the strategic nerve-centre of government policy was always the Cabinet, directed by the Prime Minister. This did not mean, of course, that a group of fifteen or so ministers was continually checking upon what the Foreign Office was up to. Since they each had their own departments, they usually had little time for a study of foreign affairs; and, especially during Liberal administrations, they deliberately preferred to concentrate upon domestic issues, thus leaving the Foreign Secretary of the day a relatively free hand. At times of crisis, however, and when fundamental issues of external policy were being decided, the Cabinet's role was all-important. Over such vital questions as the Schleswig-Holstein crisis of 1864, the Belgian neutrality declaration of 1870, the Eastern Crisis of 1876–9, the Egyptian imbroglio of the early 1880s, the Heligoland-Zanzibar treaty of 1890, the Congo quarrels of 1894, the consideration of a German and then a Japanese alliance around the turn of the century, and the thorny and interrelated questions of a naval and political settlement with Berlin in the years 1908–12, the Cabinet had the final word and the Foreign Secretary – although a most influential voice – had but one vote. The awesome decision for war in August 1914 also belonged to the Cabinet alone.

In addition, and somewhat more frequently, foreign

policy was influenced by individual ministers. The most important of all was the Prime Minister himself, not merely because of his office but because so many of them – Disraeli, Gladstone (in a way), Salisbury, Rosebery and Balfour* – took a deep interest in international affairs. Then there were those departments whose own purview embraced the outside world. The War Office and the Admiralty were the most obvious examples here, for British *external* policy meant more than diplomacy alone: the navy in the Mediterranean, for example, by its war plans, dispositions and even fleet visits to foreign ports, was a constant projection outwards of British power. The India Office and, by extension, the Indian government, was another influence, especially in respect of policy towards Russia; and the Colonial Office, in an age of imperial rivalries and of moves towards closer ties with the self-governing colonies, engaged in regular consultation with the Foreign Office. The Treasury, with its tight hold upon the purse-strings of government, and even the Board of Trade, concerned about foreign tariffs, fishing disputes and other similar matters, could be added to this list. Finally, the creation of the Committee of Imperial Defence (CID) in the post-Boer War 'shake-up' of British strategic and imperial policy provided a forum for key ministers and their advisers to come together so as to work out larger questions on an interdepartmental basis.

Apart from this formal correspondence and consultation, agreement between these various departments was often reached by means of informal meetings of ministers at Westminster or, more usually, by an interchange of private letters sent from one country house to another. Even where the matter seemed purely a diplomatic one, the Foreign Secretary might consult some of his senior colleagues because it could have political implications: Bismarck's

* Salisbury, indeed, usually combined the post of Foreign Secretary with his premiership; Rosebery was an ex-Foreign Secretary; and Balfour held the Foreign Office during Salisbury's absences.

alliance 'bid' of 1879 was handled, for example, by Disraeli, Salisbury and Northcote. All this was normally done on a friendly and intimate fashion, as between equals. Under Liberal administrations, however, where radical ministers suspected that Kimberley or Grey were not carrying out a 'truly Liberal' diplomacy, there might be a demand for a full Cabinet debate in order to define the proper policy. These were infrequent events, but they reminded all concerned of the Cabinet's ultimate responsibility, to the monarch, to parliament, and to the country, for the external policy of the government of the day.

Subject to these overall limitations, then, the Foreign Secretary and his advisers supervised the nation's diplomacy and had a considerable freedom of manoeuvre. Yet this is by no means to say that the 'Official Mind' was something aloof and unaffected by domestic pressures. Precisely because the Cabinet was composed of senior politicians whose interests did not usually lie in the field of foreign affairs, they took account of all sorts of influences which were funnelled towards them: ministers were aware of the demands being made in the Commons or the constituencies, of the urgings of interest groups and the attacks (or encouragement) in the press, of the quiet advice from the party Central Office about a forthcoming bye-election, of the alarm expressed at certain events overseas by their military and naval advisers, and of the signs of 'no confidence' made by the stock markets. A detailed analysis of, say, the Egyptian crisis of 1882 or the naval 'scare' of 1908–9, would reveal all these influences at work. Not all of them would prevail – some, indeed, were contrary in direction – but ministers usually took them into account, in the light of their own perception of the particular international crisis, before moving to some Cabinet decision. On occasions, the differences within that body were so great that a decision was shelved: for years, and mainly because of *domestic* factors, Asquith's Cabinet 'decided not to decide' whether or not Britain would support France in the event of a European war.

This mention of Cabinet differences raises a further point about the 'Official Mind': namely, that even if ministers and their advisers generally managed to hammer out a compromise on policy, the actual process usually revealed the existence of conflicting schools of thought within the governmental machine. The shared assumptions of a homogeneous élite, and their 'high calling to mediate between jarring and selfish interests',[35] was not noticeably in evidence during the last years of Disraeli's and Balfour's ministries or during all the post-1880 Liberal administrations. Instead of unity, the historian finds a series of rival perceptions about national priorities and the world order; but these respective positions were held by groups of people *in* and *out* of government. There was much more cohesion about foreign policy in the 'collective mind' formed by Cabinet ministers such as Lord Loreburn, John Morley and Louis Harcourt, senior civil servants at the Treasury and Board of Trade, certain City financiers and Nonconformist businessmen, Liberal backbenchers and a cluster of radical journalists, than there was in the perceptions of all those *within* that formal boundary which divided officialdom from everyone else. The strategical details might be known only to a few, but the debate upon, say, the 'continental commitment' before 1914 was carried on inside and outside of government offices, inside and outside of parliament, in leader-columns and party resolutions and pressure-group pamphlets as well as in country houses and sub-committees. In other words, the dynamics of British politics point to frequent struggles between what one might term sub-groups of the establishment, with each sub-group striving to have its viewpoint accepted as the national policy. It is within this larger framework that one needs to set the study of the external aspects of governmental policy.

The Role of the Crown

There was one further significant influence upon the conduct of British foreign policy which, however, declined over the course of time: that of the monarch. The importance of Victoria's role at the beginning of our story is easy to understand. As a constitutional monarch, her prerogatives were admitted to be restricted by parliament in the form of the Cabinet of the day; but there was no clear demarcation of powers and the ministers' duty to consult the Queen was not disputed. Consequently, a large 'grey area' lay between what was improper interference and what was justifiable influence on her part. This Victoria successfully exploited, partly because she remained while successive British administrations came and went, and partly because of the prominent role which European and especially German affairs occupied in the 1860s and 1870s. (The western hemisphere, or the Orient, were to her of far less interest.) Not only was the Queen intimately acquainted with the major problems of European diplomacy, but she also carried on an extensive correspondence with her many relations; and since many of the latter were the sovereigns of foreign states, who actually did decide their country's foreign policy, the Queen represented a source of additional information and, even more important, a potential means of influencing other powers which the Foreign Secretary often found useful.

Despite these advantages, there is no doubt that the Queen often added to the complications of conducting British external policy. In 1864, she had aroused other members of the Cabinet into opposing Russell and Palmerston over Schleswig-Holstein; two years later, she herself had to be dissuaded from a more interventionist course during the Austro-Prussian War. 'The Missus', as Clarendon irreverently termed her behind her back, always insisted upon being consulted on British policy towards Germany, a country which she (and some of her family) sometimes found it difficult to regard as 'foreign'. Only when it was clear that Bismarck's political dominance within Germany was unshakeable did Victoria's feelings towards that country cool somewhat. By that time, however, she had become a great supporter of Disraeli's imperial mission and in consequence a warm advocate of 'firm' policies towards Britain's potential enemies. This considerably affected her attitude towards succeeding Liberal governments, whose Prime Ministers and Foreign Secretaries she frequently upbraided for an alleged neglect of British interests. In the final decade or so of her reign, the Queen was not as capable as before of interfering in the day-to-day processes of diplomacy; and, happily trusting in Salisbury's judgment, she felt much less need to exercise what vague constitutional prerogatives she still possessed. Nevertheless, the Prime Minister consulted her frequently, respecting her experience and good sense, rather as if he were dealing with some senior Cabinet colleague. But for this personal rapport between the two ageing leaders, it is likely that her influence would have declined much more quickly.

Superficially, the actions of Victoria's successor give the impression that the monarchical role in British diplomacy was then revived. Edward VII was certainly keen to uphold what he thought to be his rights in this, as in other aspects of policy; and, by his frequent visits to foreign courts and his cultivation of the *entente cordiale,* he earned the title of 'uncle of Europe' and the enmity of Berlin. Closer inspection, however, suggests that the King's importance was not as great as that attributed to him by contemporaries or by some historians. His diplomacy was frequently influenced by personal motives, rather like that of his nephew and pushful rival, Kaiser Wilhelm II. The consequence was that Edward's influence upon British external policy was rather inconsistent, a fact which occasionally threatened the diplomatic course which Lansdowne and Grey wished to follow. In 1903 the King paid that spectacular visit to Paris which has often been seen as the 'breaking of the ice' in Anglo-French relations and the beginning of the 'encirclement' of Germany; but by the summer of the following year, Edward had re-established good relations with the Kaiser and assumed that Anglo-German tensions were over. The King was also ambivalent, rather than consistently supportive, towards the *rapprochement* with Russia and appears not to have understood why the new Liberal government was tending against Germany until Eyre Crowe wrote to him a famous memorandum of January 1907 justifying the 'new course'. Consequently, although the interpretations which others (especially the French and the Germans) placed upon Edward VII's influence and intentions have an importance of their own, G. W. Monger is surely correct to argue that he 'never showed understanding of the larger, impersonal forces bearing upon the relations between states' and had 'no real influence upon the formation of policy'.[36]

George V, his young and inexperienced successor, wisely did not even attempt to play a major part in the formulation of Britain's pre-1914 external policy.

Conclusion

What do these influences upon Britain's external policy indicate about the nation's place and role in the global political order? Studied one by one, such impulses would not enable the scholar to draw broad conclusions about the whole. After all, some of them, as mentioned earlier, were contradictory: the interest of the City or the desire of the Nonconformists for peace could well clash with the urgings of the Imperial Maritime League or a 'jingo' newspaper for assertive actions. Although all these should legitimately be seen as groups seeking (with a greater or lesser degree of success) to influence policy, the only way that the overall course of British diplomacy can be understood is by looking at the totality, and by comparing the country's position with others.

When that is done, some general conclusions may be stated. Britain at the time of Palmerston's death was an advanced nation in industrial terms – indeed, *the* industrial trail-blazer for much of the nineteenth century. Financially, it played a unique role at the centre of the world's system of credit and exchange. In maritime and colonial affairs, it had many emulators but no rival for pre-eminence. Its overall strategic position, even as late as 1914, was also rather special: it alone possessed, among the great powers, territories and interests in every part of the world. Taken together, all this meant that Britain occupied a very favourable situation, and one much envied by other nations as they sought in turn to climb to the top of the power-political and industrial ladders.

But this position as 'Number One' was also the essential British problem. Having achieved the pinnacle of worldly success, it had nothing to gain and much to lose from changes in that global order. Britain was now a *mature* state, with a built-in interest in preserving existing arrangements. It is true that British statesmen, especially on the Liberal side, retained a belief in change; but what they had in mind was 'progress', change for the better, the development of political and social and economic tendencies *on British lines* and not, of course, to Britain's detriment. The cold and unrelenting alterations in the economic, colonial and strategic spheres from about 1870 onwards did not generally accord with such assumptions. This, in turn, increased the British preference for the *status quo,* even while they recognized that newer rivals would hardly be satisfied with a stabilization of that order. As Churchill, in a remark doubtless intended to unsettle his radical Cabinet colleagues, pointed out: 'We have got all we want in territory, and our claim to be left in unmolested enjoyment of vast and splendid possessions, mainly acquired by violence, largely maintained by force, often seems less reasonable to others than to us.'[37] By the same token, the British would have liked to remain 'in unmolested enjoyment' of their traditional naval mastery, and of their older share of the world's .production of manufactures. Yet as time went on, it seemed ever less likely that this wish could be satisfied.

This overall picture of Britain as a *'status quo'* power – but one now under challenge – did not relate to external developments alone. The second great force for change lay in domestic politics, where a growing pressure for constitutional and social improvements appeared to threaten the old order. Although the internal and external challenges ran in parallel, they also interacted upon each other, as explained above; and they therefore posed a dual problem for the traditional managers of British politics.

To those 'managers', there seemed to be two alternative forms of response to such trends. The first, and most consistently used form, was what may be termed the 'liberal' alternative – in the broader and non-party sense of that word. It implied an external policy which was pragmatic, conciliatory and reasonable; and one which was predicated on the assumption that, provided national interests were not too deleteriously affected, the peaceful settlement of disputes was much more to Britain's advantage than recourse to war. It may be possible to argue that this pacific disposition derived from early Whig traditions and the basic canons of Victorian evangelicalism; or that it was instead a self-interested way of preserving one's material interests; but the most probable interpretation is that, given their awareness of the country's economic situation, domestic sentiment and strategical over-extension, it simply made good sense for Britain's leaders to pursue a policy of moderation and compromise. This applied also, of course, to the parallel domestic challenge. Here, too, by attempting to satisfy the justifiable grievances and claims of the lower orders, British statesmen believed that they had found a method of preserving political stability; the concessions made, whether in terms of a wider franchise or various social reforms, would not be begrudged if this larger aim was secured. Judging by results, such a strategy of pragmatic adjustment was an eminently successful one.

To Cobdenite radicals and to the later 'New' Liberals and Labour representatives, however, this record was spotted with black stains. In external policy, successive governments had deviated far too often from the straight and narrow, leading the country into unnecessary colonial annexations, involving it in the dangerous entanglements of European diplomacy, and spending excessive amounts upon armaments instead of domestic reform programmes or (the Cobdenites' choice) 'economical' retrenchment. There was a lot of truth in this criticism, especially in respect of colonial policy, where it is clear that British governments applied the double standard of the day; the annexation of Matabeleland was far less contentious than the seizure of Belgium or Switzerland would have been. In other respects, however, this viewpoint was rather utopian. The realities of power, the constraints upon statesmen in office, the natural impetus towards 'continuity' in foreign policy and piecemeal change in domestic policy, and the need felt even by reformist-Liberal governments to balance what was ideal with what was practicable, were not considered by these critics. In any case, although the latter could be very formidable 'trouble-makers',[38] they did not occupy the citadels of power. An alternative strategy on the lines they proposed was not, therefore, a practicable proposition.

Much more significant was the form of response adumbrated by imperialists and others on the right of the political spectrum. Holding that the idea of a world living in permanent harmony was unhistorical, that might rather than right had usually more influence in international affairs, and that governments should possess adequate armed force to uphold national honour and interests, these circles felt that Britain's response to external challenges should be firm and resolute. On internal and economic affairs, however, the right was likely to be divided, some preferring a negative stance, others a more interventionist package of 'imperialism and social reform'. There are hints of this strategy in Disraeli's own actions, and in the movement of discontented Unionists who gathered behind Chamberlain in the pre-1914 years. Obviously, with such sentiments residing within the establishment, it had a larger prospect of becoming official policy than that offered by the left. Nevertheless, this alternative remained an incipient one, never managing fully to develop; and Conservative policy under Derby, Salisbury and Balfour generally following the pattern of caution, compromise and pragmatic change.

In regard to external trends, this response ultimately hung upon the assumption mentioned above, that it could be made without national interests being too deleteriously affected. Although there were many good reasons to preserve the peace, it was in no way an *absolute*; under certain conditions, and despite protests from radicals and pacifists, despite even their own awareness of the financial strain and domestic-political unpopularity which war might bring, British governments would undoubtedly lead the nation into war.

What were those likely conditions? The first and most obvious would be for purposes of self-defence against any direct attack upon the British Isles or the overseas territories of the Empire: the British would certainly fight for India against Russian assault, more reluctantly (and with some despair) for Canada in the event of attack by the United States, and it was likely that they would also risk a great-power war to defend perceived national interests in parts of Africa. The decision-making élite might possibly be brought close to war if British naval supremacy was threatened – although since battleship-building took many years, there was little prospect of a sudden challenge, so the natural response was simply to increase the size of the Royal Navy.

Finally, it had always seemed axiomatic to the majority of British statesmen that the balance of power in Europe should not be so deranged as to allow one hostile nation or coalition of nations to dominate the continent. This axiom, however, needed definition. Exactly when the danger-point was reached, how one would detect the hegemonial aspirations of the challenger, which areas of Europe should be fought for (apart from the few, like Belgium and Portugal, defined in ancient treaties), and whether all this should be anticipated by preparatory arrangements or even alliances with other nations interested in preserving the *status quo*, were aspects over which the various groupings of British politicians and their advisers would easily be divided. What would or would not constitute the *casus belli* would to a large degree depend upon the circumstances of the moment.[39] This, in turn, allowed the British Cabinet to take into account those many internal and external influences mentioned above which would bear upon such a momentous decision.

2. Debates and Policies

The Re-casting of Europe, 1865–75

During the decade following Palmerston's death in 1865, the old European order was transformed: in place of the traditional 'power vacuum' at the centre, there emerged a united and formidable force, a German Empire under Prussian leadership. This 'German revolution', as Disraeli termed it, was in his view more significant for European politics than the French Revolution seventy years earlier; yet Britain remained passive and aloof while the continental balance was being re-cast. To certain contemporary and later critics, and to those peoples like the Danes and the French who suffered from this transformation, London's policy of non-intervention appeared both unwise and inexplicable. In the circumstances of the time, most members of the British establishment thought it sensible and understandable. Their reasons for believing this provide a good insight into their perception of the country's political priorities and international role at that time.

Perhaps the most immediate reason for the British government's passivity was its awareness of the lack of success which had attended its previous military and diplomatic interventions on the continent. The Crimean War had been disappointing in both military and naval terms, and had aroused doubts about the efficacy of the traditional aristocratic leadership. In addition, while it had probably not made many new converts to the Cobdenite orthodoxy, it had obviously given strength to the claim that war was economically wasteful as well as being morally dubious.[1] (A similar materialistic conclusion was drawn about the American Civil War of 1861-5, especially when Lancashire felt the effects of reduced cotton supplies.) Non-intervention therefore became the policy of the day. For example, although the Polish uprising of 1863 evoked considerable British sympathy, the issue was not so vital that the government could even think of making a *casus belli* out of it; and non-military pressure against Russia's rule was also impracticable, given Berlin's support for St Petersburg and the fear that France might use this affair to expand elsewhere. A year later, Palmerston and Russell were greatly aroused by the Austro-Prussian action against Denmark over Schleswig-Holstein, but there was no clear echo in the country at large to their calls for intervention. The press was divided about it, the Queen violently opposed to it, business circles were aghast at the very idea of war, and the Conservatives under Derby preached caution. Most important of all, the 'two dreadful old men' (as Victoria labelled her Prime Minister and Foreign Secretary) were repeatedly restrained by a Cabinet majority of moderate Whigs and 'Manchester school' liberals.

If the Schleswig-Holstein *débâcle* did not completely deal the death-blow to that 'foul idol', the balance-of-power policy, it did cause subsequent ministries to recognize that a warlike posture could only be adopted in the future when the vast majority of the nation supported the government. Since unanimity of opinion over foreign affairs was not usual, this precondition virtually ruled out the resort to war in all but the most pressing circumstances. Thus it was that when Bismarck provoked a conflict with Austria in 1866, and when the latter power was swiftly crushed by the efficient Prussian Army, London sat still and did little apart from Victoria's own private pleas to King William of Prussia. 'We are willing to do anything for the maintenance of peace,' Clarendon, the Foreign Secretary, informed the British ambassador in Paris, 'except committing ourselves to a policy of action . . .'² When the Conservatives took office in late June 1866, Derby assured the Lords that his government's policy was 'above all to endeavour not to interfere needlessly and vexatiously with the internal affairs of any foreign country . . . [and] studiously to maintain a strict and impartial neutrality'.³

There was, of course, much more behind this policy of abstention than the shadow of the Schleswig-Holstein affair. How could the British intervene in the Austro-Prussian War, even had they wished to do so? Naval forces could play no role in central Europe, and the army was small by continental standards – and became even less impressive as other states began to imitate the Prussian practice of recruiting a mass force of reserves. Furthermore, British forces were required elsewhere: in the aftermath of the Mutiny, fully 65,000 troops were needed to 'stiffen' the now-suspect Indian Army; others were stationed in Crown Colonies across the globe, or being held in readiness to deal with possible troubles with the Maoris, Ashantis, Abyssinians – and the Irish. The activities of other powers also turned the gaze of British statesmen from Europe. French designs upon Egypt were suspected. Russia, recovering from the Crimean War, seemed restless in Asia and ambitious in the Balkans. Above all, there was the problem of preserving fair relations with a United States still bitter at Britain's stance during the Civil War. All this reminded Whitehall that it had imperial responsibilities of much greater importance than its concerns in central Europe.

In any case, what possible motive could impel Britain to contemplate intervention? Following the Schleswig-Holstein affair, both Prussia and Austria were regarded with disfavour, and the press portrayed them as two bullies now quarrelling over the 'spoils' of the Danish duchies. Why should either of them be helped? Apart from the royal family itself, few Britons were concerned about the fate of those German states which took Austria's side and paid the penalty for it. The only thing which could have aroused

British concern was a threat to the balance of power, and even that argument would have been bitterly contested by the radicals and other isolationists. As it was, however, most Britons who interested themselves in European politics held that the equilibrium was in no great danger. A few observers, it is true, warned of the long-term growth of Prussian power and a still larger number disliked the Bismarckian habits of domestic reaction and external aggrandisement; but in general a unified and strong Germany was not opposed. Such a solution would accord well with the Liberal belief in national self-determination: and, as *The Times* urged, it would also make that country 'more capable of preserving peace within its limits and repelling aggression from abroad'.[4] This, indeed, was the crux of the matter: for the balance of power would be strengthened, not undermined, by the creation of a solid nation-state in the centre of Europe instead of the existing fragments. Moreover, it would probably act as a restraint upon the *extra-European* activities of the two 'flank' powers, France and Russia, and thus ease Britain's global position.

Finally, there was the domestic motive. Public attention was concentrated not upon the actions of Berlin and Vienna but upon the post-Palmerstonian manoeuvres by both Liberals and Conservatives over the pressing issue of parliamentary reform. An active foreign policy would, Gladstone feared, distract 'the mind of the public and the Parliament'; but, far from dampening reform agitation, such a distraction was likely to be widely resented. The passing of the Second Reform Act in 1867, and the advent of Gladstone's first 'reforming' ministry, occupied the attention of all but the professional diplomats in these years. Stanley, the Conservative Foreign Secretary, and Clarendon after him, certainly partook in a regular interchange of views with the European powers, but the high points of this activity – the carefully restricted Luxembourg neutrality guarantee of 1867, and the secret, unavailing efforts of Clarendon to secure an arms-reduction treaty between

France and Prussia in 1869–70 – revealed yet again the limited and non-committal role which Britain wished to play in Europe.[5]

All this forms the necessary background to an understanding of Britain's policy of neutrality during the Franco-Prussian War. The swift defeat of France was a watershed in European politics, dividing the two centuries of Paris's claims to continental hegemony from the seventy or so years of Berlin's bid for that same position. Admittedly, only with the benefit of hindsight does one measure the true significance of this war, but even at the time observers talked of Europe losing a mistress and gaining a master. The military operations, the abdication of Napoleon III, the proclamation of the German Empire, the establishment and crushing of the Paris Commune, were events which turned the heads of even the most purblind 'little Englanders'; and Britain's policy of neutrality was warmly debated in the press and parliament by those who favoured it and those who opposed it.

Although this debate was far more heated than that of 1866, the result was the same: Britain would not interfere in a European quarrel. Many of the reasons which applied earlier were still valid in 1870–1, in particular the widespread dislike of the waste and horrors of war, and the 'Whiggish' concern for Britain's global obligations: the fact that Russia took advantage of the war unilaterally to denounce the Black Sea restriction clauses of the 1856 Treaty of Paris reminded many that the real threat to the Empire lay elsewhere. Furthermore, it was still not evident to most British observers that the balance of power had been endangered by Germany's rise. With France bitter and Russia suspicious at this new power, an equilibrium between the centre and the periphery now prevailed. In addition, both belligerents had respected Belgian neutrality, the one point which London might have regarded as a *casus belli* had it been violated. All this does not mean that the changes which occurred in Europe were received quietly, but those who agitated on behalf of one belligerent or its opponent cancelled each other out. With Germanophiles such as Carlyle urging the government against France, and Francophiles like Frederick Harrison pleading for action against 'Prussian militarism', the non-interventionists occupied a strong middle position. It was only once threatened, by Gladstone's deep-felt indignation at the idea of transferring Alsace-Lorraine to Germany, but even on this issue Granville and the other Cabinet 'moderates' insisted that intervention was out of the question. Britain might disapprove of events; but it should not act. On this, Liberal and Conservative leaders were agreed.

Although this policy of neutrality held firm, two further remarks need to be made. First, it is possible to point to a rising public disquiet at what appeared to be national self-effacement. The clear signs that Britain had counted for little while the European order had been reshaped, the failure of the Liberal government to stop the Russian denunciation of the Black Sea restrictions, the rumours of withdrawals from colonial garrisons, and Gladstone's willing acceptance of the judgment against Britain of the *Alabama* claims in the summer of 1871, provoked a rising tide of criticism. The classic Liberal recipes of non-intervention, armaments reductions, anti-imperialism, appeals to 'moral forces' and a diplomacy of what in another age might be termed 'appeasement', disturbed not only the Queen or rebel Tories such as Salisbury but also a considerable number of Whigs, permanent officials and diplomats, newspaper editors and others. The heated discussion over the best-selling 'invasion scare' story, Colonel Chesney's *The Battle of Dorking* (1871), was another pointer to this unease. It would be wrong to exaggerate the change of mood, especially when most public attention was directed at the further reforms of Gladstone's ministry; but it was significant that that arch-tactician Disraeli was already sensing that political capital could be made out of a programme of imperial pride and diplomatic boldness. Here, in his earlier urgings to Stanley and in his famous speeches of 1872 at the Crystal Palace and elsewhere, were the first hints that the 1870s would see a far greater division between politicians over external affairs than in the 1860s.

The second remark is that the British neglect of the European power-balance was *not* total: it operated within broad but recognizable limits determined by centuries of experience and concern at the possibility of one state becoming dominant. This was not too clear in the early 1870s, when the Liberal government simply wished to be on good terms with all and for practical reasons did not desire to alienate either Paris or Berlin while its own relations with St Petersburg and Washington were so delicate. The advent of Disraeli's administration in 1874 did not at first alter this apparent abstentionism. Indeed, the new Prime Minister's belief that Britain was really much more of an 'Asian' than a European power, and that its attitude towards the continent should be one of 'proud reserve', made the Conservatives keen to see a stable balance in that region. Far from distrusting Germany, the Foreign Secretary, Derby,* looked to Berlin to preserve the European order and to temper Russian expansionism: only if Bismarck provoked 'an aggressive and an unnecessary war'[6] against France would London's attitude change.

Ironically, this is what did happen only a short while after the Conservative accession, when a flood of reports in the spring and early summer of 1875 suggested that the military party in Berlin was urging a preventive war against France before the latter fully recovered its strength. Skilfully utilizing this 'war-in-sight' crisis, French diplomacy succeeded in persuading both Russia and Britain to express concern in Berlin at the rumours, which Bismarck indignantly denied. While the exact intentions of the German government in 1875 remains a mystery, and the probability is that Russian rather than British pressure concerned it

* That is, the 15th Earl of Derby, the Stanley of the 1860s, who succeeded his father in 1869.

most, the interventionist mood of Disraeli and (even more) his royal mistress was unambiguous. Both they and their advisers made meaningful comparisons between Bismarck and 'the first Napoleon', and hinted at Britain's traditional regard for the European equilibrium. Many observers at the time suspected that German territorial aims had not been completed with the establishment of the united *kleindeutsches* (small-German) *Reich* of 1871.

Looking forward to the Triple Entente of Russia, France and Britain in the years before 1914, some historians have pointed to the 'war-in-sight' crisis as the first manifestation of the combination which would one day hold German expansionism in check. In the circumstances of the 1870s, however, such a prospect was scarcely anticipated, except perhaps by the far-seeing and resourceful Bismarck himself. His protestations that he sought no war with France were almost immediately followed by a fresh and prolonged crisis in the Eastern Question, which inevitably attracted elsewhere the attention of Russia and Britain. By the time that that crisis was 'stabilized' in the early 1880s, interest would be switching to colonial and naval rivalries; and, apart from private anxieties felt by Salisbury in the period 1886–9, it would be another thirty years after the 'war-in-sight' affair before the question of Germany's latent capacity to dominate west-central Europe became once again the central issue of international politics. Almost by definition, therefore, the lengthy absence of this issue ensured that British diplomacy over the next few decades would be influenced more by Mediterranean and imperial concerns than by west-European considerations.

Constantinople and Cairo, 1876–82

The series of crises running through the eastern Mediterranean and the Middle East in the final quarter of the nineteenth century was primarily caused by the seepage of west-European ideas, culture and finance into societies whose rulers were unable or unwilling to handle these new agents of change. In the Balkans, for example, Occidental concepts about national self-determination were readily appealed to by various ethnic groups, but the attempts by any one people to implement those concepts (i.e. by the creation of nation-states with clearly recognized boundaries) usually conflicted with the claims of neighbouring peoples and always conflicted with the existing position of the transnational Ottoman Empire, the disappearance of which would produce as many problems as it solved. Along the North African coast, Muslim societies virtually independent of their Turkish suzerain were reacting against the 'materialistic' West at the same time as certain of their own élites were succumbing to the temptations of bank loans, railway and canal development, and other forms of modernization.

To this chain of events, the late-Victorian establishment was noticeably ambivalent. Few, if any, doubted the correctness and inevitability of the modernizing process itself; all retained the Macaulayite assumption that the spread of Western (and particularly British) ideas, institutions, religion, culture and trading links would be good for those indigenous recipients as well as beneficial to its disposers. What was at issue was the balance which should be struck between these liberating tendencies on the one hand and the requirements of political order and security on the other. The latter consideration had a twofold aspect: a concern that the possible demise of a native polity might threaten those Western interests (missionaries, planters, traders, financiers) who were, consciously or unconsciously, contributing to its collapse; and an even greater concern lest any European rival exploit this local crisis to the detriment of British interests. Either of these twin fears might prompt military intervention on the part of the government in Whitehall. In the Balkans and in Egypt, both existed simultaneously – in contrast, say, to the more distant crises in Fiji, Malaya and the Gold Coast, where British intervention in 1874–5 had been almost solely motivated by the collapse of the native order.[7] Predictably enough, the 'pessimists' – or, as they liked to be termed, the 'realists' – identified themselves by calling for intervention as occasions arose, and by warning of the dangers of native unrest or foreign intrigues: their ranks included almost all the Conservatives, and many of the Whigs. By contrast, the 'optimists' or 'idealists' – that is, the great bulk of the Liberal Party, and especially its dissenter and Cobdenite circles – were opposed to the suppression of human rights and disliked the all-too-ready turn to belligerent postures and colonial annexations.

This clash between 'conservative' and 'liberal' responses to external events became so heated in the decade after 1875 for two reasons: outside developments crowded rapidly upon each other, often interacting with a speed which took British governments by surprise; secondly, those two protagonists, Disraeli and Gladstone, each perceived that such events brought with them the possibility of political gain or, if not handled properly, of electoral disaster. The best example of this was undoubtedly the Bulgarian crisis of 1876, when reports of the atrocities committed by Turkish irregulars against the Bulgarians brought a reluctant Gladstone out of retirement to lead a national crusade against the Conservative government's cynical support of the Sultan's rule. Once out of retirement, the Liberal statesman was excited by the sheer extent of the popular agitation – 'the greatest public incursion into the official conduct of foreign affairs in British history',[8] it has been said – and he determined to go with this movement, to the embarrassment of Whigs and Tories alike.

For Disraeli, this was a particularly upsetting flank attack. Up until then, he had been successfully cultivating his package of *Imperium et Libertas*, making gestures to the working classes and satisfying fellow-patriots with his adroit purchase of the Suez Canal shares and his act of giving Victoria the new title of Empress of India. More particularly, he had just enjoyed torpedoing the proposals of the Three Emperors League for reforms within the Ottoman Empire (the so-called 'Berlin Memorandum' of May 1876), hoping thereby to retain prime influence for Britain at Constantinople and, more distantly, of discrediting that Bismarck-led combination. Now, all chances of achieving a 'national consensus' in foreign affairs had been ruined by this moralistic and demagogic campaign, and his very diplomacy was in danger of being derailed by domestic sentiment. It was for this latter reason that many diplomats, intellectuals and other members of the 'upper ten thousand' not usually sympathetic to Disraeli felt disturbed by the atrocities agitation: an external policy based upon the emotionalism of the masses in place of the rationality of an élite was to them the most dangerous of all Gladstonian innovations.

But Disraeli held firm, encouraging his shaken Cabinet to stay with him until the tides turned. By the spring of 1877, relief was at hand: the Russian government, carried along by pan-Slavic agitation, declared war on Turkey and began its laborious military advance towards Constantinople. While this attempt to punish the 'unspeakable Turk' was welcomed by Gladstone's followers, the threat to the Palmerstonian tradition of upholding the Ottoman Empire from its northern neighbour alarmed many other Britons. The balance between liberty and security tilted in the latter direction: here was the prospect, which Disraeli took up with relish, of arousing the country against the Russian 'threat' *and* of dealing a hefty counter-blow at Gladstone. As 1877 gave way to 1878, the war crisis heightened. In the process, the pacific and inert Derby chose to resign, but Disraeli gained Salisbury instead as his Foreign Secretary. He also gained Cyprus as a possible troop base in any counter-stroke through the Straits; and he gained the support of Austria-Hungary, which could no longer bear the thought of Russian successes in the Balkans, and wriggled free of Bismarck's restraining hands. Faced with the prospect of an Anglo-Austrian war against an exhausted but still formidable Russia, the German Chancellor felt that he had no option but to intervene and smother the dispute in the paper and protocols of an international conference. His mediation above all else ensured the successful conclusion of the Berlin Conference, from which Disraeli and Salisbury could return in July 1878, the former publicly claiming 'peace with honour', and the latter privately wondering how much longer the ramshackle Turkish sovereignty could be maintained.

There is no doubt that the Conservative leader, after a bad start, gained politically from the Eastern Crisis of 1876–8; but Gladstone, too, was terrible on the rebound, and Tory policy elsewhere in the world could not be rescued by Bismarckian assistance or sustained domestically by pointing to the threat of Russian expansionism. There were too many 'crumbling frontiers' across the globe, and impulsive British officials seeking to 'stabilize' them, for a distant and unimaginative metropolitan power to deal with by the late 1870s. In southern Africa, where successive British administrations had wavered between periods of passivity and periods of expansion in a vain effort to establish a natural border somewhere in the limitless hinterland, the clash between Afrikaner imperialism and Zulu imperialism pulled in the colonial authorities; and the Zulu War of 1879 not only produced its crop of military reverses and an increase in income tax, but it also patently failed to stabilize the situation. In Afghanistan, an army under General Roberts had asserted British influence at Kabul, been withdrawn, and was then sent in again when the British mission was slaughtered. All this gave Gladstone ample opportunity to inveigh against 'Beaconsfieldism' – that is, reckless wars and threats of wars, needless loss of blood, squandering of British funds, aggressive annexations, and disregard of the rights of other peoples – when he conducted his famous Midlothian campaigns of 1879 and 1880.

It is difficult to say just how far the Liberal landslide in the 1880 election was caused by arguments over imperial and foreign affairs, as opposed to the influence of the current trade depression or the issue of church disestablishment; but it is clear that many observers believed that the contest *had* been about rival perceptions of external policy. This, certainly, was Gladstone's own conviction and he had repeatedly called for a return to 'normality', that is, to a rational and conciliatory diplomacy free from the forced assertiveness and aggressions of his rival. In its place, he promised, would be seen the high principles of maintaining peace, respecting the freedoms of others, avoiding unnecessary entanglements, and working with the powers in a true Concert of Europe.

Instead of these fond hopes, the external policy of Gladstone's second ministry was beset by one intractable problem after another, by external disasters and internal wrangles, with the Cabinet stumbling into Irish bogs and African quagmires. Some of the reasons for these difficulties were, perhaps, foreseeable even in 1880. The first was that the Whig majority in the Cabinet, although agreeing with Gladstone's criticisms of Disraelian adventurism, were by no means inclined to put their trust in moral force to solve external problems; if trouble threatened, their response would be Palmerstonian, not libertarian – and this preference for securing order by force if necessary was heightened by the Whigs' apprehensions of Gladstone's earnest resolve to deal with the Irish question on the same principles as he was applying to the Afghans and Afrikaners.

Secondly, it was illusory to expect that there existed – outside of Gladstone's imagination – a European concert of powers waiting to respond to Liberal suggestions. What did exist was an isolated France in the west, and a Bismarck-dominated *bloc* in the centre and the east. The Berlin Conference of 1878 may have split the Three Emperors League, as Disraeli had hoped, but not for long. In the following year Bismarck drew Vienna away from London's influence by offering a full-scale Austro-German alliance. He did, it is true, accompany this move by hints of a similar compact with Britain, but he abandoned this approach before Disraeli could respond and before the Queen, Salisbury and others needed to press the domestic and diplomatic objections to such a pact. Although the Conservative leaders had consoled themselves with the thought that the Austro-German alliance would restrain Russia, Bismarck actually used its existence to induce St Petersburg to return to a revived Three Emperors League in 1881. In the following year he pulled the Italians into his diplomatic orbit, by persuading Vienna to join him in offering membership of a Triple Alliance to Rome. All this might not have mattered to those radical Liberals who wished to remain aloof from Europe; but it affected Gladstone's hopes a great deal, for Bismarck had seen in them a threat to his own European order and therefore wielded his immense influence among the other powers to ensure that such aspirations would never be realized.[9]

Internally and externally, therefore, there existed formidable obstacles to a Prime Minister intent upon applying the principles enunciated in his 1879–80 'Midlothian campaign' to whatever foreign-policy problems might arise. And these were years, as mentioned above, when problems cropped up thick and fast. Moreover, even if Gladstone and his colleagues genuinely struggled to find what seemed to them honourable and rational solutions, the blunt fact was that the forces for change were not always susceptible to

Western, Liberal arguments. This was already being made clear by the Irish, who declined to accept Westminster's notions of property rights or parliamentary procedures; but it was even truer of Egyptian nationalists, Boer farmers, Afghani tribesmen and Balkan insurgents. All this, in turn, caused those Britons anxious about stability to call for firm government before self-government.

At first, 'Midlothian principles' prevailed. The Afghan campaign was wound down and, with British honour already restored by Roberts, only the diehard imperialists were eager to persist with a 'forward' policy in that unpromising region. There was more opposition, however, to the Liberal government's Indian policy, where the efforts of the new Viceroy, Lord Ripon, to win native affections aroused the wrath of the Anglo-Indian establishment. Reaction also threatened in South African policy, where Boer impatience at continued British rule had led to the proclamation of independence and a successful attack upon British forces at Majuba; but, brushing aside the cries for revenge, Gladstone concluded a treaty with the two Afrikaner republics (Transvaal and Orange Free State) which reduced Whitehall's control to a minimal and vague 'suzerainty'. This by no means settled the internal struggle between Briton, Boer and Bantu in southern Africa, but it did induce a temporary stability; it also marked the last gesture of a 'Liberal' external policy, before it was overwhelmed by the forces of revolution and reaction.

The real graveyard of Gladstonian diplomacy was Egypt, a country towards which, one suspects, the Grand Old Man had scarcely given a thought before the early 1880s. Unlike Afghanistan and the Transvaal, Egypt was as much a matter of European diplomacy as of imperial policy. It was, after all, technically a part of the Ottoman Empire, and thus of the intricate Eastern Question; it was also a major factor in Anglo-French relations, since commissioners appointed by the two powers had been virtually running Egypt since its bankruptcy in 1875 and the establishment of an international debt control; thirdly, the question of settling the seething discontents within its population was one which, Gladstone felt, appropriately belonged to the European concert, which was dealing with similar problems in the Balkans. But Egypt had, of course, one further attribute: it lay athwart that line of communications to Britain's eastern empire which the newly established Suez Canal had opened up. When the nationalist revolt against foreign controls in Egypt gathered pace, therefore, Gladstone found his political recipes opposed in a number of respects. The social turbulence, and threat to European residents and interests, made even an unorthodox Whig like himself apprehensive of continued instability and doubtful of indigenous self-government; the incompetence and unpopularity of the Turks, the French opposition to any resumption of their rule, and the studied neutrality of Bismarck, made a 'European concert' solution impossible; and the insistence of the Whigs upon restoring law and order could not, in the final analysis, be resisted by one who had always maintained that the process of emancipation had to take place within a context of respect for traditions, property, trade and social stability.

Slowly, agonizingly, the Liberal government moved towards intervention in Egypt, with the Whigs pressing forward and the radicals applying the brakes in vain. The situation become more complicated diplomatically, and simultaneously easier in military terms, when France backed out of the proposed joint action against the Egyptian nationalists in July 1882, just as Britain had nerved itself to act. The swift overrunning of the country by Wolseley's troops produced that 'stability' which the Whigs and Tories desired, but the erection of a single British control was soon to alienate the French and drive them into two decades of persistent hostility. Thus, the Anglo-French liberal *entente*, a major plank in the party's programme in 1880, was one further casualty of the Egyptian imbroglio. Since Gladstone characteristically insisted upon the maintenance of an *international* control of Egypt's finances (partly on the assumption that British troops would soon be withdrawn), the new antagonism between Paris and London gave even further influence to Berlin. While this did not seem so important in 1882 – it was difficult then to see Bismarck taking France's side in this affair – the diplomatic leverage which the international supervision of Egyptian finances offered to Germany was soon to be revealed. John Bright, that quintessential anti-imperialist, had resigned at this betrayal of principles; but the Liberal ministry, although rent by the inter-related disputes about legitimacy and reform in Ireland, Egypt and franchise matters, resolved to stagger on regardless.

Under Pressure, 1883–90

Gladstone's 'bondage in Egypt', as it has been neatly called,[10] was the consequence of the Liberal government's desire to have its cake and eat it: although committed to an early withdrawal, it also wished to provide security for the Suez Canal against attack, and to give some stability to the country's chaotic finances, which implied administrative reforms and the establishment of an 'Indian'-style bureaucracy. The more the British searched for that firm indigenous basis upon which 'good government' was to rest, the more they sank into Egyptian quicksands – not to mention Sudanese deserts, where a Khedival army of 10,000 men was annihilated by the Dervishes in November 1883. Here was a crumbling frontier which apparently stretched all the way up the Nile valley. As the Cabinet wrangled about the merits of staying in or abandoning Egypt, and simultaneously argued about the merits of 'Roman' or 'liberal' solutions to the parallel chaos in Ireland, French resentment grew and Paris slowly moved towards counter-measures, carefully observed by a German Chancellor never opposed to deriving benefits from the misfortunes of others.

It will not do to make the Egyptian crisis the sole or even the chief cause of the European 'scramble for Africa'. The reasons for that phenomenon had long been developing, and lay in the altering relationships (especially the economic and power relationships) between Europe and the tropical world. By July 1882, when British warships commenced their bombardment of Alexandria, the scramble was already under way. Expansionism in southern Africa, where Boers, Britons and Bantu rivalled each other, had a long history and a momentum of its own. Moreover, even in the late 1870s the French were moving into the hinterland of Senegal, and both they and King Leopold of Belgium were eyeing the Congo. In 1881 France had annexed Tunisia, in anticipation of a similar Italian step. If such actions had dismayed certain Britons and coloured the Whig fears about Egypt in the following years, the French in their turn had long suspected London's ambitions, and in particular the assertion of British 'paramountcy' in various regions by Disraeli's Colonial Secretary, Carnarvon.[11] What the British entry into Egypt and failure to withdraw from there *did* do, however, was to open up a new zone of rivalry and to make impossible any earlier hopes of an agreed Anglo-French supervision of the colonial scramble.

With France (and, inevitably, Russia) now intent upon applying diplomatic and other pressures to compel Britain to leave Egypt, Gladstone's government desperately needed the support of the Bismarck-led Triple Alliance on the international debt commission in order to secure a majority vote for proposed financial reforms. Thus was Bismarck, no great friend of English Liberalism, offered the chance to apply the *bâton égyptien* against the unfortunate Gladstone just at a time when Germany, too, had colonial demands to make upon Britain. In this respect also, it should be noted, German enterprises had already been active in Africa and the Pacific and domestic pressure groups had been calling for colonial annexations long before the summer of 1884; but it was only in that year that Bismarck perceived electoral and other internal-political grounds for abandoning his traditional aversion to overseas territories; and the Anglo-French split now offered him the opportunity to insist upon getting his own way in the quarrels which German firms had with their British rivals and the self-governing British colonies in Africa and the Pacific. When Gladstone, his benign Foreign Secretary, Granville, and his lethargic Colonial Secretary, Derby, did not see the cold logic behind Bismarck's messages, Germany's full diplomatic weight was thrown on to France's side over the Egyptian talks and during the Berlin West Africa Conference (1884–5) upon the Congo and Niger issues.

Berlin's intervention ripped aside any pretences the British Cabinet may still have held about preserving their overseas interests by claims to 'paramountcy' or the use of weaker clients like the Portuguese or the Sultan of Zanzibar. London had either to annex, or to get out; and even where it (or the sub-imperialists at Wellington, Brisbane and the Cape) wished to annex, this could no longer be done if it offended the malevolent genius in Berlin. The crux of the matter, as Gladstone informed Derby in December 1884, was that Germany could do 'extraordinary mischief to us at our one really vulnerable point, Egypt'.[12] In consequence of this, the British had already given way over South-west Africa, Togoland and the Cameroons, and were soon to give way also in New Guinea and East Africa. Moreover, all these were merely concessions made to buy the neutrality of a third power while London faced up to the implacable opposition of its chief rivals, France and Russia, which could damage British interests right across the globe; such bids for Berlin's goodwill brought only a negative benefit, together with widespread attacks by domestic and colonial critics for this further example of Gladstonian appeasement.

The last twelve months of the Liberal ministry were, in truth, fraught and unhappy. The Cabinet was already sufficiently split from top to bottom over Ireland and domestic affairs (including the Third Reform Act, and redistribution) without needing a further series of quarrels about imperial policy. Inevitably, these internal and external crises continued to affect each other – usually for the worse. Whig ministers, alarmed at disorders in Ireland, determined that order should be maintained in Egypt; but even that stance presumed that London was in control of events, which was patently not true. In early February 1885, for example, it became known that Gordon's mission to Khartoum had been overwhelmed by the Dervishes. In the outcry and confusion which followed, Gladstone confessed to the Commons 'that the difficulties of the case have passed entirely beyond the limits of such political and military difficulties as I have known in the course of an experience of half a century.'[13] In the midst of Sudanese disasters, it was not easy to recall that happy Midlothian spirit of five years earlier.

Yet there was worse to come. Already in December 1884, under the public pressure instigated by the *Pall Mall Gazette*'s revelations about naval weaknesses, the government had nervously authorized a supplementary fleet-construction bill: even so, it could not possibly produce fresh vessels for another three or four years. Moreover, the really intractable problems concerned the *land* defences of the Empire. Only a few weeks after the news of Gordon's death, Russian troops established themselves at the head of the Zulficar Pass, threatening not only Afghanistan but also the security of India. The Anglo-Russian war which Europe had expected for over two decades was now in sight, and it appeared to be a virtual certainty when London received word on 8 April 1885 of an Afghan defeat by the Russians at Penjdeh. The panic on the stock market, the vote of extraordinary credits, the occupation of Port Hamilton (off Korea) and other precautionary measures (including the printing of posters announcing the beginning of hostilities!) were all signs that a great-power conflict was closer than at any time since 1878. The only lingering form which Gladstone's hoped-for Concert of Europe now took was the united warning delivered by the powers (under Bismarckian coaching) to the Turks against allowing the Royal Navy to enter the Black Sea as a riposte to the Russian actions in Afghanistan. But the Liberal government was quite beyond appreciating the irony of all this. The Cabinet was by now exhausted and bitterly divided, and resigned in relief when defeated on a chance vote in the Commons in June 1885.

The accession of a Conservative government under Salisbury did not mean a return to an external policy of bombast and belligerency *à la* Disraeli: far from it. In the first place, Salisbury, who had never possessed much enthusiasm for his former leader's style, infinitely preferred a diplomacy of calculation and quiet persuasion, tendencies which could only be reinforced by his growing appreciation of the size of Britain's global problems. The major constraint upon Salisbury, however, was the state of internal politics, particularly in the confused years 1885–7. The Conservative government of 1885 was a minority one, sustained only by the opportunist votes of Parnell's Irish Home Rulers. By the end of the year, when Gladstone's conversion to Home Rule was made known, the Parnellite vote switched and the Liberals returned to power. The latter were no more united over Irish policy than previously, however, and when the Home Rule bill was laid before the Commons, Hartingtonite Whigs and Chamberlainite radicals joined the Conservatives in voting it down in July 1886. This balance of forces was reflected in the country at large during the subsequent general election: Salisbury's party had the biggest number of seats, but it could only outvote the combined Liberal and Irish parties with the help of the seventy-nine dissident Liberal Unionists. Since these by no means assumed that their break with the Liberal Party was final, and were only committed to supporting the Conservatives on Irish issues, Salisbury's administration was bound to be as cautious and uncontroversial as it possibly could. To the Queen, who frequently urged a more decisive diplomacy in Europe in these years, the Prime Minister was courteous but firm:

> The prospect is very gloomy abroad, but England cannot brighten it. Torn in two by a controversy which almost threatens her existence, she cannot in the present state of public opinion interfere with any decisive action abroad. The highest interests would be risked here at home, while nothing effective could be done by us to keep peace on the Continent.[14]

Both here and elsewhere, Salisbury testified to the influence of domestic affairs upon foreign policy; yet it is worth noting that his reaction was not that one could paper over such internal fissures by appeals to national sentiment as Disraeli had done (and as Bismarck was now encouraging him to do), but that Britain's external policy would have to be more reticent than ever.

Reticence did not, however, imply isolation. Indeed, Salisbury's major complaint against the Liberals' diplomacy was that it had left Britain perilously close to war, virtually without a friend in Europe. Naval and military deficiencies, even if repaired as quickly as possible, needed to be supplemented by political action: some problems, as noted earlier, were probably insoluble by military means. In the western hemisphere, where quarrels with Washington occurred in these years over such disparate matters as the Bering Sea seal fisheries and the Sackville-West affair, the ever-sensitive Anglo-American relationship required careful cultivation, if only to prevent a further worsening. But the weakest flank, at least in the early stages of Salisbury's administration, was the inherited crisis over Afghanistan. Only in September 1885 was an agreement signed which brought Britain and Russia away from the brink of war, although mutual suspicions remained.

The Anglo-Russian tension, and the parallel problem of overcoming French hostility to Britain in Africa and the

Mediterranean, dictated a policy of leaning towards the Germanic powers. At first, this brought few dividends: although happy to see the end of Gladstone's ministry, Bismarck was not going to aid Britain if that should lead to any disturbance in the delicate Russo-German relationship; and even if he was much more willing to help London against Paris now that the short-lived Franco-German colonial marriage was over, he expected compensation overseas for this support. Nevertheless, Salisbury persisted in wooing Berlin and Vienna – there being nobody else left to woo. He was aided in this strategy by events which at first sight seemed another threat to British interests: the reawakening of the Eastern Question late in 1885, and the possibility of a move by Russia against its ungrateful protégé in Bulgaria, Prince Alexander of Battenberg. Because such a move would in turn outrage the Austrians and possibly lead to a great-power struggle in the Balkans, Britain's stock steadily rose. Although Bismarck had no intention of confronting Russia himself, he could secretly hope that an Anglo-Austrian *bloc* would deter St Petersburg from military intervention in the Balkans; and, further, that Russian rage at being so deterred would be vented chiefly on London, somewhat less on Vienna, and not at all on Berlin. In addition, he was also alarmed at the growing tension between France and Italy, and hoped that the Royal Navy might be persuaded to support the latter in the Mediterranean. Finally, a patriotic revival in France with strong anti-German overtones made Bismarck even more eager to have affairs in the east kept in check by others so that he could attend to the revanchist threat in the west.

Such were the presuppositions of the grand casting-master in Berlin, to whom Britain now appeared as a likely candidate for a leading role in the European drama. Salisbury, the Chancellor's intellectual equal in diplomacy at least, obviously saw things differently. He was, of course, just as anxious to secure a stabilization of the international scene, since change would only benefit the unruly powers: as he put it in 1887, 'Whatever happens will be for the worse and therefore it is in our interest that as little should happen as possible.' But this interest in stabilization must not involve extensive commitments. Any open pledges to Austria-Hungary and Germany or against France, he feared, would alienate the Liberal Unionists. On the other hand, it was far too risky to adopt Randolph Churchill's urgings that Britain should do a deal with Russia, obtaining assurances about India in return for abandoning Constantinople and falling back upon Egypt – for that was not only a violent break with the tradition of propping up the Ottoman Empire but it would destroy Salisbury's hopes for a future settlement of Anglo-French differences. Furthermore, a great if long-suppressed fear lurked in the back of his mind: namely, that if Britain, Austria and perhaps others were involved in a war to prevent Russian domination of the Balkans or the Straits, Bismarck would not remain inactive but would instead seize this opportunity to deal with France, thus producing a west-European crisis of monumental proportions.

Salisbury's task, therefore, was to devise a course which avoided both the isolation of the radicals and the danger of being pushed forward by Bismarck into conflict with Russia or France unless this became truly unavoidable; yet he also needed to lean towards Berlin in order to obtain support over Egypt. In this complex and fluid situation, there was little that could be done to improve Anglo-Russian relations: they were too deep-frozen for that. Salisbury did try, however, through the services of his roving intermediary, Drummond-Wolff, to reach a settlement with France over Egypt, which would provide for a British withdrawal but also admit London's right to re-enter if imperial security was threatened. But here, as in other colonial issues, Salisbury found the French intransigent: and, to strengthen his own bargaining position by securing Bismarck's goodwill, he made concessions to German demands in Zanzibar, East Africa and Samoa. At almost the same time, he persuaded the Cabinet to agree to what was known as the First Mediterranean Agreement (February-March 1887), a secret exchange of notes with the Italian and Austro-Hungarian governments about diplomatic co-operation to preserve the *status quo* in the Mediterranean, Aegean and Black Seas.

A few months later, the failure of the Drummond-Wolff negotiations over Egypt, which occurred when France and Russia applied combined pressure upon the Sultan of Turkey (as the legal suzerain of Egypt) to refuse the deal, eliminated Salisbury's hopes of improving Anglo-French relations and drove him even closer to the Triple Alliance. In December 1887, the Cabinet agreed to the Second Mediterranean Agreement, a secret promise to work with Vienna and Rome for the defence of Turkey and the Balkans against a Russian assault, which at that time appeared quite likely. This was 'more nearly an alliance with a group of Great Powers than any Great Britain had ever made in time of peace and more formal than any agreement made with France or Russia twenty years later.'[15] Not surprisingly, the Liberal Unionists had qualms about such secret dealings, and Salisbury worried about German intentions towards France, where public opinion was being recklessly stoked up by General Boulanger and fellow chauvinists. On the other hand, French belligerency was not directed solely against Germany. By 1888, indeed, both the British press and many politicians were anxiously discussing the chances of a 'bolt from the blue' in the light of revelations about the country's military and naval deficiencies against a surprise invasion. Furthermore, there were increasing signs that France and Russia were moving closer together, perhaps towards a secret alliance, which in wartime could make the British position in the Mediterranean untenable. In such worrying circumstances, the British Cabinet felt that it had little alternative but to consort with what Salisbury termed the 'satisfied' powers against the designs of the 'hungry' states.

In retrospect, one can see that it was from about this time onwards that Britain's diplomatic position actually began to improve. The Russians prudently resisted the impulse to move into the Balkans, and another critical phase of the Eastern Question began to ebb. The British government, unable to get out of Egypt on adequate terms, resolved to stay and build up its position. Thirdly, apprehension of maritime weakness led to the passing of the famous Naval Defence Act of 1889, which increased the battlefleet so as to assure it of future superiority against the next two largest navies. Although all this scarcely brought immediate security for Britain, its position was far better than that of Germany and its allies, which felt increasingly threatened *on land* by the growing Franco-Russian combination. In particular, the steady worsening of relations between Berlin and St Petersburg in the 1880s, which the accession of the impulsive Wilhelm II in 1888 only hastened, indicated the end of Bismarck's European order, the demise of that Three Emperors League which had kept France isolated and had also restricted British influence on the continent.

The symbol of this change was the secret approach which Bismarck made to Salisbury early in 1889 for an Anglo-German alliance. This the British government politely turned down, with explanations of the constitutional difficulties of entering a fixed military commitment; until it actually contemplated war, London would have to remain on friendly but uncommitted terms with Berlin, a reply which probably satisfied Bismarck privately even if it may have disappointed Wilhelm and the 'military party' in Berlin. The real reasons for the British reply were, however, domestic and strategical rather than strictly constitutional: the Anglo-German alliance proposed by Bismarck was directed against France, but such a treaty would have outraged the Liberals, disturbed the Queen and the Liberal Unionists (not to mention Salisbury himself), and in no way have benefited Britain in the event, say, of a Russian assault upon India. It made far better sense to avoid an alliance, but to rely instead upon a growing naval strength and the continued benevolence of the Triple Alliance which, as it transpired, was to increase when Bismarck was dismissed early in 1890 and the secret Russo-German 'reinsurance treaty' of 1887 was allowed to lapse.

This gradual and undramatic securing of British interests also occurred outside the European field. With the French in Africa, as with the Russians in Asia, there was little scope for agreement: temporary settlements might be achieved over the New Hebrides, the Suez Canal or the Pamirs, but the fundamental disagreements over the future of the Nile valley and the hinterlands of India meant that London was always wary, and sometimes felt it had to counter these rivals with 'blocking' annexations of its own. This had also been the British attitude towards Germany's expansion in East Africa and the Pacific, although Salisbury was at first much more tolerant of those actions – less out of any warmth for German imperialism, of course, than out of his pressing need to buy Bismarck's goodwill over Egypt and the Balkans. By the time the weights had shifted in this 'diplomatic duel',[16] Berlin was being forced to consider purchasing London's goodwill in Europe by concessions in colonial disputes. Moreover, it would hardly do to portray the British as being under pressure and acting defensively *everywhere*. In West Africa, Goldie's Royal Niger Company was keen to expand up-country; from southern Africa, Rhodes and his colleagues were determined to push northwards, regardless of opposition from Boers, Matabele, Portuguese and others; and in the Pacific, politicians in Wellington and Sydney and entrepreneurs in the islands urged a forward policy. All these, moreover, had their various supporters at home – certain business interests and Chambers of Commerce, the influential missionary societies, Tory MPs, and the imperialist press. By 1889 or so, all these groupings were showing concern about the British position in central and eastern Africa, and it was perhaps fortunate for Salisbury that by then Bismarck and his successors were more interested in securing Germany's European position than in advancing the programme of the *Kolonialgesellschaft*.

The high point of Salisburian colonial policy came in the Anglo-German treaty of July 1890, whereby, in exchange for the island of Heligoland, Britain gained Zanzibar and large tracts of East Africa, thus securing the southern approaches to the Nile valley. A little later, the Italians were persuaded into a demarcation treaty which kept them out of that valley as well; and at almost the same time the Portuguese were compelled by *force majeure* to agree to British claims in central Africa. All these gains were achieved without many concessions by Britain and, indeed, with the Triple Alliance still hoping to develop even closer ties with the island-state so as to deter the French and the Russians. This was a rather impressive improvement in the country's fortunes since 1885, and the more so when Salisbury's domestic difficulties are taken into account.

Nevertheless, Salisbury's diplomacy represented a sensible but temporary adjustment, not a fundamental reversal of trends which, being rooted in the rising power of other states, were outside British control. For a short while this was not clear and many observers felt that the position had been nicely stabilized. The truth was soon to reveal itself during the period of the short-lived Liberal government of 1892–5, and would be amply demonstrated by the fact that even the Conservative administration which followed it could not handle the more pressing external problems without a series of further and more drastic adjustments.

Guarding Imperial Frontiers, 1890–7

Perhaps the most important of the changed conditions of the early 1890s was the conclusion of the Franco-Russian Alliance. Its effects were various, and even contradictory at times, but could never be ignored. At first this new combination had alarmed the Triple Alliance, which therefore hoped for British support; whereas, from London's viewpoint, it simply meant that there now existed two power-*blocs* in Europe, which balanced off each other and allowed Britain to remain uncommitted – and, indeed, to try once again to settle its outstanding disputes with France and Russia. This was Salisbury's private conclusion, even though he graced his replies to Berlin and Rome's more extensive requests for help with polite regrets and occasionally made some gestures to reassure the Italians. It was also his successor, Rosebery's, conclusion, but radical-Liberal pressure and the new Foreign Secretary's own more arrogant style soon disillusioned the Triple Alliance. Moreover, as these partners slowly reconciled themselves to the new European order and to Liberal reticence, they also perceived that the Dual Alliance was working against Britain *outside* Europe, in that it had finally brought together London's two most formidable naval and colonial rivals. Rather than chase after the British, therefore, one could wait until Franco-Russian activities forced even a purblind Liberal government to see that it needed the Triple Alliance as much as, perhaps even more than, the latter needed England. This, certainly, was the conclusion of the directors of foreign policy in Berlin, who by 1893 were trying to mend their fences with St Petersburg. (It was not so strongly shared by Italy and Austria-Hungary, because they needed British support more in the Mediterranean.) Finally, since the balance between the two *blocs* could only be altered by a great war, each side tacitly accepted the situation and turned more of its attention to the extra-European world; and this, inevitably, could only be to the discomfort of the established global power, Britain itself. A heightened pace of battleship building, increased agitation by imperialist pressure groups, and renewed colonial endeavours by France, Russia, Germany and Italy, were notable features of the early-to-mid-1890s.

The brunt of these changes fell upon the unhappy fourth and final ministry of Gladstone, which was already divided enough over Home Rule and domestic issues without having to deal with such external problems. A bitter Cabinet quarrel between Rosebery and 'economists' such as Sir William Harcourt over the retention of Uganda in 1892–4 set much of the tone. Russian military expeditions in the Pamirs and pressure upon Afghanistan increased British anxieties about Asia. Exchange visits by the French and Russian navies, and the basing of a Russian fleet at Toulon, challenged British maritime dominance in the Mediterranean: even in 1891, the intelligence departments had pointed out how difficult it would be to defend Constantinople from a Russian attack, since any British fleet sent through the Dardanelles might be followed in by the French. By 1893, many newspaper writers advocated 'scuttling' from the entire Mediterranean and, although this strategy was never adopted, the pressure grew for yet another massive naval increase – the Spencer Programme, over which Gladstone resigned and was succeeded as Prime Minister by Rosebery in April 1894. All this should have pushed the British closer to the Triple Alliance, as should have the Siam 'war scare' of July 1893, which arose when it was falsely reported that the French had ordered British vessels out of the Mekong river. But the majority of the Liberal Cabinet was opposed to any military commitments, especially against France; and the leader of the Triple Alliance, Germany, was by now so suspicious of London's aims that it prevailed upon its partners to stay aloof from Rosebery until he pledged his firm support – an impossible demand by that time.

These disagreements between Britain and the Triple Alliance over Mediterranean policy were further disrupted by a fresh outburst of colonial quarrels. The breakdown of the 'patched-up' Samoan tripartite settlement of 1889 was already leading to claims and counter-claims by New Zealand and by German nationalists for control of that group. Even more seriously, Germany and France were combining together again – rather as in their colonial *entente* of 1884–5 – to frustrate British plans in West Africa and the Congo; and a deal which Rosebery and his Foreign Secretary, Kimberley, concocted with King Leopold of the Belgians came under such criticism from Paris, Berlin and (not least) radical Cabinet members led by Harcourt that it had to be abandoned in June 1894. This humiliation so enraged Rosebery that he warned Germany's allies that he would respond by giving no help in the Mediterranean. By the end of 1894, London and Berlin were also bitterly quarrelling over events in southern Africa, where the British suspected German intrigues with the Boers, and the Germans feared that Rhodes and his fellow-expansionists would change the *status quo* in the Transvaal and then move northwards upon Portuguese and German territories.

During the final twelve months of the Liberal government's rule, the foreign-policy problems multiplied. A revolt in Armenia, cruelly suppressed by the Turks, provoked public calls for action; but that in turn raised the whole Eastern Question and, although Rosebery at first hoped for an accord with Russia on this issue to complement a recent Anglo-Russian settlement over the Pamirs, basic disagreements soon appeared. The Russian government, and those of the other powers, regarded the stability of the Ottoman Empire as a far higher priority than the fate of the Armenians, which so exercised the British evangelical conscience. Furthermore, although London was at least engaged in talks with St Petersburg and Paris over the Armenian issue, it diverged markedly from them over the Far East, where Japan was beginning its own expansionist course in 1894 by defeating and then acquiring parts of China. Fearing that this might damage their own aims in that region, Russia, France and Germany joined together diplomatically to compel the Japanese to disgorge Port Arthur. Here was further evidence that, outside Europe at least, members of the Dual and Triple Alliances might work together; but it was a sign of the altered times that Britain, traditionally the leading western power in the Orient, was not a party to this settlement of the Sino-Japanese War. In part, this paralysis was induced by the fissures within the Liberal Cabinet; but it was also caused by the sheer weight and number of the external problems that Rosebery faced, which compelled the utmost caution. As he himself put it to Kimberley, Britain should not intervene in Far Eastern quarrels unless its interests 'imperatively' demand it:

> Imperatively, I say, because our commerce is so universal and so penetrating that scarcely any question can arise in any part of the world without involving British interests. This consideration, instead of widening rather circumscribes the field of our actions. For did we not strictly limit the principle of intervention we should always be simultaneously engaged in some forty wars.[17]

Here was a nice confession that a power occupying the Number One position in trading and colonial terms had nothing to gain, and much to lose, from any serious disturbances to the peace. In a world where challengers lurked everywhere, it was extraordinarily difficult to decide in which theatre to stand and fight, because of the implications this would have for general trade and for Britain's position in other regions.

When Salisbury returned to office in June 1895, he not unnaturally complained of the Liberal government's 'disastrous inheritances'. Yet even if one can point to errors of judgment on the part of his predecessors, it is clear that most of the problems were not of Gladstone or Rosebery's making alone: they were also reflections of the new, twentieth-century world breaking through the cracking surface of the old. Japan was on the move in the Far East, the United States was about to flex its muscles in the western hemisphere, the Ottoman Empire was decomposing, the Germans were embarking upon their *Weltpolitik*, the trans-Siberian railway was steadily coming closer to the Orient. How the Conservatives would react to all this was not clear.

They had, it was true, proclaimed an attachment to the Empire which might make the abandonment of older commitments difficult: but they also had a reputation for flexible *Realpolitik*, for the pragmatic response to new circumstances when it became evident that older methods no longer sufficed. Both these characteristics, in their turn, were to be witnessed in the coming decade of Conservative external policy.

The most pressing of the Liberal 'inheritance' was the Armenian question. The continued massacre of Armenians, and the inability of the Turks to reform themselves, tempted Salisbury into considering the use of naval force to coerce the Sultan and also into musings about the possibility of solving the age-old Eastern Question by a wide-ranging partition of the Ottoman Empire. How serious this latter idea was and under what circumstances Salisbury thought it could be effected are not clear; but the reaction of the other powers was unmistakable – any alteration in the *status quo* was unwelcome because it might resurrect old rivalries and spread them across Turkey's borders into the Balkans and elsewhere. If the Sultan could not be persuaded into reforms, he certainly should not be forced into them. It was a sad commentary upon those confident mid-century Liberal hopes of converting other powers to English ways, that no nation except their own was all that perturbed by the fate of the Armenians. What gave Salisbury even more food for thought was the way this crisis had exposed weaknesses in the traditional assumption about British strategy towards Turkey. When, for example, he contemplated the unilateral despatch of a fleet to overawe the Sultan, he was strongly opposed by the Admiralty itself and then overruled in the Cabinet: the sea lords again feared that any force sent to Constantinople might be confronted by a Russian navy ahead of it and a French fleet behind it; and in any case it was now altogether more hazardous to steam through the Dardanelles, for the Turks had strengthened the defences there while neglecting those around the Bosphorus – the

Sultan now clearly feared the British more than the Russians. All this, incidentally, also threw doubt upon that older assumption that Russian pressure upon India could ultimately be answered by strikes into the Black Sea. The 'soft underbelly' of the Russian Empire had now acquired protection.

The military difficulties of reaching Constantinople, and the British public's dislike of rendering any aid to the Sultan, obviously undermined the Disraelian belief that the defence of the Straits was both practicable and desirable. This certainly affected Salisbury's thinking when he discussed with Vienna the possibility of renewing the Mediterranean *ententes* of the 1880s, and he disappointed the Austrians by his unwillingness to pledge a British commitment to the defence of Constantinople. On the other hand, Goluchowski (the Austro-Hungarian Foreign Minister) and his colleagues, although still worried about Russia's distant aims, were much more anxious to preserve the existing situation than to force reforms upon the Turks, and by 1897 Vienna and St Petersburg secretly agreed to put the Balkans 'on ice'. Apart from permitting the Russians to concentrate upon Asiatic expansion, this deal indicated that the Austrians, like Salisbury, had perceived that the earlier Anglo-Austrian identity of interests had now disappeared. By that time, indeed, the British government had privately recognized that it would make much more sense to base its defence of the route to India upon Cairo and not upon Constantinople, although for understandable reasons it was felt necessary to keep this change of strategy secret.

In the midst of the Armenian issue, around the turn of the year 1895–6, Salisbury was also unpleasantly surprised by a sharp worsening in Anglo-American relations when President Cleveland insisted upon intervening in a boundary dispute between Venezuela and British Guiana. Washington's claim that such forceful mediation was justified under the Monroe Doctrine did not much impress Salisbury, who argued that that doctrine had no basis in international law; but the prospect of a serious quarrel with the United States worried other members of the Cabinet and many British imperialists who favoured the cause of Anglo-Saxon harmony. Also alarmed were the stock markets, for more material reasons; and the strategists, since Canada was the obvious 'hostage' in an Anglo-American war and since the Royal Navy, although superior to any American fleet, could only be superior in the western hemisphere by abandoning the Mediterranean.

In addition, Cleveland had scarcely uttered his Venezuelan challenge when news arrived that Rhodes's partner, Jameson, had attempted and failed in an impetuous 'raid' against the Transvaal government, and that the Boer leader, Kruger, had received a congratulatory telegram from Wilhelm II. This German intervention in a region which the British considered their own enraged the Tory press and many backbenchers, who applauded the government's creation of a 'flying squadron' ready to sail to any threatened point of the Empire. In the circumstances of this more serious quarrel with Germany, it was not difficult for the Cabinet to agree to American arbitration in the Venezuelan issue, a decision which seemed even wiser when British Guiana was later awarded the lion's share of the disputed territory. Nonetheless, this double crisis was full of meaning. Britain had given an indication of some sort that it recognized American political predominance in the western hemisphere; and it had clashed with Germany for the first time on an issue – the supremacy of southern Africa – which London, at least, regarded as vital. Since Berlin did not have such critical interests at stake, it was soon seeking a *modus vivendi* in that part of the globe; but the quarrel had aroused German nationalists and their Kaiser, both of whom drew the conclusion that a much larger fleet was needed in anticipation of some future confrontation with the arrogant British.

Perhaps the most interesting aspect of the Venezuelan and Transvaal clashes was that they were *not* with the powers which most British imperialists considered to be the country's really serious rivals. Lurking in the background, the Cabinet and the press knew, was that formidable Franco-Russian combination, whose battlefleets were almost as large as the Royal Navy's and whose ambitions clashed with Britain's everywhere from the Mediterranean to the China Sea. If the Dual Alliance was the real foe, could the country afford the luxury of quarrelling with the other powers? And was it not a comment upon Britain's troubled world position that it had disputes with rivals right across the globe? The popular newspapers at this time might proudly take up that political catch-phrase, 'splendid isolation', but a growing number of British and foreign politicians were less convinced that such a state was all that splendid. Continental journals, sneering at London's misfortunes, portrayed the British as alone and unwanted. Perhaps it would be necessary to reduce Britain's obligations, or even to think of abandoning isolation and entering one of the alliance *blocs*, thus admitting that its interests could not be protected by its own resources alone? This was the atmosphere, it should be noted, in which contemporaries anxiously debated the claims (in, for example, E. E. Williams's book, *Made in Germany, 1896*) that German and American manufacturers were displacing British goods; and also debated, more optimistically, the prospects of some form of imperial federation with the self-governing colonies during the warm glow of the 1897 Diamond Jubilee celebrations. All these were signs, not that the decision-making élite was about to order a change of course, since no one really knew which was the best direction to take; but that an increasing number of Britons, impressed by the difficulties of guarding imperial frontiers, believed that the existing manner of conducting external policy could no longer be maintained.

Isolation or Alliance, 1898-1902

The above facts formed the background to that confused debate around the turn of the century about the relative merits of isolation or alliance. The matter was argued inside and outside the Cabinet, across party lines and in all the newspapers. Although many minor variations of stance existed, two main schools of thought predominated. The first solution was to seek, by all reasonable means, to come to an agreement with the powers whose expansion seemed most likely to threaten British interests, viz. France in Africa and Russia in Asia. A surrender of those interests (whatever the arch-patriots charged) was not intended; but this policy was based instead upon the belief that with some 'give-and-take' such colonial rivalries could be amicably settled. It presumed, therefore, that there was little need for a drastic alteration in British foreign-policy habits. This, certainly, was Salisbury's position and he had frequently given hints to Paris and St Petersburg that he was willing to discuss points at issue; even when disappointed by the replies and forced back to a policy of 'preventive' annexations and naval increase, he never fully abandoned his hopes of a future *detente*. It was a view also taken by most of the Liberal leaders, especially the Liberal Imperialists, who had shared Salisbury's dislike of too heavy a diplomatic dependence upon Berlin.

The alternative conception of external policy, held by a growing number of Conservatives and Liberal Unionists, was that the time had now arrived for Britain to re-examine its traditional policy of isolation from the European power *blocs*. In the circumstances of the late 1890s, when France and Russia pressed hard at imperial interests, this always meant a British commitment to Germany or to the Triple

Alliance as a whole. Yet this restiveness with traditional assumptions and belief that changes *had* to be made, a feeling best personified by Joseph Chamberlain and his admirers, did not logically require a commitment to Germany. When those Britons were eventually disappointed by Berlin, they were to seek an accord with France and Russia with the same enthusiasm and energy as they had earlier devoted to an Anglo-German alliance. The keynote of the movement was its search for radical measures rather than its traditional attachment to any particular alliance *bloc*. Its basic strength lay in the sense of alarm which many now felt at the threats to Britain's world position. Even if they portrayed the situation in gloomy, almost apocalyptic colours characteristic of social-Darwinistic notions of 'struggling for survival', this was an assessment which appeared to many Tory editors, backbench MPs and others to be more plausible than the passive and sceptical views of Salisbury, who was generally reckoned to be losing his touch.

The first push for change by these dissatisfied elements came with a worsening in the Far Eastern situation in late 1897/early 1898. The German seizure of Kiaochow, followed by Russia's move upon Port Arthur, seemed to presage the carving-up of a region where British influence had traditionally been dominant and to which British traders attached great importance. Although the Cabinet was under considerable domestic pressure to do something, it was also acutely aware of the perils of going to war to preserve the Chinese Empire; and Britain's own leasing of Wei-hai-wei early in 1898, described sarcastically by Salisbury as a 'cartographic consolation', was no real answer. It was at this point that Chamberlain decided to push for a change of policy, by speeches arguing that the age of isolation was over and by private (and rather clumsy) attempts to achieve an Anglo-German alliance. This solution scarcely appealed to Salisbury, but in any case it foundered upon German reservations: no one in Berlin wished to deflect Tsarist expansionism back to Prussia's eastern borders from the Orient simply (as Bülow, the State Secretary for Foreign Affairs, put it) '*pour les beaux yeux de* John Bull'; and, in addition, Bülow, the Kaiser and the Naval Secretary, Tirpitz, had plans for future expansionism which made an Anglo-German alliance impossible. The bid for a German alliance was much more a symptom of the strains within the British 'Official Mind' than a harbinger of a revolution in the existing power system.

Later in 1898 Chamberlain and Balfour believed that they had come closer to Berlin by concluding a secret agreement to divide the Portuguese Colonies if that nation, because of impending bankruptcy, should be forced to give up its overseas possessions in the future. While Salisbury was clearly more sceptical of the utility of such a deal, he could see that it at least had the effect of eliminating German claims in South-east Africa. Moreover, it would not do to be impolite to Berlin at a time when Anglo-French relations were worsening so swiftly that the two powers seemed on the point of war by late 1898. During the preceding two years, British forces had been slowly reconquering the Sudan. In September 1898 Kitchener's army crushed the Dervishes at Omdurman, just as it became known that a small French expedition had crossed from the west and established itself on the upper Nile at Fashoda. The climax of the Anglo-French duel for the Nile had finally arrived, but all the best cards were in Britain's hands. Kitchener had a decisive local military superiority. The Royal Navy, mobilized for war, was far stronger than a poorly administered French fleet – despite all the alarmism of the British Navy League. Russia, unwilling to fight for so distant an object, intimated that its alliance with France applied only to Europe. While British public opinion was united, indeed markedly bellicose in tone, the French political nation was almost torn in two at that time over the Dreyfus affair. In any case, French governments had never believed that they could expel Britain from Egypt by force; they had simply hoped to put pressure upon London to restore the former shared influence. In 1898–9 the French bluff was called, and they had to retreat. They, too, would only fight over European issues.

Salisbury's diplomatic victory at Fashoda appeared to justify his confidence that Britain could still look after itself without recourse to allies, and temporarily stemmed those right-wing critics who had thought him 'soft' in China and West Africa. The breathing-space gained, however, was short in duration. During the summer of 1899 relations worsened between Milner, the British High Commissioner in South Africa, and Kruger, the President of the Transvaal, neither individual being willing to accept the other's vision of the region's future. In October, seeking to gain a military advantage before British and imperial forces could arrive, the Boer armies struck. Yet another of the long-maturing legacies of the early Victorians had culminated to Britain's disadvantage. The South African campaign of 1899–1902 proved to be far longer and more costly than anyone in London had imagined possible. A series of early disasters revealed that the British army was deficient in numerous respects. Even after the main Boer forces had been contained, a lengthy guerrilla war ensued. At the height of the conflict, the British had around 300,000 troops in South Africa, and its defences elsewhere in the world – especially at home – were severely weakened. With a few exceptions, all of Europe appeared to enjoy Britain's discomfiture and to applaud the Boers; and ominous rumours circulated about secret attempts to construct a continental league against the arrogant and isolated island-state. Early in 1900, a fresh 'invasion scare' swept the country. As it was, the European powers were too divided among themselves to unite against Britain, and the Germans in particular had no wish to oppose the Royal Navy until their own battlefleet was ready; content to secure a favourable settlement of the Samoan question late in 1899 by 'diplomatic blackmail', Berlin looked forward with confidence to the coming century.

That mood was not shared by most Britons. They had had, in Kipling's words, 'no end of a lesson'. In fact, the war had acted as a catalyst in a variety of ways. It divided public opinion more than any event between the Eastern Crisis of 1878 and the decision for war in 1914. Judged by the size and volume of parliamentary and press utterances, of course, the domestic critics of the Boer War were in a distinct minority, especially in its early stages; but the persistent assertions by J. A. Hobson and others about the role of financial interests in causing the conflict, and the later revelations of women and children dying in concentration camps, brought together various sections of the left and produced a critique of government policies from which Chamberlain and Milner would never really recover. Ironically, the war was also disliked by many of the major institutions in the City, for the vast rise in 'unproductive' expenditure, the increase in taxes, the government loans and consequent rise in the National Debt, and the temporary corn levy, all offended the principles of orthodox finance. Yet it was less the economy which was dealt a blow than national self-confidence. Underneath the assertive jingoism of the day, there lurked gloom and dismay. All of the inner fears about the loss of Britain's global primacy welled close to the surface of the late-Victorian consciousness and, in some cases, burst into the open. There were calls for a government of non-party men, applying the principles of 'national efficiency'; hints that the parliamentary system was 'rotten' and needing to be replaced by something altogether more *dirigiste* and decisive. There were also calls for conscription and, remarkably, for widespread social reforms when it was revealed how many working-class volunteers for the army had been turned away as unfit and undersize. The newspapers, and a parliamentary commission, solemnly investigated the 'deterioration of the race'. This harsher, more fearful social-Darwinistic tone suggests that the war had caused even more convulsions on the right of the political spectrum than on the left. In the sum, it had been an unsettling and disturbing process; and the need for changes – in the army, in defence co-ordination, in the foreign-policy process – could no longer be postponed.

While the shake-up in defence administration could only be effected over time, the re-evaluation of foreign policy showed itself more swiftly – if only because fresh crises compelled diplomatic action. In June 1900, with the greater part of the British Army bogged down in South Africa, the uprising of the nationalistic Boxers in China provoked the great powers into sending forces to crush that movement. Apart from the temporary damage to British trade in China caused by these operations, the great worry in London was that some of the powers (notably Russia), once installed upon Chinese soil, would maintain their hold after the war. Consequently, Salisbury's colleagues pressed for a deal with Germany for the maintenance of the territorial *status quo* in China. The Prime Minister was again doubtful of the benefits of such an agreement, as well he might have been, since the Germans had no intention of standing up to Russia and were secretly more concerned to get Britain to promise that it would not make preventive annexations in the Yangtse valley. However, Salisbury's suspicions were not shared by his colleagues and he was overruled. In October 1900 an Anglo-German treaty on China was signed. Within another month, Salisbury had been prevailed upon to hand over the Foreign Office to Lansdowne and to concentrate his fading energies upon the duties of the premiership.

By the beginning of the following year, events had vindicated Salisbury's scepticism. Russia was tightening its hold upon northern China but the Germans, when approached about a possible joint protest against this, declared that they were neither committed nor willing to act in that region. Despite this blow, some British ministers were interested enough when misleading hints came from the counsellor of the German embassy in London, Baron von Eckardstein, that a fuller Anglo-German alliance was still possible. This was a message which Eckardstein was also conveying to Berlin, and the comedy of errors which followed upon his intrigue need not be detailed here.[18] What was noticeable was that the Cabinet, although still terribly anxious to find a partner to assist in stabilizing the Far East, became very dubious when Berlin insisted that any alliance should not be with Germany alone but with Austria-Hungary and Italy as well, for that would tie Britain to the defence of central Europe. Even the broadminded Lansdowne thought this 'a big fence to· ride at', and Salisbury's arguments against any such alliance gained ground. The essential problem therefore remained: even if a change of course was necessary, which direction should it take? By the end of 1901, with the Germans apparently insisting upon 'all or nothing', the course would clearly not be in the direction of Berlin.

The solution, ironically, came by default. The country with which the British would most have wished to act over the China crisis was the United States; but, although friendly, that power still preferred its policy of isolation. Germany had been the next choice, but its price had been too high. The only other country interested enough in the fate of China and willing to fight to prevent its being swallowed up by Russia was Japan. A decade earlier, such a solution could hardly have been contemplated by the British; but by now Japan had a considerable navy, certainly large enough, if joined with the Royal Navy's ships in the Far East, to deal with the combined Franco-Russian forces in those waters. It was surely symbolic that the Admiralty, whose vessels best represented the age of *Pax Britannica*, was now the department most eager to see an agreement reached with Japan. Even Salisbury showed himself less opposed to this notion than he had been to an Anglo-German alliance. Its attractiveness lay, to a large degree, in the fact that it would be a local pact (which a treaty with the Triple Alliance could never have been); and, secondly, that it would carefully limit the possibility of Britain being drawn into hostilities. According to the treaty, which the two powers signed on 30 January 1902, each signatory pledged mutual aid in the event of the other being engaged in a conflict over China or Korea with *two or more* countries, but benevolent neutrality if it was a conflict with only one country: the benefit to the Cabinet from this was that, while securing Japanese help if ever Britain should have to fight the Dual Alliance in the Far East, the treaty did not commit London to hostilities should Japan and Russia alone quarrel.

The news of the Anglo-Japanese Alliance provoked many comments inside and outside Britain: almost all concluded, like the *Spectator*, that it marked the end of that 'fixed policy of not making alliances'.[19] As Lansdowne himself admitted, this was a pledge to go to war at some future time under circumstances which could not (despite the specific restrictions) be strictly foretold and were likely to be outside British control. It was precisely for this reason that many Liberals and other traditionalists were disturbed. On the other hand, this new policy did not mean an end to the country's European position; in fact, it reinforced Britain's isolation from the continent, for it eliminated that need for a suitable partner for Far Eastern purposes which had lain behind the various attempts at a German alliance over the preceding four years. Yet, as will be discussed below, the conditions of the 1902 treaty had implications for London's relations with Paris, which suggested that in the long run the Oriental and the European aspects of Britain's external policy could not be separated. But all that was in the future. What seemed important at the time was that, in a year when the Victorian age had already been replaced by the Edwardian, when the Boer War was finally brought to a close and when Salisbury also was to bow out of the premiership, Britain at last seemed to be making moves away from its traditional diplomatic policy.

Diplomatic Revolution, 1903–7

Before returning to the story of Britain's changing relations with the European powers, it is necessary to note a most significant elimination of a long-standing strategic and diplomatic problem elsewhere, in the transformation of the Anglo-American relationship from one of incipient or open rivalry to friendship. The cultural and economic bases for a *rapprochement* had existed earlier, but they by no means fully predetermined the political decisions. Mid-Victorian statesmen such as Palmerston and Clarendon had frequently worried lest American expansionists take advantage of Britain's difficulties elsewhere in the world to push the imperial power out of the western hemisphere. Although such a drastic eventuality had not occurred, it was becoming clearer that the United States was determined upon a monopoly of political influence in its part of the globe. The Venezuelan crisis of 1895 had shown this, as had the victorious war against Spain in 1898. In addition, the American capacity to overrun Canada was now being complemented by the construction of a battlefleet which would shortly give the United States clear numerical superiority in western waters.

If Salisbury regarded these tendencies with some disquiet, imperialists of the Chamberlain and Kipling sort were much more optimistic: here was the opportunity, after all, to persuade the Americans to join Britain in carrying the white man's burden, especially in the settlement of the China question, where both London and Washington were keen to see the 'open door' preserved. No great interests would be lost, and much goodwill gained, by a graceful withdrawal of British strategical and political influence from Latin America; and, although somewhat later American 'dollar diplomacy' in that region was occasionally to use questionable methods, it did not seem at any time openly to wish to eliminate rival commerce (as Russian expansion in China did), and political stability could be guaranteed by a Rooseveltian 'big stick'. All these positive calculations, together with the overwhelming negative realization that if the United States was really intent upon getting its own way it could hardly be opposed, influenced Lansdowne and his colleagues in 1901 into abandoning Britain's treaty right to claim a half-share in the construction of any Isthmian canal; and, two years later, into acceding to a settlement of the Alaskan boundary dispute which favoured American claims. Smaller points of discord remained even after this time, of course, and the United States preferred isolation to alliance; but, as with the Anglo-Japanese settlement, the British were to reap long-term benefits from their willingness to recognize the claims of a rising power to a larger share of political influence in its own locality. On the other hand, the suspicion entertained by Salisbury and, decades later, by Neville Chamberlain that the USA would be a difficult and demanding ally and, commercially, at least as great a challenger as Germany, was also proved correct in the course of time. However, few Britons thought this way around 1900.

While Britain's relations with the United States were being placed on a better footing, those with Germany were worsening rapidly after 1902. This deterioration was, however, predominantly at the 'unofficial' level and had been chiefly occasioned by British imperialists' resentment of German press attacks upon the Boer War. This criticism was vigorously rebutted by *The Times, National Review, Spectator* and other journals, some of which argued that Germany was 'Britain's secret and deadliest foe', pointed meaningfully to the rising German battlefleet, and suggested that it was now time for London to compose its differences with Paris and St Petersburg. These were sentiments now shared by Joseph Chamberlain, who, disappointed by the failure to achieve an Anglo-German alliance, became involved in a furious open dispute with the German Chancellor, Bülow, about the respective practices of British troops in South Africa and German troops in France in 1870–1. This exchange of insults did not appeal to the cool Whig mind of Lansdowne, nor to that of the new Prime Minister, Balfour; but a growing suspicion of Germany was detectable among the 'newer' men at the Foreign Office such as Bertie, Hardinge and Crowe; and it was also no coincidence that, from the spring of 1902 onwards, the strategic planners at the Admiralty began to consider the need to attend to Britain's North Sea defences in response to the expanding German fleet.

The interaction between public opinion and 'Official Mind' was repeatedly illustrated during 1903, when these trends intensified. At the beginning of that year, Britain and Germany had been engaged in a joint act of 'gunboat diplomacy' against Venezuela for its loan defaults and treatment of foreign nationals. This enterprise was exciting United States' opinion and, in turn, all those British imperialists who favoured close Anglo-American links – including, incidentally, Liberal Imperialists such as Grey. With the attacks from newspapers and Tory backbenchers against the government's co-operation with 'the shameless Hun'* mounting, Lansdowne and Balfour were forced to pull out of this action. Fresh from their victory, the anti-German forces began an agitation in the spring of 1903 for the construction of a North Sea base; and then, even more dramatically, attacked the government for encouraging British banks to join their German counterparts in financing the Baghdad Railway. To the bankers themselves, and to Balfour and Lansdowne, there were good practical reasons for this co-operation with Berlin – quite apart from the more general consideration that the government still regarded the Russian threat to India as the greatest foreign problem with

* This was, of course, the phrase Kipling used in his poem 'The Rowers', published in *The Times* during this agitation.

which it had to contend. All this made no difference to the radical-right press nor, in fact, to Chamberlain, who threw his considerable weight in the Cabinet against the Baghdad Railway project. Once again, to their embarrassment, the Prime Minister and Foreign Secretary had to change their policy. It was perhaps no coincidence that Chamberlain was at this time poised to make his break with traditional fiscal policy, too, by proclaiming the cause of tariff reform, the propaganda for which was to focus heavily upon German commercial competition. And it was certainly no coincidence at all that the imperialist press was urging an *entente* with the French, who in that same month of May 1903 were being favoured by the blandishments of Edward VII during his famous visit to Paris.

There was much more than Germanophobia behind the growing Anglo-French amity, however, even if that motive was uppermost among the arch-imperialists in the two countries. After all, it was a traditional Liberal aspiration to be on good terms with the French republic, and business interests were also keen on this. Furthermore, a settlement of the many outstanding colonial quarrels between London and Paris was a good thing in itself, and was urged upon the British government by the influential Lord Cromer, who required French support for his planned financial reforms in Egypt. Above all, there was the Asiatic factor. An agreement with France, Lansdowne observed, 'would not improbably be the precursor of a better understanding with Russia',[20] this being the only practicable way of settling the Indian defence problem. As the year 1903 drew to a close, this calculation appeared even more pressing, for the signs multiplied that Russian and Japanese aims over Korea and Manchuria were no longer reconcilable by diplomatic means. In February 1904 the Japanese struck at Port Arthur. Now, at last, the longer-term consequences of the Anglo-Japanese Alliance were beginning to make their impact. The conditions both of that treaty *and* of the Franco-Russian Alliance bound their respective signatories to aid each other against two or more enemies, but to remain neutral if only one enemy was involved. This meant that if a Russo-Japanese conflict occurred, both Britain and France had a compelling interest in persuading each other to stay aloof; they had to remain as 'seconds', and not participants, in such a war, for if either gave assistance to its Far Eastern ally the other would also be obliged to come in, thus destroying all hopes of Anglo-French friendship. This was as urgent a motive to Delcassé, the French Foreign Minister, as it was to Lansdowne himself.

Although there were still difficult negotiations over certain colonial issues, the British and French governments managed to settle their differences within a couple of months of the outbreak of the Far Eastern war. In April 1904, to the acclaim of Unionists and Liberals alike, the old *entente cordiale* was restored. Yet another challenger to the British world position had been pacified, in the main by the British agreeing to French predominance in Morocco in exchange for the termination of Paris's objections to the British hold over Egypt. Although both signatories pledged future support for each other's purposes, Lansdowne at least did not see in this an anti-German move; but it was an immense satisfaction to many in Britain and France that Berlin could no longer take advantage of the colonial tensions between the two western powers. On the German side, the new Anglo-French friendship was clearly seen as a blow to the earlier confident hopes of a successful *Weltpolitik* and, along with Italy's tacit defection from the Triple Alliance and the news of a serious native uprising in South-west Africa, as one of a number of setbacks to German ambitions. The fact that, at the very end of 1904, the British right-wing press commenced a further agitation against the German fleet – including irresponsible calls to have it 'Copenhagened' before it became more powerful – could only deepen the gloom in Berlin. This was all the more significant since it followed the notorious 'Dogger Bank' incident of October 1904, when a Russian fleet heading for the Far East sank some British trawlers. Here, if ever, was the spark for an Anglo-Russian war, and a large segment of public opinion angrily pressed for revenge; but Balfour and Lansdowne coolly kept their heads, and allowed the issue to go to the International Court at The Hague. They were supported in this by various individuals in the government and the press who felt that a war with Russia (and, of course, France) would only benefit the Germans, who, it was alleged, were secretly working for such a conflict.

But the greatest alteration in the diplomatic and stra-tegical balance was yet to come. To the surprise of most commentators, including the British, Japan proved to be more than a match for Russia at sea and on land, and as 1905 unfolded these external blows to Russian military might were compounded by serious internal unrest. While British radicals were pleased that all this might lead to domestic reforms within Russia after the war, imperialists were overjoyed at the implications for their country's world position. The annihilation of the Russian Black Sea fleet at Tsushima altered the maritime balance at a stroke, for the Royal Navy became considerably larger than the next two navies. Although the Admiralty and the right-wing press were worried about the rising German fleet, Japan's victories in the Far East allowed the recall of five battleships from those waters to join the others which had been withdrawn from the Mediterranean into the North Sea. Overall, then, Britain's maritime position by the second half of 1905 was more favourable than it had been for the previous two decades, although this was not to prevent the admirals from asking for more funds. Even more comforting was the elimination of that Russian threat to China which had obsessed British statesmen and traders since the 1890s. While some observers now feared that Tsarist expansionism, expelled from the Orient, might turn towards India and the Persian Gulf, Balfour's government sought to take care of that contingency by persuading Tokyo to agree to a revision of the Anglo-Japanese Alliance so that it was extended to cover India and would become operative in the event of a signatory being at war with *one*, instead of two or more foes. Although the Unionist administration was tottering towards its end, it could console itself with the thought that its imperial problems had been considerably eased since those harrowing days of 1900.

On the other hand, it was precisely in these months that some members of the British government slowly began to realize that a major new problem in foreign affairs had arisen: for the first time in thirty, or perhaps a hundred years, the continental balance-of-power was seriously threatened. The collapse of Russia as a first-class power also meant the disappearance of that equilibrium which Derby and Salisbury's generation had virtually taken for granted. Germany was now, in military as well as industrial terms, unequalled in Europe and, under its nervous but ambitious leadership, keen to recover some of the ground it had lost over the previous two years. In particular, Berlin was anxious to make a lesson of its arch-foe, Delcassé, who was held chiefly responsible for the 'encirclement' of Germany by arranging the Anglo-French *entente* and frustrating the secret German efforts to conclude an alliance with Russia in the winter of 1904–5. With Russian power now weakened, Germany did not hesitate to exploit this favourable opportunity. France's plans to absorb Morocco were rudely shattered by the Kaiser's landing at Tangiers in March 1905 and by the plain threat that, if Germany's own Moroccan aspirations were not respected, the issue might be settled militarily. This pressure so frightened the French government that Delcassé was obliged to resign. A few months later, in July 1905, the Kaiser met Tsar Nicholas II at Björkö and secretly agreed upon a draft treaty of alliance. This latter action caused considerable confusion and argument within the German leadership, both as to whether such an alliance should merely be confined to Europe and as to its latent contradiction with the anti-French Moroccan policy, but the details are not important here. What was significant was that the British government, suspicious of a Russo-German accord and worried about the German pressure upon France, was forced to reconsider its traditional European policy.

There had been, as mentioned above, no deliberate anti-German motive in Balfour and Lansdowne's minds when they concluded the *entente* with France, and even in early 1905 they were hoping to remain on reasonable terms with Berlin. But if, as it seemed, Germany was deliberately seeking to break up that *entente*; if, furthermore, it was actually contemplating an attack upon a much weaker France, then counter-action could become necessary. As a joint sub-committee of British strategic experts pointed out:

> a second overthrow of France by Germany ... would end in the aggrandisement of Germany to an extent which would be prejudicial to the whole of Europe, and it might therefore be necessary for Great Britain in her own interests to lend France her active support should war of this nature break out.[21]

While it is by no means clear that the Prime Minister and Foreign Secretary had also reached this conclusion, such thoughts led to a flurry of operational planning by the Admiralty and War Office in the latter part of 1905, with the former contemplating a second Trafalgar in the North Sea and amphibious strikes against the German coast; and, more significantly, with the latter exploring the possibility of dispatching an expeditionary force to fight alongside the French. The diplomatic revolution was bringing a military revolution in its train.

It was during this complex international crisis that Balfour's government finally resigned and gave way to a Liberal administration under Campbell-Bannerman, which in January 1906 won a 'landslide' electoral victory to confirm it in power. Although the right-wing press portrayed the Liberal Party as composed of unpatriotic and appeasing 'little Englanders', this change-over had little effect upon external policy because of the key Cabinet positions which the Liberal Imperialists occupied. In particular, the new Foreign Secretary, Sir Edward Grey, was much more suspicious of Germany than his Unionist predecessor had been and was certainly more concerned with the European equilibrium than with imperial issues *per se*. Although partly constrained by the radical-Liberal majority in the Cabinet, Grey was swift to give sustained support to the French during the Algeciras conference, which had been called to settle the dispute of the powers over partitioning Morocco and which ended with a humiliating diplomatic defeat for Germany. He also warned Germany that an unprovoked attack upon France would excite public opinion and thus make it 'impossible for England to remain neutral'. Furthermore, he gave his backing to secret military conversations which were just then taking place between the British and French General Staffs, although Grey always maintained that any strategic contingency plans which were evolved by the experts should not determine the larger political decision of *whether* Britain should fight on France's side. That delicate and all-important question, although overshadowing many of the Liberal Party's internal quarrels over the next few years, was not to be settled until 1914 itself.

Of equal importance, and much more controversial to the radicals, was Grey's pursuit of an understanding with Russia. This, indeed, was an old Liberal Imperialist aspiration and one which had also been favoured by Salisbury and Balfour, the more especially when they realized that India could not be defended by a naval *riposte* into the Black Sea. Where Grey differed was to attach a European aspect to such a settlement: as he wrote at the height of the Algeciras Conference, 'An *entente* between Russia, France and ourselves would be absolutely secure. If it is necessary to check Germany it could then be done.'[22]

This was, predictably enough, the hope of the French government also. The obstacles to an Anglo-Russian *rapprochement* lay elsewhere: in Russia itself, where the government was not anxious to be pushed against a powerful Germany, and was reluctant to give up its ancient ambitions of southward expansion; and in Britain, where the great majority of Liberals disapproved of close relations with a regime which was abandoning its promised reforms of 1905–6 in favour of reaction, and where many traditional imperialists like Curzon believed that a lasting settlement with Russia was impossible. Some Liberals, however, could be tempted by the argument that an Asian agreement would eliminate the prospect of an enormously costly war for the defence of India, just as certain Russians could be tempted by the benefits, financial and otherwise, which might flow from the creation of an Anglo-French-Russian *bloc*. The protracted negotiations upon a demarcation of British and Russian spheres of influence in Persia and upon the status of Afghanistan and Tibet were not concluded until August 1907, and it could be regarded – and justified by both Foreign Offices – as one of those territorial compromises typical of the age if imperialism. To some other participants and observers, however, it had wider implications.

The Balance of Power in Europe, 1908–14

In 1900, with the majority of the Cabinet seeking an Anglo-German accord, even an acute student of foreign affairs could hardly have imagined that within seven years Britain would have drawn closer to France and Russia and would be regarding Germany as its most dangerous enemy. In 1907, however, such an observer would probably not have been surprised at the prediction that within another seven years Britain would decide to enter war on the side of France and

Russia, and against Germany. It was true that Liberals and many others would have been horrified at such a prediction; and it was also true that there was no inevitable path to war from 1907 to 1914. But the basic structure of European politics did not change in that period (apart, perhaps, from Turkey's further weakening), nor did any significant shift occur in that domestic-political constellation within Britain which would ultimately determine the country's reaction to a possible violent change in the European state system.

Above all, it transpired, no settlement could be reached in the two major issues which divided Britain and Germany: the naval race, and the question of British neutrality or intervention in the event of a European war. To radicals and socialists, to pacifists and churchmen, and to certain cosmopolitan financiers as well, it was inexplicable that the British government could come to an understanding with the United States in the western hemisphere, with Japan in the Far East, with France in Africa and with Russia in Asia – but not settle differences with Germany. The answer to this was partly to do with ideology, but chiefly explained by geography. Neither American fleet expansion, nor Japanese, threatened Britain's vitals: Germany's navy did, even more than France's had done a decade or so earlier. A rising German battlefleet in the North Sea automatically cast doubt upon British naval supremacy in home waters, unless the Royal Navy stationed a much larger fleet there. When that was done, the Germans were in turn prevented from securing their promised 'world-political freedom' unless they built even more vessels – including the new *Dreadnought* types after 1906 – and sought again to alter the maritime balance in their favour. The obtaining of one country's naval aims meant the failure of the other's: hence a construction race which seemed to have no ending. Despite the radicals' hopes, a naval limitations treaty was never acceptable to Berlin, for that always implied a stabilization of the existing fleet ratios.

The Anglo-German disagreement over the European

balance was also greatly determined by geographical factors. Seeking a successful strategy in a likely two-front war, the Prussian General Staff had adopted Count Schlieffen's plan to strike westwards first, via Belgium, at France. Irrespective of whether Germany's motives were aggressive or defensive, this would mean the violation of Belgian neutrality, the probable eclipse of France, and the presence of German troops on one flank of the English Channel – that is, the troops of a country whose leader proclaimed himself 'the Admiral of the Atlantic' and whose battlefleet grew without ceasing. Quite apart from any treaty, or moral or cultural considerations for Belgium and France, therefore, influential Britons argued that it was necessary to uphold the continental equilibrium for a vital and selfish reason – the preservation of British naval superiority in the future, and of Britain itself. Grey and the other Liberal Imperialists, the permanent officials in Whitehall, the Unionist Party and their newspapers all believed that, in checking German domination on land, they were ensuring their own hegemony at sea. The independence of France was not – unlike that of Persia or Venezuela or West Africa – something about which these Britons could compromise. A built-in incompatibility of national aims and strategic war-plans kept London and Berlin apart. As the *Spectator* (20 May 1911) put it, 'There is an inevitable conflict of ideals between Germany and Great Britain, between the satisfied nation and the unsatisfied nation, between the nation which desires to maintain the *status quo* and the nation which desires to alter it.'

Although this incompatibility underlay the Anglo-German relationship in the decade before 1914, it was not always so manifest. Various attempts were made by unofficial bodies after 1906 to dispel mutual suspicions, and in 1907 the Liberals placed great hopes in the arms-reduction schemes being discussed at the Second Hague Conference. Alas, it was not to be. Not only did Germany reject the 'artificial' and 'hypocritical' notion of slowing down armaments production, it also announced a little later an increase in its battleship-construction rate, to four vessels per annum. This decision, and the Cabinet quarrels about how many ships Britain should build in response, convulsed national politics for much of 1908 and early 1909 – with navalists agitating for eight or more battleships, and the radicals campaigning against such a programme and in favour of social reforms. This was by far the most momentous of the late-Victorian and Edwardian 'navy scares', and was not cooled by Asquith's compromise of laying down four battleships immediately and four more later in the year. Indeed, the internal aspects of this debate were stimulated further when, partly to pay for the increased naval costs, Lloyd George introduced his 'Peoples' Budget', which, when rejected by the Upper House, in turn led to the House of Lords crisis and the two general elections of 1910.

At the diplomatic level, however, the essence of the matter was unchanged. Germany was intent upon building more battleships; and Britain, to preserve the power ratio, was responding in kind. In addition, Grey and his staff worried about a Franco-German quarrel over Casablanca in November 1908, which seemed to bring war closer; and were extemely concerned in March 1909 when Berlin deliberately humiliated the Russians by insisting that they must recognize the Austro-Hungarian annexation of Bosnia and Herzegovina. Not only did this indicate that Russia still felt too weak to face a confrontation with Germany, but it also suggested that the German government was seeking to force other powers to admit its preponderance in Europe. This made the Foreign Office eager to remain on close terms with Paris and St Petersburg, even to the extent of ignoring Russian misdeeds in Persia. It also meant that, when Bülow and then his successor as Chancellor, Bethmann Hollweg, approached London for a political and naval understanding in 1909, the British reaction was very cautious. Although Grey, under considerable pressure from the 'left' of his party, was willing to improve Anglo-German relations, he drew back at Berlin's new offer: for what the Germans were suggesting was that they would not increase their battlefleet further, provided Britain pledged itself to stay neutral in a European war. While this was a perfectly natural desire from Bethmann Hollweg's viewpoint (although not from Tirpitz's!), it greatly alarmed the Foreign Office. If neutrality was pledged, would not Berlin take advantage of the next opportunity to crush France – and then, dominant in western Europe, resume naval construction at a faster pace? This suspicion appeared to be confirmed when, during further negotiations, Berlin insisted that a British offer not to join an 'unprovoked assault' upon Germany was insufficient. In any case, a German pledge not to introduce additional fleet increases still meant that the High Seas Fleet was steadily growing, under the existing navy laws; and what Britain wanted was an absolute reduction in numbers. Spasmodic negotiations over the next two years could not overcome this incompatibility.

This concentration upon the German factor ordered all other aspects of official policy. The army, relieved by diplomacy from the defence of India, could be discreetly prepared for continental operations, a motive which also underlay Haldane's creation of the Territorials. Although there was frequent reference to the term *imperial* defence, and in 1909 the Chief of General Staff became the Chief of the *Imperial* General Staff, both British services were concentrating their interest upon north-west Europe, and far less upon Singapore or the Hindu Kush. British commerce and possessions in distant parts of the world had increasingly to be looked after by others, which is why London was to insist upon renewing the Anglo-Japanese alliance in 1911 despite the reservations of Australia and New Zealand. The European angle determined the extra-European strategy. As the *Standard* put it (29 May 1912), 'We are in the position of Imperial Rome when the Barbarians were thundering at the frontiers ... We have called home the legions.'

The Anglo-German talks had already run into the sand

when the second Moroccan crisis erupted in the summer of 1911. By this time, British fears that Germany might browbeat France into political submission were such that even Lloyd George and Churchill shared the alarm, and the former contributed to a heightening of the tension by his famous Mansion House speech, insisting that British interests must not be ignored. At one stage the crisis seemed so acute that Grey warned the Admiralty that 'the Fleet might be attacked at any moment'.[23] More significant still in the long run was a meeting of senior ministers and their advisers in the Committee of Imperial Defence on 23 August 1911, which discovered that the two services still possessed rival strategies to check Germany, the navy favouring amphibious operations and the army planning to fight along the French and Belgian borders. Finding the navy's scheme inadequate, the meeting gave its preference to the 'continental commitment' strategy. As before, this was a debate upon *how* to support the French, not *whether* to support them; but, implicitly, the favoured strategy indicated a concern for Europe and a likely rejection of neutralism and isolationism should Germany move westwards.[24]

The great bulk of the Liberal Party was much more shocked, however, at the thought that Britain had been on the brink of a great-power war, and radicals in the Cabinet were outraged at the revelation that secret Anglo-French staff talks had been held since 1906. From September 1911 onwards, therefore, Grey and his fellow Liberal Imperialists came under very heavy pressure to improve relations with Berlin and avoid further commitment to France. At the same time, reports were arriving that, despite Bethmann Hollweg's opposition, Tirpitz was planning yet another naval increase to take advantage of German nationalist indignation over the Moroccan crisis. For internal and external reasons, Whitehall was moved to resume its previous negotiations with Germany.

The exact form these talks took was the mission of Lord Haldane to Berlin early in 1912. While it was true that both governments had a massive secular interest in exploring the possibility of a naval agreement, they were also aware of the restrictions upon their freedom of manoeuvre. For example, the German Chancellor had no chance of reducing the High Seas Fleet, since Tirpitz had the support of the Kaiser and the German nationalists; the most that could be done was to cut the number of additional vessels planned for the 1912 navy law. Even this gesture required a political *quid pro quo* from Britain – as before, it was asked to pledge neutrality if either signatory became entangled in a war with third parties. This the Cabinet could not agree to, but instead tended towards a compromise: 'although we cannot bind ourselves under all circumstances to go to war with France against Germany, we shall also certainly not bind ourselves to Germany not to assist France.' The first part of the formula consoled the radicals, the latter part reassured the Liberal Imperialists. In consequence, Berlin was again assured that Britain would join no unprovoked attack upon Germany. Since the German implementation of the Schlieffen Plan would most probably be regarded by Britain as an aggressive act, such a statement gave Berlin no guarantee of London's neutrality. The talks broke down again. The 1912 naval increase went ahead as planned; and the following period also saw large-scale additions to the Prussian Army, giving it (for the first time) the numbers necessary to implement Schlieffen's scheme.

Furthermore, Tirpitz's new navy law inadvertently drove Britain even closer to France. The key clause in that bill was not the small increase in total battleship numbers, but the large increase in German warships which would now be on constant *active* service. To meet this, Churchill (the new First Lord of the Admiralty, and as energetic a navalist as he had been a social reformer two years earlier) proposed to withdraw Britain's remaining battleships from the Mediterranean to home waters. Although those vessels would in any case soon be eclipsed by the new *Dreadnought*-style battleships which Austria-Hungary and Italy were building, the thought that there might be no Royal Navy protection for British trade routes and garrisons in the Mediterranean – a weakness inconceivable in the pre-1905 period – convulsed many of the older imperialists and navalists, whose criticisms of the Admiralty's policy were joined by those of the radicals concerned at the obsession with the German danger. For much of 1912 the Cabinet and Committee of Imperial Defence argued over the alternative solutions. The end-result was a curious one. Seizing their chance, the French offered to protect Britain's Mediterranean interests if London would do the same for French interests in the Channel and southern North Sea, from where Paris intended to withdraw its ships. Such a 'deal', if effected, would avoid an enormous rise in naval expenditure, maintain Britain's lead in the North Sea, and preserve its interests in the Mediterranean – and for all those reasons the Cabinet finally settled upon this option.* In turn, it had to concede the French demand that this naval understanding also required some agreement about consultation in the event of a threat to either party. Although the Cabinet indulged in repeated drafting exercises in order to pare down the extent of its commitment, it was the whole body and not merely a Liberal Imperialist clique which agreed to the Grey-Cambon exchange of notes of November 1912; in them, the staff talks were acknowledged and automatic consultation in times of crisis agreed upon. This still did not bind Britain to fight alongside France in any eventuality, but it did increase the moral tie and the psychological expectation that the two powers would stand together.

The next two years formed virtually a diplomatic

---

* Admittedly, the Cabinet also instructed the Admiralty to maintain a one-power standard (excluding the French) in the Mediterranean, provided 'a reasonable margin of superior strength' was always kept in the North Sea. In actual fact, this gave Churchill the freedom he wanted, and he left only a couple of battlecruisers at Gibraltar.

epilogue to this story. The gap between British and German perceptions of their national interests remained as wide as ever. No fresh attempt was made to discuss a neutrality treaty. A naval agreement – in the form of a 'holiday' in shipbuilding by both sides – was occasionally proposed by Churchill, but all this did was to irritate Tirpitz and the Kaiser. The British and French staffs continued to work upon a synchronization of their operational plans, which now included their navies as well as their armies, and extended to the China Sea as well as the Channel and the Mediterranean. By the early summer of 1914, the British Cabinet cautiously agreed to naval conversations with the Russians, news of which depressed Bethmann Hollweg immensely. Germany, in its turn, was intensifying its support for Austria-Hungary in the Balkans, adding further to its army, and finally abandoning the last remaining alternative operations scheme to the Schlieffen Plan. Whatever the *casus belli* in Europe, the Germans would strike westwards.

On the other hand, a number of events between 1912 and 1914 suggested a contrary trend, that a *detente* was occurring in Anglo-German relations. Precisely because there was no discussion of a neutrality agreement and little about naval limitation, the two governments were not reminded of the chief points of disagreement. Instead, they could talk about the prospect of a redivision of the territorial spheres covered in the secret 1898 treaty to divide the Portuguese Colonies; this was a matter over which Grey was willing to make some concessions, but the tricky issue of publishing the earlier treaties* prevented a successful conclusion to these talks. On the other hand, the two countries did manage to settle their long-standing difference over the Baghdad Railway, and an agreement was reached in June 1914. Furthermore, although

---

* *Treaties*, because in 1899 Salisbury had concluded an agreement with the Portuguese which contradicted the spirit, although not the letter, of the Anglo-German pact of the previous year. Understandably, the German government was not anxious to see these earlier actions publicized.

the Balkan Wars of 1912–13 had more than once threatened to escalate into a great-power conflict, Britain and Germany frequently co-operated to 'cool' the situation. Bethmann Hollweg continued to hope that Britain's links with its *entente* partners might slowly dissolve – a not entirely impossible development, since Anglo-Russian quarrels over Persia were severe and depressed those members of the Foreign Office such as Sir Arthur Nicolson, the Permanent Under-Secretary, who greatly feared an estrangement with St Petersburg. All this unnerved the French as well.

Although these two trends appear contradictory, what they really indicated was the very delicate and relatively flexible position which Britain occupied within the European power structure. While generally associating with France and Russia, it was not bound by any legal treaty automatically to give military assistance to one or the other of the alliance *blocs*. It could make attempts to improve relations with Berlin, and co-operate as joint 'ringmasters' during the Balkan Wars. The French could never be certain of British assistance – that would depend upon the government and parliament of the day. The radicals, for all their suspicions, could not accuse Grey of having pledged the country in advance. At the same time, however, Britain was not committed to neutrality and had repeatedly warned that it reserved its freedom to intervene. Its diplomacy involved a fine balancing act. Yet it is also important to note that in reality such an act did *not* mean that Britain would tilt in two directions: it would not fight on Germany's side. Its so-called 'flexibility' meant that it would *either* elect to stay neutral, *or* it would intervene to aid the French (and, by extension, the Russians) against Germany.

Whether Britain would intervene in a European war depended, then, upon two main factors: first, upon what the Germans did; and secondly, upon the balance of domestic forces which would bear upon the government's reaction to Germany's action. The chain of events in Europe in the summer of 1914, from the Sarajevo assassination to the activation of the Austro-German and Franco-Russian alliances, is a well-known tale which need not concern us here.[25] What is significant is that by 1 August it was clear that Germany and France would be at war; and, by 3 August, that German troops were invading Belgium. This latter act antagonized a great number of Britons, including many in the Liberal Party, and made them much more inclined to approve entry into war than would otherwise have been the case. Others had moved towards intervention by 2 August, even before the invasion of Belgium. The Unionists, urged on by their Chamberlainite backbenchers, were firmly in favour of war for the sake of France (that is, the balance of power) alone; the radicals, Labour, most middle-of-the-way Liberals, and the City, desired neutrality. The press, depending upon its viewpoint, argued strongly for intervention or abstention.

The key body, as ever, was the Cabinet, which was at last confronted with the decision it had for years hoped to avoid. The interventionist stance of the Liberal Imperialists was easily predictable. So, too, was the opposition of the committed isolationists and radicals like Burns and Morley. But what of the critically important middle group, including Lloyd George? Although most of them at first declared that Britain should stay out, days of discussion upon the meaning of the *ententes,* the military conversations, and the November 1912 arrangement with the French began to affect the 'waverers'. Perhaps some had always secretly felt that they were committed morally, politically, to fight if France was attacked. Tactfully, Asquith postponed the whole issue of the dispatch of a British Expeditionary Force, no doubt aware that the prospect of naval warfare would seem less shocking to his colleagues than continental operations. Furthermore, Grey and the other Liberal Imperialists – including, significantly, Asquith himself – indicated that they would not stay in office if France was abandoned. The prospect of another Liberal 'split', and of the country being run by a coalition of Liberal Imperialists and Unionists who would obviously enter the war and prosecute it in an 'illiberal' way, was a powerful factor to many Liberal ministers, who could accept Asquith's argument that it was better to go into war united than to hand over 'policy and control to the Tories'.[26] As the Cabinet, with a few exceptions, was moving towards this standpoint, reports of German pressure upon Belgium began to increase. Since it had already been agreed on 2 August that a 'substantial violation' of Belgian neutrality by Germany would be a *casus belli*, the Cabinet found it much less difficult to convince the party and the country to abandon neutrality for this reason. In other words, Belgium was important in keeping the Liberals united; it is doubtful whether it was decisive in causing British intervention.

The British government and people went to war in 1914 for a whole variety of reasons. Some genuinely believed that the country had a duty to fight on Belgium's behalf and, more generally, to oppose that 'Prussian militarism' which had been so frequently portrayed in the press as the chief danger to the peace and liberties of Europe. Others, especially in the Liberal camp, joined in reluctantly, feeling that they had been swept along by the pace of events or by the threat of a coalition government. Contrary spirits, however, proclaimed themselves in a state of euphoria and welcomed the war as a release from Edwardian complacency and sterility. If this appears odd nowadays, it has to be remembered that few people had any sense of how long and bloody the conflict would be.

But there was, in certain quarters, a further significant reason for entering the war: fear of what might happen to Britain if it stayed out. Decades of facing various challenges, of anxiously steering through crises, had sapped much of that confidence felt by the mid-Victorians that Britain was strong enough to stay aloof from European conflicts, if it so wished. Paradoxically, perhaps, the apprehensions of British weakness were most in evidence among those who favoured a strong national policy. Some, like Nicolson, were afraid of what Russia would do to Britain when Germany was defeated. A much more widespread fear, however, was that the Germans would win and then, all-powerful in Europe, resume their naval challenge with greater energy and resources than before. Conservatives in general, and the Chamberlainites in particular, who had worried about Britain's long-term decline and feared Germany's advance, were convinced that Britain should not stay out of the war. Yet Grey, too, for all his Liberal scruples, had been haunted by the idea that Germany would overrun France one day. Perhaps *The Times* put this thought best when it argued (20 July 1914) that intervention '. . . is not merely a duty of friendship. It is . . . an elementary duty of self-preservation . . . We cannot stand alone in a Europe dominated by any single power.'

On 6 August, after certain hesitations, the Cabinet agreed to the dispatch of the greater part of the British Expeditionary Force to France; the General Staff's plan had prevailed. The Royal Navy had already imposed its blockade upon the North Sea entrances. British, French and Dominion troops assaulted the German colonies. On 23 August, British and German forces clashed near Mons and began to kill each other in large numbers. The long age of peace in western Europe was over, and the great-power war anticipated by many had arrived.

II

Total War and its Impact, 1914–19

3. Structures and Attitudes

War as a Catalyst?

It is difficult, even from this distance, to get a true sense of the impacts of the First World War upon Britain, its people and its place in the global order. If the conflict was entered for the most part willingly, and in many cases light-heartedly, the growing strain and losses and horrors of mass destruction gradually made themselves felt. Perhaps to other, less comfortable societies, this orgy of war and death did not produce such a profound psychological and physical shock; but to many Britons, especially those in better-off circles, the years 1914–19 were cataclysmic, disrupting and in some instances destroying traditional habits and assumptions. Even after the coming of peace, this impression did not fade and it was in certain ways deepened by the later tendency to ascribe to the war the chief responsibility for current problems – the weakening of the world economy, unemployment, the rise of Labour, the breakdown of order in Ireland and growing unrest in India, and so on.

On the other hand, with the benefit of hindsight the historian may wonder whether the First World War really was so momentous. The losses in the trenches were certainly appalling, but civilian casualties and the damage to property were to be much more severe in the 1939–45 conflict, the consequences of which were also wider-ranging geographically and socially. Moreover, in surveying the whole sweep of the past hundred years and its major historical features – the rise of the USA, the collapse of the European empires, the relative eclipse of British industrial productivity, the growth of the welfare state, the rise of organized Labour, the emancipation of women, etc. – it becomes difficult to argue that the First World War really acted as an 'instigator' or a catalyst; it was, rather, an accelerator of some already established tendencies. Furthermore, the dismantling of economic controls in 1919–21, and the withdrawal of women from industry, suggest that what was 'accelerated' could also be slowed down, or even reversed, afterwards. In certain other respects, such as the checking of the German bid for European mastery for another two decades, or the advent of internal disorders in Russia, or the revived emphasis upon the solidarity of Britain and the Dominions, the war may well have had a *retarding* effect.

On the whole, the present study inclines towards the view that the war was not as decisive in its impacts upon Britain as contemporaries and many later historians believed. In holding such an interpretation, however, it is necessary to be wary of one great methodological danger: that of forgetting the subjective feelings and reactions of statesmen and the public, and instead taking the historical 'objective' reality for granted. For example, the 'Bolshevik menace' of 1918 might not appear very great in retrospect; but we shall only understand its impact properly if we view it through the eyes of worried politicians in London and Paris. Again, the cause of Imperial Federation may seem to us today to have always been a 'non-starter'; in 1917 or thereabouts, many influential people held it to be a distinct and desirable possibility. The very fact of *their* holding something to be important gives it a historical significance too.

The Economic Impact

The chief reason why great bankers like the Rothschilds tried to prevent the war was no doubt a selfish one; but they, perhaps more than any other section of the community, were also aware of the intermeshing of Britain's economy with those of the other European states (especially Germany) and of the damage which war would inflict upon the cosmopolitan world order. This, after all, had been the message of Norman Angell's best-selling work, *The Great Illusion* (1910), although he had optimistically argued that since a great-power war was so costly, statesmen would not resort to it; as Lord Esher remarked, this assumed that the businessman's viewpoint would prevail over the warrior's. Yet even those who gave some thought to the possible economic impact of war had no idea that the war would last so long or cost so much. From about the second Moroccan crisis onwards, the CID had made certain preparations for the financial and trading world which would parallel military measures such as the mobilization of reserves, requisition of merchant ships, censorship of cables, and so on.[1] But little of this related to a long-drawn-out conflict; the great concern was to prevent a sudden economic collapse – caused, say, by a run on the gold stocks, or the closure of foreign exchanges and credit – and few thought beyond the six months which such a conflict was generally supposed to last. Thus, while politicians and their advisers had worked out a War Risks Insurance Scheme for shipping, and consulted the railway companies about the transportation of troops, they never contemplated the harnessing of the country's entire industrial resources, or puzzled about how to finance a conflict which (by 1917) was to cost £7 million per day. Had they known in advance of the costs, they would probably have died of shock.

For several reasons, the British enjoyed a gradual, indeed reasonably cosy transition towards total war. The first was that, by and large, the precautionary measures taken to preserve credit and commerce were successful: shipping was not laid up, foodstuffs and raw materials continued to move, and the disruption of British trade with the Central Powers was soon compensated for by military orders and by the ending of German competition in third markets. Secondly, the fact that the French armies took the brunt of the fighting on the Western Front meant that there was time for the small British Expeditionary Force (BEF) to be built up: only in 1916, in fact, were Haig's forces to total over one million men. The chief problems were not so much financial and budgetary, as organizational – how to cope with the flood of volunteers, or how to increase shell production. In consequence, the first two war budgets (November 1914 and April 1915) did not contain any dramatic measures because the economy was not evidently under strain.

Only after the first year of war did its economic impact begin to be felt; thereafter, the pressure intensified. The outlay upon the armed forces, which had been £91.3 million (29.9 per cent of total government expenditure) in 1913, rose to £716.6 million (74.8 per cent) in 1915, and to a staggering £1955.8 million (80.6 per cent) in 1918.[2] Although a general price-inflation of around 250 per cent explains part of this, the expansion in real terms was still enormous. During the nineteenth century, government expenditure had normally been under 10 per cent of the Gross National Product, and even during the period of the pre-war Liberal administration it was only about 12½ per cent: yet by 1918, it had come to compose 51.7 per cent of GNP. Total war brought with it major economic changes, and induced what seemed to some contemporaries to be a budgetary revolution. Income tax rose from 1s. 3d. in the pound to 6s. in the pound by 1918. An 'excess-profits' tax was hurriedly introduced by the new Chancellor, McKenna, in 1915 to meet Labour criticism of profiteering; and, even more disturbing to the fiscally orthodox, protectionist duties were imposed upon certain luxury imports. Although there were various increases in taxes upon consumption (tobacco, sugar, and especially alcoholic drinks), the chief burden of the increased war revenue was placed upon the better-off. Direct taxes, which in 1913–14 brought in £94 million, raised £721 million in 1919–20 and by then formed about 80 per cent of tax revenue. At the time, these levels seemed horrific. What it suggests in retrospect was that there was ample wealth and capacity within the country to sustain this vast increase in taxation without severe discomfort or social unrest.

Some politicians and financial experts held, indeed, that taxation could have paid for an even greater share of the costs of the war, especially in its early stages. As it was, revenue only covered 36 per cent of expenditure (over the whole period 1914–15 to 1919–20), and the total deficit on the war budgets amounted to an enormous £7186 million. This deficit was covered by that traditional reserve mechanism of British governments in wartime – heavy borrowing from the City and, after 1917, through the issue of War Bonds. Again, one could argue that it was a testimony to the sheer financial strength of the country that these vast sums could be provided without much effort, in that there were both individuals and institutions rich enough to subscribe to government loans (and, of course, to gain a good return because of the interest rates offered). Only in the post-war period did the nation begin to suffer from this elevenfold rise in the National Debt, when the annual interest payments upon it consumed a very large share of central government expenditure.

The impact of the war upon Britain's global trading position was also cushioned for a long time by the country's enormous reserves of wealth and by its established hold in many overseas markets. Despite early fears, shipping was adequate to maintain an (admittedly reduced) flow of imports and exports as well as to satisfy the demands of war. The elimination of German competition certainly helped

British shippers and British exporters in some markets; and the Foreign Office and Board of Trade, fearing a revival of that competition after the war, abandoned their *laissez-faire* attitudes and urged industry to eradicate German rivalry forever. There was also, fortuitously, an improvement in the terms of trade, so that although the *volume* of British exported goods decreased, the *earnings* upon them steadily rose. This was also true of 'invisible' exports, such as the fees from shipping, insurance and banking. Thus, in 1916 the deficit of £345 million in 'visible' merchandise was still handsomely covered by 'invisible' earnings of some £520 million.[3] Only in 1917 and 1918 did it prove impossible to match the colossal rises in imports for the pursuance of total war with the export of manufactures and the earnings upon invisibles.

Taking the war years as a whole, however, the balance of payments as traditionally calculated remained favourable, although only just. Where it was deranged was in the substantial amounts loaned to Allied governments – a cool £1741 million (of which the largest share, £568 million, went to Russia). To cover this capital outflow, Britain was simultaneously borrowing, to the amount of £1365 million (of which £1027 million came from the USA); and also selling off foreign investments, although much less than was feared at the time.

At the general level, then, Britain managed to pay for the war out of its own resources, and its financial balance remained intact. In certain *specific* areas, however, there were severe and deleterious consequences. The most significant was the growing deficit with the United States, which supplied an ever-increasing proportion of British imports but required few goods in return. In order to prevent a collapse of the dollar exchange rate, the Treasury was forced to arrange the sale of dollar securities, to transfer gold and to maintain high interest rates. Nonetheless, the war transformed the USA from a major debtor into a major creditor nation, and permanently shifted the world's financial centre from London to New York, just as it had moved from Amsterdam to London during Britain's own rise in the eighteenth century. No doubt this, too, was a predictable development in the long run, given America's eclipse of Britain on the industrial and commercial fronts; but the exigencies of war ensured that it happened at this time, and at two levels simultaneously – for the massive British orders not only financed the further growth of American industry, but its borrowing in New York reversed the traditional debtor-creditor relationship.

The second major disadvantage was the loss of specific overseas markets, which a hard-pressed British industry could not maintain against foreign competition by the later stages of the war. Furthermore, shipping shortages restricted trade with distant markets. Thus, in Latin America, domestic producers and United States firms made great gains against British goods – or, rather, took advantage of the lack of them. In the Far East, a fast-industrializing Japan challenged Britain in many traditional Asian markets. Furthermore, the Indian sub-continent – which was Britain's leading market in 1913, which took almost half of Lancashire's textile exports, and which funded the British trade deficit by its own surpluses – was affected in numerous ways by the war. Its profitable sales to central Europe were hit, and the contributions it was required to make to the imperial war effort could only be raised by instituting tariffs, thereby giving protection to its own manufacturers and dealing a severe blow to Lancashire. In sum, the war eradicated a large part of that peculiar supportive position which Indian had occupied in the Edwardian global trading structure.[4]

In a similar way, British industry seemed to show up reasonably well during much of the war, but to be seriously hit in the longer term. In spite of nearly 6 million men being mobilized for the armed forces, industrial output hardly dropped at all. This was achieved 'largely by longer hours of labour and more intensive work, by better organization, better equipment and better management'.[5] Old industries were rationalized and new industries created under government direction, and the state also entered the tricky field of labour relations by negotiating with the trade unions for a 'dilution' of the skilled trades and a no-strike pact. In consequence, many of the pre-1914 industrial deficiencies of the country were repaired – including that embarrassing reliance upon neutral or even German production of vital items like ball-bearings, magnetos, aircraft-engines, optical equipment, drugs and dyestuffs which had to be imported during the early part of the war. On the other hand, the dismantling of so many government agencies after 1919 meant that much of the industrial ground gained during the war was lost in its aftermath. The same was true of British agriculture, which achieved a commendable switch from pasture to grain production, only to see a reversal to the pre-war proportions by the 1930s. Moreover, the prolonged conflict deleteriously affected the British merchant marine and the shipbuilding industry – both traditional earners of foreign currency – because of the losses caused by U-boats and because of the fact that British yards had to give priority to warship construction, leaving the Americans, Japanese and Scandinavians to fill the gap in merchant vessels. In 1914 the British Empire had produced 71 per cent of that year's merchant-ship launchings, the USA a mere 8 per cent; in 1918, the British Empire's share had slumped to 29 per cent, the American proportion had risen to 56 per cent. The coming of peace did not lead to a recovery of that Edwardian predominance. Finally, the war gave an artificial stimulation to certain of the established industries (iron and steel, coal, textiles), which then collapsed the faster when hostilities were over, the government-inspired capital investment was withdrawn, and foreign competition revived. An immediate post-war boom was to make the subsequent contraction in the early 1920s seem that much more severe.

In these five areas, then: the enormous growth of the National Debt, the cession of financial leadership to the

United States, the loss of overseas and Indian markets, the damage to shipping and shipbuilding, and the distortion of traditional basic industries, the war had a deleterious effect. Against this could be set various advantages, so that the exact balance-sheet remains a matter for debate.[6] What is clear is that instead of boosting the country to the front rank of the world's military-naval and commercial-industrial powers as the Napoleonic conflict had done, it had caused grievous strain. If this was not evident to all observers, then it was because Britain's position still appeared favourable when compared with the chaos reigning in Russia, the severe economic problems facing Germany, and the emaciation of French industrial power by 1919. When measured against the United States, however, it was clear that there had been a distinct and irrecoverable waning of Britain's relative industrial and financial strength.

Social, Psychological and Party-political Impacts

By comparison with these economic aspects, the other consequences of the war upon British society are more difficult to quantify. This does not mean that they were less substantial. On the contrary, since they pertained to people's beliefs, expectations, daily routines and general social relations, they were more likely to have a lasting impact than the loss of overseas investments or the waste of so much war material. The conflict shaped citizens' lives in ways scarcely contemplated earlier. Millions of men responded to the call for volunteers; when the flood dried up, millions more were conscripted. A growing casualty list – 750,000 dead and 1,700,000 wounded was the final, horrific total – affected almost every family. Belief in a Divine presence rose, and then fell off. Family life was strained, and social mores challenged. Women were 'liberated' – chiefly to work in the factories. Industrial relations were 'frozen' into an uneasy, and occasionally broken peace. Freedom of movement, and of drinking, was curtailed; cricket, the Boat Race, football and horseracing stopped, at least for the duration of the war. On the other hand, the more the state demanded from its citizens, the more it felt the need to proffer compensations, especially when peace came in sight again: the Education Act (1918), the Ministry of Health Act (1919), the Housing Act (1919) and the National Insurance Act (1920) were all variations on the theme of 'homes fit for Heroes' – however limited the implementation of social-reform policies turned out to be by the early 1920s. Taxation, and the decline in domestic service, brought further change, and uncertainty, into social relations. Yet at the same time as it caused internal tensions, the war was also intensifying national unity by the shared war effort, the rationing, and the suspension of certain political activities.

Psychologically, the impact of war was perhaps even more important, and more intangible. The first response, predictable enough in an age where the individual's identification with his nation-state was emphasized in all manner of ways, was that surge of patriotism recorded by so many observers: the cheering crowds around Whitehall and Buckingham Palace, the immense popularity of George V, the ready abandonment of civilian occupations or university studies to enrol in Kitchener's 'New Army', the flood of poems and speeches dedicated to the Empire and to the cause of victory; and, on its dark obverse side, the bitter feelings against anything German, the attacks upon domiciled German shopkeepers and other businesses, the vendettas against Haldane, Battenberg and (most ironic of all) Eyre Crowe, the cartoon portrayals of Wilhelm II as the devil incarnate. This campaign, kept alive by the radical right and by the press agitations of Horatio Bottomley, *Punch* magazine and other publications (including many Liberal ones), lasted throughout the war: the more casualties suffered at German hands, the more the Germans were hated; and the coming of unrestricted U-boat warfare, Zeppelin and aircraft raids, and the occasional shelling of east-coast towns intensified the animosity.

By the later stages of the war, however, patriotic emotions were mingling with, and in some cases overshadowed by, feelings of despair, frustration, pessimism. The sheer cost and horrors of war cast gloom upon all but the most unimaginative of chauvinists. An apathy towards the conflict became more noticeable, especially among the workers; so, too, did the resentment in certain trades against the bosses and the government, as could be seen in sporadic outbreaks of strikes. Much of the frenzied enjoyment of night-life and the change in sexual mores can be ascribed to a search for release from the drabness and restrictions and increased labour of wartime Britain; and, on the part of the troops home on leave, this was clearly an escape from the futility and slaughter of the Western Front.[7]

It was this latter image especially which unsettled, and sometimes overwhelmed the British consciousness: millions of men struggling through the mud, or impaled upon barbed-wire fences, in an effort to gain some small redoubt. It was this image, too, which was preserved in the national consciousness after the war by a whole host of writers. It may be true, as one critic has argued, that with few exceptions the war poets and novelists came from 'sheltered, well-off, upper- or upper-middle-class backgrounds, the products of an upbringing at home and at their public schools which had given them little knowledge or understanding of the real world of their time, but rather a set of unpractical idealistic attitudes';[8] but it was precisely those classes – the 'upper ten thousand' once again – who held power and whose Liberal political culture was most placed under stress by the war. Moreover, this sense of shock at trench-warfare and mass casualties was evident in all classes, and acute members of the establishment watched nervously as the evidence of public disenchantment and *ennui* mounted. Others, less wedded in any case to that Liberal political culture, were often more optimistic, perceiving that the war offered an emerging possibility of reconstructing national politics either in a rightward or leftward direction. All, however, sensed the dissolving certainties. As the editor of the *Daily Express* noted in his diary, 'the war has simply turned the whole world topsy-turvy'.[9]

Some of these tendencies – especially the turn against war in any form – were not to take full effect until some time after the conflict was over; and while the German challenge remained, and the fighting continued, national solidarity generally held firm. However, the parliamentary political scene, acting as a seismograph to these deeper tremors, recorded a considerable number of important changes in consequence of the war. A strengthening of the right, new fissures and possibilities on the left, the eclipse of Irish representation at Westminster, were but some of the longer-term results of the Cabinet's decision in early August 1914 to enter the European conflict.

All these political consequences were in some degree linked with that larger event, the decline of Liberalism and (more specifically) of the Liberal Party itself. The extensive historical debate about whether English Liberalism had suffered a 'strange death' even before 1914, or whether, by contrast, it was purposefully reforming and redefining itself until thrown off course by the misadventure of war, is not of direct concern here.[10] Neither school of thought would deny that the prolonged world conflict hurt the movement; as many Cobdenite and social-reform members of the party had warned beforehand, war was fatal to Liberalism. Although the cause of 'poor little Belgium' and the defence of European liberties was a more acceptable justification than any reference to the balance of power, the very act of intervention was seen as a blow to some Liberal traditions; Morley's resignation, and the disaffection on the left at the Cabinet's decision for war, testified to this. On the other hand, the Conservatives, already pressing the government hard before 1914, were given new opportunities by the coming of war. The party's stress upon national interests, upon military preparedness, upon harnessing the resources of the whole nation for an unconditional victory over Germany, now appeared to serve better than those traditional Liberal recipes of international understanding, tolerance, concern about civil liberties and dissent, and repugnance of war. Above all, the ending of peace gave a chance to the many frustrated and articulate followers of Milner and (the now-deceased) Chamberlain to push ahead with their attack upon 'our blindness, indolence, and lack of leadership', upon government by pedants and lawyers (i.e. Asquith), upon the 'enemies within', and in general upon the shibboleths of a bygone, *laissez-faire* Liberalism.[11]

There were three main stages in this Conservative advance towards power. First, the formation of the Coalition government in May 1915, when the broadsides of the Northcliffe press against the shell shortages and the discontent within and without the government at the Gallipoli failures caused Asquith, Lloyd George and Bonar Law (all for differing reasons) to agree upon a merging of the front benches. Although this was by no means to the full satisfaction of Conservative backbenchers, it greatly dismayed many Liberals because of the implications for their party and its traditions, a dismay which intensified when Asquith was compelled to accept conscription a year later. This period also gave the opportunity to Lloyd George, who had no such scruple for traditions, to demonstrate his ability to organize munitions production with the aid of businessmen and unions – a task at which which the older governing elites appeared to have little competence. The second, and most spectacular, change came in December 1916 when Asquith, supported by traditional Liberals and traditional Conservatives, found himself out-manoeuvred by Lloyd George, who was supported by Bonar Law and backbench Conservatives, and a considerable number of Liberal MPs organized by Addison. A little later, and with some reluctance, Arthur Henderson and much of the Labour movement also agreed to support the new regime. A national leader, willing to wage total warfare and supported by those eager for change, was now in power. Since Lloyd George was bitterly opposed by Asquith and his followers, the bulk of the coalition consisted of Conservatives; thus, although he frequently dazzled Bonar Law and his colleagues, the new Prime Minister was also ultimately dependent upon them. This became clearer than ever during the third stage, the general election of December 1918, when he needed to bargain hard to ensure that a sufficient number of his coalition Liberals were not opposed by Conservative candidates and thus would avoid the fate of the Asquithian Liberals, who were nearly wiped out.

While the Liberal Party was split into two factions, both of which waned in the face of this swing towards the Conservatives, it also lost support in other directions. The most obvious loss was of Redmond's Irish Party, which had sustained the Liberals at Westminster since 1910, and before. The suspension of the Home Rule Act, the Easter Rebellion and its suppression, the coming of the coalition, the further failures to effect Home Rule by negotiation, and finally the extension of conscription to Ireland, led to a steady weakening of Redmond's position and a corresponding enhancement of the Sinn Fein 'irreconcilables'. Of course, Irish support in the Commons for the Liberal Party had not always been reliable, but in the past it had often and usefully kept the Tories at bay. By 1918 it was gone for ever.

Even more significant in the long term was the decomposition of the 'left' of the Liberal Party. There were already signs of this at the outset of war, when that hard core of radical Liberals who had earlier harried Grey for his *ententes* policy endeavoured to keep Britain neutral and, having failed to do that, formed the Union of Democratic Control to promulgate an alternative conception of foreign policy. At the same time, MacDonald and various Independent Labour Party (ILP) members showed themselves willing to oppose the war, although the trade unions and the majority of the parliamentary Labour Party supported Asquith and then, somewhat more suspiciously, Lloyd George. Whatever the Labour movement's commitment to the cause of victory, however, it was determined to preserve its domestic political independence, just as the unions were determined to hang on to their industrial rights even while tolerating certain deviations in wartime.

By adopting this stance, Labour too was a natural beneficiary of the larger processes of war: it gained the adhesion of those social-reform Liberals and intellectuals who regarded the Asquith Cabinet's decision for war as a betrayal of their hopes to improve British society; it also gained the support of an increasing number of trade unionists* when public disenchantment mounted after the first few years of the war and resentment against 'dilution' and profiteering grew; and it was inevitably assisted by the great public debate and concern about domestic reforms, since such aims naturally appeared to have a better chance of realization if power rested in the future with a working-class party rather than with hastily converted Conservatives and their unorthodox Liberal coalition leader. Above all, Labour benefited in the long term from the Representation of the People Act, which became law in June 1918 and increased the electorate from around 7 million people to over 20 million. In a franchise which was much more closely a democracy than ever before, the party obviously had a much better chance of electoral success. Not surprisingly, Labour under Henderson's leadership preferred to develop its own party programme, including 'common ownership of the means of production', and to refuse Lloyd George's plea to remain in the wartime coalition. If, in the 'jingo' atmosphere of that time, it was lucky to gain the number of seats it did

* Trade-union membership itself doubled during the war from 4 million to 8 million. Moreover, the war itself ironed out certain distinctions between the skilled and unskilled trades, and produced a stronger sense of identity within Labour, at least *vis-à-vis* the establishment.

(fifty-nine) in the 1918 election, it had received over $2\frac{1}{4}$ million votes and was well positioned to take advantage of any post-war disillusionment and yearnings for change.

Since, in sum, the war strengthened those forces both to the right and to the left of Asquithian Liberalism, it is scarcely surprising that the debate upon external policy witnessed an intensification of that divide between 'idealists' and 'realists' which had existed in the pre-1914 decades. To a much larger degree than in, say, the Second World War, the arguments about the country's proper aims and the means it should employ to achieve those aims were ideologically charged and polarized. In one sense, this was very predictable, for despite the manifestations of popular enthusiasm at the outbreak of war there had been much more reluctance to accept a state of hostilities than was to be the case in 1939. Once it became clear that the conflict would be long and hard, and was forcing all manner of changes upon British society, then the debate was bound to intensify. It was also going to be affected, as we shall see, by significant external influences.

It would be wrong to represent this disagreement over British external policy as one held by two equally strong political groupings. The desire for victory, the belief in the righteousness of Britain's cause, the hatred of Germany, were altogether too strong to be checked by those who thought differently. The substantial increase of support within the parliamentary Liberal Party for Lloyd George as the man who could 'win the war' was testimony to this, as was that growing Conservative strength noted above; even in Labour and trade-union circles, it was the *minority* and the *unorthodox* who questioned the aims of British policy. Furthermore, since a truce prevailed in by-elections and the parliamentary battleground was subdued by the coalition of the party leaders for most of the war, 'public opinion' seemed to manifest itself more than ever in the views expressed by the newspapers, which probably reached the height of their political power during this period. And the press, with a few exceptions like the *Manchester Guardian* and the *Nation*, was strongly nationalistic in tone. In particular, the influence wielded by the owner of the *Daily Mail* and of *The Times*, Lord Northcliffe – or, to be more precise, the influence which politicians believed he could exert – was such that all feared his press broadsides, and the more so as the Conservative influence in the coalition grew. Thus, although Lloyd George benefited from the assault of *The Times* and *Daily Mail* against the 'shell shortages' in 1915, he also found himself as Prime Minister severely constrained by this extra-constitutional force; getting rid of Haig, for example, was impossible unless he was willing to risk violent press attacks and a Tory revolt. Similarly, that arch-intriguer and military correspondent of *The Times* (later, of the *Morning Post*), Repington, was always ready to aid the generals by publishing *exposés* of civilian interference in strategic matters. In consequence of all this, the dominant tone of 'public' opinion remained one of resolute commitment to total war and total victory.

The dissenters from this tone were more influential after the war than during it, for the strength of their case rested upon the belief that the conflict was futile, wasteful and unnecessary. Since few in authority accepted, or at least professed to accept, that argument while the battles raged, these critics had correspondingly little influence; their intellectual heritage was so obviously that of the 'trouble-makers' of the past,[12] those Cobdenite or quasi-Marxist critics of militarism and *Realpolitik* who had often been a thorn in the side of governments but had never been able to implement their own policies. In the harsher atmosphere of 1914–18, however, even ineffective dissent could not be tolerated and the leader of the Union of Democratic Control, E. D. Morel, paid for his activities with a spell in prison. The very notions of a negotiated peace, the renunciation in advance of any territorial or material gains, the repudiation of secret treaties and the assertion of democratic control over foreign policy would, if propagated widely, doubtless shake national unity; and, as a Cabinet Committee on War Policy warned, 'the maintenance of a helathy public opinion is a factor of great importance in the consideration of our war policy . . .'[13] Quakers and other conscientious objectors also found themselves subjected to 'illiberal' treatment, and indeed to disenfranchisement for five years after the war.

The real area of concern to the government was not so much the opinions of Morel, Arthur Ponsonby, C. P. Trevelyan and other intellectual 'defectors' from the establishment, or the religiously motivated objectors to the war; but rather the potential influence which pacifist and international ideas might have upon Labour. MacDonald's own retirement from the official Labour leadership in 1914 and, more significantly, Henderson's resignation from the War Cabinet in March 1917 over the specific issue of Labour's attendance at the international socialist conference in Stockholm, were indications that not all of the leaders of the working classes would accept official British policy. Of course, the growth of Labour's reservations about the foreign policy of the war cannot be understood outside the domestic resentment of the privations and restrictions which that conflict was imposing by 1917; the shortages in food and fuel, the temporary decline in the workers' standard of living, and the strikes against 'dilution', represented the *material* side of the coin, the propaganda against an 'imperialist' and 'capitalist' war the *ideological* side. Because these ideas were growing among Labour, the Cabinet's concern also increased; yet, by the same token, it hesitated to take action. Just as in the industrial field, so also in this political issue of war aims, Lloyd George and most of his colleagues felt that it was necessary to conciliate rather than to repress. With the right clamouring for a more vigorous prosecution of the conflict, and the left beginning to show increasing hostility to it, even the wily Prime Minister was to find it difficult to steer a middle course between these pressures.

The Influence of Wilson and Lenin

The Cabinet's task of evolving a coherent grand strategy which would satisfy both the country's external *and* internal needs during these years of prolonged strain was further complicated by certain outside influences upon British opinion. Such influences, by their nature, could not be physically controlled in the way that domestic forces could; only adroit counter-propaganda could neutralize the effect of these foreign impulses, which by the closing year of the war were threatening to upset government policy in a number of ways.

Although Morley, as the keeper of the Gladstonian conscience, had resigned in protest at the entry into war, there was a new Gladstone waiting in the wings, on the far side of the Atlantic. As the European conflict intensified, the American President, Woodrow Wilson, felt drawn into a mediating role; given the economic importance of the United States this was perhaps inevitable, but Wilson, like his hero Gladstone,* was a natural interferer. The President's oratory, moral fervour, and belief in national self-determination, democracy, international co-operation and arbitration delighted the radicals in Britain, who had despaired of finding a domestic statesman willing to campaign for such ideals. In fact, so isolated did they feel that many of them had rejoiced when Lansdowne published his famous letter in the *Daily Telegraph* in November 1917, urging moderate peace terms before the war destroyed the traditional social order; Ponsonby, for example, wondered how Lansdowne could be made Prime Minister! Yet Wilson was clearly a much better ally than an ex-Whig grandee

* Wilson, who called Gladstone 'the greatest statesman that ever lived', had a portrait of the Englishman on his desk.

whose views on social reform and Irish Home Rule were, to say the least, not very progressive. With most British leaders committed to a fight to the finish, the President appeared as a saviour to the opponents of militarism and imperialism. Even C. P. Scott was forced to admit that the attitude of his friend and confidant Lloyd George 'savours rather of the "real-politik" of Bismarck than of Wilson's idealism which we are supposed to share.'[14] Moreover, the President's appeals, like Gladstone's, appeared to strike deep into the hearts of many of the lower-middle and working classes, and thus were likely to be more influential than the rather academic pamphleteering of the Union of Democratic Control.

All this might not have mattered so much had Woodrow Wilson not been President of the United States. By his office, he posed a double challenge to the policy which Lloyd George and his colleagues preferred: first, by offering a much-publicized alternative conception of war and peace aims to the *internal* British audience; and secondly, by being the leader of what was now seen to be the most powerful state in the world, he could exert an *external* pressure upon the Western Allies. This latter point was, indeed, the rub. In October 1916, the Chancellor of the Exchequer, McKenna, warned that 'by next June or earlier, the President of the American Republic will be in a position, if he wishes, to dictate his own terms to us.'[15] This was the more alarming because, quite apart from Wilson's impact upon British morale and the will to victory, he had also shown himself opposed to the Allied naval blockade; and he was more than likely to object to French and Italian hopes of reshaping European boundaries, and to the Dominions' wish to retain the German colonies.

On the other hand, Britain especially was becoming dependent upon American financial and industrial assistance, and the Allied war effort as a whole would crumble if that assistance were withdrawn. Secondly, there was always the hope that the United States might be tempted into the war itself: by 1917, with Russia collapsing, this was the only chance the Allies possessed to win the war – indeed, to ensure that they did not lose it. Yet the eventual American entry as an 'associated power', while a great military boost, also meant that Wilson was now a direct participant in the debate about war aims and peace terms; and this in turn meant that Lloyd George had to take an ever-greater account of this distorting trans-Atlantic influence. From around 1915–16 onwards, it is fair to argue, successive British governments were rarely to be able to decide upon a major item of external policy without some deliberation of the American factor.

Even more disturbing to the War Cabinet were the events in Russia, where the Tsarist regime was replaced in March 1917 by a democratic republic, which in turn was challenged by the Bolshevik uprising. Once again, the impact was not merely upon external policy but upon domestic politics as well. For decades, organized Labour had been anti-Russian in sentiment; now, with the change of government, this feeling altered dramatically. Moreover, while the new Russian leaders embarrassed their Western Allies by proposing a peace with 'no annexations and no indemnities', the Bolsheviks were altogether more categorical in their attack upon an imperialists' war and in their determination to retire from the conflict. The call to the working classes of all the belligerent nations to co-operate in reaching a peace which their rulers, on selfish class grounds, had refused to consider, found a ready response in Britain – not merely from the ILP and the (Marxist) British Socialist Party, but also from more moderate leaders such as Henderson and MacDonald, and from the Union of Democratic Control. Of course, many held rather confusing notions of what the Bolshevik Revolution represented, and freely mixed Russian proposals with those emanating from Wilson; but the point was not the precision and coherence of these new ideologies so much as the fact that they challenged the old assumptions.

If the British government's apprehensions about these

developments were excessive, they are easy to understand in the context of the time. The war on land had raged for so long and cost so much, yet the victory was as far away as ever: with the French army mutinies after the Nivelle offensive, and Russia's defection, it was even further away than in 1914. At sea, there was a grave danger of losing control of the Atlantic trade routes. All this doubtless made people think of, if not openly advocate, a negotiated peace. At home, the Liberal Party was slowly dissolving to the left and the right, and the political scene was polarizing. Trade-union unrest was high and public morale was low. 'Combing-out' more men for the army was meeting with Labour resistance. The Shop Stewards' Movement suggested that, even if the national leaders of the unions still supported the government, there was now a danger of a rank-and-file breakaway. In addition, the Leeds meeting of the United Socialist Council, which had called for the creation of workers' and soldiers' *soviets* (councils), and the resignation of Henderson from the War Cabinet, seemed very disturbing to a predominantly Conservative and arch-imperialist British government. In June 1917, Milner wrote worriedly to the Prime Minister: 'I fear the time is very near at hand, when we shall have to take some strong steps to stop the "rot" in this country, unless we wish to "follow Russia" into impotence and dissolution.'[16]

By the end of the year, with the Bolsheviks attempting their *coup* and appealing for similar actions by workers elsewhere, Smuts was writing of 'the grim spectre of Bolshevik anarchy ... stalking to the front'.[17] Even the army, it was feared, might not be immune to these influences. In such circumstances, *all* criticism of the establishment appeared suspicious, and few in authority perceived that the British Labour movement, led by Henderson and MacDonald and broad-based upon the trade unions, would concern itself predominantly with industrial aims and was in effect a brake upon a genuine and violent social revolution. On the other hand, parts of the Labour movement were now increasingly suspicious of *any* external policy which appeared annexationist and aggressive. Whatever the actual aims of the British government, therefore, they would have to be phrased (and perhaps disguised) to cope with these new American and Russian influences and their impact upon domestic politics.

The Influence of the Empire

In the seven or eight years prior to 1914 the imperial aspect in British policy had receded somewhat, due to the defeat of the Tariff Reform campaign and to the concentration of attention upon either the threatening state of European affairs or upon such domestic issues as social reform, Ireland and the House of Lords crisis. The coming of war increased the Empire's significance at a stroke. This was, no doubt, natural enough: the existence of a foreign foe is always likely to induce a sinking of differences within a community. Furthermore, although the King-Emperor had declared war on behalf of the whole Empire, the Dominions at least were free to determine the *extent* of their own participation; and it was therefore heart-warming to Britons that their kinsfolk overseas responded so readily (with the exception of diehard Afrikaners).

Quite apart from emotional considerations, the Empire's material contribution to the war was such as to command respect and gratitude. Of the 458,218 Canadians who served overseas, 56,639 lost their lives; of the 331,814 Australians, 59,330 lost their lives; of the 76,184 white South Africans, 7121 lost their lives. New Zealand, always the most loyal of Dominions, sent overseas 112,223 troops, which represented a massive 19.35 per cent of its European male population; 16,711 of them lost their lives. One and a half million volunteers enlisted in the Indian Army, and 62,056 of those died. There were smaller contingents from Newfoundland, West and East Africa, and other parts of the colonial Empire. In all, 2½ million 'colonials' fought for Britain. Their campaigns ranged from the assaults upon the German colonies, the push into Mesopotamia, the Anzac effort at Gallipoli, and many famous battles along the Western Front, as well as smaller naval operations. Finally, the Empire was economically important, not only in offering direct grants of money to Britain, but in supplying a vastly increased amount of raw materials. For example, British imports from Canada in the period 1910–14 averaged £29 million per year; in the period 1915–20, this shot up to an annual average of £86 million. Imports from British possessions in Asia also jumped from an average £89 million per year in the first quinquennium to £164 million per year in the second. At last, so it seemed at first glance, Chamberlain's dream of exploiting the colonial estates was being realized.

This evidence of the Empire's unity and utility was greeted with joy by many in the Conservative Party, who thought that their hour had come on the imperial front as well as in domestic affairs; inevitably, as Liberalism weakened and the Tories became the dominant force within the Coalition government, the significance of the overseas Empire was bound to be enhanced. The challenges of total war, and the inability or unwillingness of leading Liberals to handle those challenges, brought the old proconsuls into positions of power. In Lloyd George's streamlined War Cabinet, for example, one of the five members was Milner, another Curzon; later, Smuts was added. Balfour, as Foreign Secretary, was also likely to give great attention to imperial matters. Equally important was the penetration of the government by members of Milner's former South African staff (the 'kindergarten') and other younger imperialists. For example, Lloyd George's own secretariat contained Waldorf Astor, Lionel Curtis and Philip Kerr (later Lord Lothian), the latter being the Prime Minister's adviser upon imperial affairs; Leo Amery and Mark Sykes were advisers on Middle East matters to the Cabinet secretariat; and John Buchan was deputy director in the new Ministry of Information. All these – and that other ex-'kindergarten' member Geoffrey Dawson, editor of *The Times* – could be guaranteed to sing the high song of Empire and to argue that weight should be given to the interests of a Greater Britain.

In retrospect, it may no doubt seem clear that the Milnerites failed to perceive the centrifugal forces at work in the Empire, and also exaggerated the extent to which even the most developed of their overseas territories could buttress British power. Notwithstanding their contributions of men and money as mentioned above, the fact remains that the United Kingdom provided 79 per cent of the whole Empire's combat casualties between 1914 and 1918, and an even higher percentage of war expenditure – 43.8 billion dollars to the rest of the Empire's 5.8 billion dollars.[18] Nevertheless, it is easy to understand why, in the middle of a great war, British imperialists should rejoice at the benefits derived from the Dominions and the dependent territories.

To the more traditional British leaders, even to Lloyd George himself, such tendencies were not without complications. Along with these increasingly valuable contributions from the Dominions went a demand for a say in the conduct of the war, the more especially after military disasters at Gallipoli and on the Western Front. As the Canadian Prime Minister, Sir Robert Borden, complained:

It can hardly be expected that we shall put 400,000 or 500,000 men in the field and willingly accept the position of having no more voice and receiving no more consideration than if we were toy automata. Any person cherishing such an expectation harbours an unfortunate and even dangerous delusion. Is this war being waged by the United Kingdom alone or is it a war waged by the whole Empire?[19]

In a word, the war had raised again the ancient issue of taxation without representation, the 'taxes' in this instance being paid by the blood of Dominion troops. To imperial federationists, the matter could be resolved by developing a truly organic union between the motherland and its offspring. However, to a considerable number of other participants, including the majority of Dominions' politicians, the chief aim was to redefine inter-imperial relations so that the requirements of collective self defence did not obliterate their own claims for greater autonomy. This was the critical issue which Smuts sought to resolve in 1917 and 1918 when drafting his ideas about a 'British Commonwealth' of nations, bound by ties of history and sentiment rather than tight constitutional bonds.[20]

While this problem of federation *versus* decentralization could hardly be settled in the heat of battle, there were certain areas of policy where the Dominions' influence was more immediately felt. Discussion upon war aims, for example, was affected by the Dominions' unanimous insistence on retaining the captured German colonies. More important still, perhaps, was their inclination against a purely Eurocentric grand strategy: if, indeed, this was a war fought by and on behalf of the entire British Empire, then the European equilibrium could not be the sole or even the overriding concern.

These voices from Australia, New Zealand, South Africa and (after it had secured its own representation in London in 1917) India suggested that Britain needed to interest itself once again in those issues and regions which had obsessed Salisbury's generation – the future of East Africa, the defence of the approaches to India, the security of British trade and possessions in the Far East.[21] In the great strategical debate between 'Westerners' and 'Easterners', the Dominions were almost universally Easterners; not only did they possess a positive interest in the non-European aspects of policy, but they manifested strong *negative* feelings towards France and towards the French insistence that absolute priority had always to be given to the defeat of German military power in the west.

If the British were encouraged by the Empire's ready offerings of men, money and materials, they were later perturbed by the signs that the lengthy conflict was causing strains overseas similar to those at home. In that half-domestic, half-imperial problem of Ireland, the war at first suppressed, but by 1916 and even more by 1918 had exacerbated, ancient antagonisms so much that civil war could no longer be contained. In India, too, the many advantages which the British derived from their rule over the sub-continent (from large-scale assistance with war loans and free grants, to the recruitment of so many native troops, to the reduction in the size of the British garrison there to a mere 15,000 troops at one stage) were gradually over-shadowed by a variety of disadvantages. The loss of India's trading surplus for the sterling area and the creation of domestic tariffs were the lesser evils; more important was the resurgence of Indian nationalism, which by 1917 had become, in the words of the Secretary of State for India, Edwin Montagu, 'a seething, boiling, political flood, raging across the country', and which provoked that belated British gesture, the Montagu-Chelmsford reforms proposed in 1918.[22] In Egypt, too, resentment against British rule had markedly increased when London declared that country to be a formal protectorate after Turkey's entry into the war.

Nor were the Dominions themselves unaffected by internal dislike of the imperial connection and the pursuit of an imperial war. In South Africa a rebellion against commitment on Britain's side was hastily suppressed in 1914, but even so, by no means all Afrikaners shared the wish of Botha and Smuts for a lasting reconciliation with London. Elsewhere, the main bone of contention was conscription. Volunteering to assist Britain in its struggle was one thing; being forced to fight unwillingly on some distant and dangerous foreign battlefield was quite another. This in particular was the view of the Labour movement and of many Irish immigrants in Australia, where two successive referenda could not secure a majority for conscription. Yet even that row paled by comparison with the one which took place in Canada during 1917 following Borden's decision to introduce conscription there: the bitter resentment of national service shown by the French Canadians, with riots in Quebec, not only revealed a considerable lack of commitment to the war but also exposed – and widened – the cultural and linguistic cleavage in the country as a whole. In such circumstances it was inevitable that even the most loyal of Dominion statesmen felt bound to warn London that continued participation in the war depended upon due regard being paid to colonial opinion and interests.

The effect upon the British government of these controversies and growing problems was twofold. In the first place, ministers and officials were constantly reminded that theirs was not a purely European state but one possessing global responsibilities which needed careful attention; the Empire not only distracted Whitehall's gaze from the continent, but it also on occasions tempted many Britons to dream of the possibility of an eventual return to a policy of isolation, so that a firmer imperial basis could be constructed, unhampered by European obligations. Secondly, this pressure compelled the provision of *ad hoc* adjustments to the constitutional and decision-making processes of the Empire even while the war was waging. Eager to harness the goodwill of the Dominions upon which ultimately depended the prospects of their continued support for the military struggle, Lloyd George was willing to admit a certain sharing of power by creating an Imperial War Cabinet. This, indeed, was a significant response, and quite unprecedented in British constitutional history. Since, however, the First World War led to a number of important changes in governmental structures, it will be more practicable to consider them all together in the section following.

Government Structures and the Decision-making Process

Although the unwritten British constitution which had evolved in the preceding centuries made for a flexible decision-making process, and one which was sensitive to most of those forces which sought to influence the decision-makers, it also rested upon habits of lengthy and leisured consultation and upon a preference for reasoned compromise rather than decisive and perhaps contentious action. The subordination of the military and of permanent officials to their political masters, the careful deliberations of a Cabinet of some fifteen to twenty members, and the fact that even when that body had fashioned a policy it was often required to justify it in the Commons and secure the support of a majority of that assembly, were all suitable to a slowly evolving society whose establishment hoped to obtain government by consent. By the same token, however, it was not a very satisfactory instrument for handling a world crisis, which put a premium upon decisive leadership, swift action, considerable secrecy, and a certain disregard of traditional scruples about the means used.

It was for this very reason that the new imperialists of the post-Salisbury era, believing that even in the decade before 1914 Britain faced such a global crisis, had been critical of the elaborate procedures of parliamentary government and party politics; and for the same reason that traditionalists and left-wingers had suspected the ulterior motives behind such arguments about 'national efficiency', and even mistrusted the mild 'streamlining' of decision-making which the Committee of Imperial Defence represented. Once the country faced the challenge of total war, it became clear that governmental structures would need to be much more extensively amended and streamlined in order to secure ultimate victory.

The institution most noticeably eclipsed by the advent of hostilities was parliament itself; as Liberals had feared, democratic and deliberative assemblies would always be at a discount in wartime. Apart from voting the credits required by the government, the Commons had little other role. The requirements of secrecy meant that a great deal of government policy could not be openly discussed even after an event, and it was of course quite impossible to have the Commons debate operational planning or a change in future diplomatic strategy. It was also true, however, that the Conservatives' decision to support the Asquith ministry in August 1914 and their later entry into a coalition meant that the Commons' powers to interrogate, to vote in opposition and to pass censure motions had been largely given up by the party leaders themselves. This did not, of course, prevent strong feelings being vented in the House by Sir Edward Carson, W. A. S. Hewins and other discontented Tories, and there were occasional secret sessions; but the only time the 'official Opposition' divided the Commons during the war was in the censure motion by the Asquithian Liberals (the so-called Maurice affair) in May 1918 – although the unofficial left did the same three times in 1917 with motions upon war aims.[23] The party truce also operated in the related field of by-elections, so that they, too, offered no forum for arguments about alternative policies.

All this did not mean that backbench MPs lacked power and influence during the war, but rather that the pressures they exerted now tended to be diverted from the floor of the Commons itself and were instead transmitted via the party machine to their own leadership. At that level, they were still immensely effective and perhaps the more so for being less quantifiable than a Commons division: witness, for example, Bonar Law's own unease at backbench discontent over the scandal of a shells shortage in May 1915, or the powerful Liberal counter-pressure placed upon Asquith and against the conscriptionist movement in the following year. Lloyd George, even at the peak of his influence, always acted in recognition that an unholy combination of voting blocks in the Commons *could* bring the government down and dissolve the precarious coalition. However, since neither he nor his various opponents knew what results the subsequent general election might produce, each side usually backed down from a confrontation which would make an election unavoidable. These unusual circumstances gave a considerable amount of influence to those political operators who had the ear of great men and laid claim to 'know' what the party or the country at large was feeling – Beaverbrook, for example, or even Horatio Bottomley.

The war's impact upon the great departments of state was extremely varied. The Treasury, for instance, found its position severely circumscribed; for while it was true that it had the critical task of steering the wartime economy, it no longer had that tight control over the armed services which in peacetime gave it a substantial, if negative, influence over external policy. Its task now was simply to find the money to meet the demands of the army and the navy. Obviously, this is another way of saying that the two latter departments found their positions immensely boosted by the war, since upon their performance the fate of the country depended. Of the two, the army's rise to power was the more dramatic. This followed inevitably from the decision for a 'continental commitment', and from the consequent fact that the army consumed by far the greater share of men and munitions.

What excited controversy both at the time and afterwards, however, was that it was not the successive civilian War Ministers who gained in power, but rather the General Staff and the Commander-in-Chief in France. Indeed, when the formidable Sir William Robertson became Chief of Imperial General Staff in December 1915 he demanded – and got – full operational control of the army.[24] Even this might not have been so controversial had not the holders of those posts remorselessly advocated the overriding strategical priority of the Western Front. That issue cannot be understood outside the arguments between 'Easterners' and 'Westerners' which will be examined in the following chapter; but it is worth remarking at this point that the army's unprecedentedly strong position rested less upon its military case than upon its ability to mobilize powerful domestic allies in its defence. Among the latter were the Conservative leaders and most of their backbenchers, the Northcliffe press and, last but not least, the King himself. Indeed, as compared with his low profile in the pre-1914 period, George V's stature and influence appears to have risen considerably during the war; not only was the monarch the chief beneficiary of an enhanced patriotism which sectarian politicians could never themselves completely command, but his involvement in appointments to the higher military offices was obviously much more significant now than in peacetime.

The effects of the war upon the Foreign Office and diplomatic corps were also various, although it would be true to say that both branches suffered a decline in power, especially in the early stages of the conflict. Once hostilities had commenced, Grey himself clearly believed that diplomacy was to be subordinated to military requirements and he rarely attempted to query or influence the decisions of the generals. Although the Foreign Secretary had been firmly in favour of Britain's intervention, the war immensely depressed him and undoubtedly accelerated his premature ageing and growing loss of sight; and, while he himself could not provide decisive leadership, his subordinates found themselves grappling with a host of new problems and a vast increase in business which took a heavy toll of their ranks as well. Furthermore, the Office itself was the object of suspicion and dislike from various quarters: from the right, which remembered the pre-war negotiations for a *detente* with Berlin and suspected officials of having pro-German sympathies; from the left, which now felt more than ever that the clerks had captured Grey and perverted all attempts at a

Liberal foreign policy; and from others who were frustrated at the failures of diplomacy in the Balkans and elsewhere.[25]

In certain respects, however, the war created new possibilities and new areas of responsibility which actually enhanced the work of the Foreign Office. For example, Crowe was soon moved sideways to run a new sub-division handling the problems of wartime commerce and trade, and it was from these small beginnings that the important Ministry of Blockade was to grow. Simply because total war involved mercantilist policies, all aspects of diplomacy which related to commerce increased in significance – as witnessed, for example, in the work of Sir Francis Oppenheimer, formerly the commercial attaché in Frankfurt, when he was sent to the Netherlands to monitor neutral trade and to prevent any gaps in the blockade of the German economy.[26] Even the Board of Trade rose in importance, since it overlapped with the Foreign Office on matters of overseas trade policy and blockade.

Secondly, the increasing need to formulate British war aims by 1916 or so – whether a compromise peace or an all-out victory was assumed – and the possibility of attracting new powers to the Allied side or detaching others from Germany's side naturally increased the role of diplomacy. In European affairs especially, this gave the Foreign Office the chance to regain its old position by presenting memoranda on war aims – an activity reinforced near the end of the war by the creation of the Political Intelligence Division, for its recruits from academe such as Lewis Namier and R. W. Seton-Watson were highly respected for their knowledge of east-European questions. On the other hand, and despite the replacement of Grey by the more influential Balfour in 1916, there were by then many rival sources of information and opinion about the proper aims of British external policy – Hankey, for example, as secretary to the War Cabinet; the Ministry of Information under Beaverbrook; and the ex-'kindergarten' imperialists surrounding Lloyd George, who himself had little respect for the traditional diplomats.

Finally, of course, there were the opinions of the other members of the War Cabinet, where the really important issues of external policy were settled; here, too, it seems clear that people such as Milner and Smuts shared the Prime Minister's disregard of the Foreign Office staff and the major ambassadors, and preferred to use private individuals for secret negotiations and missions in Europe.

The rise of the War Cabinet was indeed *the* most significant institutional response to the extraordinary demands of wartime. Since the majority of the twenty-two members of Asquith's Cabinet at the outset of war ran civilian departments, the body as a whole was unsuitable for the conduct of grand strategy, especially on a day-to-day basis; that task fell to those individual ministers chiefly concerned with external policy. In any case, the direction of the war required that a much more prominent role be given to non-Cabinet 'outsiders' such as generals and admirals, and it was therefore not surprising that the Committee of Imperial Defence with its efficient secretariat under Hankey was pressed into service. In November 1914, in fact, the CID was converted into a War Council, a mixture of senior civilian ministers and strategic advisers. Even so, it did not supercede the ordinary Cabinet altogether, nor did it meet very often; and the coming of the first Coalition government in May 1915, which led to the replacement of the War Council by the Dardanelles Committee, hardly improved the efficiency of decision-making at the top. Only with the triumph of Lloyd George was the system decisively altered.

The War Cabinet which the new Prime Minister headed was intended to be a small but all-powerful group which would run the war unimpeded by departmental burdens. It would meet almost daily, and summon individual ministers to attend it; and it would be serviced by Hankey, although Lloyd George himself possessed his own staff in the so-called 'Garden Suburb'. In certain respects, this new system also remained defective; it was even more detached than before from the service ministries, which therefore made it difficult to get control over the General Staff. On the other hand, it did centralize the direction of British diplomacy, almost to the point of taking control on occasions. It was the Labour representative on the War Cabinet, Henderson, who was sent to report on conditions in Russia; and Smuts who was allowed to explore secret peace negotiations with Austria-Hungary. Although the War Cabinet frequently consulted Balfour, it was clear that many of the traditional forms of advice-giving and decision-making in external affairs had been eroded by the creation of this new body.

But Lloyd George and his colleagues represented more than a structural alteration within the governmental process. They reflected the new need for and new emphasis upon decisive leadership, and this enhanced the powers of the Prime Minister's office especially. They also seemed to symbolize the weakening of the traditional democratic and consultative processes in consequence of the war. The very membership of the War Cabinet was a clue to all this. Apart from Lloyd George, it contained his chief political support, Bonar Law, to represent the Conservatives; Henderson (after 1917, Barnes) to speak for the Labour interest; and the former pro-Consuls, Curzon and Milner, who inevitably skewed the political flavour of the whole body. This was even more true when Smuts, representing no British 'constituency' at all, became a member in June 1917.* In addition, during March-April 1917 and in the summer of 1918 the War Cabinet was expanded to become an Imperial War Cabinet, with Prime Ministers and representatives from the Dominions and India. All this suggested that a much more autocratic, decisive and imperial body had now taken supreme command, which was true enough. But while that state of affairs lasted until the Versailles Conference, the War Cabinet (although not the Cabinet secretariat) vanished in its aftermath, not least because the most powerful and

* There were certain other changes. Carson became a member from July 1917 to January 1918, and then Austen Chamberlain took Milner's place in April 1918 when the latter went to the War Office.

traditional political party (the Conservatives) distrusted the emphasis upon charismatic leadership – just as the Imperial War Cabinet also vanished, because of the Dominions' dislike of maintaining such a supra-national body after the coming of peace. The Cabinet, like much else in British politics and society, was altered by the war but soon re-emerged when times were deemed 'normal' again.

4. Debates and Policies

The Debate upon Strategy

To all the great powers, including such a well-prepared state as Germany, the actual course of the military operations during the Great War came as a surprise and a disappointment. Every General Staff had not only predicted victory but had also forecast that the enemy would be defeated within a short time, following a campaign of rapid movement. It was the image of the Elder Moltke's three swift wars against the Danes, the Austrians and the French, rather than that of the long-drawn-out campaigns of attrition during the American Civil War and Russo-Japanese War, which the pre-1914 strategists favoured. Even at sea, both the British and German navies had expected that decisive encounters between the main battlefleets would take place soon after the war had begun.[1] In consequence, few if any governments had made the necessary preparations for a war which might last more than six months; even the stockpiling of shells and raw materials, and the measures to prevent bank collapses, had been postulated upon the assumption of a short struggle. When the early military operations became bogged down in trench warfare, and the surface war in the North Sea produced a similar stalemate, each side was slowly forced into a new appreciation of the dimensions of the conflict. Obviously, ominously, the premium in future had to be placed upon stamina, upon the total mobilization of resources and – in all probability – upon the capacity to endure vast losses of men while bludgeoning a way through the enemy's lines and compelling surrender.

Of all the belligerents, the British felt the most affected by this. The continental powers, after all, had little choice but to fight on land and each of them already possessed an army of millions; it was the indecisiveness of the battles and the duration of the war which upset *their* calculations, and even then their General Staffs continued to insist that they were only a short distance from victory. Britain, however, had neither possessed a large army nor anticipated the mobilization – and later, the conscription – of millions of men. Above all, very few people before the war had imagined that the country would undertake such an extensive commitment to military operations far from the sea. Many imperialists and navalists who had feared German expansionism had nonetheless expected that it would be checked by the traditional 'British way in warfare' – the peripheral, maritime-based strategy which was supposed to have been so successful in the eighteenth-century struggles against France.[2] The despatch of the six divisions of the BEF across the Channel in August 1914 was not regarded as a major breach of that tradition, since it had been justified as a short-term but necessary means of helping the French to withstand the early German assaults until the fabled Russian 'steam-roller' drove westwards. The first blow to such assumptions came with the evidence that the Russian Army, absurdly overrated by most pre-war observers, was incapable of sustaining a prolonged offensive; the second came with the transformation of the campaigns in the west from bold sweeps and counter-strokes to static trench warfare with mounting casualties, requiring ever more replacements. Over the same six-month period, it had become clear that the hopes of a swift and decisive naval battle in the North Sea were also too optimistic.

Not all of the early fighting by Britain took place in north-west Europe. Cruiser squadrons swept the shipping lanes and cut off German overseas trade. The *Goeben* and *Breslau* were chased, unsuccessfully, through the Mediterranean and into the Straits; and, to much greater satisfaction, Graf von Spee's squadron was finally caught and destroyed at the Falkland Islands. With the exception of German East Africa, the German colonies were overrun by early in 1915 and, when Turkey entered the war, operations were also started in Mesopotamia. Nevertheless, the greater part of the British Army was being concentrated along the Western Front, and the casualty rate there was much larger than elsewhere – without any apparent gains. This fact, more than anything else, was at the heart of the furious debate which developed within the British government about war strategy. Could the struggle against Germany only be fought and won in the trenches of Flanders, as the 'Westerners' argued? Or was there an alternative way of bringing down the enemy at less cost, as the navalists and the 'Easterners' thought? And – an important point – was there not more profit to be gained from an assault upon Turkey's possessions than upon operations in north-west Europe?

This latter school of thought was not altogether right in its contention that a large-scale and permanent commitment to European battlefields was a break with tradition – they tended to forget, for example, the campaigns of Marlborough and Wellington – but the military involvement in Europe was difficult to accept because most Britons living in 1914 had been brought up in that post-Crimean War period of military isolation. The 'Easterners' were also right in holding that continental warfare was bloody, expensive and might ultimately weaken the country's power beyond repair. The flaw in their own argument, however, was the assumption that a viable alternative strategy actually existed which would ensure the defeat of Germany as well as securing colonial gains. If it did, the British government never found it.

To a large extent, Britain here can be seen as a victim both of geography and of changing technology:[3] other nations also suffered, of course, but the impact of the strategical revolution upon them was less far-reaching because even in the past they had rarely possessed a *cheap* way of winning wars. In the British tradition, most campaigns had been chiefly maritime and colonial, which were relatively economical – in certain cases, even beneficial. By 1914, circumstances had altered. A second 'Trafalgar' was not likely in the North Sea, since the Kaiser's beloved High Seas Fleet was unwilling to face its much larger opponent, whereas the Grand Fleet was unlikely either to split itself up for the enemy's benefit or – despite Fisher's ideas of amphibious raids along the German coast – to sail into waters now made dangerous by minefields and submarines. Chance naval encounters did occur – at the Dogger Bank (January 1915) and at Jutland (May–June 1916), but the results did not alter the strategical stalemate. The Royal Navy held the exits to the North Sea, and the German Navy would not contest control of those exits. Britain was protected from invasion and was not losing the *surface* naval war, but that host of battleships at Scapa Flow could do nothing positive to bring down Germany.

Colonial and economic warfare was also far less effective against this new foe than it had been centuries earlier against, say, Spain or the Netherlands. By 1914 the German colonial empire took only 3.8 per cent of the fatherland's foreign investment and contributed to only 0.5 per cent of its foreign trade; losing such possessions was hardly a mortal blow to Berlin. Even the blockade of the enemy's overseas trade by the Royal Navy, which many held to be *the* great weapon in the British armoury, was not particularly effective against a country such as Germany. About 19 per cent of its national income came from exports, but only one fifth of that was extra-European trade and a large amount of business could be diverted to military production; and only 10 per cent of its national income was in overseas investment, the returns from which contributed a mere 2 per cent of national earnings each year. In other words, Germany could not be mortally wounded by the loss of overseas trade. It could, of course, be badly hit by the lack of certain vital raw materials, but the Central Powers already possessed most of their requirements, gained other ones by conquest (e.g. Rumanian wheat and some oil), and secured the rest from neutrals or even from the production of *ersatz* (substitute) goods. In foodstuffs Germany was virtually self-sufficient – it imported a lot, but also exported considerable amounts before the war – and its allies produced a surplus. The loss of nitrates for fertilizer was a blow to German agriculture, but the civilian sufferings near the end of the war which were generally attributed to the 'inhuman' naval blockade would scarcely have occurred had not the great military campaigns swallowed up such astronomical amounts of foodstuffs, industrial products, and especially the men and the horses needed to farm the land. It was the bloody maw of the Western and Eastern Fronts, rather than the naval blockade, which chiefly caused the 'hunger' in Germany. If this was only fully established by later investigations,[4] it was becoming clear to the British during the war that maritime pressure was having no apparent effect upon the German bid for victory.

The only solution remaining was for the navalists to press for joint operations, which were also felt to be a cheaper form of warfare than fighting in Flanders. As Lord Esher argued in 1915, 'our military power, used amphibiously in combination with the Fleet, can produce results all out of proportion to the numerical strength of our Army . . .'[5] Yet this, too, foundered upon geography and the new technology. Those very instruments (mine, torpedo, submarine) which made it increasingly difficult for the Grand Fleet to operate safely in the North Sea also made it impossible to mount an assault upon Heligoland, let alone upon the Pomeranian coast. Even Germany's far-from-efficient allies, the Turks, were now made much less vulnerable to the influence of sea power than before, as the British and French fleets found when they steamed into the Dardanelles Straits in March 1915 and suffered heavy losses from mines and coastal gunnery.

This Gallipoli *débâcle*, as it soon turned out to be when the troops who landed there found themselves confined to the beaches until the ignominious evacuation at the end of the year, was the most spectacular of all the efforts to hit upon a strategy of 'indirect approach'. Controversial at the time, it has remained a matter for intense historical debate since, partly because of what it revealed about the disorganized decision-making process of the Asquith government in wartime, partly because it led to Churchill's eclipse and the coming of the first Coalition government, and partly because of the tantalizing thought that with a little better execution and more resolution the operation might have succeeded.[6] Even if the Gallipoli venture had been successful, however, it is hard to believe that it would have grievously affected *Germany's* capacity to wage war, or that it could have saved the Russian Army from the disasters it was suffering on its Western Front. In effect, all of these attempts at a maritime, peripheral strategy contained one basic flaw. As A. J. P. Taylor cleverly remarks, the protagonists of sea power held that it

> could somehow be used to turn the German flank without the sacrifice of millions of men. They wanted a dodge in a double sense: a clever trick which would evade the deadlock of the Western Front. They sought a field of action where the Germans could not get at them, and forgot that they in turn would not be able to get at the Germans.[7]

The Gallipoli disaster by no means ended the debate over strategy within the British government. How could it? That campaign cost 250,000 casualties, but they were still light compared with the losses which were suffered by the armies under General French and (after December 1915) his successor Haig along the Western Front. The Second Battle of Ypres had virtually finished off the original BEF, and the autumn 1915 offensives were just as bad – little more than a fortnight's fighting at Loos cost 50,000 casualties. Under such circumstances it was inevitable that the civilian leaders would 'seek other paths to victory than the terrifying record of attrition tempered by misplaced optimism which was all that the generals had to offer'.[8] Alas, little comfort came from these alternative campaigns. An Anglo-French army had been landed at Salonika in October 1915, but it too had been unable to move far from the beachheads. An offensive into Mesopotamia under General Townshend led to the disastrous surrender at Kut in April 1916. At the end of the following month the Battle of Jutland revealed certain weaknesses in British warship design, and suggested that no end was in sight to the strategical stalemate in the North Sea.

To the army leadership, all this simply confirmed the folly of trying to win the war elsewhere; they instead were confidently preparing for a massive attack in the west which would crush the Germans, relieve the French (who had suffered heavily at Verdun) and coincide with summer offensives planned by the Russians and the Italians. That 'massive attack' became known as the Battle of the Somme. On its first day, 1 July 1916, the British Army suffered almost 60,000 casualties – 'the greatest loss in its history'.[9] Barbed wire and machine-guns on land, like the new technology of mines and torpedoes at sea, made it much more difficult to achieve victory without appalling losses. The entire Somme campaign cost the British just under 500,000 casualties, of which about 120,000 were fatal – approximately the same as those the British suffered fighting Germany during the *entire* Second World War. Was this, the critics could ask, any better than losing lives in the eastern Mediterranean? Even if the somewhat lower German casualties at the Somme shook Ludendorff, was it a sufficient compensation for this dreadful haemorrhaging of British manpower?

The British strategic dilemma can therefore be expressed as follows: they could either fight directly against Germany, which was after all the main enemy, but at a horrific cost; or they could search for alternative theatres of war, which would probably be cheaper but would certainly not lead to that 'destruction of the military domination of Prussia' which the government had openly pledged. Being thus impaled on the horns of a dilemma, it was not surprising that more politicians than Lansdowne felt by late 1916 that a compromise peace should be considered. His moderate plea for a reconsideration of what they were doing was, however, rudely rejected by the generals and within a fortnight Lloyd George had taken over as national leader committed to a war to the finish.

Asquith's departure in no way ended this argument. With the change in the premiership and the creation of the War Cabinet, there was now assembled all the forces on each side of the debate. The generals, that is, Robertson in London and Haig on the front, were implacable in their opposition to any proposals to downgrade the main theatre of operations. They could rely upon the support of most of the Conservative Party, including Curzon and Bonar Law within the War Cabinet – less so upon Milner, who had never been an orthodox Tory; and, curiously, upon the embittered Asquith and some of his supporters, who soon detected that Lloyd George was at odds with the military and preferred to support the latter against their arch-foe. There was also the King, who had sustained Haig during his early career and was unlikely now to prefer a dubious Welsh solicitor to a well-endowed officer who had actually married one of Queen Alexandra's ladies-in-waiting. George V was discreet, operating through intermediaries to keep the 'frocks' from ruining the schemes of the 'brass-hats'. Northcliffe, the uncrowned 'king' of the press, was much less so. Every quarrel Lloyd George had with the army leaders was soon transmitted into print, in the form of newspaper salvoes against any wavering. In January 1917, for example, the new Prime Minister returned home from fruitless efforts to develop the Italian front to find *The Times* warning: 'It is on the West . . . that the main decision must take place . . . The German armies must be broken up, captured, or destroyed

. . . We trust [these considerations] are constantly present in the minds of those who are responsible for the conduct of the war.'[10]

More distantly, but just as persistently, there were the French themselves, hypersensitive to the diversion of forces from the Western Front and suspicious (not unjustifiably) that the 'sideshows' favoured by the 'Easterners' would lead to the further enhancement of the British Empire. Yet, although this French insistence was another obstacle to Lloyd George, he respected their generals more and feared them less than his own. Robertson and Haig were furious, for instance, when the War Cabinet agreed that British forces should be in a *supporting* role to the French during Nivelle's offensive, and that pledge was soon undermined. As it turned out, the Nivelle attack was a disaster which so weakened the French Army that it was only half-effective after April 1917. This, together with the collapse of Russia, allowed Haig to argue for that large-scale operation near the Belgian coast which was to become the Battle of Passchendaele.

Most of the War Cabinet, and many others usually found on the side of the 'brass-hats', felt that this would be a disaster; yet Haig's view again prevailed. The 'push' began late in July but the frequent rains, and the massive strength of the German Army in defensive positions, took their inevitable toll – a further 300,000 casualties. Only the parallel disaster to the Italians at Caporetto in October 1917 and the transfer of five divisions there from the Western Front compelled Haig to abandon his futile assaults. By this stage, even Northcliffe and his papers were beginning to be upset by this strategy of attrition.

The opposition to the 'Westerners' was always disparate and never as strong. The navy, after the departure of Fisher and Churchill over Gallipoli, was a weak reed. It had been Jellicoe's fears about Channel defences, for example, which had finally caused a reluctant War Cabinet to sanction the Passchendaele operation. Moreover, it was during this period that the inadequacy of the navy to deal with the U-boat menace was becoming ever more apparent. Early in 1917, many in the British government feared that a paralysis of the trade routes would lead to an Allied surrender; between February and June, 3.3 million tons of shipping were sunk and the situation was only stabilized by Lloyd George's act of forcing convoy upon the Admiralty. Nor could the Prime Minister, for all his optimism and intrigues, discover an alternative 'front' on the European mainland: the Austro-Italian struggle threatened to be just as bloody and futile as that in Flanders; Salonika remained a stalemate; and Russia – even if it could somehow be reinforced – was virtually finished.

The only alternatives, and possible bright spot, lay in the ideas now being put forward by the 'new imperialists'. Foremost among them, in suggestions at least, was Amery, now in government service, who urged upon Lloyd George the importance of military advances in East Africa and throughout the Middle East so as to 'enable that Southern British World which runs from Cape Town through Cairo, Baghdad and Calcutta to Sydney and Wellington to go about its peaceful business without constant fear of German aggression.'[11] These were appealing ideas to Milner and Curzon, as well as to their new colleague, Smuts. Their real strength, however, lay in the fact that they seemed to offer tangible victories. By the end of 1917, British Empire forces were at last able to drive Lettow-Vorbeck's forces out of German East Africa. At the same time, Allenby's troops had crushed a Turkish army and entered Jerusalem. Other British forces were pushing through Mesopotamia, or into Persia, or even into the Caucasus. All this compared well with the disastrous losses on the Western Front, which appeared to depress even Haig; and overseas gains were nice to have if, as seemed likely, a compromise peace had to be worked out with the Germans.

This strategic debate was, to most participants, one of emphasis rather than of an absolute divide. Few people shared the view of Robertson and Haig that campaigns other than on the Western Front were totally irrelevant. Few if any 'Easterners' argued that there should be a complete withdrawal from France and Belgium. Smuts, although disliking the French and concerned primarily with the Empire, was a soldier enough not to want to attack Haig. Curzon may have been an ex-Viceroy of India but he also possessed a Tory loyalty to the army. And Lloyd George himself, although opposed to the generals, was often indecisive about strategic priorities and doubtless aware of the awful and basic question: 'How could an Easterner deliver the knock-out blow? How could one be an Easterner and expect to win the war?'[12] What he most writhed at was the lack of civilian control, the awful losses on the Western Front, and the failure to discover alternative ways of fighting the foe. By early 1918, with Robertson at last replaced as Chief of Imperial General Staff by the more pliable Henry Wilson, with the Western Front relatively quiescent while both sides took breath, with an Allied Supreme War Council established (a means, so Lloyd George hoped, of further controlling Haig), and with 750,000 Empire troops operating, for the most part successfully, in Mesopotamia, Palestine and Greece, the balance was altogether more satisfactory in the Prime Minister's eyes.

It was just as well that there was this policy of balance, with no absolute commitment to the Easterners' cause, for in March 1918 Ludendorff began his last great offensive in the west, forcing Haig's troops towards the Channel while the French army prepared to fall back upon Paris. Here, ironically, was the supreme occasion for Haig to be sent all the forces possible, although the British government, aware of earlier wastage, was not at first keen to do this. When the seriousness of the situation became known, however, Allenby's campaign was stopped, troops were pulled out of Greece, and reinforcements hastily despatched across the Channel. Fortunately for the Allies, Ludendorff's offensive was held by the early summer and, under the general direction of Foch and using improved tactics, many of the new tanks and an increasing flow of American troops, a successful counter-assault was mounted and kept up. As the German armies retreated, their High Command was unpleasantly surprised at the news that Bulgaria was collapsing after an attack from the Greek front, and that the Turks, too, were on the point of surrender following this threat from Greece and the fresh defeats at the hands of Allenby's troops and Lawrence's irregulars. With Austria-Hungary unsettled both by the Bulgarian defection and by the defeat on the Italian front at Vittorio Veneto, the Central Powers appeared to be cracking on all the other theatres at the same time as the defeats and withdrawal in the west. Affected at least as much by the news from the Balkans as from France, Ludendorff advised the German government early in October 1918 that the war must be ended. The Western and the Eastern fronts had interacted with each other, therefore, until the very end. Whether the British government would continue to take a keen interest in each region now that a peace settlement had to be negotiated was quite a different matter.

Wartime Diplomacy and the Search for Allies

Although Liberal members of Europe's pre-1914 élite may have winced at the Clausewitzian dictum that war was a continuation of policy by other means, all agreed that strategy and diplomacy were interrelated. After all, it was the alliance system which, technically, had transformed an Austro-Serb quarrel into a great-power conflict; and, now that the rival *blocs* were engaged in struggle, it was inevitable that their governments should concern themselves more than ever with a harmonization of these two spheres of policy. The Foreign Offices of the powers might be subordinate to their General Staffs, but both were pursuing victory at their own level. The very fact that the combatants were fairly evenly matched, and the dawning realization that there would be no sudden victories on land or at sea, put a premium upon successful wartime diplomacy. If a neutral state could be tempted to join one's own side, or an enemy induced to defect from the opposing coalition, then the military balance would be altered and the cause of victory enhanced – or so it seemed.

The first gains in this search for allies, or defecting foes, went to the Triple Entente. On 3 August Italy declared its neutrality, explaining that its treaty with Berlin and Vienna only applied to a 'defensive' war. This had been a predictable response since the formation of the Anglo-French *entente* in 1904 – for the entire Italian coastline was vulnerable to naval bombardment – but it was nonetheless a morale blow to the Central Powers and it also meant that France did not need to deploy strong forces in the south. Rumania, too, declined to fight with Germany and Austria-Hungary, for it hoped to gain Transylvania if the Habsburg monarchy should collapse; and this, in turn, took the pressure from the southern flank of the Russian Army. Thirdly, the Japanese, liberally interpreting the clauses of the Anglo-Japanese Alliance, took advantage of the European war to overrun the German territories at Tsingtao and in the central Pacific. Again, while it was not a severe blow to Berlin in material terms, it was psychologically important in showing the isolation of the Central Powers.

Japan's action was not, however, an unmixed blessing so far as the British were concerned, for there were certain indications that Tokyo would prove to be an embarrassing partner, if not a threat, in the future. Its traders challenged the British for Asian markets, and in 1915 its 'Twenty-one Demands' upon China suggested that it sought to monopolize foreign commerce and influence in that region; it was suspected of encouraging seditious ideas in India; and the continued existence of the Anglo-Japanese Alliance prejudiced Britain's relations with the United States, which looked with some alarm at Japanese expansionism, and it also complicated relations with the Dominions, which shared American suspicions. On the other hand, the British concentration upon the European struggle was leading to an almost total dependence upon Japan for naval security east of Suez; in the latter part of the war, Japanese warships were not only patrolling the Indian Ocean but even assisting in anti-submarine patrols in the Mediterranean. In return for this, the War Cabinet felt that it had no alternative but to support the Japanese wish to retain the territories it had seized from Germany early in the war, the more especially since Australia and New Zealand wished to do the same south of the equator. Although some robust Britons felt that this eclipse of their traditional political and naval influence in Asia was but temporary, others feared that the war was accelerating an already established decline of British power in the Orient which was probably irreversible. The Japanese factor in British diplomacy was not perhaps a major one in the First World War, and it is often ignored in historical accounts; but it is worth noting, since it later added weight to the arguments of those circles in the Official Mind who felt that it was necessary for Britain to measure its European commitments against its imperial obligations.

The great diplomatic gain which the Germans achieved in the early part of the war was an alliance with Turkey. This, they hoped, would assist the Central Powers in the Balkans, and it might also cause trouble among the many Muslims within the British Empire. More directly, it cut Russia off from the west. To be sure, Britain and France had few munitions to spare; and even if Russia had received war supplies, it is doubtful whether its rickety army and delicate internal structure could have sustained a prolonged campaign against German and Austro-Hungarian forces; but without the possibility of such supplies, Russia's defeat was virtually inevitable. On the other hand, Turkey's entry into the war opened up the prospects for enemy operations in the vast Middle-Eastern region over which the Turks still claimed suzerainty. The British, for example, having declared Egypt now to be a full protectorate, were keen to expand into Mesopotamia and the Levant. This was an advantage to Germany in one way, for it drew British Empire forces from the Western Front into imperial 'sideshows'; but on the other hand it meant that Berlin had allied with a country which it would be difficult, to say the least, to preserve intact.

With the war raging, the value of neutrals in the market rose rapidly. Italy, especially, was wooed by both sides and, as it had no pressing need to enter the conflict, it bargained hard. Eventually, the Allies bid the most for Italy's favour; they, unlike the Germans, could offer large chunks of southern Austria as the future reward for entry. In April 1915 this 'deal' was clinched in the Treaty of London. A month later, Italy declared war upon Austria-Hungary. At the time, this seemed a significant step: Italy was a great power or, at least, almost a great power. Its entry would divert considerable Austro-Hungarian forces from the Eastern Front and the Balkans. Very soon, however, it became clear that the Italian Army was in no position to destroy the Habsburg Empire, indeed, it required support from Britain and France in order to avoid defeat itself.

This did not halt the diplomatic struggle to win new allies. Late in 1915 both sides were striving for Bulgaria's hand. This time the Central Powers won, by applying the same principle of bidding more than their rivals: Germany could offer Macedonia to the Bulgarians; the Allies, obligated to Serbia, could not. Instead, they tried more muscular persuasion. The Anglo-French expedition to Salonika was meant to warn Bulgaria to keep out of the war, and to pull Greece into it. Everything went wrong. Bulgaria entered the war in October 1915; Greece stayed out, at least until 1917; Serbia was overrun; and the Allied expeditionary forces, the so-called 'gardeners of Salonika', remained in their beach-heads. Bulgaria's action also delivered the final blow to the

Gallipoli venture, which now appeared pointless. A year later, the Allies thought they had secured their revenge, when Rumania was at last tempted into the conflict; again, the highest bidders won, for Berlin could hardly offer parts of the Austro-Hungarian Empire which the Rumanians demanded. In this case, the Allies paid for their hubris and the Rumanians for their greed: German troops overran the country by the end of 1916 and seized its foodstuffs and raw materials – although not its oil-wells, which were mainly destroyed by British agents. With the German armies firmly holding their lines inside France and Belgium, the last Russian offensive disintegrating, Bulgaria and Turkey as allies, Serbia and Rumania eliminated, and Italy held on the south-Austrian front, a Teutonic *Mitteleuropa* seemed closer than ever before.

The mutual search for allies always contained two flaws. The first was that the smaller states, rather than adding to the strength of one side, required support in the shape of munitions and men. Belgium, Serbia, Rumania, even Italy, were a drain upon the Triple Entente; Turkey, for its part, required German arms and soldiers, as did Bulgaria. Consequently, the British gained potentially much more from the *loss* of Turkey to the Central Powers than from their own acquisition of smaller European allies. The second disadvantage was that even the least of these new recruits demanded territorial compensations, which in turn complicated diplomacy, especially when it became necessary to consider a compromise peace or to detach one of the enemy powers. Turkey's entry into the war, for example, offered strategic alternatives to British navalists and imperialists; but before they could assault the Dardanelles, they had to promise that the entire Straits region would go to Russia – by that time, simply to keep up Russian morale. Italy's entry was an even greater diplomatic embarrassment to Whitehall: Rome had been promised the Tyrol and Istria – which made a separate peace with Austria-Hungary impossible – and part of the Balkans (Albania) and Asiatic Turkey, which complicated any future settlement of those already complicated areas. The same was true of the promises to Rumania. The exigencies of war made Foreign Offices liberal in their offers, while the very uncertainties of the moment allowed them to console themselves with the thought that these cheques might never be drawn.

Perhaps the greatest – certainly the longest lasting – set of contradictions in British diplomacy related to an area which had hardly ever featured on the Cabinet's agenda in the years before 1914: Palestine. The Turkish entry into the conflict opened up possibilities for British expansion in the whole Middle East; but it also caused other powers, especially France, to demand compensations in that region – hence the secret Sykes-Picot agreement of early 1916 which allotted Syria to France while Britain took Mesopotamia as a sphere of influence. Later, the British felt compelled to offer territorial compensations – from Turkey's lands, of course – to the Russians, the Italians and even the Greeks. As those claims involved Asia Minor, and the whole matter was theoretical at the time, it seemed of little concern to London, just so long as all could agree when the actual carve-up took place. Further south and east, however, the British were very concerned, especially after their defeat at Kut. To strengthen their actual campaign on the gound, they had established links with Arab groups hostile to Turkish rule and promised that Britain would 'recognize and support the independence of the Arabs'. From June 1916 onwards, therefore, combined British and Arab military pressure pushed the unpopular Turks out of the Middle East. Given Whitehall's traditional concern about the security of India and the Suez Canal, and its newer concern about the oilfields of the Persian Gulf – given, too, the military failures on the Western Front – it was not surprising that its enthusiasm for expansion in this region grew.

The chief problem was not a military but a diplomatic one. The vaguely worded assurances about 'the independence of the Arabs' conflicted with the terms of the Sykes-Picot treaty; to preserve harmony with the suspicious French, the British had to disappoint the Arabs. Their double-cross was, moreover, a double one, for in November 1917 they gave their blessing – in the Balfour Declaration – to 'the establishment in Palestine of a national home for the Jewish people'. It is possible to see this gesture instigated by personal and religious motives – influential Zionists had won the sympathies of various figures in the British government, including Lloyd George himself. But there is every indication that, although unclear about Arab feelings over Palestine, the British *were* clear about the political advantages which would accrue from the establishment of a Jewish bulwark in that area: it would protect the approaches to the Suez Canal, eliminate Turkish control there forever, and also reduce France's prospects of expanding south from Syria. Finally, it would gain the applause of Zionists everywhere from the United States to Russia. Here were sufficient arguments of expediency and possible advantage to outweigh scruples concerning the Arabs; and so confused and ambiguous was the language of these various pacts that even those who tried for an honest reconciliation between them found it difficult to make much progress. In the heat of war, few wished to think about it. The eventual settlement, whatever it turned out to be, would only be worked out when the fighting ceased. In 1917–18, enjoying the support of both the Arabs and the Jews, Whitehall was not anxious to unravel these contradictions.

By the middle stages of the war, there remained one neutral power whose alliance would be an unquestionable gain in military terms: the United States. Competitive bidding for that support was by no means equal. Despite the considerable number of German-Americans and despite certain cultural affiliations, there was no real prospect of an alliance between Berlin and Washington. Common elements of language, ideology and culture made the majority of politically conscious Americans identify with the cause of Britain and France, and share their dislike of 'Prussian militarism' – a sentiment which was heated by the German despoliation of Belgium and by extremely clever Allied propaganda. Economic ties also linked the United States much closer to Britain (especially) and to France than to Germany, and the massive orders for munitions and foodstuffs – together with the loans floated in New York – bound American businessmen, farmers and bankers ever more tightly to the fate of the Entente powers. In addition, the British were reaping the long-term benefits of that turn-of-the-century withdrawal from the western hemisphere, which had convinced most American expansionists that London no longer posed a military threat. The only remaining area of controversy lay at sea, where the Allied maritime blockade clashed with traditional American conceptions about 'freedom of the seas' and aroused the suspicions of Anglophobe navalists such as Admiral Benson. Nonetheless, the Foreign Office did its best – often to the disgust of the Admiralty – to pacify the Americans on this issue. In any case, in the United States' eyes British misconduct paled in comparison with Germany's, whose bouts of unrestricted submarine warfare and intrigues with Mexico – nicely intercepted by British intelligence – aroused American humanitarians and imperialists alike.

This diplomatic wooing of the United States was not an easy task, quite apart from the quarrels over the naval blockade. Judging from the manifestations of public opinion, most Americans wished to stay out of the conflict, which was often portrayed as an Old World quarrel fought between two equally guilty and unregenerate *blocs* of states. This was more particularly the case when Tsarist Russia appeared the military leader of the Entente, and it also seemed confirmed when the British took harsh revenge for the Easter 1916 rising in Ireland. Wilson, too, in his mediation diplomacy showed that he did not wish to be identified with one side or the other. In the end, however, Britain was aided – as so often in the first half of the twentieth century – by German clumsiness. The High

Command's decision to order unrestricted U-boat warfare caused the United Stated to sever diplomatic relations in February 1917; and the revelation of the 'Zimmermann Telegram' to Mexico, offering an anti-American alliance, later that month proved the final straw. On 6 April Congress gave its approval to a declaration of war.

American entry into the conflict produced positive and negative effects so far as the British were concerned. The chief positive consequence, of course, was to make an eventual Allied victory certain – provided that the collapse of Russia did not lead to a defeat in the short run. The sheer economic strength of the United States by 1917 or so was almost beyond belief: its population of almost 100 millions would provide a vast army within a year or two, and one with far better equipment and morale than that recruited from the 120 million Russians; its iron and steel production was more than that of *all the European powers combined*; its ship-building capacities such that it could launch vessels faster than the U-boats could sink them; and half of the world's vital food exports came from its farms. Here was the one ally recruited by the British and French which, although not properly equipped for war at the outset, would not require men, munitions or any other form of assistance: a prize catch, indeed.

But the power of the United States, combined with the peculiar political preconceptions (as European statesmen saw them) held by Wilson, brought a large number of problems as well. Although entering the war, Washington intended to maintain a considerable distance between itself and its new partners. It became an 'Associated Power', not an ally. Wilson refused to look at the existing secret treaties. The notion of being the arbitrator or mediator in Europe's quarrels was not given up; and it was clear that Wilson would have distinct views upon extra-European issues as well. Even the dispute over the 'freedom of the seas' was merely postponed, and in the meantime the US navy was going ahead with the construction of a fleet 'second to none' – an aim which even Tirpitz (though he privately hoped for it) had never publicly outlined. Above all, as we shall see below, the United States was to differ from its European partners in the question of war aims and territorial gains. All this time, European dependence upon the Americans for foodstuffs and especially for money was rapidly increasing; between August 1914 and April 1917, Entente purchases of American goods totalled around $7 billion, of which $2.4 billion came from credits; but between April 1917 and the armistice those purchases totalled $10.3 billion, of which an enormous $7.1 billion were credits.[13] Handling this awkward, slightly unpredictable and extraordinarily powerful new colleague was now one of the most difficult diplomatic tasks facing the British government as it entered the later stages of the war.

War Aims and Peace Feelers

Although the United States was ultimately to exert a considerable influence over British war aims, its impact was more upon the appearance than upon the *substance* of those ideas, which had been developing within Whitehall since early in the war. The one specific territorial aim, openly proclaimed since 3 August 1914, was the restoration of Belgium's independence: it was, after all, the chief legal ground for Britain's entry into the conflict, and it rested upon both moral and practical considerations. In order to reassure domestic Liberal – and perhaps American – opinion, Asquith declared on 2 October that the British Empire had no desire to expand. So far as he and most of his colleagues were concerned it was important not to disturb public morale or to upset Britain's allies by open speculation upon the possible terms of a peace settlement. In any case, once it became clear that the conflict would be a long one, this issue fell into the background compared with the much more pressing matter of evolving a military strategy to achieve victory. Peace terms would follow upon a decision in the field, and not precede it.

Yet it was also true, as one scholar points out, that 'The fact of war meant that the map of the world was open for redrawing. Aims that could not have been avowed as a reason for going to war now became attainable, indeed, perhaps inevitable, since the alternative to a British solution for the new problems would have been one less favourable to Britain, or actually damaging to the Empire's security.'[14] For example, London had not gone to war to dismember Austria-Hungary; but, in the course of time, that became a matter for earnest discussion and calculation. The possibilities of 'redrawing' the map were even greater *outside* Europe, of course, for there the military and political situation was much more fluid and less under the shadow of the grinding stalemate of the Western Front. There had been little resentment of the German Colonial Empire in pre-1914 British policy, at least as compared with the fears aroused by the expansion of the High Seas Fleet or the latent threat to the balance of power; British traders had operated freely in the German colonies, and an extension of Germany's overseas possessions had been seriously considered as the price for a lasting Anglo-German reconciliation. The coming of war in Europe changed all that: on 5 August 1914, Asquith assented to a series of operations to conquer the German colonies, with the military justification that this would protect imperial maritime communications. Once those territories had fallen, however, it became ever less likely that they could easily be returned to Germany.

In the first place, some parts of the German overseas Empire had been seized by Japanese and French forces, and were not Britain's to dispose of; and, in the case of German East Africa, Belgian troops moving from the Congo had occupied a portion, much to the alarm of Smuts and fellow South Africans. This introduces the second factor: the influence of the Dominions. Pacific territories such as New

Guinea, the Bismarck archipelago, Nauru and Samoa had been taken by Australian and New Zealand forces, and South-west Africa by South African troops, whose politicians also evinced a keen interest in the fate of German East Africa. Once those lands had been occupied, it was going to be immensely difficult to dislodge this Dominion grip, particularly when London was so eager to emphasize the solidarity and common future of the whole Empire. The vigorous Australian Prime Minister, 'Billy' Hughes, flatly asserted that no one would take away his country's gains, which were vital for security reasons – which was what New Zealand said about Samoa, and South Africa about South-west Africa. These arguments were reinforced by voices within the metropolis: the Admiralty, which claimed that the German colonies possessed bases for future operations by surface vessels or, more ominously, U-boats; and imperialists like Amery, eager to see the consolidation of that 'Southern British World' – an intention which was also at the forefront of a Cabinet sub-committee on 'Territorial Desiderata' which Curzon chaired in 1917. If other British politicians were less committed to full-scale annexations, fearing American disapproval or the prospect of having to return those territories as part of a compromise peace, they were not inclined to oppose the imperialists while the conflict raged.

It was the spoils accruing from the campaigns against Turkey, however, which attracted the greatest British interest. The primal instinct to defend the approaches to India by 'preventive', 'forward' moves, and additionally to protect the Royal Navy's oil supplies, led to an expedition by the Indian Army to capture the head of the Persian Gulf on the day after war was declared upon Turkey. In British eyes, the whole Middle East was now a power-political vacuum which, if not filled by themselves and their protégés, would assuredly be filled by others: either by their age-old imperial rivals, the French (from the Levant) and the Russians (from the Caucasus), or by the Germans, whose successes on the

Eastern Front might tempt them to realize the dream of an empire stretching from Berlin to Baghdad. Furthermore, gains by Britain in the Middle East were less likely to have to be surrendered in a compromise peace with Germany; and in the racially ordered mentality of most British imperialists, the Turks had lesser claims to rule over other peoples. Confident that the Arabs would be happy to exist under British suzerainty, the government in London showed a growing desire to gain compensations in the Middle East for the losses of men and materials in Europe. The capture of Baghdad and Jerusalem, as Lloyd George openly admitted to the Commons in December 1917, was the modern-day equivalent to the Battle of Plassey and the scaling of the Heights of Abraham during the Seven Years War. Then and now, he added, 'the British Empire owes a great deal to sideshows.'[15]

British war aims inside Europe, apart from the restoration of Belgium, were altogether less concrete. This was because they were expressed in terms of political aspiration rather than strict territorial objectives: what was wanted, Asquith had stated in the autumn of 1914, was the eradication of that 'Prussian militarism' which was held to be the underlying cause of the war. Although such an emphasis upon the Hohenzollern traditions of military autocracy and aggrandisement was increasingly made for domestic and American consumption, it should not be assumed that this motive was regarded cynically in private: on the contrary, Liberals and Liberal Imperialists held it to be the overriding aim. When, therefore, a tentative German offer to withdraw from Belgium was made in December 1914, Grey insisted that in addition, Britain and its allies 'must have security against any future attack from Germany'.[16] But how was that to be achieved without a substantial reduction of Germany's capacity to wage war – perhaps by territorial transfers, or reductions in the size of its armed forces? And how could 'Prussianism' be eliminated without forcing a change in Germany's domestic constitution, by deposing the Kaiser?

Although many Britons* – and, still more, many Frenchmen – would have agreed with the logic of those questions, this was an open-ended goal, impossible to achieve without total victory. By comparison, haggling over the future of, say, Togoland was an easy chore.

Furthermore, there was another strand in British imperial thinking which in some respects contradicted this desire to eliminate Germany as a future force in Europe. In July/August 1914, dedicated pro-Russians like Nicolson at the Foreign Office and Buchanan at St Petersburg had urged intervention because they wished to keep on good terms with the Tsar's government and thus avoid pressure upon India if Germany was defeated. To others, however, it was precisely the fact that Britain possessed vital extra-European interests which made them nervous about the destruction of German power altogether. Even Robertson, although committed to the prosecution of an all-out military campaign against Germany, conceded that ultimately the real British aim was to ensure a *balance* in Europe, rather like that which had existed in Bismarck's time, before the 'artificial' Wilhelmine striving to become a world power:

> . . . as Germany is the chief European competitor with us on the sea, it would be advantageous to make such terms of peace as would check the development of her navy and of her mercantile marine. In other words, it would be in the interests of the British Empire to leave Germany reasonably strong on land, but to weaken her at sea.[17]

These were obviously not the sentiments of the French, or of the 'jingo' press which howled for the total defeat of Germany, but they did receive support from New Imperialists like Milner and Amery who – whatever their pre-1914 hostility to German expansionism – were essentially

* Curiously, *not* Haig and Robertson, who had no wish to fight for German 'democracy': the generals wanted victory for its own sake, not for ideological reasons.

interested in the establishement of an organic imperial union. Thus, in Amery's view,

> This war against a German domination of Europe was only necessary because we had failed to make ourselves sufficiently strong and united as an Empire to be able to afford to disregard the European balance. When it comes to the terms of peace and after, we have to get back to a British point of view and get rid of the echoing of French and Russian ideas cemented together by denunciation of Germany.[18]

Along with this often went an appreciation of the talents, cultural unity and industrial achievements of the Germans, which it would be foolish and unfair to suppress once the Junker establishment had been shown the folly of its ways. Here was an echo of those late-nineteenth-century ideas about how much the British and German peoples had in common, which reminds one how comparatively recent the turn towards France and Russia had been.

Although these two strands of British thought about Germany existed simultaneously throughout the war, the relative strength of each was naturally affected by the fluctuating military circumstances. When the Cabinet had received some confident prediction from the General Staff about Germany's exhaustion in the near future, or when they considered French rivalry in the Middle East, concern grew about a post-war world in which Britain alone would be facing a Franco-Russian combine over a large number of contentious issues. On the other hand, when it appeared that the most that could be achieved was a compromise peace in Europe, with Berlin's power unchecked, or the possibility arose of a German drive through the Balkans or southern Russia towards the Persian Gulf, then the British correspondingly needed to stand closer to their Entente partners. What the whole thing suggests is the relatively flexible and non-ideological attitude which the greater part of the government had towards all foreign powers; more specifically, it suggests also that a future policy of restoring links with Germany was not a total impossibility.

It was with these ideas in mind that the British approached the problem of Germany's relations with its territorial neighbours, especially in disputed border regions. It was easy to reply to Wilson's peace enquiry of December 1916 that the Entente required the restoration, not only of Belgium, but also of northern France, western Russia, Serbia and Rumania; but this – even if Berlin and Vienna had accepted – simply meant a return to the *status quo ante,* with German power unchecked. The European balance would not be secured by it, nor by the additional and quite new call for the principle of 'national self-determination' to be applied to the territories of the Central Powers. Much of the inherent strength of imperial Germany derived from the fact that it was a homogeneous ethnic unit which, whatever the Kaiser and the Pan-Germans felt, would not suffer much from the loss of dissident Danes, Alsatians and Poles.

Consequently, it was not upon Germany but upon Austria-Hungary that the Entente concentrated its diplomatic efforts, especially after Francis Joseph's death in November 1916 brought to the throne a new Emperor, Karl, who was far less committed to a fight to the finish. The prospect of breaking up the Austro-German alliance greatly interested Lloyd George and his colleagues, who pursued this in secret negotiations with the Austrians via intermediaries such as Prince Sixte of Bourbon, the Pope, and the Spanish government. This goal, if achieved, would destroy German hopes of a *Mitteleuropa* and block Berlin's aims in the Balkans and Near East, a matter of some urgency when Russia was collapsing fast; it would take Europe back to before 1879, or even before 1870, when Prussia-Germany was surrounded by three suspicious neighbours. Yet, although a delicious idea, it was ridden with difficulties. Quite apart from the fact that Berlin simply might use force to prevent such a defection, any deal with Vienna would involve a diminution in the territorial aims of Italy, Serbia and Rumania. After all, the Austrians and Hungarians would not conclude a separate peace merely to be dismembered by diplomacy; it was going to be difficult enough to persuade them to grant 'Home Rule all round' to the Czechs, Slovaks, Croats and other minorities within the Empire which was deemed essential in London and Paris to prevent a complete internal fissuring and the loss of this planned anti-German bulwark. Furthermore, the French soon began to dislike the prospect of a peace settlement on the Italian and Balkan fronts whilst the great struggle in the west continued, and therefore insisted more than ever upon the return of Alsace-Lorraine. Such a price would never be accepted by a German government dominated now by Ludendorff and Hindenburg and, when Berlin publicly stated this on October 1917, Lloyd George in turn responded by making the recovery of the French territories lost in 1871 a *British* war aim as well.

By the end of 1917, therefore, the prospects for a negotiated peace were foundering at the diplomatic level, even if the military situation in Italy and in the west was one of mutual exhaustion. Unable to detach Austria-Hungary, the Entente thus turned to the alternative policy: a dismemberment of that multinational state into a cluster of smaller ethnic units. This was an idea being urged by the Slav peoples themselves and and by their representatives and supporters in the west. The 'splintering' or 'balkanization' of east-central Europe would, so it was argued, lead to a considerable reduction in Germany's eastern frontiers (in Poland) and the creation of a set of buffer-states between Berlin and Asia. Considerable doubts were expressed in Whitehall about this strategy, especially by Milner and some of his circle and by the Foreign Office staff, who not only suspected that these 'buffers' would be weak but also pointed out that a strict application of the principle of national self-determination would permit the Austrian Germans to join the *Reich*, which would more than compensate Germany for the loss of Alsace-Lorraine. By early-to-mid-1918, when it became clear that Vienna would not be split from Berlin's attempts to achieve victory through Ludendorff's offensive, the British government slowly succumbed to the urgings of domestic Slavophiles and of Northcliffe's propaganda advisers that an open commitment to national self-determination would arouse great support and unrest in east-central Europe and thus 'explode' in Germany's back. Since this tactic coincided with Wilson's idealistic support for self-rule, Allied policy hardened in this direction as the war drew to a close. In so doing, it obviously sealed the fate of the old Turkish and Austro-Hungarian empires; whether it would effectively cramp German power in the future was much less likely.[19]

The Approach to Versailles

Although the sudden collapse of Germany's allies and Ludendorff's insistence that his government must seek an armistice in the late autumn of 1918 came as a surprise to the British, the calculations uppermost in the War Cabinet's mind as it tried to formulate peace terms and prepare briefs for the Versailles Conference* had been long maturing. Those calculations, as the above analysis has sought to show, were many and mixed, in part even contradictory; the problems confronted were complex; and the pressures upon Lloyd George's government, from within and without, introduced further 'variables' into the workings of the Official Mind.

* The conference itself developed from a preliminary inter-Allied meeting in early January 1919. Its final terms were worked out on 16 June and accepted by the Germans on 23 June. Five days later the Treaty of Versailles itself was signed, and Lloyd George and Wilson left Paris.

The *first* factor was doubtless a joy at the enemy's surrender mingled with a fervent desire to see this victory in the field translated into peace terms which would reflect that triumph. This was both the cause and a consequence of the sweeping governmental gains in the election of December 1918; and, since the real beneficiaries were the Conservatives, Lloyd George was more dependent than ever upon the support of a party flushed by nationalistic fervour and a desire for concrete gains. To this lobby, a compromise peace was regarded as execrable: in April 1919, for example, the Prime Minister had to rush back to defend himself from backbench Tory complaints that he was 'soft' over reparations and towards Bolshevism. As against this, however, he and his advisers had to take note of a *second* consideration: public relief at the ending of hostilities, a war-weariness, and an associated agitation among organized Labour for peaceful reconstruction at home and the abandonment of overseas military operations, especially in Russia. Industrial unrest mounted; in February 1919 the old pre-war 'triple alliance' of railwaymen, miners and transport workers was revived, their leaders determined to reverse the temporary drop in their standards of living.

In Glasgow, always a centre of political as well as industrial radicalism, the red flag was raised on the town hall; and the War Cabinet, setting up a special 'Industrial Unrest Committee', felt that a Bolshevik revolution was being attempted at home.[20] Discontent among the troops pressing for demobilization alarmed the War Office. All these were signs that any return to full-scale hostilities, now that the armistice had come, would produce tremendous domestic ructions. To that extent, and despite all the threatening language used to the German negotiators, it was becoming doubtful whether Britain could force terms upon Berlin. In other words, to achieve the desired 'social peace' at home by means of demobilization and reconstruction, it was necessary for Lloyd George to secure a satisfactory 'European peace' which all nations accepted and which eliminated likely causes of future war.

This apprehension about domestic discontent was reinforced by the knowledge that the German army itself had not been beaten in the field, nor had any part of Germany's territory been captured by military operations. If it had taken so much effort to compel Berlin to withdraw, under the armistice, to its 1914 frontiers, how much more would be necessary in order to overrun that country? Had Britain the physical power to do this, if even Germany's new 'moderate' leadership refused the Allied demands? Just a few months earlier, Smuts had pointed out that 'It may well be that, by the indefinite continuance of the war, we shall become a second- or third-class Power, and the leadership, not only financially and militarily, but in every respect, will have passed on to America and to Japan.'[21] For much of 1918, indeed, British and Dominion statesmen had worried about the looming manpower shortages and the inevitable future contraction of their military operations. By this stage of the war, therefore, the British were made increasingly aware of this *third* element, the fact that they had reached, and probably passed, their military zenith – and not merely in terms of armies, for by that time the American and Japanese battleship-construction programmes had reached enormous proportions.

The *fourth* aspect in the British mind was concern for the European balance. During 1918 itself, this variable had fluctuated enormously: some members of the War Cabinet such as Smuts and Milner had argued that since it was militarily impossible to beat Germany, it would be necessary to permit Berlin to keep its gains in eastern Europe in return for concessions to the Allies in the west and overseas; others, fearful of the *furor teutonicus* which Ludendorff had unleashed and of a simultaneous German drive towards India, pressed desperately for the elimination of this colossal German power. By the end of the war, however, this argument was being affected by the *fifth* element, the widespread fear of Bolshevism, which had not only laid

Russia low but was spreading into central Europe. The unrest in Germany, the demise of the Hohenzollerns and the Habsburgs, the Communist regime in Hungary, and Lenin and Trotsky's appeals to workers everywhere to join in the revolutionary movement, all combined to convince the British government that 'Our real danger now is not the Boches but Bolshevism.'[22] As Hankey later explained, 'Bolshevism was the greatest danger to Europe . . . Germany and Austria were the only countries capable of providing a line of resistance unless the Peace Treaties were so drastic as to deprive them of the power to do so.'[23] Just how 'soft' the peace terms imposed upon Germany should be in consequence of this, and just how vigorously the Allies should prosecute the various campaigns in Russia against the Bolsheviks, were matters of heated debate. To the French government, and to many right-wing Britons, both 'Boches' and Bolsheviks should be crushed; to the more liberal-minded, including Lloyd George himself, an extreme policy against either was unwise – the more especially when economic and domestic-political factors were taken into account.

The *sixth* variable, also discussed above, was the influence of the imperialist faction in British politics – now stronger than before following the Tory gains in the election, and also because of the Dominions' insistence that they be a full part of the decision-making process when the peace settlement was made. (In fact, at the Versailles Conference itself, the Dominions each obtained separate representation – like, say, Belgium and Rumania – but also were part of the British Empire delegation and thus able to influence decisions at the highest level.) Since by the time of the armistice imperial forces were making striking advances throughout the Middle East and the Dominions' hold upon the German colonies had been consolidated, it was easy to predict what items on the Versailles agenda would most interest them. Conversely, their earlier concern about German power in Europe had almost evaporated and their eyes were now gazing uneasily at new threats. By the autumn of 1918, British forces were operating in the Caucasus and trans-Caspia, and by the end of the year some officials were arguing for protectorates in those regions, so as to establish yet another buffer against a possible Soviet threat to India. At the same time, Curzon was nervously writing, 'I am seriously afraid that the great Power from whom we may have most to fear in the future is France . . . She is powerful in almost all parts of the world, even around India.'[24] The Anglo-French *entente*, tested and strengthened by the common fear of Germany, was now wearing thin.

The *seventh* and final variable was, inevitably, the United States. Wilson's attitude was not merely important to Lloyd George because of American economic strength and Allied dependence upon it, but also because the President's philosophy and appeal posed a challenge in almost all aspects of policy. The Fourteen Points which he proclaimed in January 1918, and which evoked such a widespread response on the British domestic front, represented a bid for a new order of international politics. Out would go the 'old diplomacy' and the balance of power; in would come a new institution, the League of Nations. Out, too, would go annexations and control over other peoples, which was a deadly blow to the Turks and the Austrians, and would also remove German control from Alsace-Lorraine, Poland and Schleswig; but it might also rule out the acquisition of colonial territories, and the gains planned by the French and Italians inside Europe. Equally worrying was the reappearance in the Fourteen Points of Wilson's old idea of 'Absolute freedom of navigation upon the seas'. Some of this, particularly the last-named point, might be stoutly contested during the meetings of the 'Big Four'* at Versailles; but

* Lloyd George, Wilson, Clemenceau, and Orlando of Italy. This was originally a grouping of the 'Big Five', but Japan's representative soon dropped out. A little later, disgusted by Italy's share of the spoils, Orlando faded into the background and the 'Big Three' dominated the proceedings.

others would have to be carefully handled, with concessions made to this internationalist philosophy whilst in practice preserving traditional national interests. To a clever politician like Lloyd George, Wilson's pressure was not totally disadvantageous, for it could be directed against defeated foes and intransigent allies; and the Prime Minister, sensitive to strains on his own domestic front, could recognize in the President's programme an extremely plausible counter-bid against Bolshevik appeals to the peoples of Europe.

In sum, Lloyd George and his colleagues were seeking to evolve what one scholar has described as a 'peace strategy',[25] containing both domestic and foreign components. If they succeeded in all their individual aims in late 1918/early 1919, they would have produced an *international* settlement which protected the enhanced position of the British Empire, and avoided a return to hostilities which would produce economic uncertainty and internal unrest; and, simultaneously, by pacification measures on the domestic front they would forestall discontent and *reestablish that harmonious social base* which was the prerequisite for a sensible and successful external policy.

The Peace Settlement

The results of the Versailles Conference were, so far as the British were concerned, the product of all the above intermingling forces which the War Cabinet and in particular its leader juggled with, almost on a day-to-day basis. At times Lloyd George was in angry disputation with the American leader – as in the issue of naval blockade and neutral rights; at times, though, he could sit by and watch with some amusement while Dominion leaders such as Hughes bluntly told Wilson that they must have the German colonies; and at other times he himself, rather than the

President, had to oppose the French demands for punitive peace terms against Germany. The alliances forged, and the arguments adopted by the main personalities at Versailles often changed from issue to issue, and few members emerged without having to compromise on their aims to some extent. So far as Lloyd George was concerned, however, Britain and its Empire could be happy with the overall result.

For a start, the Admiralty was quite delighted at the elimination of German naval power, the more especially since in October/November 1918 it had encountered considerable resistance from both Lloyd George and the French over its demand to see the High Seas Fleet and the U-boats surrendered. That was a condition, Foch and Clemenceau felt, not justified by the inconclusive naval war and likely to provoke a resumption of the conflict on land. As it turned out, the Germans were willing to surrender their fleet but, neutral Spain having declined to intern it, the vessels were ordered instead to Scapa Flow; and it was there that the skeleton crews, fearing that this prize would be divided among the victors, scuttled the fifteen capital ships and fifty-one smaller ones on 21 June 1919. Although at first outraged by such a trick, the British soon came to see that this was a far better solution than sharing out the warships with the French, Italians and others. The terms of the Versailles settlement further sought to ensure that Germany would remain merely a continental nation by banning the future construction of heavy warships and U-boats, and by ordering the destruction of coastal fortifications. And, by mutual consent, the Anglo-American 'naval battle of Paris' over blockade rights was postponed until some later time.

In the colonial sphere, too, the British could be pleased with the results. Although the conflict of opinion between Wilson and certain Dominions leaders remained, a compromise formula was devised by that great wordsmith Smuts, who suggested that the ex-German colonies be held by their present possessors on a 'mandate' from the League of Nations. In the course of discussions, various categories of mandated territories were specified; from the 'A'-class ones in the Middle East, where the prospect of creating independent nations in the near future was admitted, to the 'C'-class territories, which were much more directly administered by a neighbouring state, as the Dominions did to South-west Africa, New Guinea and Samoa, and Japan did to the central Pacific groups. (The 'B'-class mandates, as the term implies, occupied a middle status: these were the ex-German colonies of Togoland, the Kamerun and German East Africa, which France and Britain divided. In practice, they scarcely differed from the 'C'-class territories.) The essence of the compromise, in other words, was that lip-service was paid to the ideals of international trusteeship but the occupiers of the German colonies were left virtually undisturbed in the running of these new possessions. In the case of the ex-Turkish territories in the Middle East, the settlement was not fully recognized until 1923, but it was already fairly clear before then that London's control over Palestine and Mesopotamia would ensure the security of that fabled Southern British World around the Indian Ocean.

The future of the Balkan region was not decided at Versailles either, but at certain later ceremonies: namely, the peace treaty with Austria (at St Germain, September 1919), with Bulgaria (Neuilly, November 1919), and with Hungary (Trianon, June 1920). Essentially, they followed upon the Wilsonian principle of national self-determination and thus marked the decomposition of the Habsburg Empire into its ethnic sub-sections – although the drawing of borders to reflect those divisions inevitably lacked precision. This was not a region in which the British government took a great deal of interest and, having earlier abandoned the hope of preserving an Austro-Hungarian bulwark against Germany, it had little difficulty in recognizing the successor-states of Austria, Hungary, Czechoslovakia and Yugoslavia. By the same token, it was not deeply concerned about the readjusted boundaries of Rumania, Bulgaria and Greece, or the Italian agitation over Fiume, or the creation of an independent Finland and the three Baltic states of Estonia, Latvia or Lithuania, all of which were formed out of the lands of the old Russian Empire.

The crux of the peace settlement, and the most heated issue of all, was the German question, that is, how to deal with the country which – so the Allies felt – had been chiefly responsible for the First World War and whose population and industrial resources had enabled it to prosecute that war for so long. To the French, who had twice within a lifetime suffered at German hands, the answer was clear: Germany's power should, by various devices, be so reduced that all prospect of a future military revival was eliminated. To the Americans and the British, secure behind oceanic barriers and thinking of a re-created international order in which all nations should work for peace, prosperity and stability, thinking too of the possible Bolshevik threat to that order, it seemed unwise to persecute a whole people. During the election campaign itself, Lloyd George had joined in the calls to 'hang the Kaiser' and make Germany pay for the war; but later he modified his position on both counts when he saw the practical difficulties involved. Now that the Hohenzollern dynasty had gone, the British were pleased to see Germany ruled by parliamentary leaders, whose delicate authority would be undermined by too severe economic and other pressures from outside. Furthermore, all the Allies were agreed upon the reduction of the formidable German army to a small internal-security force, the disbanding of the Prussian General Staff, and the banning of most of Germany's armaments production. This having been achieved, the Anglo-Saxons were less keen to press for further punitive measures.

This disparity between the victors came out very clearly in the discussion over reparations, where the French demand for a truly colossal sum was based partly upon an assessment of the physical damage the Germans had wrought upon northern France and partly upon the calculation that the transfer of such sums would permanently weaken the German economy. Precisely because of this latter point, the British, eager to see the restoration of international prosperity, demurred. After neatly slipping into the reparations tally the cost of war pensions – which shifted the *proportion* of the claim away from France and Belgium and towards the British Empire, which obviously had not suffered physical invasion – Lloyd George then proposed that a team of experts be set up to assess the total amount of these various categories of 'damage' and also Germany's capacity to pay. Since, in the tense months of early 1919 the victors' and losers' estimates were very far apart indeed, the British hoped by this proposal to postpone the matter until tempers had cooled sufficiently to allow for a proper compromise. Reparations, and the related issue of war debts among the Allies, was to be the substance of many conferences and the cause of much disagreement throughout the 1920s; but it was a great relief to the British at Versailles to have the issue pushed into the uncertain future.

Boundary settlements could not be so easily postponed, however, and these led to the greatest of the quarrels between Clemenceau on the one hand and Wilson and Lloyd George on the other. In the west, the French at first demanded a frontier up to the Rhine, which, as the British government pointed out, would create an 'Alsace-Lorraine in reverse' and be the cause of constant German resentment. After furious rows, this boundary readjustment was reduced to the following: the return of Alsace-Lorraine itself to France; the cession of the Saarland to the League of Nations for fifteen years, during which time the French could work the coalmines and at the end of which a plebiscite would be held to determine the wishes of its inhabitants; while the Rhineland was to be permanently demilitarized and temporarily occupied by Allied troops, but to remain German; and some small border zones were transferred to Belgium and, in the north, to Denmark.

Germany's eastern boundary turned out to be an even more contentious matter, since the ethnic groups were very mixed and the French supported the most extreme Polish territorial claims – to the west against Germany, and to the east against the Bolsheviks. The latter problem could obviously not be settled while the war was raging within Russia and along its borders, but the German-Polish boundary could be dealt with at Versailles. Here it was Lloyd George, rather than Wilson, who fought against the Polish claims and French arguments, warning of the fateful consequences of incorporating millions of Germans within new boundaries. In his famous Fontainebleau memorandum of March 1919, the Prime Minister grimly forecast the origins of the Second World War:

> I cannot imagine any greater cause for future war than that the German people, who have proved themselves one of the most powerful and vigorous races of the world, should be surrounded by a number of small States, many of them consisting of peoples who have never previously set up a stable government for themselves, but each containing large masses of Germans clamouring for reunion with their native land.[26]

It was because of Lloyd George's pressure that the key port of Danzig was made a Free City under the League of Nations and that a plebiscite was held (in 1921) in upper Silesia, about one-third of which then went to Poland and a small portion to Czechoslovakia. If this disgusted the Poles and the French, it did not please the Germans: apart from those losses, Memel had to go to Lithuania and, above all, there now existed the infamous Polish Corridor, which split East Prussia from the west and contained many (though certainly not a majority of) German inhabitants. To cap it all, the 'Big Three' refused to permit the Germanic 'rump' state of Austria to join the *Reich*, for that would enhance its power. The principle of national self-determination, it appeared, was only being applied selectively.

One reason why Clemenceau, who was under intense pressure from his own agitated and anti-German public opinion, agreed to abandon his earlier position towards Germany was that in March 1919 Wilson and Lloyd George had offered France a pact of guarantee against unprovoked German aggression. It is doubtful whether the British leader took this pledge all that seriously at the time; it was, in his view, a 'stopgap' measure to reassure the French until there was a return to European harmony and prosperity, which would make the guarantee unnecessary. Perhaps this was also the reason why it received its second reading in the Commons on 22 July 1919, with hardly a debate at all. Nevertheless, in its written form this treaty – signed in June alongside the Treaty of Versailles – marked an unprecedented British and, even more, American military commitment. The pact was, however, to be approved by both the British and the American legislatures, and Lloyd George's government would certainly not regard it as valid if the US Congress refused to accept this pledge. That, in fact, was exactly what was to happen, although few at Versailles in the spring of 1919 foresaw such an outcome. Since there were still many more quarrels to come, especially over Polish issues, it was clear that the French government did not feel very enthusiastic or grateful to the British for this offer, and frequently expressed its dismay at London's selfishness and relative lack of concern about the future European balance now that German naval and colonial power had been disposed of. To those Britons who, like their forbears in the 1860s, looked to a stable and strong Germany to offset France and Russia, this was hardly a complaint with which they could sympathize.

The final item dealt with at Versailles was the establishment of the League of Nations. This was less controversial than certain other points, but the debate about it again revealed a gap between the views of the French and of the east-European 'successor states', which desired the League to have an international military force to preserve newly established boundaries, and the Anglo-Saxon stance, which favoured a more flexible institutional arrangement. To the Liberals and Labour in Britain, the creation of a world body to prevent future wars and aggression would be admirable, but its strength would primarily derive from enlightened public opinion. To Tory imperialists, an international police force detracted from British sovereignty and would place the Royal Navy in an awkward position. Finally, to all those aware of the unavoidable defects in the Versailles settlement and of the complicated disputes still outstanding, it was important that the League should function as an instrument for the peaceful *adjustment* of international boundaries and other disputed matters, and not as a force committed to oppose all change. Few outside the corridors of power were fully aware of these two divergent viewpoints and were instead impressed by the rhetoric and spectacle of creating this new organization; and it was not for Lloyd George, who always hoped these differences would resolve themselves in the future, to prick this bubble of public hope.

The settlement of so many complicated and contentious issues in such a relatively short time could not possibly satisfy everyone. Even at the time, British radicals were beginning to complain that it deviated from Wilson's Fourteen Points, an argument put even more forcibly by outraged German nationalists. Vast numbers of ethnic minorities were placed on the wrong sides of new borders. A patchwork quilt of small, unstable states had been established throughout east-central Europe in place of the old Empires, but these new units were only likely to survive so long as German and Russian power remained weak. The reparations question was fobbed off, not settled. Imperialist annexations, disguised by the fig-leaf of the mandates system, had occurred on a widespread scale. Above all, it was later said, the 1919 peace settlement had failed to solve the Franco-German antagonism and was in fact the worst of both worlds, being too severe to be permanently acceptable to most Germans yet too lenient to check a resurgence of German power.

All this was true; but it was equally true that there were few simple solutions to these problems which all sides would happily accept. The 'Big Three', jumping from question to question and often under severe domestic pressures which made a 'fair' settlement impossible, were not unaware of the deficiencies in their handiwork. But this was precisely why, so far as Lloyd George was concerned, the League of Nations was created. As he said to the Commons, in July 1919, 'I look forward to the League of Nations to remedy, to repair and to redress . . . [it] will be there as a Court of Appeal to readjust crudities, irregularities, injustices.'[27] This was not a watertight excuse, since it was difficult to see how an organization created to prevent future aggressors could properly function when it lacked enforcement powers and had as yet no machinery of collective security. Yet to governments needing to deal with critical domestic problems and aware of the public weariness of war, it seemed a good enough justification at the time.

III
The Politics of
Appeasement,
1919–39

5. Structures and Attitudes

Perceptions of Britain's Post-war Position

In the winter of 1920/1 the German historian, Erich Marcks, noted bitterly:

> In the world Russia and Germany have now collapsed, a colossal gain for England . . . She has secured the double aim of her imperialism, to dominate the route from Cairo to the Cape, and from Cairo to Calcutta . . . the Indian Ocean in its totality, has become an English sea. In India itself England has deployed powerful forces. She has strengthened her power and her trade, has gained valuable new regions in Mesopotamia, Persia and Africa, and her world empire has increased in land-size by around 27 per cent and in population by almost the same. This has resulted in a global power and position as never before; England is the only winner from this war, England together with North America: one can see an Anglo-Saxon world mastery rising on the horizon . . .[1]

It is worth bearing in mind this particular perception of Britain's favourable post-1919 position, since it is all too easy for the student of the period to anticipate its global decline and only to take note of those early signs of economic weakness and political uncertainty which would be much more dominant by the late 1930s, or the 1960s. To a German nationalist crushed by the terms of the Versailles Treaty, or an Indian shocked by the shootings at Amritsar in 1919, or a

Palestinian experiencing the newly established British suzerainty, it would have been inconceivable to regard the British Empire as in a state of irreversible decline. Nor, it must be said, would most Britons have held such a gloomy view. The Admiralty, for example, still assumed that the Royal Navy should be the largest in the world. Right-wing Conservatives, keen to see Bolshevism destroyed, advocated a 'forward' policy rather than a defensive one. Imperialists looked with hope to the further strengthening of the links with the Dominions. And neither the political centre, which had little enthusiasm for the unpopular posture of over-extension abroad, nor even the left, which was more outspoken in its attacks upon power-politics, questioned the assumption that Britain was still a great world power. What was at issue, as it had been under Gladstone and Disraeli, was the *manner* in which that British influence was exerted.

While the early 1920s were years when the term 'appeasement' was already creeping into the political vocabulary,* it is evident that it meant something different to this generation than it did to a later one. The appeasing of Germany, which was already being urged by those who felt guilty at the Versailles settlement, was understood by its advocates to demonstrate British magnanimity, fair-mindedness and wisdom, not cravenness. These were gestures – prudent gestures, admittedly – from those in a position of strength to the forlorn and defeated. The governments of Lloyd George, Bonar Law and Baldwin were facing pressing internal and external problems, to be sure; yet to a political élite which had managed to emerge victoriously from a world war, such problems hardly appeared insurmountable and paled into insignificance compared with the tasks confronting their German, Italian, Russian or even French equivalents.

As in the years after 1815, in other words, Britain's global position was enhanced negatively by the internal fissures and

* For example, at the time of the Versailles Conference itself, C. P. Scott of the *Manchester Guardian* wrote of the need for a 'peace of appeasement'.

introspection of its traditional rivals. Although this goes a long way towards explaining why contemporaries assumed that its external situation was reasonably strong, there was no guarantee that this cosy and artificial state would last forever. Germany, despite its short-term problems, was still potentially the greatest military and economic power in Europe: once it had recovered, the balance would inexorably tilt against France – and Britain – just as it had done in the decades before 1914. This equilibrium would be further upset by the expansion of Japan in the Far East. Moreover, behind such shifts in the relative strength of the *middle-range* nations, there was also occurring that long-term growth of the two future superpowers, the USA and Russia. When one examines the period between 1914 and 1945 in its entirety, as political scientists have pointed out, the fundamental transformation was that of a multipolar great-power system being replaced by a bi-polar one.[2] Seen from this perspective, the British effort to preserve their position, not only *vis à vis* revisionist nations of a similar size, but also *vis à vis* the two continent-wide states, was bound to produce serious difficulties, however great the statesmanship displayed in London; and was also foredoomed, one suspects, to failure.

All this, inevitably, makes it difficult to arrive at a correct perception of Britain's post-war position. *Subjectively*, most of those who bothered to think about external affairs probably retained a certain confidence throughout the 1920s even if they recognized some immediate difficulties. *Objectively*, the depressed condition of most other powers and the American retreat into isolationism justified such optimism. Yet with the benefit of hindsight the historian also knows how short-lived the British advantage was and can detect, beneath the various efforts of its leaders to return to an already mythical Edwardian normalcy, the signs that things had irretrievably changed.

Economic Strain and the Demand for Retrenchment

The handling of the nation's economic problems after 1919 nicely illustrates this distinction between the short-term and long-term outlooks, and between subjective and objective measurements of British power. Economically, the war had of course been a great strain. Quite apart from the massive expenditure of men and materials, and the wearing-out of much industrial plant, the economy had been deranged from a structure designed to pay Britain's way in the world to one intended to support an enormous war-machine. By the end of the war, for example, the army totalled $5\frac{1}{2}$ million men, the newly established Royal Air Force already boasted of 20,000 aircraft and 290,000 personnel and the navy possessed 438,000 men and a force of 58 capital ships, 103 cruisers, 12 aircraft-carriers, 456 destroyers and 122 submarines. Although Britain had sustained such military strength in the short term by borrowing – in 1918, total government expenditure had been £2,579 million and revenue only £889 million – it was now imperative for the country to live within its means. Spending, particularly upon the armed forces, would have to be cut right back. Here, in one sense, was clear evidence of economic weakness affecting external policy; from now on, the availability of funds would determine defence strategy, and not *vice versa*.

On the other hand, this could also be viewed as a predictable and very traditional measure of budgetary stabilization, little different from the retrenchments which had occurred after the Napoleonic, Crimean and Boer Wars. What the government intended, with the active encouragement of the City of London, was a balancing of the books so as to recover the economic (and, by extension, the military) strength Britain had possessed in 1913. In other words, it was an old rather than a new vision of national economics which prevailed in Downing Street, as the 1925 decision to return to the Gold Standard vividly illustrated. American reticence in claiming the leadership of either the global economic or political order, and the near-collapse of the German economy, seemed to confirm – albeit by default – that the British might successfully recapture their Edwardian position.

These early assumptions about a return to prosperity were never matched by economic reality. It is true that short-lived booms occurred, and that the inter-war years as a whole witnessed the growth of many new industries; but a persistently high rate of unemployment and a poor export performance already existed before the world-wide slump after 1929 shook the ailing economy to its roots. Textile production, which provided over 40 per cent of British exports, was thereafter cut by two-thirds; coal, which provided 10 per cent of exports, dropped by one-fifth; shipbuilding was so badly hit that in 1933 production fell to 7 per cent of its pre-war figure; steel production fell by 45 per cent in the three years 1929–32, and pig-iron production by 53 per cent. Although the prosperity of other states was also hit by the depression and the unemployment rates in some cases were even more horrific, Britain seemed to be affected most in world-trade terms, its share of global commerce continuing a downward trend, from 14.15 per cent (1913) to 10.75 per cent (1929) to 9.8 per cent (1937). Most significant of all, this decrease in *visible* trade was accompanied by a ravaging of the service industries of the City of London, which required a high level of international commerce and prosperity in order to achieve its invisible earnings. Instead, the profits from shipping, insurance and overseas investments fell steadily, and in 1931 visible and invisible exports together were an alarming £103 million less than imports. Although that year and the next two were in many respects the economic nadir, these sorry trends meant that the consciousness of the inter-war polity was increasingly dominated by fears of financial weakness, even when production began to rise again.

Because the 1931 crisis was in so many respects a climacteric – simultaneously destroying the two-party balance within Britain and weakening the international economy – it at least exposed the folly of successive post-war governments in searching for a restoration of the pre-1914 situation. From this time onwards, politicians and their advisers were more concerned about coping with a new world than restoring an old one. But since the actual circumstances of this break with the past had been so harrowing, they generally did not look to the future with confidence and continued to fear a breakdown of the international economic order and national bankruptcy.

Several other structural features of the British economy were also worrying. First, that elevenfold increase in the National Debt between 1914 and 1918 meant that by the late 1920s the annual *interest payments* alone on this account consumed around 40 per cent of central government spending as compared with around 12 per cent in 1913. Not only did this divert expenditure from other possible areas, but it led the economically orthodox to argue that a reduction in the debt and a recovery of the government's credit should be the first priority. It also reminded those who influenced policy of the awful costs of any future war.

The second structural feature was that Britain's central place in the global commercial system and the reliance of its stable industries upon less-developed markets made it much more difficult for it to follow the example of the USA, Russia and Germany in rebuilding national strength by concentrating upon domestic production and consumption. The watered-down system of imperial preference which was finally adopted at the Ottawa Conference of 1932 could hardly give much of a stimulus to the metropolitan economy. What it did do, though, was important enough. The relative increase in inter-imperial trade during the 1930s reinforced that strand of the British political consciousness.

which preferred to attend to the Empire rather than to Europe; and, in a somewhat similar way, it reinforced the old concern about British naval strength – since the British alone among the great powers imported half their required foodstuffs – and thus correspondingly played down any strategical worry about the size of the army and the state of the European equilibrium. Furthermore, both the background to and the effects of the move to imperial preference were not free from Anglo-American economic jealousies, which in turn explains a considerable amount of the early British mistrust of Roosevelt. On the other hand, Britain's massive reliance upon imported foodstuffs and raw materials from the 'underdeveloped' world meant that its own economic (and social) problems were cushioned to a very considerable degree during the depression years by the marked fall in the prices of non-manufactured wares.

This characteristically British dependence upon trade with distant parts of the globe had a further consequence; it meant, ironically, that it needed more than ever to protect, say, the China market or Malayan rubber or investments in south-east Europe even as its ability to act as the world's policeman was declining. In November 1923, Baldwin had declared:

> The interests of the British Empire in foreign countries are first of all economic and commercial. When we speak of peace being the greatest British interest, we mean British trade and commerce, which are essential to the life of our people, flourish best in conditions of peace.[3]

Yet this in turn meant that whereas the British were on occasions to be found willing to recognize the claims of other great powers to a specific *political* sphere of influence – Germany's in eastern Europe, or Japan's in the Orient – there is much less sign that London thought of ceding its *economic* interests in such regions. Indeed, it was often to be found clinging on determinedly to its commercial rights after it had made open acts of political 'appeasement'. This could suggest either a strategy of Machiavellian cunning (ceding the form but not the essence) or, more likely, that the liberal-cosmopolitan mind did not see that political control by Nazi Germany or Japan of a certain region would automatically mean economic monopoly since the state and cartelized big business were working together on quasi-mercantilist lines.

Finally, it is worth noting that while this governmental concern to balance the budget by cutting down armaments expenditure hit the armed services in the short term, the longer-term consequence was that, when the decision for *rearmament* was made in the more threatening circumstances of the 1930s, industry itself could not adequately respond. The long lean years of virtually no construction, the lack of incentive for technological innovation, the unwillingness to invest capital in fields regarded as unprofitable, and in general the steady decay of the country's industrial sinews during the depression, produced their own results. The productive capacity of the country as a whole, and those of specialized armaments firms in particular, were too run-down to be reversed without major investment in factories and machine-tools. Thus, even when money for new weaponry was released, it proved impossible to construct, say, as many fighters and bombers as was desired; and until 1939 the Admiralty could do little more than supervise the construction of vessels to bring the navy's strength up to what it should have been in 1930, even under international treaty restrictions.

The Role of the Treasury

The role of the Treasury, as the official comptroller of national accounts and custodian of economic orthodoxy, was therefore vital throughout this entire period. Although its views were not substantially different from those of its political masters and of a generally pacifist public opinion, its position at the centre of the governmental machine virtually gave it a day-to-day voice in matters which affected external policy if finance was involved. The famous Ten-year Rule of 1919, whereby the armed services were instructed to prepare their estimates 'on the assumption that the British Empire would not be engaged in any great war during the next ten years', and the later refinement which put this rule on a daily shifting basis, allowed the Treasury to demand that everything asked for by the defence chiefs be justified in terms of immediate need, which was a difficult case to develop in the relatively placid global circumstances of the 1920s. Defence spending thus tumbled, from £766 million in 1919–20, to £189 million in 1921–2, and to £102 million in 1932.

When the Japanese occupation of Manchuria in 1931 and the Nazi seizure of power in 1933 caused the Cabinet to decide upon a review of Britain's defence deficiencies and a modest increase in expenditure, the Treasury's function became both negative and positive. On the first count, it was still concerned to put a brake upon any swift upward movement in armaments spending and, the gloomier the international outlook became and the more defence chiefs called for additional funds, the louder grew the warnings of the Chancellor and his advisers about the deleterious consequences of giving in to such demands. More positively, the Treasury quickly perceived that since a sudden rush of defence orders would cause all sorts of blockages in a British industrial machine incapable of responding swiftly to this demand, then it was important not merely to regulate the pace of armaments expenditure in general, but also to decide which orders had priority. While the latter was really a strategic decision, the plain fact that the Chiefs of Staff could not agree among themselves which of their rival demands (and alternative strategies) had precedence placed an enormous power in the hands of the Treasury; and under the forceful Chancellor, Neville Chamberlain, and his influential Permanent Under-Secretary, Sir Warren Fisher, some requests were discouraged and others were more warmly received. The army's wish for a European field force had little prospect of success, for example, and the Admiralty's hope for a two-ocean fleet was repeatedly delayed, with the Treasury attempting to compensate for that naval deficiency by its own efforts to secure good relations with Japan, thereby encroaching not a little upon the Foreign Office's role as well. On the other hand, the RAF was generally encouraged in its rebuilding plans, for it was hoped for a long while that its bombers would act as a 'deterrent' against German aggression, and, later, that its fighters would protect the homeland from the much feared *Luftwaffe* when the policy of deterrence seemed to have failed.

Until recently, the Treasury's impact upon British interwar defence and foreign policy has been regarded as obstructionist, appeasing and to a large degree responsible for the military unpreparedness of the country during the crises of the late-1930s and the disastrous early years of the war itself. Now a more balanced view is being taken of the role of that institution. Its argument that it was no use ordering goods that British industry could not produce is seen as valid and as one which directs attention to the real areas of economic weakness. There was a massive shortage of skilled labour but trade unions such as the engineers' refused to accept 'dilution' without concessions which the government in turn found unacceptable. There was also an intense dislike by the employers of state direction and coercion, which made a Conservative administration naturally prefer voluntary co-operation from industry, despite its drawbacks. Although a state of war would ease the acute political problems of introducing 'compulsion' over labour and 'controls' over management, neither the Cabinet nor its advisers were eager to grasp that nettle in a period when they still hoped for peace.

Above all, the Treasury's stated fears that the halting revival in production for exports and the restoration of a budgetary balance after 1933 would be ruined by an armaments race were by no means implausible. When it conceded in 1932 that the Ten-Year Rule might have to be abandoned, the Treasury was not exaggerating in simultaneously warning that 'today's financial and economic risks are the most serious and urgent that the country has to face'. The great increases in governmental spending a few years later, and the large defence loans of 1937 and 1939, did cause inflation; the orders abroad for steel, machine-tools, instruments and other items which British industry could not itself produce on time, did add to that worsening of the balance of payments which followed upon the hard-won surplus year of 1935; and the transition of production from peacetime export goods to armaments for home consumption reduced still further Britain's capacity to pay its way in the world. To the Chiefs of Staff, the Treasury no doubt usually appeared obstructionist; but that obstructionism was based upon a genuine concern for a straitened economy, the so-called 'fourth arm of defence' upon which the other three arms depended. As one Treasury official remarked, when the Air Ministry presented an upward revision of its building programmes after the Munich crisis, the real difficulty was

that we cannot say whether we shall be able to afford it. Indeed, we think that we shall probably not be able to without bringing down the general economy of this country and thus presenting Hitler with precisely that kind of peaceful victory which would be most gratifying to him.[4]

Ultimately, some have argued, the Treasury's perception of British 'grand strategy' was more sophisticated and realistic than those who simply called for more armaments. If war was to come, a British victory would depend upon the careful husbanding of resources, which would then be steadily channelled towards an all-out war effort; the peacetime mobilization and control of national resources which was occurring in the dictator states was reckoned impossible in a democracy for both economic and political reasons. Moreover, there still existed that much-revered tradition (dating back to the 'great War' against Napoleon) which assumed Britain's role was less that of an immediately engaged combatant on land than the arsenal and paymaster of the coalition against the mutual enemy. Since, by this time, British resources were increasingly inadequate to match the military calls made upon them, and since American neutrality legislation made it unlikely that succour could again come from that source (as in 1917–18), a conservation of British wealth and a control over armaments expenditure was even more necessary than before – always provided, of course, that one did not lose a short war through having planned only to fight a long one! Hitler's *Blitzkrieg* strategy, for example, was particularly unsettling, because British armaments production was not timed to deal with it.

On the other hand, despite the recent literature defending the role of the Treasury, the fact remains that many of *its* assumptions were also false. Could it really still believe that Britain might again act as 'the arsenal and paymaster' of the democratic West? Did it really think that orthodox finance would restore the ailing British economy to health? Did it actually accept that Hitler – of all people – would be impressed by this adherence to orthodox finance and normal measures? Finally, did it at any time squarely face the basic dilemma of the late 1930s: either to follow a policy of all-out preparation for war, or to accept a junior role in a Hitler-dominated Europe?

The most cruel dilemma facing British decision-makers as they contemplated the various external threats of the 1930s was, therefore, that the defence chiefs and the economic 'watchdogs' at the Treasury and Bank of England were both correct – and both wrong. The country could either have a balanced economy but with inadequate forces to protect itself and its overseas interests against those threats; or it could have much larger armaments and a bankrupt economy. It could not have both, and the post-Munich decision to abandon Treasury controls on defence spending simply meant that one hazard had been replaced by another.

Economic considerations as put forward by the Treasury, the Board of Trade and the Bank of England impinged upon British external policy in a second major way in these years, namely, in attitudes towards international trade. On the whole, and excepting those interests tied to imperial preference, the British government, bankers and business-men pressed for a liberalization of commerce on grounds which were quintessentially Cobdenite. A prosperous world comity would, it was hoped, heal the wounds of the past, make nations more dependent upon each other as markets and suppliers, and thus less ready to go to war, and produce an atmosphere of international friendship and understanding. More specifically, it would aid the commercial recovery of Britain itself after 1919, since so many parts of its economy depended upon foreign trade and investment. This, after all, had been one of Keynes's chief arguments in his philippic *The Economic Consequences of the Peace,* which reminded its readers how important Anglo-German commerce had been for their mutual prosperity before 1914. The recovery of the German economy, which the French feared on strategic gounds, was thus regarded in British eyes as an advantage on commercial grounds. This sentiment was not changed by the rise of Hitler: indeed, the possibility that Nazi extremism was a product of the depression reinforced the argument that, if Germany was treated kindly in trade treaties and led away from autarkic economic policies, it would recognize the benefits of international prosperity and interdependence. Consequently, the 1930s witnessed numer-ous British attempts to draw the teeth of German discontent at the existing order by proposals for economic co-operation, a possible loan, access to tropical raw materials, a mutual reduction of tariffs, improved exchange arrangements, and so on. All rested upon the flawed assumption that Nazi demagogues – or, for that matter, Japanese *samurai* – had the same healthy respect for peace, prosperity and stability as the cautious, satiated élites of the Western democracies.

Failing to comprehend that their own faith in the liberal political culture was not shared by all foreigners, most Britons did not perceive until after Munich or Prague that the dictators wished to destroy the international club rather than negotiate entry into it. This was a curious blindness since, as many historians have pointed out, British statesmen did recognize that they had most to lose by a severe dislocation of the existing global economy and territorial distribution, from which they benefited so much. As Neville Chamberlain himself admitted: 'We are a very rich and a very vulnerable Empire and there are plenty of poor adventurers not very far away who look on us with hungry eyes.'[5] This being the case, it was a trifle naïve to assume that those who did not have all they wanted would find the appeal to 'live in peace' equally attractive.

The Rise of Labour and the Turn to Domestic Reform

The post-1919 arguments in favour of peace, retrenchment and a cautious, non-committal external policy so far presented have all been essentially economic. They were reasons which could have been, and indeed were, put forward by people with impeccable Conservative credentials – bankers, industrialists, Tory MPs and the like. But there was a parallel and even more powerful argument arising from the social and political realm where, however much a return to 'normalcy' was preached, fundamental changes had occurred since the period before 1914. The first of these was in the sheer size of the electorate: in 1906 it had been a mere $7\frac{1}{4}$ million; in 1929, it was nearly 29 million, a parliamentary *democracy* for the first time ever.

The crude fact that politicians could only gain and preserve power by winning the support of a far larger constituency, and one with different or at least additional expectations of what governments should do than those of an earlier generation, became all the more significant because of the steady rise of a Labour Party which did, literally, promise a transformation of society. That Labour politicians, once in the citadels of power, should actually turn out to be more 'moderate' and less 'revolutionary' than the established classes feared did not alter the impact much: the very existence of a left-wing party *within* the parliamentary system, capable of attracting as many votes as any other party, was to amend traditional political habits and thinking in various ways. Above all, it caused such astute political animals as Lloyd George, Baldwin and also Neville Chamberlain to bid for what they considered to be the 'popular' vote in the 'middle' ground of politics, an electoral region into which the Labour Party itself and its far-from-revolutionary leader, Ramsay MacDonald, equally needed to make advances. In one sense, then, the rise of a mass working-class party, its proclaimed commitment to socialism, the bitterness engendered by the General Strike of 1926 and many smaller industrial conflicts, and the controversy surrounding the formation of the National government in 1931, indicated a polarization of society along class lines. In another sense, however, the political dynamics of inter-war Britain as fashioned by its electoral geography meant that *all* the parties needed to move towards the centre so as to pick up additional support, since a slight shift in national voting percentages could often mean a dramatic change in the number of parliamentary seats held by each party. If ideological purists of the left and the right disliked this tacking to the wind of electoral popularity, there is little sign that their arguments gained much of a hearing among the power-brokers and the pragmatists.

But what exactly constituted this middle ground of the political stage towards which both Baldwin and MacDonald were edging, leaving imperialists like Churchill and ILPers such as James Maxton in the wings? There were, predictably, those common demands from Conservative-voting clerks and Labour-voting miners: better housing, improved roads, enhanced educational opportunities etc. There was also a wish for less taxation, a reduction in unemployment, and an escape from economic uncertainties. But even in these areas there could be party disputes, over direct *versus* indirect taxation, or over private *versus* public housing schemes. Where 'consensus politics' could be most easily achieved was over external issues, by a paring-down of overseas commitments, a swingeing reduction in defence expenditures, and the avoidance of any policy which could bring even the faintest risk of another conflict like that of 1914–18 which the majority of the British people now abhorred. Unlike 1878 and 1900, no electoral advantage could be gained after 1919 by waving the flag and beating the drum. On the contrary: as Baldwin, then Chancellor of the Exchequer, warned in 1923, defence expenditures had to be cut still further, otherwise 'the inevitable result will be the stabilization of taxation at something very near to its present level (5/- in £1), the consequences of which may easily be the substitution for the present Government of one whose regard for the armed services is not particularly marked.'⁶ Or, as Churchill himself put it only a little later, 'I cannot conceive of any course more certain to result in a Socialist victory . . .' than higher naval estimates.⁷

Admittedly, it becomes more difficult to get a firm grasp of the domestic-political matrix during the 1930s, since contradictory indications exist about party opinion on the one hand and political practice on the other. On the industrial front, Britain appeared far more peaceful than in the 1920s – although this was, perhaps, a peace of exhaustion. Ideologically, British opinion seemed often strongly divided after the crisis of 1931 and the creation of a National government. The Left was nursing its wounds after MacDonald's 'betrayal' and, being free from the constraints of office and lacking firm leadership, indulged in much stronger verbal attacks upon the existing order. Unlike the 1920s, this rhetoric placed considerable attention upon international affairs, for it was now argued that Britain's own problems arose from flaws in the world economic and political order. The massive interest in Russia's planned economy, and the rising disquiet at the fascist threats also produced a ferment of ideas about a 'proper' British foreign policy. The great divisions of opinion over, say, the Spanish Civil War are a reminder that, however stable Baldwinian England appeared domestically, there was no unanimity of feeling about the conduct and aims of the nation's diplomacy. The 'middle opinion' which some historians have detected at this time concerned itself with social and economic planning, not with foreign affairs. Nonetheless, precisely because MacDonald and Baldwin wished to 'defuse' domestic tensions about external issues, they continued to avoid possibly controversial measures and kept defence expenditure to a minimum.

Had the demand for Gladstonian-style retrenchment alone been all-dominant, as some economists and business-men still wished it to be, then government expenditure *as a whole* would have tumbled. What in fact happened was that this pressure confronted, but in no way overcame, the pressure for greater state attention to the people's social and economic needs. In the latter area, indeed, expenditure continued to grow and was but slightly checked by the 'prunings' of the National government. A comparison of the breakdown of British public expenditure before the First World War and in the inter-war period is, therefore, highly instructive:[8]

Public Expenditure (£ million)

	1913		1933	
Defence	91·3	(29·9%)	112·4	(10·5%)
Social services	100·8	(33%)	497·2	(46·6%)
Economic services	39·5	(12·9%)	111·8	(10·5%)
National Debt	18·7	(6·1%)	228·4	(21·4%)
Total	305·4	(100%)	1066	(100%)

(NB. Index of current prices [1900 = 100]: 1913 – 109; 1933 – 174)

Despite the toll taken by price inflation, British defence expenditure had only increased between 1913 and 1933 because of the existence of a third armed service (the RAF), which consumed £17.1 million by the latter date. Yet expenditures in all other areas of government had risen impressively and inexorably. Like it or not, all British administrations now accepted that the days of the 'nightwatchman state' were over, and that a commitment to significant civilian expenditures was a *sine qua non* of political survival.

Public Opinion and the Revulsion against War

The fact that the armed services' share of governmental spending was sharply reduced during the 1920s and early 1930s cannot fully be explained by the concurrent growth of civil and debt expenditures, or even by the absence of any perceived threat to British interests during that period. It was also intimately connected with a widespread public revulsion against the use of military forces and even, in some quarters, against their very existence. Pacifism itself had had a long tradition in British politics, especially among the Quakers, Nonconformist businessmen and other 'dissenter' groups; but it had never possessed much political weight even in Cobden's heyday, and a succession of Tory, Whig and Liberal Imperialist cabinets had kept the ideals of unilateral disarmament, abjuration of war, and such like in check. The loss of life, and, perhaps more important, the *psychological* scars which the First World War inflicted upon the nation changed all that. With almost unanimous fervour and emotion, the British people revolted against the idea of war and all that the contemporary sources of wisdom – politicians, historians, publicists – claimed could cause it: arms races, secret diplomacy, military *ententes,* imperialism. The Union of Democratic Control, relatively ineffective during the 1914–18 conflict itself, now came into its own, and was joined by a multitude of other organizations – the National Peace Council, the League of Nations Union, the Peace Pledge Union – which together made as much noise as the National Service League, navy leagues and other patriotic organizations had done in Edwardian England.

Even the middle classes, although worried at the idea of a Labour government apparently bent upon burying capitalism, sympathized with that portrayal of war as senseless and horrid which emerged from such writings as Remarque's *All Quiet on the Western Front,* Graves's *Goodbye to All That,* and the poems of Wilfred Owen. Aldington's bitter novel, *Death of a Hero,* for example, was regarded by the *Sunday Times* as showing 'the monstrous futility of war itself', and recommended by the *Daily Mirror* 'as a useful reminder and sermon for those who are beginning to forget'.[9] Keynes's own earlier assaults upon the 'Carthaginian Peace' of 1919, and the historical accounts by Lowes Dickinson, Bertrand Russell, G. P. Gooch and other UDC members of the pre-1914 'international anarchy', all point to an intellectual revisionism against the Edwardian ideals of muscular patriotism and the unquestioned pursuit of national interests. Moreover, the Trades Union Congress added its voice, regularly and insistently, to this anti-war chorus for many years, and both the Labour and Liberal parties claimed to favour policies of international peace and disarmament.

Given this swing in popular sentiment, and the fact that the prejudice against military force was shared by the City and by many in the establishment whose progeny had been killed in the war, even the Conservatives began to shift their ground. It would be absurd, of course, to suggest that all Tories fell for this message of turning swords into ploughshares. Generals and admirals, whether retired or active, warned against placing one's trust in the League. Papers such as the *Morning Post* and *Daily Telegraph* attacked the reduction in the Royal Navy's cruiser fleets and, on a less material but still symbolic note, joined with Kipling in vilifying the Labour government's proposal to abandon Remembrance Day in 1930. The primal instincts of the arch-imperialists were aroused, not subdued, by concessions to the nationalist movements in India and Egypt. Conservatives such as Leo Amery and Austen Chamberlain could not shake off their pre-war mistrust of Germany. Popular publications such as the Ward Lock *Guide to Belgium and the Battlefields* were still automatically referring to 'Hunnish atrocities' well into the 1920s. But it was unsettling that even many Conservative newspapers now joined in the pro-appeasement chorus; that the Oxford Union voted that it would 'in no circumstances fight for its King and Country'; that the public schools seemed to be producing not simply the patriots of Victorian times but also a considerable number of disaffected radicals. To a nimble political operator such as Baldwin, this was probably less significant than the fact that – as seemed to be indicated by the famous East Fulham by-election of 1933 – the voting public preferred pacifist candidates in favour of pro-armaments Conservatives. Consequently, in the run-up to the 1935 general election he told a meeting of the International Peace Society – an interesting audience for a

Tory leader – that 'I give you my word that there will be no great armaments'.[10] The National government's pose as the guarantor of 'normalcy' meant that it needed to head off any campaign by Labour or Liberals to cast doubt upon its adherence to international co-operation and disarmament, even when it was privately becoming alarmed at developments abroad.

The Role of the League of Nations

The importance of the League of Nations in this altered post-war atmosphere was twofold. The first was distinctly practical. Whatever the defects of that body and the contradictions between various clauses of the League Covenant, it did seem to offer to more than international idealists an advance upon the pre-1914 anarchy. After all, large nations and small did come together at Geneva to discuss mutual problems. The possibilities of international disarmament were being explored under its auspices, as was the settlement of reparations. And it might well act as the mediator between other powers in quarrels where the British found it difficult or embarrassing to assume the role of 'honest broker'. More cynically, support for the League and the much-publicized attendance of British statesmen at international conferences often brought personal enhancement within the party and within the country at large, and was thus a useful corrective to mediocre achievements in domestic policy.

Yet this in turn points to the second reason for the League's importance: namely, its high esteem among so many of the British electorate, whose consciousness of that body's work was kept alive by the extremely active League of Nations Union, which kept up a running commentary upon the conduct of foreign relations and made special efforts (such as the 1935 Peace Ballot) to use the weight of public opinion to compel governments to abandon their ancient tendency towards power-politics. In 1928 Gilbert Murray could openly boast: 'All parties are pledged to the League . . . all Prime Ministers and ex-Prime Ministers support it . . . no candidate for Parliament dares to oppose it openly.'[11]

Despite Murray's optimism, it is difficult to conclude in retrospect that the existence of the League proved an advantage to Britain. Apart from Robert Cecil, very few politicians when in power and almost no permanent official really believed it to be an efficacious instrument for the settlement of international problems. Some, indeed, feared that it might restrict their traditional powers and habits. On the other hand, they also feared to express these criticisms openly because of the League's popularity. The British public by and large assumed that, since future wars (if they occurred) would involve *all* the League nations disciplining unruly states and checking aggression, Britain's own defence weaknesses didn't matter so much. Certain enthusiasts, in fact, somehow persuaded themselves that force would not be needed to uphold the principles of the League at all; goodwill and 'enlightened' opinion alone would suffice. Few people bothered to query the value of military help from the Argentines and the Portuguese and the Greeks in disciplining a powerful aggressor. The 'Official Mind', for its part, was aware of these practical difficulties but unwilling to spell them out. Thus, there existed a divorce between the outward actions and the inner convictions of the British government, carefully concealed from public scrutiny.

The results of this ostensible conversion were to be seen during the Manchurian and Abyssinian crises, when British statesmen found themselves unable to escape from the rhetoric of commitment to the League in circumstances where that body's effectiveness as a deterrent to aggressors was greatly in question. Only by the second half of the 1930s, when the League's supporters in Britain were beginning to split into their purely pacifist and increasingly antiappeasement wings, was it possible for an assertive politician like Neville Chamberlain to develop his own diplomacy, free from much reference to the League's principles. Almost simultaneously, the left had noted how useless the Geneva organization had been during the Spanish Civil War, and therefore turned towards new and different methods of securing their desired world order. Having wanted to see the League of Nations work so that it could, *inter alia,* redress German grievances in the 1920s, many British radicals realized a decade later that they needed an old-fashioned military alliance (disguised in 'Popular Front' clothes) to check Nazi expansionism.

The Impact of Bolshevism

With one exception, there were no really profound disagreements in British attitudes towards their great-power neighbours in the years after 1919. The United States was often seen as a difficult and somewhat unpredictable partner, but its sheer economic importance and the value attached to common cultural and linguistic ties generally outweighed the suspicions of the far left and the far right. Most Britons found relations with France increasingly irksome, since its constant demands for security and its unwillingness to bury the hatchet with Germany blocked their own insular wish to see the new European order stabilized without requiring frequent interventions by London. Conversely, Germany was regarded with growing sympathy despite certain unpleasant domestic-political characteristics, for most British imperialists were eager to see the return of a strong but satiated 'Bismarckian state' in central Europe whereas the proponents of internationalism wished to form a comity of western nations, freed from the taint of any pre-war alliance *blocs.*

In regard to Soviet Russia, however, opinions were much more sharply split. This itself was both a reflection of the domestic divisions within British society and a continuation of the debate which had begun in the later stages of the First World War. The armistice had brought no end to that particular debate, for the Allied support of the White Russians in 1919 was being urged by belligerent anti-Bolsheviks like Churchill and opposed with strikes by trades unions. Even when Lloyd George prudently eliminated the possibility of any further British military intervention in Russia, there was no real attempt to establish normal diplomatic relations until the advent of the first Labour government in 1924; and the 'scare' over the so-called Zinoviev Letter later that year showed how ideologically charged this issue remained. Conservative politicians such as Curzon and Churchill were reinforced in their suspicions by secret service 'intercepts' of Bolshevik encouragement of Indian subversives and British labour. Furthermore, the Labour Party establishment, keen to demonstrate its respectability, had no great regard for Stalinist Russia. In their conduct of relations with Moscow between 1929 and 1931 both MacDonald and Henderson were on their guard against possible Soviet 'monkey tricks'; but the rank-and-file of the party and a whole host of intellectual fellow-travellers thought differently.

This issue is worthy of note because it structured much of the discussion upon Britain's external policy during the 1930s as well as the 1920s. There is no doubt that an exaggerated fear of domestic communism caused many Conservatives to dislike the Soviet experiment and to wish to see Russia kept in diplomatic isolation. Conversely, it reinforced the instinct to support the rehabilitation of Germany, which might then act as a bulwark against Russian penetration westwards. This was a curious reversal of the pre-war *Realpolitik*, which had encouraged a strong Russia in order to check German expansionism; and, with the exception of those few right-wingers who came to see the

Nazi threat as the more serious, it remained a Conservative prejudice until almost the eve of the Second World War. This does not mean that appeasement should be interpreted as being *primarily* anti-Soviet in purpose, but such a consideration clearly influenced, say, Whitehall's coolness to the Franco-Russian pact of 1935, support for the Spanish republic, and its high regard for Polish fears of Russia in 1939. On the other hand, the sympathies shown towards Russia by Labour activists and by many anti-establishment critics such as the Webbs who claimed to have discovered in Soviet Russia 'a new civilization' meant that the left's regard for Germany noticeably waned after 1933. Instead, it joined with enthusiasm in the Russian-backed mobilization of a European 'popular front', whose propaganda (especially during the Spanish Civil War) represented a certain replacement for the fading belief in the League of Nations and simultaneously offered a constant critique of British official policy. Since these calls for action against fascism were mingled with continued criticism (until 1937) of the British government's decision to accelerate rearmament, it is probable that this left-wing chorus merely hardened Chamberlain's belief that it should not be taken seriously. But this in turn made it all the more difficult for that proud man later to swallow the idea of a *rapprochement* with Moscow.

Imperial Isolation and Disintegration

If economic problems, the 'impact of Labour' and a swing in public attitudes against war were causing successive British governments to seek to avoid any binding military or even diplomatic commitments to continental Europe after 1919, then this aversion was further reinforced by the voice of the Dominions. The major explanation for the latter's prejudice lay of course within those self-governing branches of the Empire themselves. Despite the Anglo-French alliance during the war, that common cause had not healed the fissure between the British and French in Canada, and it *had* confirmed the doubts of those Canadians who disliked involvement in European power-politics and mass bloodshed. When the United States repented of its own interventionist role, there were thus many Canadians (including its sensitive and suspicious Prime Minister, Mackenzie King) who favoured a similar retreat into isolationism. The same could be said for the Afrikaner element in South Africa, and even the Anglophile Smuts displayed an intense dislike of France and a wish to keep Britain from committing itself to French pretensions in Europe. Australia and New Zealand, although more attached to London, were also keen to divert British attention from Europe, if only because they felt that it should be concentrated instead upon Japanese designs in the Far East. What was more, this appeal to return to the days of Victorian 'splendid isolation', for Britain to be an Asiatic power rather than a European one, accorded with the imperialist instincts of such influential personages as Curzon, Beaverbrook and the members of Milner's former 'kindergarten'.

To the imperial-federationists in Britain, the First World War had demonstrated not only the unity and loyalty of the Dominions and the importance of their contribution to the motherland's great-power status, but also the urgent need to hammer out an effective means of consultation and decision-making among the Empire's various parts. To the Canadians and South Africans, in contrast, the war had revealed the dangers inherent in too close a link with Whitehall; and, when joined after 1921 by that most reluctant Dominion, the Irish Free State, these three governments devoted much of their efforts to redefining their relationship with Britain so that the ties would be looser, not stronger. The precise nature of the constitutional changes effected by the imperial conferences of 1926 and 1931 –

milestones though they were in the transition from 'Empire' to 'Commonwealth' – need not be examined here. But at the end of it all, two facts were clear. The first was that most of the Dominions, sensitive about their own independence, preferred to develop separate foreign policies rather than be committed, even with prior consultation, to the consequences of Britain's diplomacy; by extension, they were also unenthusiastic about, and sometimes openly hostile to, suggestions of contingency defence planning. Nor were they eager to spend money upon the armed services, so that in practice 'imperial defence' still meant the deployment of chiefly British funds and personnel for the protection of an Empire covering one-quarter of the globe.

The second fact was a logical, but slightly curious corollary of the first; if British politicians, who had been brought up to assume that a unified Empire was one of life's unchanging features, wished to preserve that unity, then they could do so only by drawing closer to the Dominions' viewpoint. It would be an exaggeration to claim that pressure from Ottawa, Pretoria and elsewhere *made* the British isolationist in the inter-war years, for there already existed sufficient independent causes for that policy; but Dominion sentiment strengthened such an instinct, and simultaneously provided another good reason for it. Ironically, although frequently urging on British appeasement within Europe, the Dominions (together with imperialists like Amery) had little enthusiasm for 'colonial appeasement' since that would probably involve the return of territories seized from Germany during the First World War.

The changing relationship between Britain and the Dominions was not the only development within the Empire during the inter-war years. Quite apart from the early troubles in Ireland, there loomed ahead the enormous difficulty of handling the nationalist movement in India. The alternating strategies of repression and concession adopted there by successive British administrations indicated that perhaps no 'middle-way' solution was possible here, but the more immediate significance of this matter was that it, too, diverted London's energies from issues nearer home. This must also be said for the parallel uncertainties about the course of Egyptian nationalism, which was handled with a similar mixture of force and compromise; for the burgeoning and increasingly nasty struggles between Zionists and Arabs in Palestine; for other turbulences right across the Middle East; and for the wavering treatment of the Royal Navy's claim for a Singapore base. If the last-named issue consumed the passions of the Senior Service, the other ones absorbed much of the strength of the army and even the RAF. The envious words of Professor Marcks quoted at the beginning of this chapter can nicely be juxtaposed with the gloomy diary entries of the Chief of Imperial General Staff at precisely the same time: 'our small army is much too scattered . . . in no single theatre are we strong enough – not in Ireland, nor England, nor on the Rhine, nor in Constantinople, nor Batoum, nor Egypt, nor Palestine, nor Mesopotamia, nor Persia, nor India.'[12]

Strategically as well as emotionally, the British 'Janus' now felt the need to focus upon the overseas world and to cast but cool or irritated glances at Europe. Economically, too, as noted above, the depression, foreign tariffs and the 1932 decision for imperial preference had increased the proportion of British trade with the formal Empire and kindled the enthusiasm of Conservatives for their tropical estates. As the grand imperial structure began to crack, and as the industrial machine at the centre of this apparatus became weaker, the significance of the British Empire to many at home was paradoxically never stronger.

This concern about the possibility of imperial disintegration had one minor consequence worthy of mention. When Baldwin and his colleagues sought, in their usual fashion, to negotiate with Gandhi and later to defuse the situation in India by extending self-government to the provinces, this conciliatory stance was roundly attacked by Conservative diehards, among the most prominent of whom was Winston Churchill. Such criticisms did little injury to Baldwin, by then close to retirement; indeed, they confirmed his image as a man of moderation, against whom the Labour Party (on this issue at least) could find little to criticize. Nor did they hurt the political career of the conciliatory Indian Viceroy, Irwin, who as the Earl of Halifax would find himself as Chamberlain's Foreign Secretary in the years 1938–9. But this did damage Churchill, sending him into the political wilderness and confirming in many minds the image of him as unreliable and extreme. This, in consequence, inevitably cast doubt over the validity of his concurrent attacks upon the appeasement of Hitler, and understandably made the anti-Chamberlain forces on the left wary of associating with him.

Continuity in Government Structures?

Given the various impulses upon British policy from the public, and the overshadowing influence of economic factors, one is bound to wonder what effect this all had upon the role of ministers and their advisers within the 'Official Mind' of government after 1919. 'High politics', as some historians stress,[13] was still a game to be played out between select members of the national establishment. Similarly, one might point to the very strong continuity in the personnel and assumptions of those senior civil servants who ran the great departments of state, as well as in the functions of those offices. Hankey, Secretary to the Cabinet and to the Committee of Imperial Defence, remained to advise successive administrations in the post-war years as well. Eyre Crowe, Assistant Under-Secretary at the Foreign Office before 1914, had now (1920–5) moved up to the post of Permanent Under-Secretary. Beatty and his fellow sea lords, unshaken by Jutland, pressed as in the good old days for ever more battleships. The Treasury countered with its traditional arguments, reinforced by those of the Bank of England. Moreover, new recruits who entered the corridors of power came from an educational system which reinforced the prevailing assumptions of a post-Victorian but not post-imperial élite.

There were, to be sure, some alterations in structure and position. The Foreign Office, even under Curzon or Austen Chamberlain, never recovered the place it had occupied under Lansdowne and Grey, in part because of popular criticism of the 'old diplomacy', in part because Prime Ministers such as Lloyd George and MacDonald and, following them, Chamberlain, often wished to run their own foreign policy. The positions of the Admiralty and the War Office were also more circumscribed than before, not only by the arrival of the Royal Air Force as a separate ministry but also due to the increasing tendency towards 'defence by committee' and even, after 1936, by the existence of a Minister for the Co-ordination of Defence. The newly created Dominions Office, transmitting the views of the white parts of the Empire, soon had a recognizable place in the decision-making process, at least on certain issues. And the Treasury, as we have seen, had a much more definite voice on almost every issue. Yet, on the whole, it could be argued that the operation of politics in Whitehall and Westminster seemed to go on much the same as before, especially as compared with the upheavals in government and administration which were occurring in Russia, Germany, Italy and elsewhere in Europe. Was there not, then, that same political game by parliamentary leaders, and that same, flexible, day-to-day handling of British interests *vis-à-vis* the world outside as had existed in the decades before 1914?

Perhaps the chief difficulty with this argument about a basic continuity in British external policy – as executed by the 'Official Mind' in Whitehall, or as debated by the parliamentary groups in Westminster – is precisely that: it examines the offices and office-holders, not the issues; the plumbing, not the water; the wires, and not the electrical impulses. But it is precisely because the issues, the impulses, were in some cases remarkably different from those which had existed before the First World War; and even more, because they affected both the conception and the execution of Britain's external policy, that they have been given much more attention in the preceding sub-sections of this chapter than has the government structure. The experience of the 1920s was probably critical in this respect, since the domination of domestic issues in the politics of that decade placed foreign affairs in the shade and reduced the importance of diplomacy and diplomats, and the Foreign Secretary himself. When the international crises of the 1930s forced foreign affairs back into the centre of the stage, they were still handled by governments preoccupied by domestic concerns and thus rarely subjected to the kind of scrutiny which Salisbury and Lansdowne had been able to give to foreign-policy problems. Much as Permanent Under-Secretaries might deplore it or Conservative backbenchers shake their heads, therefore, the impact of democracy, economic strain, social reform and public sentiment upon the realm of government was substantial, permanent and far-reaching.

Continuity in Style and Purpose

What did not much change was the sheer 'style' of British politics and diplomacy, as compared with earlier generations. Arthur Henderson may have been an exception as Foreign Secretary, but the mannerisms and thought-processes of, say, Lord Halifax were not remarkably different from those of Granville, Salisbury, Lansdowne or Grey. The aristocratic pose of detachment, the tendency to understatement and irony, the appeal to reasoned argument, the avoidance of theory and 'ideology', the global perspective, were still in evidence. Given the honing of such characteristics at public school, in Oxford Union debates and in university essays, that was not surprising. It still impressed most Britons outside the establishment, and many within it; and it continued to bowl over foreign politicians – until, that is, it was replaced by the even more impressive spectacle of the jackboot and the Stuka.

These comments upon the political style of the British élite are not intended to be ironical. On the contrary, it is worth arguing that this is an extremely important aspect of any understanding of the entire political culture within which these statesmen executed their domestic and external policies. On the one hand, this system – and in particular the free-ranging nature of Cabinet discussions, the reference of tricky issues to specialist committees, and the belief in calm and rational solutions for virtually all problems – not only was a remarkably civilized mode of governing an Empire, but also an unusually effective one. It normally succeeded in considering all the major pros and cons of a particular action, and thus in achieving a certain ordering of governmental priorities. It was unlikely to lead to sudden and radical changes in policy, although admittedly that could have its drawbacks when deficiencies in the system became apparent. A row within the Cabinet, or an interdepartmental squabble, usually led the Prime Minister to postpone the issue until it had cooled; and the cost of delaying some decisions could be very expensive in the long run. Yet it was highly unlikely – indeed, almost inconceivable – that the British people would wake up one morning to find themselves on the brink of war with other powers as a consequence of the actions taken by *their* leaders.

Prudence, pragmatism, moderation, an unwillingness to be bound too closely to ideologies or rushed into actions – these were features of a governmental style which permitted the wide consideration of what were viewed as 'British interests', even in the altered circumstances of the 1920s and

1930s. Domestic pressures had to be assessed against the changes abroad, the Chiefs of Staffs' viewpoint to be set against that of the Treasury, the concern with European developments against obligations to the Empire, the costs of action against the costs of inaction. To this extent, it may indeed be argued that little had altered in the *modus procedendi* since far back into the nineteenth century. If this is so, then it deserves two further remarks. The first is that this very mode may well have helped to conceal – even to the decision-makers themselves – the extent of the global changes which had occurred since it was first developed as a political style; in particular, the continuity in outward structures and mannerisms may have taken attention from the sheer loss of British power in consequence of economic and technological alterations occurring since 1860 or so. When revelations of British military and industrial weaknesses *were* made known to the Cabinet, the system was going to appear less satisfactory; indecision, 'muddling through', and a refusal to plan ahead, would be the charges thrown against those who held the reins of power.

The second remark is that these assumptions about the rationality of politics, and the necessity of compromise, meant that it was extremely difficult for British politicians to understand that other states and other national leaders might not share these enlightened views. Perhaps this in turn was because individual British politicians such as Baldwin and Neville Chamberlain had remarkably little knowledge of *different* political systems and *alternative* ideologies to their own Western-liberal culture. But it may also be true, as Correlli Barnett suggests, that the particular educational and social mores of the late- and post-Victorian establishment made difficult a realistic assessment of other peoples – and induced a considerable amount of wishful thinking when reported facts did not accord with assumptions.[14] For example, the Cabinet was fed a number of very telling analyses by diplomats and others in the early 1930s of what the Nazi ideology implied, but years of bitter experience passed before it was fully understood that that creed could not be related to British political habits and beliefs. By then it was almost too late.

One is also driven to wonder whether the pleas in favour of moderation, maturity and compromise so frequently made by the executors of British foreign policy after 1919 were not a sign of something deeper – of an uneasy apprehension of future national decline and a private sense that the country had passed its peak. Few politicians in such a situation desire to articulate that suspicion, of course, and calls for renewal and reform are much more likely. But there clearly were many who felt, as a Foreign Office memorandum of 1926 put it, that

> We ... have no territorial ambitions nor desire for aggrandisement. We have got all that we want – perhaps more. Our sole object is to keep what we want and live in peace ... The fact is that war and rumours of war, quarrels and friction, in any corner of the world spell loss and harm to British commercial and financial interests ..
> so manifold and ubiquitous are British trade and British finance that, whatever else may be the outcome of a disturbance of the peace, we shall be the losers.[15]

Britain was a satiated power, in other words, and one with a growing awareness of the difficulties of maintaining what she possessed. In part, the dangers to the *status quo* seemed to come from within the Empire, or within the country itself following the rise of Labour; but they also came from external challenges, which grew ever more formidable as the 1930s unfolded. Given this awareness, was it not natural that the British were keen to see the League of Nations, or any other system which would stabilize the international scene, succeed?; that they felt bound to try to mediate in the antagonisms between Germany and its neighbours, before they escalated into a general conflagration?; that they were willing to make smaller concessions, if it avoided the greater (and incalculable) costs of an all-out war?; and that they wobbled precariously and frequently, as they tried to estimate how far they could appease without prejudicing that security and stability which had been their overriding motive for negotiating with the dictators in the first place?

Arnold Toynbee, perhaps thinking of Chamberlain with his umbrella and pinstripes incongruously inspecting the Nazi guard of honour at Bad Godesberg and Munich, once observed that a declining power descends the stairs like an old man in silken slippers, only to meet the rising power, clad in jackboots, on its way to the top. The contrast, for our purposes, is too sharp and too simple. It is also a-historical: other declining empires did not, in any exact sense, have to confront an Adolf Hitler abroad and a newly organized Labour movement at home. But it may help us to understand better the overall context of British policy in the inter-war years if we bear in mind that these were the actions of a country with nothing to gain, and much to lose, by being involved in war. Peace, in such circumstances, was the greatest of national interests

6. Debates and Policies

The formal signing of the Versailles Treaty did not, of course, present the British with a clean slate in their approach to external issues. The intervention in Russia was still going on. The Irish 'troubles' were worsening, as were those in India. Much of central Europe was in turmoil. The future of the entire Middle East was uncertain. The Dominions were keen to redefine their status. The League of Nations was an untried instrument.

All of these issues were to be either solved or at least 'patched up' during the following few years. The Irish Free State was established. The attempt to crush Bolshevism was abandoned. The Poles were urged to settle their border disputes to the east and the west by diplomacy. The Indian nationalist movement was smothered. The Dominions were more diplomatically appeased. A Middle East settlement was eventually hammered out with France and Italy, delayed by the Anglo-Turkish clash which led up to the Chanak crisis of 1922, and then implemented in the following year. By that time, too, the League of Nations was apparently working and was certainly very busy. In some cases, it may be argued that the 'solutions' were a mere postponement of the problems; but even if that were so, the British Cabinet was still pleased to see these matters disappear from its agenda for a while.

Two further outstanding diplomatic issues were also temporarily patched up in these years: the question of British policy towards Japan and the United States in the Far East, and the question of Franco-German relations. Their significance was such, however, that they both deserve a little closer scrutiny.

The Appeasement of the United States

The Anglo-American quarrel over 'the freedom of the seas' at the end of the First World War was, to the two navies concerned, by no means an academic or legal one. To the Admiralty, the most worrying fact was the remorseless growth of the US Navy, regardless of the coming of peace – and this at a time when the Treasury was pressing for more and more cuts in British defence expenditure, and when the Royal Navy's own battlefleet was ageing by comparison with the more modern (post-Jutland) vessels constructed by the USA and Japan. To those in charge of British foreign policy, the threat of a naval race with the Americans was complicated by the introduction of another issue: the Anglo-Japanese Alliance. From Washington it was reported that a larger fleet was not only regarded as necessary for the United States to ensure that its oceanic commerce was properly respected in future disputes; but also that its size had to be measured against the hypothetical contingency of a war against the British (whose pretensions to continued maritime mastery were detested by American navalists such as Admiral Benson) *and* simultaneously against the Japanese (whose ambitions in the Pacific had been revealed by its seizure of the German colonies and by its Twenty-one Demands upon China).

These American suspicions of Japanese intentions were shared in part by Australia and New Zealand, and even more by the government of India, but the fact remained that to Whitehall Japan's friendship during the war had been vital and should be preserved if at all possible. Yet although the British repeatedly attempted to persuade the Americans that the Anglo-Japanese Alliance would never be implemented against the USA, such arguments were in vain: clearly,

London would soon have to choose between Washington and Tokyo. At the same time, the Royal Navy was itself eager to reassert its position in the Orient by the creation of a great naval base at Singapore, where it was hoped a modern battlefleet would be stationed. While the decision to construct that base was made in June 1921, the Cabinet was still squabbling over the extent of any naval rebuilding plans when President Harding sent his famous invitation to the powers to confer in Washington on naval disarmament and Far Eastern affairs.

The chief decisions of that conference, based mainly upon American proposals, were simple enough. Henceforward, the five greatest naval powers would only be permitted to possess a fixed ratio of capital ships: 525,000 tons for Britain and the USA, 315,000 tons for Japan, and 175,000 tons for France and Italy. All construction work, with a few exceptions, would stop and there would be a ten-year 'naval holiday' as regards replacements. There would also be strict size limitations. However, due to French insistence, no restrictions were placed upon the size or the use of submarines, which had been the bane of the Royal Navy during the war. In addition, the British agreed not to renew the Anglo-Japanese Alliance, although this was partly concealed by a Four-Power (Britain, USA, Japan, France) Treaty to respect each other's possessions in the Pacific and Far East. To this were added clauses forbidding fortifications in that region, with certain exceptions such as Singapore and Pearl Harbor.

The sea lords and their supporters violently objected to a great deal of this. It meant that for the first time the Royal Navy was to be content with mere parity rather than numerical superiority over another navy; and that its size was determined by international treaty rather than an assessment of Britain's own strategic needs. Furthermore, the halt in capital-ship building would leave the navy with an obsolescent fleet by the time construction was again permitted, and during the interval the shipbuilding industry would almost certainly have decayed. In the Far East the consequences also seemed risky, since very few, if any, large vessels could be stationed there without weakening the British naval presence in the Atlantic and Mediterranean. Yet at the same time British interests in the Orient would no longer be protected as they had been for two decades, by the alliance with Japan; and the vague assurances from Washington offered no real substitute especially when many Japanese were visibly upset at this white man's front against their own imperial ambitions.

Why, then, did the British government accept the American terms? Partly because of Canadian and South African pressure at the 1921 Imperial Conference, for those Dominions were aghast at the idea of any Anglo-American antagonism. Partly because the civilian Cabinet was more optimistic about future relations with either Japan or the USA than their strategic advisers, who by training and inclination assumed the worst. Partly because the immediate post-war boom had broken, the unemployment level had risen above 2 million, and the Treasury and the newly formed Geddes committee were insisting upon further massive cuts in the defence budget – which, if accepted, would have scarcely left the Royal Navy much larger even had there not been that naval limitations agreement at Washington.

But the overriding reason, of course, was the haunting fear of an Anglo-American naval race, the costs of which were incalculable. The budget would, especially in the existing circumstances, suffer far greater strains from this than it had from the pre-1914 race against Germany. The public, if required to carry crushing taxation burdens and to see the expected spending upon social services curtailed, would respond angrily: just how angrily, no one wished to predict, but an electoral defeat would be the least of the possible domestic evils. And in any case, if the Americans were really serious about 'a navy second to none', Britain could not hope to compete with them indefinitely. To engage in open rivalry, as Lloyd George warned, was conceivably a decision greater than that taken in August 1914: 'We should be up against the greatest resources in the world.'[1] The eventual financial collapse of the country, hastened by the American demand for the repayment of war loans, would be a blessing compared with the alternative course – war with the United States itself, a war which Britain could not possibly win. The prospect, the Cabinet agreed, was 'ghastly', 'horrible', 'unthinkable'. Against it Washington temptingly held out the offer of a naval limitations treaty, set within an attractive though admittedly vague framework of international goodwill and co-operation in the Pacific and Far East. In view of this, it is not surprising that the British were willing in the last resort to abandon the alliance with Japan and to clutch at the establishment by treaty of naval parity with the United States – which, after all, would serve to disguise Britain's actual weakness, to stabilize the territorial *status quo* in the Far East, and even, perhaps, to 'control' the actions of an American republic which had always seemed a little wayward and unpredictable and was now quite independent of pressures which might be exerted via the League of Nations.

Seen in long-term perspective, this was but one in a whole series of acts of British deference to the Americans, which began (at the latest) with the *Alabama* settlement of 1871 and was to continue through to the Suez crisis of 1956 and beyond. As such, it can also be viewed as a steady tilting of the scales from the older, declining power to the newer, expanding one: as a pragmatic adjustment to realities, conditioned by a regular assessment of Britain's economic needs, affected also by the more intangible factors of culture, language and ideology, and made possible by the laws of geopolitics – for the USA, unlike France or Germany, was far enough away to be able to expand without directly encroaching upon British national security. Although expansionist at the commercial level (e.g. Middle East oil, tariffs, China trade), the Americans did not appear to wish to crush the British Empire by force, a conclusion which could not be so easily drawn about the intentions of certain other rivals in this period.

Nevertheless, however prescient these adjustments to reality may have been, they often left successive British governments with a considerable number of shorter-term problems. The only concession made by Washington in 1921 was, as so often, a negative one: that it would cease its naval construction. It offered no promises of helping to preserve the territorial order in the Far East, let alone in Europe, where its attitude over war debts in the early 1920s left (in the British view) much to be desired: London was compelled to make substantial concessions, for example, in the Anglo-American debt settlement of January 1923. Washington also strongly objected to the idea that the League of Nations, in implementing economic sanctions against an aggressor, should interfere with American oceanic commerce. This left many Britons keen to maintain harmonious relations with Japan, which could still be seen as a stabilizing force during the 1920s, and be sympathized with when it took action against the turbulent Chinese nationalists. For those Britons and, still more, Australasians who suspected Tokyo's aims, however, it was difficult to contemplate maintaining a stand against Japan without knowledge of how the Americans would react. Certain harder-nosed individuals, such as Neville Chamberlain, had little patience with this frequent 'deference', as they saw it, to Washington's susceptibilities; but British policy on the whole sought to maintain friendly relations even at some cost, as MacDonald did when offering concessions over cruiser numbers at the 1929–30 talks prior to the London Naval Conference. In sum, the 'American angle' added to the number of uncertainties with which British diplomacy had to contend in the inter-war years, but brought no positive advantages.

The Avoidance of a Continental Commitment

The rapid retirement of the United States into isolation after 1920 left the joint Anglo-American guarantee to France in ruins, and accounted for the latter's feverish search for alternative structures of security – in the League of Nations, in an east European *bloc* of anti-revisionist and anti-German states, and in a fresh commitment by Britain alone. By the same token, this American retreat increased those tendencies already in evidence within Britain to keep the country's hands free of any obligations, especially military obligations, on the continent of Europe. London's dilemma, however, was that it could not throw aside its European role as easily as Washington had done. Dominion and domestic sentiment might urge isolationism, and troubles in Ireland and India reinforce the need to concentrate elsewhere, but there always remained good reasons for British involvement in European diplomacy. The League of Nations, if it was to succeed at all, clearly required Britain's participation; and politicians were aware that, however much sentiment had swung against the 'old diplomacy' and power-politics, the British public did applaud the efforts and appearances of its leaders at Geneva. In much the same way the growing sympathy for Germany and dislike of French actions suggested British mediation there rather than non-involvement; and the economic arguments in favour of the restoration of German industry and wealth also implied intervention by Whitehall so as to ensure the recovery of Europe. What was desired, therefore, was a judicious policy of balance, securing British interests in Europe while avoiding the extremes of isolationism or binding military pledges.

This ideal policy was easier to describe than to achieve.

For example, hammering out the League of Nations' position towards the permanence – or otherwise – of the territorial boundaries of its member states after 1919 always involved Anglo-French differences, as did discussions about a military response by the League to any attempt to alter the *status quo* unilaterally. The British, hoping for machinery which would keep the peace by regularizing inter-state co-operation and on occasions permitting *peaceful change,* found themselves at odds with France and its allies, who continued to see in the League an instrument to ensure, by forceful means if necessary, the settlement of 1919.

This is hardly the place to develop a defence of the French viewpoint, but it undoubtedly contained a certain hard, cold logic. German strength had merely been damaged, not eradicated, by the terms imposed at Versailles; and despite its temporary economic distress it still had the potential to regain its place as the power-house of western Europe. Even in 1921, it may be noted, Germany's crude steel production was over three times that of France's. To keep this potential force from developing, it was felt necessary by Paris to weaken the German economy by insisting upon the full repayment of reparations, by encouraging separatist movements in the Rhineland and Polish claims in Silesia, by fashioning the League into a military alliance for the implacable defence of the Versailles boundaries, and by establishing a further obstacle to change through an alliance with Germany's fearful eastern neighbours. Alas for this French logic, it also directly contradicted the British hopes of lessening nationalist tensions within Europe, dissolving all pre-war alliance *blocs,* bringing (a prosperous) Germany back into the European concert, and using the League to arrange and monitor any necessary subsequent alterations in the hastily contrived boundaries of 1919. Given the influence of economic pressures and public sentiment and domestic-political calculation upon British statesmen, and upon their French equivalents, it was not surprising that relations between the two countries were often strained in the early 1920s.

The full history of these quarrels – over the French occupation of the Ruhr, over reparations and war debts, over disarmament *versus* security – is well covered elsewhere.[2] What they all revealed was that, whereas the French feared a strong Germany, the British had by and large abandoned their pre-1914 suspicion of Berlin. British appeasement, at least in these years, revealed not an awareness of weakness *vis-à-vis* Germany but a certain optimism about the future, always provided that it was not ruined by French intransigence. Of course, this very 'intransigence' would have been less had the British government given Paris the assurances which it sought. In the circumstances of the 1920s, there was no chance of that. This wrangle began only a short while after the Anglo-American guarantee had collapsed, and it was soon exacerbated by the quarrel over the French move into the Rhine (spring 1920) and over France's support of Polish claims to Silesia (summer 1921). By then, Germany's first payment of reparations was causing such a weakening in the value of the mark that Lloyd George, fearing repercussions upon the international economy, had almost abandoned his earlier belief that the Germans could and should pay for their wartime aggression. Although hoping that some carefully-defined alliance offer would ease France's hard-line policies in Europe and also secure concessions in the Middle East, the British immediately baulked when they learned Paris's views during the winter of 1921/2. It was made clear by the French that a British guarantee to intervene against a future German strike *westwards* was insufficient, for it failed to take into account the probability that the first direction of expansion might be to the east. What was required, Paris felt, was British help in deterring another Sadowa as well as another Sedan.

Nothing was more likely to weaken the fast-receding British desire to be involved in Europe than this demand for aid against 'indirect aggression' upon France. Throughout the nineteenth century, London had openly admitted that it could not intervene in eastern Europe, and many Britons now bitterly resented the fact that the First World War, arising from a Balkan quarrel, had dragged in the western nations because of the rigid alliance system and fixed military plans. That Britain should bind itself in perpetuity to preserve the newly cast and somewhat questionable boundaries of eastern Europe seemed unthinkable. Lloyd George's offer to Briand of reciprocal assistance in January 1922 therefore firmly ruled out participation in military enterprises in central and eastern Europe. The replacement of Briand by Poincaré as French Prime Minister brought a hardening of attitudes, with Paris tightening its links with the east-European 'little Entente' (Czechoslovakia, Yugoslavia and Rumania) while the British looked on disapprovingly; and with these bilateral disagreements between French and British Foreign Offices paralleled by the wider quarrel at Geneva between those states which saw the League as a conciliator and those which stressed the need for collective resistance to any change of existing boundaries.

The fall of Lloyd George's coalition and its replacement in 1922 by Bonar Law promising 'tranquility and freedom from adventures and commitments both at home and abroad' meant that Britain's continental policy was more than ever like that of the mid-to-late 1860s: advice and criticism were freely proffered to European capitals, but binding military pledges were anathema. Lloyd George's 'adventures' and rash moves during the Chanak crisis, where he appeared willing for a while to go to war to keep Turkish forces from the international zone on the Straits, were as much approved of by domestic opinion as Palmerston and Russell's blunder over Schleswig-Holstein had been; and Dominion opinion was even more critical of the idea of fighting the Turks at London's behest. Similarly, British attitudes to Poincaré's policies (especially during the Franco-Belgian occupation of the Ruhr in 1923 following

Germany's default on coal and timber reparations) echoed in many respects the earlier dislike of Napoleon III's Rhine strategy. Only with the advent of MacDonald's administration in January 1924, American assistance through the Dawes Committee (which proposed a reorganization of German finances and a two-year halt to reparations until its economy was stronger), the replacement of Poincaré by the socialist Herriot, and France's concern at its own economic problems, did there emerge a compromise and indeed a vast improvement in relations between London and Paris. Yet these promising signs obscured the fact that the British policy against military guarantees remained unaltered. Despite its proclaimed adherence to the League, MacDonald's Labour government rejected that body's so-called 'Draft Treaty of Mutual Assistance' in July 1924 on grounds similar to those advanced by Conservative administrations. While in theory it obligated all member-states to act against aggressors in their region, in practice the Draft Treaty would always involve some of the world-wide forces of the British Empire, and place a particular strain upon the Royal Navy. Again, when the substitute mutual-aid scheme known as the Geneva Protocol was drafted, it was rejected by Baldwin's Conservative government and by the Dominions for the same reason: all disliked binding and universal pledges.

If this dogged wish to avoid such obligations was partly concealed in the rosy year of 1925, when the Locarno Treaty was signed, it nevertheless remained unshaken. The treaty to which the British government appended its signature was more significant for what was *not* guaranteed than for what was offered. In the first place, London joined Italy, France, Belgium and Germany only in guaranteeing the inviolability of the Rhine borders, and steadfastly refused to make a similar pledge in the east – which could be easily interpreted as an indirect recognition of German claims against Poland and Czechoslovakia, and also as a sign that some clauses of the Versailles settlement were less important than others.

Even so, various groups in Britain were opposed to the obligations they believed were contained in the Locarno Treaty, and the Dominions insisted that no obligation should be placed upon them by it – another step in the emergence of their separate foreign policies. It is worth remarking that throughout this period British ministers such as Austen Chamberlain and Leo Amery refused point-blank to discuss German colonial claims: that aspect of the 1919 settlement, unlike eastern Europe, was non-negotiable.

In many respects, Locarno represented a major French defeat. Not being an old-style, formally defined military alliance but a general pledge against 'aggression' from one side of the Rhine or the other, it meant that there was now no danger of Whitehall being drawn into Anglo-French staff talks: the aggressor, after all, would only be known when he had committed his act. It was also impossible for the French army to plan any future offensive into Germany without breaching the treaty, which gave the generals the excuse they needed for adopting a defensive, 'Maginot Line' strategy. As for the British military, Locarno might not have existed. In the following year, the Chiefs of Staff revealed that they had no plans and few forces to give practical effect to that new obligation, yet no one in the British government appears to have been too disturbed by this revelation. Locarno was not really about military commitments, even in the West. It served to patch up the European concert and to allow Britain to concentrate upon domestic and imperial issues. In the same bland fashion, Baldwin's government was willing to 'outlaw war' by signing the innocuous Briand-Kellogg Pact of 1928, although with the significant proviso about taking action if necessary in defence of the Suez Canal zone and other vital points of the Empire.

Finally, it is this complex of domestic-political, economic and imperial factors determining Britain's inter-war external policy which explains the government's lack of enthusiasm for a bold stroke to solve the disarmament talks deadlock of the late 1920s and early 1930s. Ostensibly, the country had everything to gain from a further reduction of armaments – and knew it. Not only did Baldwin and MacDonald find the frequent criticisms of British defence policy by the centre and left politically embarrassing, but orthodox economic opinion also disliked the diversion of the nation's resources from 'productive' to 'unproductive' ends. It was the pre-1914 arms race, historians and others argued, which had made that conflict inevitable. If contemporary suspicions and antagonisms in Europe and the Far East were to be eased, then a *status quo* power like Britain had an obvious interest in seeing that arms limitations talks succeeded. This motive was clearly to the fore in the government's handling of the 1930 London Naval Conference: despite the Admiralty's fears, it seemed a larger wisdom to agree to cut the number of cruisers and to prolong for five years the 'naval holiday' in capital ship construction, rather than to risk a naval race with the USA and Japan.

Securing agreement upon land armaments was altogether more difficult. In part, this was because, whereas the three leading naval powers all had good reasons of their own at that time for accepting continued restrictions upon their fleets, no such mutual pressures existed to defuse the quarrel between the Germans and the French over the size and type of their armies. To French political and military leaders, who were well informed of Germany's secret rearmament steps, it would be both national and political suicide to reduce their own large forces without water-tight guarantees of security: they were, therefore, unwilling to take the Germans on trust or to consider proposals to change their own army from a mass-conscription one to a much smaller, long-service force. On the other side of the Rhine, it was felt intolerable that the 'natural' claim for Germany's equality with other powers, which was now freely conceded in such things as membership of the League, should continue to be denied in the military sphere. Although still bound by the Versailles Treaty, each successive German administration knew that it could not long survive nationalist pressure unless it obtained concessions from the French. Between these two adamantine positions the British wavered, attracted (since their own army was so shrunken in size) to the German notions of smaller 'qualitative' forces rather than larger 'quantitative' ones, yet simultaneously appreciative of French feelings of insecurity and personally irritated by the German arrogance in negotiations and the violence of their domestic politics.

In view of the latter, and of the driving-forces within National Socialism, and of the economic potential which Germany possessed, it is doubtful whether London could have done anything to forestall a Franco-German clash in the long run. But it is clear that the British were not eager to pay much to prevent a breakdown. In September 1933, even as Hitler was consolidating his hold internally, the French reluctantly agreed to 'level down' their armaments in the future to satisfy German demands, but only provided Britain would bind itself to various automatic sanctions – diplomatic, economic and military – if Germany should be found to be violating this proposed understanding by rearming. At this, London once again backed away, insisting that while violations by Berlin would meet with 'the moral condemnation of the world',[3] the British government could not promise to act against Germany. By the following month, Hitler had pulled out of these disarmament talks, and German preparations to expand and refurnish their armed forces were accelerated.

In sum, the British policy towards France was less than helpful: it unhinged the French strategy towards Germany, making it less consistent and effective but of course never more friendly and confident. As such, it reminds one of the way American policy distorted the British strategy towards Europe and the Far East. No doubt there were many justifications for London's reserve towards French requests for aid, just as there were good reasons for Washington's suspicions of being entangled in the defence of British imperial interests; but it also remains the case that, since the hoped-for support was not forthcoming, both the French and the British policy respectively was made that much more uncertain just at a time when bold, generous and far-seeing gestures were vital.

The Shape of British Defence Policy in the Early 1930s

The size and weaponry of the British armed forces, and the strategic plans of their respective staffs, reflected much of this attitude to external events. Although there seems to exist no full statement of defence priorities from the early years of the National government, the order of importance was certainly not different from that submitted to the Cabinet by Sir Thomas Inskip, the Minister for Co-ordination of Defence, in December 1937. In the first place, inevitably, was the maintenance of the security of the United Kingdom, the core of the Empire's strength. Then followed the protection of the trade routes on which the country depended for essential imports of food and raw materials; and, thirdly, the maintenance of those forces needed to defend British territories overseas. The final objective, to be provided only if the others were met, was 'co-operation in the defence of the territories of any allies we may have in war'.[4] Despite the coming of the twentieth century, in other words, there was little difference here in Britain's strategic priorities from the time of the 1891 Stanhope Memorandum, which had placed home and imperial defence foremost and argued that involvement in a European conflict was improbable. Forty years later, splendid isolation was still the preferred policy.

The implications of this for the three armed services were clear enough. Allocations to the army had been cut most after 1919, and the service was manifestly the most unpopular of all in the public mind, a sentiment which was unlikely to be altered by the boom in anti-war literature in the late 1920s. What was more, the army chiefs themselves, perhaps also recoiling from their 1914–18 experiences, produced no fresh Sir Henry Wilson to argue the case for a 'continental commitment'. Instead, they readily concentrated their attention upon the state of the garrisons in India and Egypt or upon the challenge posed to cavalry by new developments in tanks. A Russian threat to India, rather than a German strike against Belgium or Poland, was also more likely to exercise the minds of the army planners in this period. Since the actual size of the army was minimal, this might be regarded as a judicious adjustment to the realities imposed upon the generals from outside. On occasions, they, together with the other Chiefs of Staff, warned the Cabinet that they could only 'take note' of the obligations to European security which they understood to be contained in the Versailles and Locarno treaties. At most, they might scrape together two divisions for despatch to the continent, but that itself would imply both a reversal of the order of priorities and a (most unlikely) period of tranquillity throughout the Empire. In October 1933, indeed, just as the Germans were pulling out of the disarmament talks, the British Chiefs of Staff gloomily pointed out that, 'Should war break out in Europe, far from our having the means to intervene, we should be able to do little more than hold the frontier and outposts of the Empire during the first few months of the war.'[5]

The Royal Navy in these years was treated more favourably – or, rather, *less unfavourably* – by British governments and the public because of a general recognition of the importance of sea power for the maintenance of a world empire, because Dominion governments and Britain's own imperialists wished to maintain a 'presence' abroad, and because the service could not be held responsible for the continental slaughters of 1914–18. That said, however, it is obvious that the navy also suffered grievously during the inter-war years: there were no replacement battleships, its cruiser and destroyer numbers were steadily reduced, naval stores were run down, and its string of bases throughout the Empire was more or less totally neglected, all of which affected those industries to which the service would turn if ever it was permitted to rebuild. In addition, it suffered from a prolonged wrangle with the Royal Air Force about administrative controls over the Fleet Air Arm, which was arguably one reason why the Admiralty never developed the concept of long-range, fast carrier groups on the Japanese and American model. In fairness to the sea lords, it should be added that they probably had enough on their hands in dealing with politicians and in attempting to resolve the ancient dilemma of how to deploy their vessels so as to defend the overseas empire without losing control of home waters. Technically, this strategy seemed feasible under the terms of the Washington Treaty, for the British superiority over Japan in battleship tonnage (525,000 tons to 315,000 tons) would just permit the Admiralty to send a fleet to the Far East whilst keeping a 'one-power standard' against the next largest European navy. All this presupposed, however, the maintenance of the Royal Navy to full treaty standard.[6]

The RAF's position in the slump years was the most curious of all. It owed its survival as an independent service to the Cabinet's acceptance of Trenchard's argument that a long-range bombing force, large enough to attack the enemy's homeland and destroy his economy, should neither be in the hands of sea-bound admirals nor land-bound generals. Indeed, a sub-committee of the Imperial War Cabinet, reporting in 1917, had speculated upon the day when aerial operations 'may become the principal operations of war, to which the older forms of military and naval operations may become secondary and subordinate.'[7] Such a theory of air power was accepted by the British government, which also came to believe that a bomber 'deterrent' might be a cheaper and certainly a politically more attractive way of preventing future aggression in Europe: in taking the place of an expeditionary force, bombers would not be stationed outside Britain in such a fixed and irrevocable fashion. The only trouble with this concept was that the RAF did not possess the long-range modern aircraft with which to carry out an effective bombing campaign in central Europe. Its bombers were light, short-range craft, useful for imperial policing in the Middle East and India but for little else.

Furthermore, it took no genius to realize that if British bombers would (to use Baldwin's phrase) 'always get through', then the home country was itself threatened by the possibility of raids by foreign air forces – as the Zeppelin and Gotha bomber attacks had shown during the war. Frequent bombing attacks from continental bases, it was pessimistically forecast by a CID sub-committee in 1922, would produce so much damage and demoralization that the public would insist upon an armistice and only an adequate aerial defence could counter such a danger. Within the space of a few decades, technology had effected a revolutionary change – for the worse – in Britain's strategic position: no matter how great a navy she possessed, the 'wooden walls' of the island state had now been breached. This in turn had two consequences. The first was that politicians, always attuned to the apprehensions of the public, were likely to have a high regard for the creation of a defensive air force (i.e. fighters). In the early 1920s, therefore, a Metropolitan Air Force was established, the size of which was measured against the unlikely contingency of a French bombing attack. Only later would the more real possibility of assaults by the *Luftwaffe* arise, but essentially the impact upon the RAF was the same: it was put under pressure to direct resources from its bomber arm to its fighter squadrons.

The second implication of the military revolution was even more disturbing to the few who thought about it: namely, that the fate of any region from which bombing raids could be launched upon Britain now became vital to national security. As Baldwin was to put it in 1934, Britain's frontier had moved from Dover to the Rhine. Here was a very substantial reinforcement of the traditional strategic need to preserve the independence of the Low Countries and to keep northern France from occupation by a hostile power. Yet it was to be some years before this fact dawned upon those politicians who were striving to 'isolate' Britain once again from any commitments to the continent.

In sum, the defence policies of the British Empire suggest once again that this was now a cautious, rather introspective power hoping for a peaceful life, a restoration of prosperity and the preservation of the *status quo*. These were years of relative placidity in international politics, which seemed to those in government to justify the running-down of the armed services. As it turned out, this period of placidity was all too brief, which later led to many criticisms of the lack of foresight among British politicians and their advisers. It would, however, have taken a prophet of rare sagacity and prescience to have foreseen that the international situation would change so swiftly, and that so many *simultaneous* threats to the British Empire would occur precisely at a time when its defences were weakest and when public attention was riveted upon the domestic scene. On the other hand, there is no doubt that British decision-makers failed to see how hard it would be for a democratic regime swiftly to change gear, if it should be necessary to increase the unpopular defence spending: and that many of them ignored until the very last the possibility that their own pacific inclinations might not be shared by others.

The Beginnings of Doubt, 1931–5

One set of national leaders who clearly did not share this firm adherence to Wilsonian internationalism was that of Japan, a power eager to carve out for itself in the twentieth century an imperial sphere akin to those carved out by the European nations in earlier centuries. Holding (as most dissatisfied and rising states do) that the 'natural' processes of growth and struggle should not be artificially restrained, the Japanese Army and its domestic nationalists could only regard the League of Nations and the Washington treaties as devices to check their country's economic and territorial growth. In September 1931, unable to restrain their impatience at Chinese obstructionism or their own longer-term ambitions any longer, the army began its conquest of Manchuria, which within two years it had turned into a puppet state. Here was the first real challenge by a major power to the 'new' international system.

To this transgression the British government, despite repeated references to the principles of the League, could offer only a limp and half-hearted policy of protest. The reasons for this attitude were, at a certain level of logic, eminently rational, convincing and manifest. The United States, probably the only nation capable of playing a great-power role in the Orient had it so wished, seemed unwilling (because of its own domestic opinion) to offer anything more than verbal condemnation. Few other countries had either the strength to deter Japan, or an interest in doing so: France's gaze, for example, was unblinkingly cast across the Rhine. The Dominions indicated strong disapproval of the idea of applying automatic sanctions; and various Britons saw in this confusion of reactions a confirmation of their earlier suspicion that, whatever policy a majority of League members voted to support in principle, only in the Royal Navy was there an instrument to execute this decision in practice. Many in London, Paris and Washington – and in their embassies in the Orient – sympathized with Japan's claims against the Chinese nationalists and found the actions in Manchuria not dissimilar from, say, the British military moves in Shanghai in 1927.

More important still, even had the British government itself not possessed such reservations, it was inconceivable that domestic opinion would have permitted a military entanglement in such a distant part of the globe when it already felt so reluctant about commitments to nearby Europe. By the most cruel of conjunctures, the Japanese elected to begin their operations in Manchuria between the collapse of the Labour government in August 1931 and the National government's electoral victory in late October 1931. During the interval MacDonald and his colleagues cleary did regard their role as provisional, 'for dealing with the national emergency as it now exists'. Faced with political convulsions, the flight from sterling, the decision to come off the gold standard, spiralling unemployment, unpopular economic cuts and – as a consequence of the latter – the 'mutiny' at Invergordon, Cabinet ministers had little time to reflect upon what the Japanese were up to on the far side of the globe. As MacDonald put it to Baldwin, 'We have all been so distracted by day-to-day troubles that we have never had a chance of surveying the whole situation and hammering out a policy regarding it, but have had to live from agitation to agitation.'[8]

When, over the next few months and years, the National government did find the time to reflect upon the Far Eastern crisis, its policy of tacit appeasement of Japan became ever more confirmed in practice. Quite apart from the reasons mentioned above, the Cabinet was increasingly aware of its military incapacity to do much in the Far East. British power in that region, of questionable merit ever since the Russo-Japanese War, had been completely neutered by the Washington treaties and by the economy drives of the 1920s. The construction of the Singapore base had again been discontinued; nor was there any battlefleet to occupy it had it been ready for use. Only a few months earlier, in April 1931, the Admiralty had reported that the country's naval strength 'in certain circumstances is definitely below that required to keep our sea communications open in the event of our being drawn into a war': it was impossible to send capital ships to the Far East without jeopardizing British maritime security *vis-à-vis* a European power. Neither the army, with its garrisons stretched across the globe, nor the

RAF, with its inadequate machines and service facilities, could compensate for this weakness in the naval sphere. 'The whole of our territory in the Far East, as well as the coast-line of India and the Dominions and our vast trade and shipping, lies open to attack . . .', the Chiefs of Staff reported early in 1932.⁹ Finally, since the continued Japanese defiance of the League coincided with the rise of the Nazis in Germany and the breakdown of the disarmament conference, the British government faced the task of simultaneously dealing with two great states, at opposite ends of the world, with unfulfilled ambitions and bitter memories. Even those Cabinet ministers most absorbed with domestic affairs and suspicious of the military mind acknowledged that it was now time to re-examine the assumptions upon which British defence and foreign policy had been based for the past decade.

From 1932 onwards, this process of reassessment got under way. Resumption of work upon the Singapore base was ordered. The Ten-Year Rule was abandoned. A Defence Requirements sub-committee of the CID was established to recommend a programme for repairing the worst deficiencies in British and imperial defence. In its reports, and in the many others submitted by the three services, the picture was steadily built up of an alarming lack of military force to defend what was still the largest conglomeration of political and economic interests and commitments in the world. There was not one adequately defended base throughout the entire Empire. An out-of-date navy was not strong enough to take on the Japanese fleet, let alone preserve its maritime dominance in European waters at the same time. A run-down army could not possibly play its traditional role of preserving the European equilibrium. Britain's anti-aircraft defences were virtually non-existent. The RAF itself possessed neither the bombers to deter aggression, nor the fighters to keep the homeland safe. This was scarcely comforting news to a Cabinet which had just concluded that, while it was necessary to regard Japan as the more immediate threat to peace, a Germany under Nazi direction was 'the ultimate potential enemy against whom our "long range" policy must be directed'.[10]

The real problem for politicians such as MacDonald, Baldwin, Neville Chamberlain, Simon and their colleagues was not that this information and analysis was impossible to accept: indeed, the sober and clinical tone adopted by the Chiefs of Staff and other permanent advisers was such as to chill both sceptics and idealists. The dilemma was that this flow of reports coincided with the high point reached by all those pressures – domestic-political, economic, sentimental, and imperial – described in Chapter 5 above (especially pages 226–43). The call to re-equip the Empire's defences had, in other words, to be considered against contrary calls and thus suffer dilution through that typically British process of compromising in committee between clashing demands. With the Treasury forecasting national bankruptcy, for example, the Cabinet was compelled to warn that the cancellation of the Ten-Year Rule 'must not be taken to justify an expanding expenditure by the Defence Services without regard to the very serious financial and economic situation which still obtains'.[11] This was hardly a green light for full-scale rearmament. Nor did the domestic situation, where pacifist and internationalist opinion remained strong, suggest to the National government that circumstances were favourable for an open abandonment of the existing external policy; and cautious politicians such as Baldwin (and Roosevelt in the USA) wished not to get too far ahead of public sentiment. The fate of coalition candidates in by-elections, the sullen opposition of Labour, the agitations of the Peace Pledge movement, and the continued weakness of sterling were uppermost in the minds of Cabinet ministers.

British policy during the years 1932–5 was, in consequence, not a little confused and unreal. More and more evidence emerged of deficiencies in the defence field. More and more alarming news came from abroad – the Japanese and German withdrawals from the League of Nations, the

German rearmament programme, the 'Night of the Long Knives', the murder of Dollfuss. At the same time, the political leaders in London felt cramped by domestic forces from instituting a more active external policy and were themselves, psychologically and culturally, inclined to delay decisions and to order further reports upon the costs and mechanics of rearmament whilst they pondered on its political and diplomatic implications. Even when the majority of the Cabinet accepted that the world was now a less peaceful place than it had been in the 1920s, they were still confused about the priority which they should give to certain 'threats' and to the consequential defence measures to counter them. The Admiralty was thinking chiefly of the Japanese challenge. The Treasury recognized in Germany the greatest problem and wished to see relations with Japan improved. Vansittart, the Permanent Under-Secretary at the Foreign Office, also had his eyes fixed on Germany but disapproved of some of the ways suggested to satisfy Hitler by concessions. Appeasement, in other words, is not only to be found as a general frame of mind, but could also exist as a policy pursued towards one nation so as to allow a tougher stance against another. But since even the adoption of a 'tougher stance' required an increase in British armaments, and since the politicians hoped to discover a diplomatic solution to the grievances of the dissatisfied states in the meantime, it was not surprising that a policy of 'cunctation', as it was termed, was favoured.

Furthermore, to the vacillations within the British government had to be added the differences of opinion *between* the Western democracies. Spasmodic Anglo-American-French consultations over Manchuria had already shown how difficult it was to hammer out any common policy at all. In Europe, Britain and France had been quarrelling over the correct treatment of Germany ever since 1919. While the advent of the Nazis produced a certain revival of the old liberal *entente*, it did not lead to agreements on a positive and united approach to Berlin. In April 1935, for example, the British, French and Italian governments meeting at Stresa reaffirmed their approval of the non-aggressive pacts designed to preserve the *status quo* in eastern Europe, and condemned German rearmament. A month later, the French negotiated a pact of mutual assistance with the Soviet Union, to the evident disapproval of London which hoped to avoid the pre-1914 division of Europe into alliance *blocs* and still wished to bring Germany into the comity of nations rather than to isolate her. With this thought in mind, the British had been considering for some time a unilateral approach and consummated this by signing the Anglo-German naval agreement of June 1935 – which in turn provoked the French to complain that the solidarity of the 'Stresa Front' had been undermined. To a British Admiralty worried by its weakness in the Far East, however, a naval treaty with Germany (restricting the latter's surface fleet to 35 per cent of the Royal Navy's, and its submarines to 45 per cent) was attractive since this put an upper limit on the size of the German fleet and made the despatch of a force to Singapore in the future a little more feasible – this calculation now being all the more pressing since the Japanese had refused to prolong the naval limitations treaties. As it turned out, the Germans probably secured the chief benefits from this Anglo-German deal, since they had not only divided the Western camp but were enabled to build undisturbed for years until they were ready to breach the limits imposed in 1935; while the growth of the German fleet even to those restricted levels began to mesmerise the Admiralty, to the eventual detriment of deployments in other waters.

The Pace of Appeasement Quickens

The strategical and diplomatic assumptions upon which the Admiralty's 'two-power standard' policy was based were soon to be shattered by another event: the Italian war upon Abyssinia, and Mussolini's growing adhesion to Berlin. Hitherto, Italy's benevolent neutrality, if not support, had been taken for granted. Now, because of the aggression in Abyssinia, Anglo-Italian relations were strained almost to breaking point. This crisis, like the Manchurian one earlier, illustrated perfectly the dilemma the British found themselves in by the mid-1930s. A policy of pusillanimity, all were aware, would merely encourage the dictators. Moreover, public opinion still clung to the principles of the League of Nations, sympathized strongly with the Abyssinian appeals for assistance, and disapproved of any private deal with Mussolini – as was demonstrated by the uproar over the Hoare-Laval pact, which had proposed ceding most of Abyssinia to the Italians. What public opinion positively desired was now more difficult to decipher, however, for while Robert Cecil and the League enthusiasts called for sanctions, pacifist and isolationist voices deplored any thought of war. The tentative imposition of sanctions not only divided opinion in London and Geneva, but also caused some waverers to worry in case Washington held firm to its belief in the untrammelled rights of neutral traders. Other Britons, including 'anti-appeasers' such as Amery and Vansittart, were more worried about the possibility of alienating Italy while the more formidable threat from Germany hovered in the background; and this consideration was repeatedly pressed by the French, who had only recently come to an agreement with Mussolini about joint action to prevent a German *Anschluss* of Austria.

Finally, the British Chiefs of Staff, when consulted about the likely outcome of a war with Italy, proffered their usual catalogue of depressing facts. The Royal Navy was superior to the Italian fleet alone and the Abyssinian war could be throttled by the closure of the Suez Canal; but there the advantages ended. The prospect of Italian air attacks in narrow waters, and the fact that the anti-aircraft guns at Malta, Egypt and Aden were so few and had so little ammunition, caused the Mediterranean Fleet to be withdrawn from Malta to Alexandria. Yet to send aerial reinforcements to the region would denude the British Isles at a time when the public and government were frightened by the (alleged) massive superiority of the *Luftwaffe*. Most important of all, as the First Lord, Monsell, put it: 'We could not afford to overlook Japan.' British involvement – or worse, warship losses – in the Mediterranean would leave China and the whole of south-east Asia open to Japanese expansion. Once again, therefore, the Cabinet was reminded that Britain's interests – much more so than those of any other power – were world-wide, but that it lacked the armed strength to protect them adequately.[12]

To cap it all, Hitler took advantage of this confusion by moving into the Rhineland in March 1936, as the French had always suspected he would. And, once again, a whole cluster of reasons overwhelmed those few who wished to answer this violation of the Versailles and Locarno treaties. The French themselves had to move first, and didn't. The British public, it was claimed, would not understand a war merely to prevent the Germans from going 'into their own backyard'. The Labour Party and trades unions would be critical of any action. The Dominions would be even more disapproving. Economic uncertainties still clouded the horizon. The Chiefs of Staff, having agreed to send the country's miniscule reserves to the Mediterranean, warned that it could take two months to recall them. They were further worried at what they considered to be Britain's extreme vulnerability to air attack.[13] Ironically, of course, once the Germans took possession of the Rhineland the British government had even more cause for alarm about the proximity of the *Luftwaffe* – just as, once Mussolini had been allowed to assert himself in Abyssinia and (to a lesser extent) in Spain, the prospects of being able to send reinforcements through the Mediterranean to deal with a Far Eastern crisis became ever less likely.

By this stage, appeasement had become a very hybrid creature indeed – and it is therefore not surprising that later historians, like the apocryphal blind men feeling different parts of the elephant, have come away with varying impressions about the shape of this beast. It still possessed, for example, a very idealist and moral aspect, a belief in human rationality and justice, an abhorrence of war, and a willingness to satisfy the grievances of those wronged. It had, secondly, a continued commercial and financial motivation, the desire to preserve the existing economic order, to further prosperity by increasing international trade and reducing armaments, and to avoid the cost and turbulences of war. Equally pragmatic, it may be argued, was Neville Chamberlain's domestic-political calculation, that the preservation of the Conservative Party with himself at its head would best be achieved by the successful resolution of threatening external issues, a success which would naturally confound his critics on the left and on the right. But the beast of appeasement also exhibited negative aspects: the fear of communism, and of British and French socialism, by many Conservatives; the traditional isolationism 'from Europe, reinforced by the urgings of the Rothermere and Beaverbrook press, and by messages from the Dominions; and, spreading with some speed, an apprehension of defeat, of aerial bombardment, of catastrophic loss. It is this latter aspect in particular which must cause one to doubt whether the appeasement of Germany between, say, 1936 and 1939 was fully in that tradition of the careful maintenance of 'British interests' which some scholars have seen going right back to the age of Canning.[14] There now were signs of a nervousness, a lack of certainty, and a fear which, while not the predominant features of Chamberlain's Cabinet, would be hard to detect in the deliberations of ministers and opinion-makers in the days of Palmerston or Salisbury.

By this stage, too, it is possible to detect some fissures in what previously had been close to a 'national consensus' in the British attitude towards Germany. Few, if any, Britons were yet willing to face the possibility of war, but there were now several groups who dissented from the official policy of seeking by all means to conciliate Hitler. In part, this trend may be ascribed to the slightly earlier collapse of belief in the efficacy of the League of Nations, for that had compelled various sections of the left to reassess their tactics. Many committed socialists and communists went off to fight the fascist dictatorships on the battlefields of Spain, and many more campaigned at home for a 'Popular Front'. The trades unions, and especially such leaders as Bevin and Citrine, became increasingly hostile to Nazi internal policies and disapproved of the Labour Party's stand against rearmament. And politicians such as Attlee and Dalton now found it useful to suggest that the government's appeasement strategy was a capitalist device, just as they had alleged years earlier that the 'unfair' treatment of Germany was a consequence of the establishment's adherence to a bad old system. One may suspect, too, that these attacks were all the easier to launch because the avuncular, reassuring Baldwin was succeeded as Prime Minister in May 1937 by Chamberlain, a much colder, more authoritarian figure who displayed no wish to conciliate his domestic critics.

Furthermore, it is worth noting that the anti-appeasers were not confined to the left of the political spectrum. There were also Conservative opponents, Amery, Nicolson, Churchill, Keyes, Bracken, who were later to be joined by Eden and Duff Cooper: although before Munich they remained a small, unco-ordinated and in part unorthodox cluster, neither able to shake Chamberlain's hold over the Conservative Party in general, nor to make much impact with their criticisms of concessions in Europe and in the colonial sphere. Moreover, these critics – like many government supporters – were often divided among themselves; some favoured economic appeasement but opposed colonial concessions, and vice versa. There were few united fronts, and there was much more grey than black and white. Until Hitler himself discredited the overall policy of appeasement, Chamberlain could not be brought down by his diffuse domestic rivals.[15]

The new Prime Minister did not so much alter earlier British policies towards Germany as carry them out with more energy and conviction. He was quite certain that the public would not tolerate being dragged into a war, especially over some obscure east-European dispute. He knew from his years at the Treasury how precarious the economic position was. He preferred spending on domestic items rather than upon armaments. He had little faith in the French and still less in the isolationist Americans; and his distrust of Russia was profound. In addition, the strategic advice he received was more insistent and pessimistic than ever. In December 1937 the Chiefs of Staff argued that

> we cannot foresee the time when our defence forces will be strong enough to safeguard our trade, territory and vital interests against Germany, Italy and Japan at the same time . . . [we cannot] exaggerate the importance from the point of view of Imperial Defence of any political or international action which could be taken to reduce the number of our potential enemies and to gain the support of potential allies.[16]

While the Foreign Office thus fretted that military weaknesses restricted its diplomatic hand, the Chiefs of Staff took the contrary approach that the dilemma would only be eased when political steps were taken to buy off one or more of the revisionist powers. This, however, was much more difficult to achieve with totalitarian states than had been the case with, say, Lansdowne's conciliation of the USA and France after 1900. The summer of 1937 had seen renewed Japanese expansion into China, which further exposed the inability of the League powers or the USA to prevent this. Italy under the erratic Mussolini offered a better chance, but Il Duce's temperament made any Mediterranean deal unreliable and it was difficult to see where Britain could offer large-scale concessions in that vital region. The course of the Spanish Civil War, and in particular the Italian interventions in it, opened up yet another vulnerable 'flank' in the imperial defence system, albeit one never as serious as the looming threat from central Europe. Nevertheless, Chamberlain persisted in his efforts to woo Mussolini, this being one of the major reasons for Eden's resignation as Foreign Secretary early in 1938 and his replacement by the more pliant Halifax; but the event was also symptomatic of the Prime Minister's belief that a thorough settlement with the dictators was feasible, provided one was single-minded enough. In the meantime, it would also be prudent to push ahead faster with the rearmament programme, especially in aerial defence.

This, above all, was the two-pronged policy to be carried out towards Germany as the critical year of 1938 unfolded. A bold and decisive diplomacy, of anticipating Hitler's actions and satisfying all legitimate grievances – in return, of course, for Berlin's agreeing to be bound by a general settlement – was the best way to keep the peace; and, if a German-instigated war in Europe could thereby be headed off, then any territorial readjustment could be cemented by various forms of economic aid, possible colonial cessions, and so on. It was, in other words, to be understood as a far more sensible stratagem for preserving the international order than a purely negative stance, clinging obstinately to the 1919 boundaries as the French tended to do.

One difficulty in carrying out this policy was that Hitler might not wait while the British bustled around, negotiating concessions here and there, and hinting at a return of the

German colonies. In March 1938, for example, the German Army moved into Austria and swiftly took over that country. If this *Anschluss* was hardly unexpected in London, its timing and the speed with which it was done upset the British. Yet it was also clear that no one among the British decision-makers was going to threaten war or sanctions simply to stop Germans joining Germans, especially when Italy had acquiesced in Hitler's move and France at that moment had no government in office. As Chamberlain explained to the Commons, 'nothing could have arrested the action by Germany unless we and others with us had been prepared to use force to prevent it.'[17] Yet these were retrospective rationalizations to account for London's passivity; an Austro-German union was quite a tolerable proposition in itself. What was upsetting was the peremptory German style, which increased the uncertainties throughout Europe just as the British sought to allay them.

Partly on this account, London was much better prepared to intervene diplomatically when the next crisis arose, for it took no genius to see that Hitler would now want to settle the problem of the Sudeten Germans within Czechoslovakia. Furthermore, this was an altogether more dangerous issue, since most Czechs wanted to resist the German pressure and since France was bound to come to Prague's assistance (as indeed was Russia). German moves against Czechoslovakia, in other words, could well instigate a chain of events that would embroil the British in another great war, however much they had endeavoured to keep clear of direct military commitments to eastern Europe.

The efforts of Chamberlain and his government to defuse this situation are well known and easily told.[18] From March 1938 onwards the French were repeatedly warned that Britain had no obligation to defend Czechoslovakia, and urged to put pressure on Benes and his fellow Czechs to do all they could to avoid a showdown with Germany. By May, with the tension rising inside the Sudetenland and reports reaching London of German troop movements, the British were compelled to intervene more directly, with diplomatic messages to Berlin and Prague. In August, Lord Runciman acted as a mediator between the Czech government and the German (and other) minorities, but all to no avail. Hitler's speeches, the military preparations, and the state of near-civil war within Czechoslovakia made concessions by either side almost impossible. With a German invasion imminent, and the French apparently unable either to deter Hitler or to evade their treaty responsibilities to the Czechs, Chamberlain resolved to try to settle the issue by direct negotiations with the German leader. The Berchtesgaden talks of 15–16 September where the principle of some form of secession of the Sudetenland was agreed upon; the Godesberg nego-tiations of 22–23 September, where Hitler's peremptory demands for a takeover were so blatant as to make even the appeasing British and French statesmen declare that the terms were unacceptable, and to fear that war was close at hand; and the famous Munich meeting of 29–30 September, which modulated the timing but not the essence of the German acquisitions, were the three chief diplomatic milestones in this journey to avoid war. When Chamberlain returned from the final visit to receive the adulation of much of the press, Conservative Party and many other Britons relieved that a conflict had been avoided, he brought back with him a statement which he and Hitler had signed, affirming 'the desire of our two people never to go to war with one another again'. That was a pledge which was to be broken in less than twelve months.

Munich: the Anatomy

The Czech crisis of 1938 was not only the high point of appeasement but, as compared with the German *faits accomplis* against the Rhineland, Austria and later Prague and Poland, also the most protracted. It therefore offers, and always has offered to the historian, the largest store of evidence about the motives behind British policy. To those studying background influences upon Whitehall's diplomacy, the events of May to October 1938 offer not one or two but a whole concatenation of motives and pressures to explain the decisions taken by Chamberlain and his colleagues. There are so many, in fact, that for the purposes of clarity it may be best to list them, in no particular order of importance:

(i) *Defence weaknesses.* This is a motive much seized on by historians and especially by Conservative apologists for Chamberlain eager to demonstrate the Prime Minister's wisdom in postponing a showdown until Britain's armed forces had been further strengthened. There is, to be sure, an enormous amount of documentary evidence for this, if only because the Chiefs of Staff and CID had been cataloguing the nation's military deficiencies for some time. In a broad survey of 21 March 1938, the defence chiefs had paid tribute to Germany's increased striking power but found that France's army, air force and industrial strength had waned over the past few years. Moreover, French morale had been affected not only by domestic fissures but also by the new threat from its Spanish flank and by the withdrawal of Belgium into neutrality. The Czech forces, although significant, had had their flank turned by the German occupation of Austria. Britain's naval superiority was admitted to be useless as an influence upon the equilibrium in central Europe, and her army was so insignificant in continental terms that the Chiefs of Staff had been opposed to conversations with their French and Belgian opposite numbers early in 1938 since they had no ground forces to offer! Perhaps the most worrying message of all was that Britain's air defences were still judged inadequate against the estimated force which the *Luftwaffe* might despatch; and this argument predictably touched a sensitive nerve among the politicians. In short, the Chiefs of Staff, too, were appeasers at this time. As General Ironside noted: 'Chamberlain is of course right. We have not the means of defending ourselves and he knows it ... We cannot expose ourselves now to a German attack. We simply commit suicide if we do'.[19] Finally, it has been pointed out that during the 'breathing-space' between Munich and the outbreak of war in 1939 vital improvements were made in the British radar network and anti-aircraft-gun system, and in the number of modern fighter squadrons (Hurricane and Spitfire) available for air defence.

Against this catalogue of British defence weaknesses in 1938, it needs to be remarked that both the Chiefs of Staff and Cabinet were making some excessively gloomy predictions. None of the strategical and economic problems which so worried the advisers to Hitler at this time was mentioned; nor did anyone consider whether a Germany intent upon crushing Czechoslovakia and warding off the latter's French (and possibly Russian) ally would actually deploy the greater part of the *Luftwaffe* to attack British cities – a strategy which the Germans had given little thought to and were not very well equipped to implement. In fact, no one seems to have enquired 'What can the RAF do to attack Germany?' or posed the very interesting supplementary question, 'If very little, why should we suppose that the *Luftwaffe* can do a great deal to damage us?' No one made a proper assessment of the Czech capacity to resist or slow down a German invasion.[20] No one asked the critical question, 'What will be left of the balance of power if Czechoslovakia is dismantled?' And no one, with the possible exception of Duff Cooper, appears before this crisis to have been disturbed that the army had been *deliberately* kept small and thus incapable of carrying out a European field role. At the beginning of the Munich crisis, Inskip reminded his colleagues that 'we had based our rearmament programme on what was necessary for our own defences. We had concentrated on the navy and the air ...'[21] This was by no means an accident or an oversight. From the early 1930s onwards Chamberlain himself had been preaching that 'our resources will be more profitably engaged in the air and on sea, than in building up great armies', and this tendency was reinforced by the writings of the influential *Times* defence correspondent, Basil Liddell Hart, in favour of the so-called 'British Way in Warfare'. Even the Chiefs of Staff themselves, although on occasions to be found reminding the Cabinet of the need to preserve the European equilibrium, were also undermining that strategy by pointing out that 'The greater our commitments to Europe, the less will be our ability to secure our Empire and its communications.'[22] In other words, although one might concede that the government was *subjectively* worried about British defence weaknesses, this argument begs several significant questions about the *objective* reality of its judgement and about the alternative strategies which they avoided implementing or even examining. Whether or not the postponement of war for a year saved Britain, there is a strong case for arguing that it lost Europe.

(ii) *Extra-European obligations.* Where the Chiefs of Staff had more validity was in their frequent reference to the fact that there were other potential enemies to consider as well as the Germans. They feared a war over Czechoslovakia was quite likely to bring in Italy, and also to tempt Japan to make further moves in the Far East. Yet, as they noted, 'War against Japan, Germany and Italy simultaneously in 1938 is a commitment which neither the present nor the projected strength of our defence forces is designed to meet, even if we were in alliance with France and Russia . . .'[23] The only way Japan might be held at bay, for example, was by stripping the Mediterranean theatre of British naval and air units, which in turn left that region vulnerable to an attack by Italy. Even if there were no major conflicts overseas while war was being waged against Germany, imperial commitments still tied down a large portion of the British armed forces. More and more troops were being sent to deal with the worsening crisis in Palestine; and it was difficult to imagine that many of the forty-five battalions stationed in India could be withdrawn to Europe. In the view of that influential 'appeaser', Lord Lothian, 'Nehru is openly awaiting the next world war to let loose revolution in India.'[24] Yet while it was perfectly understandable for the British to seek to preserve their imperial position, it was equally valid for the French, Czechs and others hoping for London's aid to suspect that this was a deliberate choice of priorities, and that the obverse side of this positive preference and concern for the Empire was that well-known British . . .

(iii) *Tradition of isolationism.* Chamberlain himself put this most clearly – and notoriously – when on 27 September 1938 he openly confessed to his horror at the idea of going to war 'because of a quarrel in a far-away country between people of whom we know nothing'. But was this not a common British prejudice? Even before the British government moved forward to mediate, a *Daily Mail* article of 6 May by Lord Rothermere himself insisted: 'Czechoslovakia is not of the remotest concern to us.'[25] And Beaverbrook's *Daily Express*, which frequently asserted, 'There will be no European war,' carried a statement from its isolationist owner on 22 September: 'Britain never gave any pledge to protect Czechoslovakia . . . No moral obligation rests on us.'[26] For two decades the government and the greater part of public opinion had sought to repudiate the fatal intervention of August 1914 and to return to the Victorian policy of non-intervention in the affairs of eastern Europe, a region whose local politics and border disputes always remained a puzzle. This was why, with the exception of certain Conservatives (Austen Chamberlain, Duff Cooper, Spears, Churchill), most Britons in the inter-war years resented the French: not only did the latter interfere in eastern Europe and keep up an unjustified national resentment of Germany, but France's very existence reminded the British that they, too, could not fully free themselves from the fate of the continent. Hence the strong pressure put upon Paris during the Munich crisis *not* to fight on behalf of the Czechs.

(iv) *Dominion pressures.* For at least a generation, as we have noted above, the urgings of the self-governing Dominions had formed an important counter to the pleas of the French and other Europeans for a greater British commitment to the continent. The rationale behind the stance of Australia and New Zealand was well known, and had become even more plausible as the Japanese threats to the *status quo* in Asia and the Pacific grew (which did not stop the New Zealand government from being the only one which unreservedly accepted its obligations to fight if Britain did). The voices of isolationism were much more the consequence of domestic pressures. These views had been forcibly put at the 1937 Imperial Conference, where Mackenzie King had criticized various schemes for common defence arrangements, and General Hertzog had warned that if a European war 'did come because England continued to associate with France in a policy in respect of central and eastern Europe calculated to threaten Germany's existence through unwillingness to set right the injustices flowing from the Treaty of Versailles, South Africa cannot be expected to take part in the war . . .'[27] When the Munich crisis developed, therefore, the Dominions' High Commissioners in London were exceedingly active, and their pressure for a peaceful settlement was faithfully relayed to Chamberlain and his colleagues by the Colonial Secretary, Malcolm MacDonald, by Geoffrey Dawson of *The Times* and by other pro-Empire intermediaries. Once again, it is worth suggesting that their arguments for appeasing Hitler provided merely a reinforcement for the British Prime Minister, who had reached his own conclusion quite independently; but it no doubt proved rather useful for him to remind waverers in the Cabinet that a war might divide the Empire.

(v) *British public opinion*. Although sentiment in the country as a whole had been strongly opposed to war since 1919 and to any continental obligations which might lead to war, this national consensus was breaking up somewhat by the time of Munich. It was true, of course, that there was a massive and perfectly natural shudder of relief that a conflict had been avoided, and this mood in turn caused the Labour leaders to be wary of being cast in the unusual role of warmongers. The scenes of jubilation in the House of Commons and in the country at large upon Chamberlain's return from Munich were not manufactured, nor were the thousands of private letters of praise sent to the Prime Minister in the days following. Yet it is also true that there were substantial voices outside and even within the government who had urged Chamberlain to take a firmer stand and did not agree with *The Times*'s sycophantic greeting that 'No conqueror returning from victory on the battlefield had come adorned with nobler laurels.' In the intense Cabinet debates Duff Cooper, Stanley, Hore-Belisha and de la Warr had been much less eager to appease, and the first-named resigned after Munich, damning the settlement in a moving Commons speech. Churchill, Nicolson, Amery and a few other Conservative rebels had shared these feelings all along. The biggest seismic shift, however, had taken place among the centre-left ranks of British politics, less for strategic than for moral reasons: the same internationalist principles which had earlier caused the Labour and Liberal parties, the Trades Union Congress, the *Manchester Guardian*, Robert Cecil, Gilbert Murray and other 'idealists' to favour the League of Nations now impelled them to call for an armed bloc of peace-loving states to resist Hitler.[28]

It is difficult to see, therefore, what exactly was meant by Chamberlain's frequent warnings to the Cabinet that a war would bring national disunity. No doubt the pro-Germans within the Conservative Party, and the still considerable numbers of pacifists, would have objected – but would the left have protested? The situation was now rather altered from the age of Lloyd George and Baldwin, when it was (perhaps correctly) feared that an assertive foreign policy would antagonize the Labour Party and the trade unions. Indeed, Chamberlain's attempt to persist in his policy of securing a lasting and mutually satisfactory settlement with Germany well after Munich and even after Prague, when public opinion was turning fast against any further appeasement, suggests that his mind was made up without much regard for the 'great oracle'. To repeat: there can be no doubt of the widespread horror of war, especially for the sake of a country not well known to the British population, nor can one mistake the relief felt that the Munich deal had avoided such a conflict; but it would be naïve to assume that Chamberlain and his close colleagues were mere weather-vanes, pointing in the direction of the prevailing winds of public opinion; and just as wrong to assume that there were no contrary winds.

(vi) *Domestic-political calculation.* This is a related although significantly distinct explanation of the British government's motives in 1938. A successful termination of the outstanding tensions in Europe without recourse to war would certainly enhance Chamberlain's position within the Cabinet and the Conservative Party at large, blocking potential rivals like Eden and keeping more forthright critics like Churchill in isolation – although it is also true that there was little sign of backbench discontent before the spring of 1939. Perhaps more significantly, these successes in foreign policy could – if trumpeted by the Tory press – sustain the party's appeal in the country at large and thus deflate the criticisms made by Attlee, Bevin, Dalton and others of the government's handling of affairs as the election year of 1940 drew closer. By extension, this policy of successful and peaceful coexistence with Hitler would not only disconcert the Labour Party tactically but it would also mean the avoidance of a long-drawn-out war during which – if the 1914–18 conflict was any guide – there would be a further shift in the domestic social order towards the working classes. Already the Labour Party spokesmen and trade unions were making it clear that, if war came, the price for their full-hearted support would be the 'conscription of wealth' as well as of manpower, and the nationalization of certain key industries. Churchill, Eden and their friends might have been willing to pay this price; but there was little sign that Chamberlain, or many industrialists, or most of the Conservative Party, were. As Oliver Stanley, the President of the Board of Trade, put it to an acquaintance early in September 1938, '. . . whether we win or lose [a war], it will be the end of everything we stand for.'[29] Stabilizing the European scene, it has been argued, was another way to ensure that the domestic structure of politics and power remained intact.

(vii) *Economic restraints.* Although there is little evidence that economic factors were widely debated or referred to by British decision-makers during the Czech crisis, this is not altogether surprising. As one scholar has pointed out, the appeasement of Germany in 1938 'was not devised in the heat of the moment . . . Both the defence ration and appeasement were the result of the government's carefully calculated assessment of the economic, social, political and strategic realities that Britain faced . . .'[30] Ministers brought up in the shadow of the First World War did not need to remind each other in September 1938 just how costly another great-power conflict would be. They were already aware that the increase in armaments spending hitherto was affecting the delicate budgetary balance. In 1935 defence had taken 15 per cent of central government expenditures – £137 million out of a total £841 million; in 1937 its share had risen to 26 per cent – £256 million out of a total £978 million; and in 1938 it was to jump again, to 38 per cent – £397 million out of £1033 million. Taxes alone, although steadily increased after 1936, were unable to cover expenditure and in 1937 the Treasury had reluctantly agreed to a National Defence

Loan. Near the end of that year there occurred a commercial down-swing. The unemployment figures rose ominously, prices were increasing, the balance of payments was worsening, sterling was starting to weaken *vis-à-vis* the dollar, and the international money markets were gloomy and volatile. The early stages of the Czech crisis had seen a large-scale withdrawal of currency reserves from Britain to safer shores. Yet all this would be but a mere preliminary to the economic losses which an all-out war against Germany (and perhaps other states) would bring. The avoidance of military conflict was closely allied to the avoidance of national bankruptcy.

(viii) *Fear of Soviet communism.* Once a fairly popular interpretation, this has now lost much of its credibility except among party-line historians in present-day Russia. It is true that at Berchtesgaden in 1937 Halifax seems to have referred to Germany as an anti-communist bastion and to have hinted at British willingness to see peaceful adjustments to the *status quo* in eastern Europe in Germany's favour; and six months later he urged Ribbentrop that 'We should not let [the Czech crisis] get out of hand, for then the only ones to benefit would be communists.'[31] It is also the case that Chamberlain shared this dislike of the Soviet regime, and had no wish to include Russia in the Munich Conference. Yet, although many British Conservatives felt communism to be as bad as (or worse than) national socialism, other members of the 'ruling class' like Churchill and Eden did not, and were to urge instead co-operation with Stalin. Most important of all, the contention that appeasement was an attempt to turn Germany against the home of world communism distorts the order of the British government's priorities. Bolshevism was intensely disliked, but much less feared than in the 1920s, and Russia is hardly mentioned in the Cabinet debates during the Czech crisis, compared with the frequent references to strategic weaknesses, public opinion, the Dominions, and so on.

(ix) *Moral idealism*. This is another feature which, although partly valid, has probably carried too large a weight of historical explanation. There can be no doubt that the British Cabinet, and Chamberlain in particular, shared the widespread public abhorrence of war and desired instead peace, goodwill, stability. War, said Chamberlain on one occasion, 'wins nothing, cures nothing, ends nothing'. It was also true that many, possibly most, Britons felt that parts of the Treaty of Versailles had been unfair to Germany and that the claims of the Sudeten Germans in 1938 were not unjustified. The Prime Minister's earnest search for peace impressed many observers, and caused sceptics in the USA, Canada and elsewhere to admit that this time the British government could not be accused of responsibility for a war. Yet the notion that appeasement was essentially a policy derived from certain moral principles looked increasingly thin by 1938, not only because opponents were attacking Chamberlain's policy precisely on the opposite grounds that Hitler's demands *violated* western ideals, but also because the Wilsonian sentiments characteristic of earlier British governments had become mixed up (and watered down) with arguments of military weakness, political expediency, and economy. Halifax's high-church conscience was clearly touched, for example, by the thought that the policy towards Germany was prudent rather than right.[32]

Should one attempt at all to get these various motives in order? It is not difficult to send some interpretations (fear of Soviet communism, influence of the Dominions) to the bottom of the list, and to place others (defence weaknesses, domestic-political calculation, economic necessity) near the top. But beyond this the exercise becomes rather arcane. As one historian has observed,

If one begins to tot up all the plausible motivations for appeasement . . . one sees that these are far more than enough to explain it. It was massively over-determined;

any other policy in 1938 would have been an astounding, almost inexplicable divergence from the norm. Under such circumstances, it does not even help much to try to seek out the main cause or causes; when everything seems to lead towards a certain decision, it is often impossible even for the person who makes the decision to know what was to be the most important factor in it."

The Waning of Appeasement, 1938–9

Whatever the particular circumstances and arguments of 1938, appeasement is probably best understood in general terms as a 'natural' policy for a small island-state gradually losing its place in world affairs, shouldering military and economic burdens which were increasingly too great for it, and developing internally from an oligarchic to a more democratic society in which sentiments in favour of the pacific and rational settlement of disputes were widely held. Yet to say that appeasement was 'natural' in the sense used here need not also imply that it was the most superior and efficacious policy; for the real dilemma facing British decision-makers was not that they had to steer the right course through the storm to the safe harbour beyond, but that there was no such haven: there was no good or 'correct' policy. Appeasement had its dangers and disadvantages but so, too, did the opposite course of action. This latter fact, however, did not deter British public opinion and, more slowly and much more reluctantly, the British government from abandoning previous attitudes in the eleven months after Munich.

The policy of appeasement ultimately collapsed because of further aggressions on Hitler's part, and because the majority of the British political nation was no longer willing to tolerate such aggressions. In between this exogenous and endogenous pressure Chamberlain and his closest Cabinet colleagues manoeuvred, attempting to balance out all the considerations and to achieve their original aims with as little alteration in their methods as possible. Precautions had to be taken against a 'mad-dog act' by Hitler, but the Prime Minister still obviously hoped to the end that a pacific settlement of outstanding issues would be achieved and refused to accept his critics' assertion that Munich had been a 'disaster'.

The state of the national economy after 1938 increased, if anything, the logic of preserving peace. Whatever the optimistic pronouncements from Downing Street about the Anglo-German accord which Chamberlain brought back from Munich, there is no doubt that the Cabinet and its advisers had been shocked by the country's vulnerability during the September crisis and were resolved to accelerate the rearmament programmes of all the services. Against the pressures from the Chiefs of Staff and the anxieties of the Cabinet, the Treasury could now offer much less resistance. Nevertheless – and this is the important point – it continued to warn of the potential ruin which lay ahead as a consequence of this transformation from a peacetime to a wartime economy. The balance of payments was worsening rapidly, the standard rate of income tax was higher than at any time since 1919, and yet there was no way in which the swelling defence expenditures could be paid for except by going to the money markets once again for another large-scale loan. This itself was a delicate business since the very action placed a question mark over the country's long-term credit and weakened sterling against the dollar just as Britain was importing increased supplies of munitions and other materials to be paid for in gold or dollars. High interest rates, draconian fiscal controls, and a sterling crisis loomed before the Treasury's eyes. As one alarmed Under-Secretary there put it, in March 1939:

Defence expenditure is now at a level which must seriously call into question the country's ability to meet it, and a continuance at this level may well result in a situation in which the completion of our material preparations against attack is frustrated by a weakening of our economic stability, which renders us incapable of standing the strain of war or even of maintaining those material defences in peace.[34]

In view of such messages, which were bound in any case to echo Chamberlain's long-standing apprehensions, it is scarcely surprising to observe how the Prime Minister sought throughout the first eight months of 1939 to improve the atmosphere between Britain and Germany; and it is even less surprising that the British pursuit of appeasement by economic means was secretly accelerated. From London in this period came a whole flow of hints about a financial *détente*, an increase in foreign credits for Germany so that it could purchase British colonial produce, commercial arrangements in eastern Europe, and so on. Such measures could not only stimulate international trade and offer some potential assistance to the flagging British economy, but they could also increase confidence on the nervous bourses of the West. Furthermore, since the British suspected that Germany's own critical economic problems might compel Hitler to solve them by some spectacular foreign move, it was vital to hold out to the so-called 'moderate' Nazis the alternative possibility of surmounting those problems through international co-operation, commercial prosperity and peace. Ultimately, of course, this strategy was *still* based upon the assumption that the German leadership also adhered to the basic tenets of the liberal political economy – a remarkably myopic view at a time when, for example, the British commercial attaché at the Berlin embassy was repeatedly warning his superiors that Germany seemed only interested in having continued access to sterling so as to stockpile tropical raw materials for a future war.[35] Once again, London's dilemma – although not admitted by the economic appeasers – was that it had merely a choice between two dangerous positions: to plan for war at the risk of undermining its own economic strength; or to continue its search for co-operation at the cost of increasing the power of a potential enemy.

Britain's defence position improved, at least in part, as 1939 developed. This was, of course, a consequence of that increased spending upon the armed forces which was simultaneously weakening the economy; but it was a great relief to see the network of radar stations extended, new squadrons of Hurricane and Spitfire fighters being formed, new classes of destroyers and escort vessels joining the fleet, the construction of heavy ships accelerated, and anti-aircraft measures being improved.

The most remarkable change occurred, however, in the army's role and future capabilities. For two decades it had been emasculated so as to render impossible an effective 'continental commitment', but by late 1938/early 1939 such a policy was crumbling. The French, shattered by the collapse of their eastern alliance system, were hinting that they might give up the diplomatic struggle against Hitler unless Britain provided *military* aid; and even if they did fight alone, the French might be overwhelmed by a more powerful Germany. And, as the British Chiefs of Staff pointed out, 'It is difficult to see how the security of the United Kingdom could be maintained if France were forced to capitulate and therefore defence of the former may have to include a share in the land defence of French territory.'[36] Rumours of a possible German invasion of Holland, or of an eastward strike, increased the British fear that if they did not act swiftly the entire continental equilibrium would be deranged. In the spring of 1939 the Cabinet decided, with grudging Treasury approval, to meet the army's demand for a European Field Force of six divisions, with Territorial Army reserves and a large-scale expansion of the latter; staff talks with the French were approved; and, only a little later, under French and American urgings, conscription was introduced – the first time ever in peacetime. Things were changing at a gallop, even if Chamberlain still clung to his belief that war was not yet inevitable.

Whether the measures would be sufficient to deal with a *Wehrmacht* whose own forces were expanding – the number of the critically important German armoured divisions doubled between 1938 and 1939 – and whose industrial base had been widened by the absorption of the Sudetenland, was an open question. They might have improved the aerial defence of the United Kingdom, but would they be adequate to contain German expansionism overland? Britain could offer diplomatic support to Rumania, for example, but how could it prevent Germany from seizing the oilfields there and thus becoming less vulnerable than ever to maritime blockade? What was more, would this new British concentration upon the European theatre affect its power elsewhere in the world?

Suspicions of Germany's intentions inevitably increased London's desire to improve relations with Italy after Munich and, with differences over Spain patched up, Chamberlain visited Rome in January 1939 in an effort to win over Mussolini. The signs, however, were not promising: Franco-Italian relations were bitter, and in April Italy attacked Albania. This meant that the British needed to reinforce their Mediterranean positions, something which in turn could only be done at the expense of their Far Eastern obligations. At the 1937 Imperial Conference, the Chiefs of Staff had assured the Dominions that the United Kingdom and Singapore were 'the keystones on which the British Commonwealth of Nations depended', and that events in the Mediterranean would not interfere with the despatch of a fleet to the Far East. By February 1939, this was discreetly reversed: a substantial naval reinforcement of Singapore, it was agreed, 'must depend on our resources and on the state of war in the European theatre.'[37] Unable to trust Italy, the British were forced to hope for Japanese inactivity in the Far

East. Since the period 1938-9 also saw the continuation of Anglo-Japanese disagreements over China – where Japan, unable to defeat the Chinese nationalists, was intent upon stopping British economic and moral support to the latter – this was obviously a very shaky policy. Unwilling to abandon the Chinese, and their own very considerable material interests in China, the British were always aware that they could not threaten to use force: in June 1939, for example, the Cabinet decided to make concessions in their quarrel with Japan at Tientsin, since the Admiralty was warning that a Far Eastern war would be impossible for it.

Seen from this global perspective, in other words, London was still involved in the gigantic and risky juggling-act of preserving its interests with sorely-stretched defence forces. Only in regard to Europe did things look a little better than in 1938, and yet that optimism was based upon two rather dubious arguments: the first, already mentioned, was the improvement in Britain's aerial defences, which was no consolation to the Poles or the French; and the second was the belief, put forward by the Chiefs of Staff, but also accepted by Chamberlain, that the Western democracies were in a better position than Germany and Italy to win a long war, with the emphasis upon economic staying-power. This latter argument, with its traditional assumptions about the 'British way in warfare', was no doubt shared by many in Whitehall; but since the Treasury was *simultaneously* warning that Britain could not sustain a long war, it is difficult – indeed impossible – to believe that all of the government were confident about the nation's capacity to endure a struggle with the Axis powers.

If all this generally gave British statesmen further incentives to preserve a peaceful and non-committal policy, it was to no avail. Whenever their hopes rose that a policy of co-existence might be succeeding, that optimism was dashed by further action by the dictators. Whereas Chamberlain wished Munich to be seen as a 'peace with honour', Hitler soon began to claim it as a decisive victory, a rout of the

Western democracies. Another horrific illustration of the nature of the Nazi regime came with the detailed press coverage of the program against the Jews during the night of 10 November 1938: the *Picture Post*'s coverage of 'A New Dark Age in Europe' and unflattering portraits of the Nazi leaders were yet another reminder to the British public of the inner beastliness of the country they had sought to appease. A little later, the German government announced its intention of building up to 100 per cent of British submarine strength, a manifestly hostile gesture against the island-state. This was followed, around the turn of the year, by those rumours of a German strike westwards or eastwards which so perturbed the Cabinet that they abandoned their reservations about a 'continental commitment'. Then, on 15 March 1939, came a much greater blow: the German occupation of the 'rump' state of Czechoslovakia, a country guaranteed by the great powers at the Munich Conference only six months earlier and no longer possessing a substantial ethnic German minority in need of rescue by the Fatherland. This was expansionist power-politics, and nothing more. Not to be outdone, Mussolini, as noted above, attacked Albania in the month following.

To British statesmen seeking to 'stabilize' the European system, these were disconcerting events; to a growing segment of the British public, they were outrageous. In a really significant way, Chamberlain's critics on the left and the right were beginning to converge. Papers such as the *News Chronicle* and the *Manchester Guardian* praised right-wing Conservative rebels and called for the entry of Eden, Churchill and Duff Cooper into the Cabinet. The Labour Party, having shed its pacifism, now called for assistance to be given to all states willing to stand up to the dictators and for the mobilization of national resources. At the same time, the Conservative anti-appeasers were losing some of their traditional aversion to Soviet Russia and during the Prague crisis they and the left called for an Anglo-French-Russian *bloc* to halt German aggression – a curious return to the pre-

1914 Triple Entente. Military necessity now forced all sorts of compromises with ideological principles: 'I am not prepared to regard Soviet Russia as a freedom-loving nation but we cannot do without her now,' Commander Bower told the Commons. 'I know they have shot a lot of people but there are some 170,000,000 of them left.'[38] Churchill and not Chamberlain, it was being muttered on the backbenches, had been right all along, a suggestion which percolated upwards to prey upon the consciences of Halifax and other ministers.

This 'gap' between the government and public opinion was most clearly perceivable following the German *coup* against Prague in March. To the former, which had always assumed that eastern Europe was a German sphere of political influence at least, which was eager to keep the discussion upon Anglo-German co-operation going, and even more keen to avoid being pushed into a conflict from which probably only the USA and the Labour Party would benefit, Hitler's fresh act of aggression was regrettable but nothing more. The first reactions of Chamberlain, Halifax, Simon and Hoare were therefore complacent and anodyne: as Simon explained, it was now impossible to fulfil a guarantee to a state which had just ceased to exist. The explosion of discontent which followed, in the Conservative Party and in traditional pro-government papers like the *Observer*, forced a sudden change of tone; by 17 March Chamberlain was publicly warning that 'any attempt to dominate the world by force was one which the Democracies must resist'.[39]

In private, of course, the attempts to settle with the Germans went on; but in public, the government was being carried along into actions which it would never have contemplated a year earlier. At the end of March, under pressure from various directions to 'stop Hitler', it joined France in pledging support to Poland if the latter was attacked by Germany. This was, strategically and politically, a much more difficult obligation than those which successive

British governments had sought to avoid for the past two decades; but no one now seemed to remember Austen Chamberlain's ill-fated quip about the Polish Corridor not being worth the bones of a British Grenadier. In line with this new-found urgency to assure the potential victims of the dictator's next strike, Britain and France gave similar guarantees against aggression to Greece and Rumania a fortnight later. All these measures appeared in retrospect to be fateful steps, full of implications – indeed, the Polish guarantee was to be the legal cause for the Anglo-French declaration of war when Germany invaded that country. At the time of their creation, however, these guarantees were simply an immediate and scarcely thought-out response to demands for action.

The government's next major step was altogether more drawn-out and agonizing: an approach to Russia for joint co-operation against Germany. This was something being urged upon the Cabinet from all sides: by Churchill and the Conservative anti-appeasers, by Lloyd George, by most of the press, by the Labour and Liberal parties. That did not make the policy itself any more attractive to the Prime Minister, who already had many reasons for not wishing to see an Anglo-Russian alliance created; it would be regarded as a victory for his domestic critics, not himself; it would destroy forever the delicate attempts to improve relations with Germany; Russian support was desired, on the whole, by the Chiefs of Staff but she was also assumed to be still weak and her army ineffective following Stalin's purges; contrarily, in the view of the Poles, she was too dangerous and ambitious to be allowed the right to place Russian divisions on Polish soil as a means of protection. There is little evidence that Stalin himself was enthusiastic about a pact with the West, and soon secret negotiations had begun with Germany for an eventual Russo-German 'carve-up' of Poland and the Baltic states. Yet the fruits of the Chamberlain-Halifax policy of hesitation and delay appeared to be bad on all counts; it contradicted the policy of trying to improve Anglo-German relations on the one hand, and it failed to gain a Soviet alliance and thus to erect a strong 'peace barrier' against German expansionism on the other. Once again, the British government's diplomacy looked incompetent. Most important of all, the failure – marked by the signing of the Nazi-Soviet Pact of 23 August 1939 – allowed Hitler to proceed with his plan to crush Poland in defiance of the recent British and French guarantees. It led immediately, in other words, to the outbreak of the Second World War itself.

The reactions in Britain to the Polish crisis in the summer of 1939 were a repetition of those over Prague a few months earlier. By now the Labour and Conservative anti-appeasers in the Commons were suspicious of Chamberlain, and refused to let Parliament adjourn lest negotiations with Hitler be concluded during the recess. These suspicions appeared justified in late August, as London urged Germans and Poles to settle their differences over Danzig; and even more so by 1 September, when the German attack commenced. For two days, while Poland was being bombed and shelled, Chamberlain and his colleagues hesitated, seeking to the last to find a *modus vivendi,* and also attempting to co-ordinate moves with the French, who were even more reluctant to plunge into war. But it was not to be. The public pressure upon the government, far greater than that of March, forced it reluctantly onwards. The left insisted upon upholding the obligation to Poland, the dissenting Tories clamoured for a declaration of war, the Conservative backbenchers now also wanted it, and even a Cabinet which had probably been the most docile so far that century to its Prime Minister's wishes felt that it could no longer be avoided. By the time of his disastrous, temporarizing speech to the Commons on the evening of 2 September, Chamberlain was virtually isolated, his supporters falling away on all sides, and Labour and Conservative MPs combining openly in their attacks upon him. At the very end of the day, and disregarding further French pleas for a delay because (as Halifax explained) of 'the difficult position which had arisen in the House of Commons',[40] the Cabinet resolved to send an ultimatum. The die had at last been cast.

The precise moment at which the Prime Minister himself decided war was inevitable is difficult to pinpoint; perhaps he had privately sensed for some time that it was impossible to avoid, but still also wished to be master of the situation. Furthermore, he had to wrestle in his mind with all the disadvantages, for the British Empire and for himself, of going to war even as he was being told by others that he must take such a step. Yet, although conscious of Britain's weaknesses and desperate to avoid the bloodshed of 1914–18, he also retained the assumption that the country could act as an independent great power. As the inheritor of a great tradition, he could never be completely ruthless and insist that it was not in Britain's best interests to guarantee and to fight for Poland. The weight of accumulated prestige and habits of mind, together with the domestic pressures, made a declaration of war unavoidable once it was clear that Hitler was not going to be deterred by the Anglo-Polish Alliance pledges.

This was an ironic death for the appeasement policy. For twenty years at least, and arguably much longer, the British political nation had tended to agree that a cheap, pacific, non-interventionist foreign policy suited the national interests. Appeasement was the course favoured by public opinion; it represented the 'middle ground', so secure against the impracticalities of the left and the right; and it was the means whereby Lloyd George, Baldwin, MacDonald and Chamberlain himself could bolster up their domestic positions and supervise Britain's economic recovery. By 1939, conditions had altered dramatically. Those considerations of morality, economy, global strategy and domestic affairs which made an external policy of compromise and concession *normally* appear to be the logical one were now working against appeasement. The moral repugnance against war was overwhelmed by outrage at

Hitler's wanton aggression; apprehensions about the economic costs of war were matched by fears of the *materiel* (and other) consequences of a Germany supreme in Europe; concern for Britain's global commitments could no longer check the vital need to preserve the European equilibrium; and a public once chary of foreign entanglements and war now criticized the government for failure to act. Chamberlain, as heir to and chief advocate of the policy of appeasement, had striven to ensure its prolongation by achieving a lasting peace with Germany. When this stratagem failed, he was then exposed to the full blast of contemporary and later criticism for having executed a diplomacy which satisfied neither the moral nor the practical requirements of the nation.

IV
Defiance and Decline, 1939–80

7. Structures and Attitudes

The Consequences of Economic Debilitation

The horns of the dilemma upon which all British leaders found themselves impaled during the final stages of the country's period as a great power have been described in the previous section. Either they could rearm and fight as vigorously as was necessary to preserve the country's security and possessions, but at the cost of further weakening its financial sinews; *or* they could prefer economic stability to military power, but only by reducing the existing armed strength and making it impossible to fulfil overseas commitments and to defend itself. Either choice implied loss and disadvantage; both, it is easy to say in retrospect, implied Britain's demotion to the status of a second-rank nation. What was more, this dilemma existed both throughout the Second World War itself and into the 'Cold War' era which followed. The only difference was that in wartime the British government gave priority to the fighting services, although with many an anxious glance at the weakening economy; whereas after 1945 it sought first and foremost to secure economic stability, although with many an anxious glance at its declining military capacities.

This dilemma the Treasury brought repeatedly to the Cabinet's attention during the crisis year of 1940, when the gaze of most people was fixed upon Norway, France, the Battle of Britain or the early stages of the North African campaign. If anything, the accession of Churchill as Prime Minister increased the economic anxieties, since his rejection of German overtures for a ceasefire and his determination to 'wage war, by sea, land and air, with all our might . . . however long and hard the road may be'¹ obviously implied the abandonment of Chamberlain's policy of husbanding resources. Armament production, already spiralling upwards at an unprecedented rate, was to be increased yet again: a firm commitment was made to equip a British Commonwealth Army of fifty-five divisions by 1942; production of the (very expensive) long-range bombers for the RAF was to be vastly expanded; and more aircraft-carriers were to be laid down for the Royal Navy. But there was a twofold flaw in all this. First, it enormously increased the importation of raw materials to satisfy the demands of a wartime economy. Moreover, since British industry itself could not possibly fulfil all those fresh orders, American firms were required to make up the difference – in aircraft, machine-tools, steel, lorries and other equipment. In addition, London took over all the outstanding French orders in the USA after June 1940. The consequence was a horrendous drain in Britain's holdings of gold and dollars, since these imports could not possibly be matched by exports: in the autumn of 1940, the volume of British exports was almost 40 per cent less than in 1935. By the middle of winter, the country was close to bankruptcy; and, just before the Lend-lease Act was passed by Congress in March 1941, all fresh purchasing abroad had had to be stopped.

Lend-lease provided succour, but at a cost. Like any bank manager, the United States government felt it necessary to dictate conditions before proffering benefits upon a needy customer. Britain's gold and dollar reserves were to be rigorously controlled in order to prevent them rising above the level thought to be desirable in Washington. No lend-lease goods could go into exports, nor could similar *British-made* products be sent to overseas markets lest this provoke resentment in United States business circles. Not surprisingly, British exports tumbled further; as Keynes later admitted, 'We threw good housekeeping to the winds.' In addition, the American perception of the post-war world and the pressure from Washington to arrange Britain's place in it could not but add to the unease which London felt about its long-term economic future. The American desire to break up the Sterling Block and have full convertibility of that currency; the dislike of the preferential tariffs instituted within the Empire at the 1932 Ottawa Conference; the enhancement of the American share of Middle East oil; and the constant reference to the need to have access to the raw materials and markets of the European colonies, all caused a dubious London to try to postpone compliance with such requests. Being in such a weakened position – by December 1943 Britain's sterling liabilities were seven times greater than its gold and dollar holdings – this was not always possible. More and more, the British piper played the tunes required by his American paymaster. The terms of lend-lease demanded by Washington, notes one critical historian, rendered the British economy 'ill-equipped to resist American objectives at the end of the war'.[2] But did London have any other choice than to accept this aid, despite its unwelcome conditions?

Even the briefest survey of the country's economic position in 1945 would show how disastrous the conflict had been. There were fewer manpower losses than in the First World War, since neither Churchill nor his generals desired to re-enact the horrors of the Western Front; but in all other major respects the costs were higher. Almost 11½ million tons of merchant shipping had been lost, housing and industrial property had been extensively damaged by bombing, and the strain of six years of war had worn out a great deal of manufacturing plant. About 10 per cent of Britain's pre-war national wealth had been destroyed at home, and industry was in a poor position to recapture overseas markets. Exports had dropped from £471 million in 1938 to £258 million in 1945; but during the same period imports had risen from £858 million to £1299 million, overseas debts had increased nearly fivefold, to £3355 million, and capital assets worth £1299 million had been liquidated, this in turn halving net overseas income and making it less likely that 'invisible' earnings could cover the trading gap in 'visible' goods. In all, Britain had probably lost about one-quarter (£7300 million) of its pre-war wealth, and was in the unenviable position of being the world's largest debtor nation.

The British government had been planning a gradual transition from a wartime to a peacetime economy just as soon as the struggle in Europe was finished; but the unexpectedly swift collapse of Japan three months later, which precipitated the American decision to stop the vital lend-lease aid, destroyed such calculations and left Britain terribly weak. The Japanese surrender on 14 August 1945, coincided with the circulation to the new Labour cabinet of Keynes's hair-raising memorandum on 'Our Overseas Financial Prospects'. The country, he argued, faced 'a financial Dunkirk': its colossal trade gap, its weakened industrial base, its enormous overseas establishments, meant that without substantial American aid it was bankrupt. Without that help, indeed, 'a greater degree of austerity would be necessary than we have experienced at any time during the war,' and 'the best hopes of the new Government would have to be postponed'.[3]

As Keynes had hoped, the Americans were willing to help – at a price. The virtual cancellation of Britain's lend-lease obligations and a long-term loan of $3750 million were most welcome, but they were accompanied by the condition that London should soon arrange free convertibility of sterling, a sign that the United States still overestimated British economic strength. However, such a mistake could not be made by 1947, when convertibility was permitted: the sharp increase in the flow of funds out of London, and the pressure upon the pound were such that, after five weeks, exchange controls were reimposed. Even so, the economy appeared unamenable to government efforts to recover Britain's pre-war commercial position. Despite a certain closing of the gap in 1948, the balance with the dollar zone remained obstinately in the red and the pressure upon sterling – artificially fixed at its 1939 rate of \$4 to £1 – intensified. By 1949, even a reluctant Cripps was forced to admit that the pound should be devalued, to a level of \$2.80. The temporary relief which following this was then undermined by the onset of the Korean War (1950–3) and the decision of the Western powers heavily to increase defence expenditure, thereby diverting resources once again from productive to unproductive ends, reducing exports, raising taxes – and sealing the fate of the Labour government in the 1951 election.

By the 1950s, however, it was becoming more and more difficult to argue that it was the effect of the Second World War (and, to a lesser extent, the Korean War) which were primarily responsible for the continued weakness. If the British were financially burdened in 1945, their situation could hardly be compared with that of the Japanese, Germans and other peoples whose commerce and industry had been almost eradictated, and whose later share of 'Marshall Aid', provided by the USA for economic recovery, was less than Britain's. Nations far more severely hit by the war have since then flourished economically whereas the post-1945 rise in British prosperity, although substantial in absolute terms, is very poor relatively. Almost every figure relating to manufacturing productivity in this period – whether national rates of growth, rises in output per man-hour, capital formation and investment, and exports – has shown Britain to be at or near the bottom of the table of industrialized powers: just as the statistics now reveal its people to be among the poorer, rather than the richer nations in Western Europe.

This is not the place to conduct a post-mortem into the causes of the British decline. Certain of them are, admittedly, of recent origin, like the post-1945 overseas military expenditure or the unfavourable change in the terms of trade in the late 1940s and again in the 1970s. But most were trends which had already been detected by observers in the 1920s, and even in the 1890s: a widespread refusal to recognize that the traditional attitudes and methods of management and trades unions required modification; an inability to exploit new ideas and techniques adequately; shoddy workmanship and poor salesmanship; a distaste for science, technology and commerce in education and public life; a depressingly low rate of investment, which was probably the most significant reason of all for the relatively poor growth rate; bad labour relations; and a propensity for the nation to spend more than it was earning.

This last-named failing was by no means a monopoly of Labour governments committed to the creation and then the preservation of 'state socialism'. Indeed, it could be argued that, given the awful circumstances it faced in 1945, Attlee's administration effected an economic recovery which was almost on a par with its diplomatic successes; and that the far more popular Tory governments which followed it, by taking too optimistic a view of the situation, permitted a further weakening of the economy *vis-à-vis* other countries under the slogan of 'free enterprise'. Since the early 1960s, however, it would be difficult to say which party has most mishandled its proclaimed economic policies.

The sole justification for concentrating so much of this chapter upon the economic problems faced by successive British governments from 1939 to the present is that these difficulties have overshadowed, ominously, continually, restrictively, almost every consideration of the country's external role and have thus been the greatest influence of all in its decline as a major power. Nor should this be at all surprising. Power rests, ultimately, upon the relative wealth and strength of the country possessing it. In the heyday of British world influence, trade and industry on the one hand, and the navy on the other, had mutually assisted each other. Now an ailing economy brought the country out of the ranks of the great powers and constrained even those statesmen whose assumptions and reactions in external affairs were instinctively Palmerstonian. Like imperial Spain in the eighteenth century, there was little prospect of Britain now being able to play an important role in world affairs when its economic machine was weak and its military muscle was becoming less and less adequate.

The Coming of the Welfare State

One major difference between Britain's decline and those of the Spanish, Ottoman and Dutch empires in earlier centuries was that it was becoming, simultaneously, a democratic welfare state. The case was not simply, therefore, that 'instinctively Palmerstonian' policies were constrained by economic exigency, but also that such policies themselves carried less weight in the public mind. Apart from the select few who had the time, leisure, patriotic conviction or perhaps commercial interest to study world politics, the attention of the greater part of the voting populace was predictably occupied by such bread-and-butter issues as unemployment, inflation, wages, strikes, law and order, housing and education. This had been the case, as noted earlier, even in the 1920s; and the coming of the National government in 1931 had by no means checked these domestic concerns. Nor, indeed, did the outbreak of war itself. The country might unite behind Chamberlain's leadership and, more enthusiastically, behind Churchill's, but that did not mean that the 'condition of England' question was obliterated by the need to fight Hitler.

In the first place, there was a widespread and very natural feeling that the sacrifices endured in wartime for the defence of democracy and of Britain itself should be repaid by domestic social improvements afterwards; few wished to fight solely to uphold an unreconstructed capitalism and to protect a society which might return to the worst days of the

1930s depression. The personal popularity of Churchill was not a good guide to the working man's regard for the Conservative Party, which was often accused of being responsible for the high inter-war unemployment rate *and* for appeasement. Both these policies were rejected after 1940, and a ferment of ideas upon social reform existed alongside the public interest in the desert campaign or the struggle for Normandy. Keynesian notions of economics were much more widespread than hitherto. The Beveridge Report (1943), proposing improvements in unemployment insurance, a national health service, family allowances, and a more unified and comprehensive pensions scheme, was received with great enthusiasm – a pointer to the public mood which Churchill and the Tory hierarchy failed to see. Another pointer they ignored was a public opinion poll showing that housing was by far the most important post-war consideration in people's minds. Although younger Conservatives like Macmillan also favoured social reform, the chief beneficiary of this rise in popular expectations was the Labour Party, which laid stress upon such policies in its 1945 electoral propaganda.

It is worth arguing that, whatever the outcome of that election, the war was so altering British society that a reshuffle in the order of political priorities would have happened in any case. As Orwell noted in 1940, 'War is the greatest of all agents of change. It speeds up all processes, wipes out minor distinctions, brings realities to the surface ... We cannot win the war without introducing Socialism ...'[4] It was partly for this reason, it has been suggested, that Chamberlain was eager to preserve the European peace. A modern war would be 'a people's war', and the consent of the people would have to be bought. Agreements were again made with the trades unions, for example, to ensure uninterrupted production. Under Churchill, a Coalition government was formed, which incidentally gave Labour leaders such as Attlee and Bevin political experience and stature. It also allowed those frustrated intellectuals and bureaucratic progressives of the 1930s – Keynes, Beveridge, the PEP people – to establish themselves in the corridors of power no longer dominated by Treasury orthodoxy. Rationing of food – the most obvious form of 'war socialism' – was both a political and logistical necessity, and furthered the egalitarian tendency, as did the increases in taxation. Unemployment was largely eliminated, and many demanded that it should not return after the war. *Laissez-faire* was thrown overboard in favour of planning and interventionism in such diverse matters as secondary education, budgetary techniques, colonial development, town and country planning, and industrial management as well as in the provision of social services. The successful prosecution of the conflict had compelled the government to spend a larger proportion of the national income than ever before; and here, too, domestic expectations made a return to pre-war levels quite impossible after 1945.

Although the post-war structure of British income-distribution and class-bands suggests that this had really been less of a 'people's war' than contemporaries believed, the domestic programme of Attlee's administration did demonstrate a shift in spending priorities and public concerns. The nationalization of coal, the railways, the Bank of England and especially iron and steel might have caused more political controversy, but the coming of the 'Welfare State' – that is, the National Insurance Act, the health service, free spectacles, teeth and medical prescriptions – was much more significant. Yet apart from being so popular that the Conservatives were not keen to oppose it, it was also expensive: in 1950, for example, £2094 million (46.1 per cent) of the total government expenditure of £4539 million was devoted to the social services. Given the pressing need to restore a balanced economy (which has been discussed above) and the perceived threats to British interests during the Cold War (which will be covered below), this inevitably meant that the political nation was again faced with a choice between guns or butter.

By and large, as we shall see, the nation chose butter. There were certain well-known advocates of drastic disarmament and of an intensification of social and economic reforms on the left wing of the Labour Party, just as there were ardent defenders of *laissez-faire* and imperial rule on the Tory right; but, although noisy, both flanks were less significant than the 'centrist' political managers of the two main parties. Macmillan and Butler, just as much as Attlee and Gaitskell, were in general agreement that the welfare state should be supported but that Britain should simultaneously maintain its defence obligations, albeit over a reduced area if contractions were unavoidable. Even so, this vague consensus (often disguised by party rhetoric) could not conceal the long-term shift in spending priorities from defence to domestic services, nor the equally significant fact that external policy possessed decreasing weight as an election issue. The Midlothian campaign of 1879/80, or the Khaki election of 1900, could not be fought in post-1945 Britain. How could they be when a public-opinion poll taken in 1948 revealed that 'three-quarters of the population did not know the difference between a dominion and a colony, and half could not name a single British colony'?[5] Tories as well as Labour based their claims to power firmly upon their ability to reduce unemployment, increase spending power, control inflation, and so on:

In a National Opinion Poll, about a week before the [1964] election, on the issues considered particularly important, by far the greatest number (72 per cent) listed 'Cost of living'; 'Education', 'Housing', 'Pensions' followed in that order. At the bottom of the list were 'Independent Deterrent', 'Defence', and 'Foreign Affairs', with 13 per cent, 12 per cent, and 10 per cent, respectively.[6]

Even contentious electoral issues such as membership of the European Economic Community or 'Common Market' consisted, essentially, of arguments about economic and social policy. And it was indicative of this line of thought that when the Duncan Committee reported in 1969 upon the functions and scale of British representation overseas, it argued that diplomacy was the handmaid of commerce and that there should be a concentration upon Britain's richest trading partners. Many of these proposals were strongly contested, but it was clear at least that the committee felt that the foreign service itself should no longer be so concerned with *grosse Politik,* as in the days of Stratford Canning or even Nevile Henderson, but should be much more directly related to the country's fight for economic survival.

The Change in Budgetary Priorities

The best means of measuring this shift in public priorities is to examine once again the pattern of spending upon various services. By 1950, the proportion of governmental expenditure upon defence had fallen to 18.5 per cent (£836 million), as opposed to the 46.1 per cent devoted to social services – a breakdown not dissimilar to that existing in the mid-1930s, although the absolute sums involved were now much larger. The Korean War and the fears generated by a worsening of relations with Russia led to a temporary reversal of this trend; and by 1953 British defence expenditure had shot up to £1725 million, representing a massive 28.5 per cent of total government spending.[7] In the years following, however, the basic trend re-emerged and by the 1970s, only about 11 per cent of public expenditure was devoted to the defence forces, which had fallen from first to fourth place:[8]

Public expenditure upon defence and various other services (£ million)

	1962	1972	1978
Defence	1840	3097	7493
Housing and environmental services	967	2770	5073
Education	1173	3508	8658
National health	971	2644	7615
Social security benefits	1744	5119	15786
Debt interest	885	2286	7302
(All other services)	3433	7720	19424
Total	11013	27144	71351

In absolute terms, the figures show a rise in defence expenditures from decade to decade; but that was more a reflection of price-inflation than of anything else, and it is the relative figures which are more important. What is remarkable, and certainly in contrast with the 1920s, is the frequent and open admission by successive British governments in recent decades that they were taking seriously the potential threats posed to national security by specific and named foreign powers – in particular, the Soviet Union. This suggests a basic difference between the post-Versailles and post-Suez contractions in the relative share of public expenditure devoted to the armed forces: for the former contraction had taken place, after all, when not only the general public but also the government's own strategic and diplomatic advisers agreed that there were few dangers on the international scene. Over the past few decades, such a cosy consensus has not existed, in part because of a strong wish to learn the so-called 'lesson of appeasement', and in part because of considerable distrust (shown not only by the Conservatives) of Russian intentions.

There were three main reasons for this general propensity to accept a lower share of spending upon defence and which still apply, even despite recent efforts by the 1979

Conservative government to reverse the trend. The first was an external one: had the United States not taken a leading role in the defence of the West since 1946 or so, no West European – or Japanese – would have been able to luxuriate in this position of 'security on the cheap'. The other two reasons were purely domestic, and have been discussed previously: continued economic weakness and a widespread reluctance to engage in massive rearmament. The former explains why even Conservative administrations have usually restrained themselves, for unlimited defence spending (especially overseas) was certainly regarded as damaging to the economy. The latter explains why Labour leaders in particular have not wished to be seen as 'Cold War warriors', since that would only provoke dissension by the radicals within the party. Left-wing politicians frequently point out that Britain has been devoting much more (around 5 per cent) of its Gross National Product to defence than either France or West Germany (each around $3\frac{1}{2}$ per cent)⁹ – although it is also true that the *absolute* sums those two countries allocate towards the armed services are actually greater than Britain's total, since their Gross National Product is that much more. Obviously, this debate about 'guns or butter' in post-war Britain would have been much less contentious had the national wealth been that much larger, in consequence of the sustained economic growth which successive governments have sought, but failed to achieve. Instead, Britain has had to struggle to maintain its military obligations – rather like Austria-Hungary before 1914. And the economic and domestic-political constraints have been such that no politician seeking office has dared to suggest that defence should consume as large a share of the Gross National Product as occurs in a 'closed' society such as Russia.

The consequences of these pressures upon Britain's ability to maintain the defence forces of a 'great' power and its previous role in the world are well known. There are many instances, as will be discussed below, where London was forced to retreat from overseas territories after 1945 because the cost was too high; and other instances where it was compelled to abandon new weapons because of their soaring development costs or general budgetary considerations. The 'large army' policy of national conscription was scrapped in the late 1950s chiefly because of the expense (although voluntary recruitment could only compete with civilian employers by offering much higher wages); the burden upon the balance of payments of such events as the Indonesian confrontation in the 1960s led to demands for a withdrawal from that region; weapons-systems such as the TSR-2 bomber were cancelled because their costs escalated beyond the country's capacity to pay for them; the 1966 Defence White Paper opposed the construction of new aircraft-carriers because of the Treasury's insistence that the defence budget should not exceed £2000 million. The best-known example of all is probably that series of decisions taken by the Labour government as a direct result of the grave economic crisis of 1967–8: the abandonment of the 'East of Suez' policy with its expensive bases in the Persian Gulf and Far East, the cancellation of the F-111 aircraft, the reduction in the personnel of the armed forces and the earlier phasing-out of the aircraft-carriers, were all indications that Britain could no longer pretend to operate as a world power.

The Disintegration of the Empire-Commonwealth

While imperial retreat was often hastened by economic or domestic-political necessity within the metropolis, it is clear that centrifugal forces existed in the dependent colonies which would have led to that result in any case. The declaration of war upon Germany in 1939 by the King-Emperor was the last time that the old British Empire was to function as a single military unit. As it was, the Irish predictably remained neutral; South Africa only entered the war after an internal crisis; in Canada, Mackenzie King pointedly allowed a full parliamentary debate; and in India the nationalists strongly resented being committed to war by a distant monarch, even if they sympathized in theory with the cause for which Britain was fighting. As in the 1914–18 conflict, the common threats to security and parliamentary democracy posed by the dictator-states produced a strong and emotional sense of unity within the Empire: the impressive contribution of Dominion, Indian and colonial troops in the desert war, Italy, Dieppe, Normandy and Burma were testimony to that, as was the sentiment shown towards those forces by British imperialists from Churchill downwards. Yet this war, like its predecessor, also revealed fissures within the grand imperial structure.

The short-term effect of the war upon British-Indian relations, it has been argued,[10] was to halt the trend towards independence for that sub-continent; kid-glove treatment of Indian nationalism was discarded by the British Army when Japan was at the threshold. But of the long-term effect there could be no doubt. The widespread unrest instigated by the Congress Party, the Cripps mission and the promise of withdrawal after the war, and the persistent American pressure for concessions to the nationalists, all pointed towards the demise of the Raj. Even more alarming and humiliating was the rapid collapse of British-held positions in the Orient when Japan finally struck in 1941–2. The fall of Singapore in February 1942, Churchill admitted, was 'the greatest disaster in our history'. It was not just that widespread *military* weaknesses were exposed, for if London was surprised at how swiftly the Empire forces surrendered, there had always been an awareness that strategic security in the Far East had been sacrificed – since 1938 or, perhaps, since 1902 – in order to achieve security in Europe. The more frightening aspects were *political* and *psychological*. Japan's rule over the peoples in its newly conquered territories was neither benign nor disinterested, but some of the ideas associated with the Tokyo's proposal for a 'Greater East Asia Co-Prosperity Sphere' produced echoes throughout the continent. Apart from those hill-peoples (for example, the Gurkhas) keen to uphold their own warrior traditions, Asians from Hong Kong to Rangoon – and beyond, to Cairo – generally showed themselves sullen and apathetic rather than supportive and loyal in the face of external challenges to the Empire. From Kipling onwards, the most acute imperialists had sensed on what a thin crust of Afro-Asian deference their colonial rule rested. By 1942 at the latest, that superficial layer had been torn asunder.

The blow to European prestige caused by the collapse of colonial rule in Burma, Malaya, the East Indies and Indo-China could not be erased by the eventual recapture of those territories – which was mainly achieved by the exertions of a trans-Pacific power with little regard for anachronistic European imperialisms. In part sharing that prejudice, in part turning for the necessary military and economic sustenance to the new leader of the Anglo-Saxon *bloc*, Australia and New Zealand made haste to follow along the path already beaten by Canada in establishing their own 'special relationship' with the United States. Like a powerful new magnet entering an existing field, America exercised a more and more distorting influence upon the now-waning pulses between Britain and its overseas possessions and Dominions. A considerable part of the veiled (and sometimes open) antagonism which occurred in the Anglo-American relationship during the war can be traced, as Dalton noted, to 'the jealousy of the old British governing class at the "passing of power".'[11]

The chief elements in the immediate post-1945 world offered little hope that the decomposition of the British Empire would be arrested by the coming of peace: a Labour government in office at home, a Russian posing (or assumed to be posing) a threat to west-central Europe, a United States capable both of checking that threat and of assisting the British economy but only at a price, and a United Nations organization now infused with an even larger spirit of Wilsonian anti-colonialism. Given these circumstances, there was only one way London could handle the impending collapse of order in the Indian sub-continent: by getting out as quickly as possible. Once again, Dalton's diary offers a nice reflection: 'If you are in a place [he noted in 1947] where you are not wanted and where you have not got the force to squash those who don't want you, the only thing to do is to come out.'[12]

Forty years earlier, Curzon had plainly spelt out the consequences for the rest of the Empire if India, the 'jewel', were ever lost: 'Your ports and coaling stations, your fortresses and dockyards, your Crown colonies and protectorates will go too. For either they will be unnecessary as the toll-gates and barbicans of an empire that has vanished, or they will be taken by an enemy more powerful than yourselves.'[13] Yet when that *dies irae* occurred, Whitehall did not draw such a sombre conclusion about its control over those 'Crown Colonies and protectorates'. The British Empire receded, spasmodically, from one defensive line to the next: new zones of economic potential (especially Middle East oilfields), new frontiers of insecurity, made any outright abandonment of the colonies seem unfeasible and foolish. Only ten years later, in 1957, did a further wave of imperial withdrawals begin. Empiricism, traditional patterns of thought, and a concentration upon domestic issues, help to explain this delayed process. Because there were no considered long-term assessments by the government of Britain's place in the world, of the processes of decolonization, and of the changing military balance, its armed forces were compelled to fight a whole series of *ad hoc* 'brushfire' wars and to be despatched for various confrontations overseas: Malaya, Kenya, Suez, Kuwait, North Borneo, Cyprus, Aden, the Trucial States, East Africa, the Falkland Islands, British Honduras, Mauritius, the sheer number and geographical disparity of such places being yet another reflection of the overstretched imperial structure that the

British had erected in happier days. Even successful campaigns were often followed by events which negated their achievements; and revolutionary leaders were frequently recognized later as heads of state. The overall effect of such British interventions was to act as a delaying force, to create 'stability' for a certain length of time, rather than to recover the days of gunboat diplomacy. They were the death spasms of a sinking empire – frequent and large-scale at first, but slowly ebbing away as the patient's strength became exhausted and his muscles atrophied. One might detect the last shudder in that 1968 announcement of abandoning an 'East of Suez' role, for the marginal amendments made by later Conservative administrations can hardly be said to have revived the corpse.

Imperial Myths and the Confrontation with Reality

All the above is easy to state in retrospect. Nothing is as inevitable as what has happened. During and after the Second World War, however, there were many influential Britons who clung to the notion that their country still had a special place and mission in the world and that the Empire should continue. Not all of these were Tory diehards, aged Milnerites, or eccentric press lords: indeed, many incoming members of Attlee's administration assumed, as they had done in their 1930s criticisms of appeasement, that Britain *had* the power to play a grand role. Nor did the facts, so far as contemporaries could observe them, totally belie this assumption. The bold defiance during the early, near-disastrous stages of the war, the thousand or more bombers which later battered German cities, the hundreds of warships which kept open the sea-lanes, the millions of troops who marched and fought through Europe, Africa and Asia, above all, perhaps, the personality of Churchill, who inspired so many to think that they were still a great people, and who met on equal terms with Roosevelt and Stalin to decide the affairs of the world, were testimony to the country's claims that it should not be regarded as a second-class power. Admittedly, it was economically weakened by 1945, but no one at Yalta or Potsdam had suggested that it was not one of the 'Big Three'. Compared with the ruined state of Japan and Germany, and with the long-discredited power of France, Britain still appeared to be in a different league. It had fought longer than any other power in this war, and emerged victoriously at the end of it. Its imperial possessions had all been recovered, and its forces were stationed in places unconceived of as bases in 1939 – Austria, north Germany, Greece, Libya, Indo-China.

These visible signs of influence mingled with comforting thoughts about Britain's unique position as the 'bridge' between America and Europe, and between the developed and the underdeveloped regions of the globe. British rule over its African and Asian colonies was regarded as benign and enlightened compared with that of other imperialisms, and it would become even more so with the passing of the Colonial Development Acts of 1940 and 1945. What had been achieved in the steady metamorphosis of ties between the Dominions and the metropolis could, eventually, also occur with the non-white regions of the Empire. In any case, it ill behoved the Russians to criticize the rule of one nation over another, and many Britons also exploded at the American tendency to pontificate about London's misrule in India while maintaining its own racist society at home and laying plans for the annexation of strategic bases in the Pacific. The world would surely be a better place, it was hinted, if it were not dominated by an inscrutable Soviet dictator on the one hand and a somewhat blinkered and *arriviste* American democracy on the other.

Far from regarding the age of appeasement as one which had exposed British military and economic weaknesses, even Labour ministers such as Bevin and Alexander and many of their permanent advisers felt that it had rather been an era of *moral* cowardice, a modern version of the reign of Ethelred the Unready. The test of war, however, had rekindled the fire in British bellies, restored the high moral purpose of the Victorians, and shown that willpower and commitment were better national attributes than concession and doubt. Churchillian rhetoric lingered in men's minds long after the coming of Labour. If by the 1950s it existed alongside the dull recognition that Britain was falling from the ranks of the 'Big Three', no one in any position of authority admitted that its great-power role was totally over. West-European integration for defence and economic purposes was to be encouraged, but Britain was still not, in its own estimation, a 'European' power enough to join that club: it functioned instead as an off-shore mediator, persuading the Americans not to repeat their post-1919 turn to isolationism. At the same time, it secretly decided – and this under a Labour government in 1946–7 – to develop its own nuclear bomb so as to retain its claims to an independent say in global power-politics and thus avoid being regarded merely as an American satrapy. With nuclear weapons, moreover, Britain would counter-balance its other weaknesses and thus still lay claim to be regarded as a great power.

By and by, these assumptions were to be punctuated by reality, and many Britons began to readjust to the changed circumstances. Yet since the decline in the country's relative power in these post-war decades was so continuous and precipitous, it is scarcely surprising that many others, of an older generation, found it harder to adjust. Even those who willingly conceded that India should be granted independence found it difficult to agree, for example, that Uganda or Borneo should go the same way. As late as 1954, a junior minister, speaking of Cyprus, could still declare that 'there are certain territories in the Commonwealth which, owing to their particular circumstances, can never expect to be fully independent'.[14] Quite apart from issues of prestige and strategy, there was the not inconsiderable aspect of trade and finance. In the period 1950–4, the Empire-Commonwealth supplied 49 per cent of Britain's imports and took 54 per cent of its exports, figures which would have brought joy to Joseph Chamberlain a half-century earlier. This accentuated that twin trend of the 1930s, whereby Britain's commercial links with its far-flung possessions were becoming more important just as its power to hold on to them was receding; now the contradicition was even greater, but it is not surprising that many did not spot it and concluded instead that increased trade meant continued (or increased) imperial commitment. Only in the 1960s were the economic indices to point in another direction, towards an integrated European market.

The darker side of this continued attachment to colonial possessions could be seen in the open dislike shown by right-wing Tories of Asian and African nationalist leaders and especially of the 'betrayals' of successive British governments which gave in to indigenous pressures for independence; in the atavistic wish to crush Nasser during the 1956 'Suez affair' as thoroughly as Wolseley's troops had crushed Arabi Pasha in 1882; in the emotional attachment of the Monday Club and others to their 'kith and kin' in Rhodesia; and in the rearguard action they fought against entry into the European Economic Community. Moreover, as the Commonwealth was transformed from a white man's club into a multi-racial group of several dozen members with separate (and sometimes conflicting) interests, many Tories gave it up in disgust; and their views on the 1948 definition of 'British nationality', which allowed all Commonwealth citizens to enter the United Kingdom without restriction, also went into a sharp reverse. By the 1960s, some Conservatives had transferred their affections towards a united Europe, which constituted, as they saw it, a more attractive collection of braves waiting eagerly for the leadership which only the British chief could provide. It is difficult to say how influential the pro-Empire wing of the

Conservative Party really was; but it may have caused pragmatic leaders like Macmillan, MacLeod and Butler to move more cautiously. it complicated the approach to the European Economic Community, and it appeared to furnish evidence to Anglophobes overseas that the British were still 'racist' and 'imperialist'.

The lighter side of this attachment was the perception, shared by most Labour and Liberal as well as many moderate Conservative politicians, that the growing global tensions between 'North' and 'South' might be eased by multi-racial co-operation under Commonwealth auspices; that Britain's retreat to become merely a middle-rank European power in military terms should not imply an abandonment of interest in the non-European world; and that, even when entering the European Economic Community, it was important to secure commercial concessions for those goods (e.g. West Indian sugar, New Zealand dairy produce) which had made themselves peculiarly dependent upon the British market. Along with this went a genuine affection for the Commonwealth as a cultural unit, with its shared language, legal system, educational structure and sporting traditions. This, and the fact that so many British families had relatives who had emigrated to the older 'white' Dominions, gave a continued extra-European flavour to the national consciousness even when the bases of its political power had gone. To some observers, this was a commendable trait; to others, it helped to obfuscate the realities of Britain's weakened position, by encouraging successive administrations to assume that such cultural influence could act as a substitute for military power, thereby maintaining its extra-European role and delaying its full return to the continent to which it belonged.

There was some truth, certainly, in this latter remark. But it was also the case that such obfuscations of reality may have had a beneficial effect, at least upon domestic politics. It is surely remarkable that. despite occasional growls from the right, the collapse of the British Empire did not lead to internal convulsions or to the violence which wracked parts of French society during the Algerian War. As Max Beloff observes, 'No doubt much of human history consists in the more or less gracious acceptance of the ineluctable; but even the degree of grace is a matter of some interest.'[15] Perhaps the fact that the loss of Empire and great-power status was gradual and spasmodic, rather than cataclysmic, helps to explain this general acceptance of the new order. Perhaps it was because of the British tradition of acquiescing without violence in the policies of the elected government of the day and bowing before the views of the majority – a majority which now preferred to concentrate upon domestic politics. Perhaps it was because both the social composition of the decision-making *élite,* and the institutions within which they operated, were largely unchanged that the transformation was further disguised. Or perhaps it was that there existed a 'reserve' ideology about the Commonwealth, to step into the gap left by the discrediting of the imperial ideal? None of these interpretations totally excludes the others; all suggest that British traditionalism, although affecting clarity of vision, was not without its saving graces. In a turbulent world, it was a natural reaction to identify with that which was familiar; and there was a good deal that was familiar, and reassuring, about official photographs of George VI or Elizabeth II sitting amid the premiers at a Commonwealth Prime Ministers' Conference, even if the Empire which their grandparents had taken for granted was now at one with Nineveh and Tyre.

The Rise of the Superpowers and the Eclipse of Britain: the Basic Trend

Perhaps the most fundamental problem facing the directors of Britain's external policy during the 1939–45 war and afterwards was the way in which its power so rapidly fell behind that of Russia and, especially, the USA. This produced a strategical and diplomatic situation *qualitatively* different from anything which had occurred over the preceding two centuries. Since the end of the War of Spanish Succession (1713), it may be argued, Britain had been able to hold its own against any other great power – although whether it could by itself defeat, say, Bourbon France or Tsarist Russia was another matter. Yet, while the British Army alone was never able to decide the fate of Europe, the country's maritime and economic strength had made it virtually invulnerable in wartime, capable of enduring a long-drawn-out struggle, and a source of inspiration (and supplies) to those peoples faced by the same overweening power. Such characteristics, impressive and effective in past conflicts, now no longer worked.

In the early stages of the Second World War, it is true, this traditional pattern seemed to hold. Germany was admittedly a formidable foe – in 1938 its steel production was one-quarter greater than that of the United Kingdom and France combined – but it was reckoned to be short on economic stamina and it could not, either by sea or air, overwhelm British defences. This was true even when Germany had conquered most of western Europe, and by 1941 British aircraft production was boosted to almost twice the German output: 20,100 planes to 10,775.[16] That, however, was an artificial lead, caused chiefly by the fact that in this period the Germans were leisurely waging war and enjoying both the guns *and* the butter which a *Blitzkrieg* strategy allowed. The defeats at Stalingrad and Alamein galvanized the Germans into action, and under Speer's leadership armaments production soared well past the British: for example, in 1944 Germany had a twofold superiority in small-arms production, as compared with a British superiority of 60 per cent in 1942. Yet measuring this rivalry is, in a certain sense, an artificial exercise. Germany could only maintain its productive growth either by diverting manpower from the armed services or by exploiting even further its satellites and thus making its rule over them more precarious. And Britain could only maintain its productive growth by an ever-increasing reliance upon American resources.

In grand-strategical terms, moreover, that particular rivalry was almost irrelevant. In horseracing parlance, Britain and Germany were like two front-runners who were exhausting themselves in the early stages of the contest. By its middle stages, they were already being outdistanced. Although the Soviet Union was fighting with over half its industrial and agricultural resources in enemy hands, it was soon producing enough to re-equip vast armies. In the years 1942–4, its annual production averages of 40,000 aircraft and 30,000 tanks and self-propelled guns were far superior to the respective German totals of 26,000 and 12,000. American war production was simply phenomenal. In 1941 it was only 75 per cent of Germany's, but by the following year it was already two-and-a-half times as great and still in its early stages. Whereas the Americans had built only 2100 aircraft in 1939, this had risen to 48,000 in 1942, 86,000 in 1943 and to a staggering 96,300 in 1944. In fact, in the five years 1940–5 the United States produced 297,000 aircraft, 86,000 tanks, 17,400,000 small arms, 64,500 landing vessels and 5200 larger ships (of nearly 53 million tons).[17]

The figures for total arms expenditure alone go a long way towards explaining the eventual outcome of the war in Europe:[18]

	1939 ($ billion)	1941 ($ billion)	1943 ($ billion)
USA	0.6	4.5	37.5
Britain	1.0	6.5	11.1
Russia	3.3	8.5	13.9
Germany	3.4	6.0	13.8

These statistics, which by 1944–5 tilted even further in the direction of the USA and Russia, were scarcely affected by including the Japanese output – for that country had in December 1941 rashly attacked a power with a Gross National Product ten times its own! This meant that behind the famous and undoubtedly genuine friendship of Churchill and Roosevelt there lay a hard economic reality which made one of the partners grow in superiority over the other. In the second quarter of 1942, American military output caught up with the British; by the end of 1943, its production of aircraft was double, its launchings of merchant vessels six times, that of Britain; and by 1944, its overall armaments production was six times as large. The full potential of its continent-wide resources, its great population, its more modern industry, was at last being realized – to produce a superpower which was as far ahead of Britain as the latter had been of the declining and smaller states of Portugal, Spain and the Netherlands two or three centuries earlier. Furthermore, the British became 'clients' of the Americans, in rather the same way that their eighteenth-century allies had looked to London for aid in the struggles against France. In 1941, 10 per cent of the British Empire's munitions came from American factories; by 1944 – as Britain's own armaments output was levelling off and in some cases falling because it had been overstrained – the figure had risen to 28.7 per cent. More specifically, the United States supplied 47 per cent of the Empire's total consumption of tanks, 21 per cent of small arms, 38 per cent of landing-craft – yet this enormous aid formed only a small proportion of total American output. In 1945, true to the lend-lease agreement, Washington generously agreed to wipe out the $21,000 million of American material which Britain had consumed in the war effort. It is difficult to imagine how the British would have fought *without* that assistance, or how they could ever have paid it back.

But Washington's generosity alone could not alter the new global balance. Even when the war was at its height, American planners were able to sketch with confidence the coming bi-polar system:

The successful termination of the war against our present enemies will find a world profoundly changed in respect of relative national military strengths, a change more comparable indeed with that occasioned by the fall of Rome than with any other change occurring during the succeeding fifteen hundred years . . . After the defeat of Japan, the United States and the Soviet Union will be the only military powers of the first magnitude. This is due in each case to a combination of geographical position and extent, and vast munitioning potential . . . Both in an absolute sense and relative to the United States and Russia, the British Empire will emerge from the war having lost ground economically and militarily.[19]

In the post-war world, this prediction was well confirmed. In the late 1940s, the United States possessed a Gross National Product around six times that of Britain, and the Soviet Union about two to three times as large. If Britain was still in third place then, the following decades saw it slip further down the league table as the economies of the other 'middle-range' states revived:[20]

	Gross national product of the powers ($ billion)					
	USA	Japan	West Germany	France	Britain	Russia
1952	350	16	32	29	44	113 (?)
1962	560	59	89	74	81	229 (?)
1972	1152	317	229	224	128	439 (?)
1977	1890	677	508	374	263	645 (?)

The most interesting point here, then, is not so much that Britain has been outdistanced by the USA and Russia, but that it is economically so much weaker than France (for the first time in 150 years) and Japan (for the first time in centuries), and quite eclipsed by the western portion of Germany.

The significance of this steady, relative decline is twofold.

In the first place, concern about 'slow growth' and attempts to recover a higher annual pace of increasing the national wealth became the Number One aim of all British post-war administrations, to the possible neglect of non-economic issues. Secondly, and more directly, it affected Britain's capacity to afford an adequate defensive system, especially in an age of expensive missile delivery systems and spiralling inflation. Even if, as mentioned above, it devoted a larger share of its Gross National Product to the armed forces than either France or West Germany, its spending was considerably less in absolute terms; and was, of course, quite eclipsed by the three big military powers:[21]

Military expenditures ($ billion)		
	1967	1976
USA	75·7	91·0
Russia	50·0	127·0
China	15·7	34·4
West Germany	8·6	16·0
France	7·7	14·2
Britain	6·9	11·0

The consequences of Britain's decline in the ranks of the great powers were most immediately – in a sense, most *physically* – felt in its post-war military policy. Everything had become relative, and thus more complex and intangible. After all, the two-power naval standard, although measured *vis à vis* other nations, had an absolute end in view, the maintenance of an unchallengeable status as the first maritime nation: the Washington Conference reduced this to a one-power standard, but the principle remained. For a country halfway up – or down – the great-power scale, such absolute aims become impossible. Should it attempt to maintain a spending parity with, say, West Germany, even if it was steadily becoming less wealthy; or agree to devote, say, one-fifth of the monies spent on armaments by the Soviet Union? If its wealth was only a fraction of that of the superpowers, should it be devoted to each area of defence or concentrated upon certain aspects, with others abandoned; upon submarines at the expense of aircraft-carriers, or the RAF at the expense of the army? Is it worthwhile to maintain an 'independent' nuclear deterrent even when the country's security is bound up with that of the entire Western alliance? If the problems and burdens of being the Number One world power (or the Number Two power striving to take the first place) were immense, then the practical difficulties facing a medium-size power in the formulation of a coherent defence policy were at least as great.

The same could be said, and with equal emphasis, about the conduct of British diplomacy after the war. Its leaders – educated for the main part in Edwardian England – simply did not have any experience of playing outside the 'first division' of nation-states, and many could not shake off the consciousness that Britain was still a great force in world affairs. Even those politicians willing to readjust found it difficult to get a measure of their country's new place in the changed global order. Should it seek to uphold its imperial traditions, albeit through the evolving Commonwealth, and to be at the centre of the North-South dialogue? Should it stress its trans-Atlantic links, hew to Washington's diplomatic line, and play Greece to America's Rome? Or was its place really in Europe? Each of these potential strategies, however attractive, possessed disadvantages and aroused doubts. Nor was it possible for Britain permanently to remain still, neatly enclosed (as Churchill described it in 1948) by the three overlapping circumferences of the Commonwealth, the United States and Europe.

Nevertheless, the eventual option was by no means clear to British or to foreign observers in 1945, or even perhaps in 1955. It was to require several decades of slow economic growth, the Suez *débâcle* of 1956, an appreciation of the 'wind of change' sweeping the Third World, a recognition that it could not compete with the superpowers militarily, and an awakening to what possibilities existed in the field of

European unity, before the path became clear. But in the intervening period – the period covered in the narrative chapter following – the British leadership was involved in picking its way through, and frequently stumbling upon, the debris and dust which had arisen from the collapse of the four-hundred-year-old Eurocentric global order. For contemporary critics and later scholars who felt that the conduct of British external policy in these decades was often confused and mistaken, it may be proper to recall that wartime comparison made by the American planners about the fall of the Roman world. In both cases, one suspects, a great deal of the difficulties and uncertainties statesmen faced was caused by the loss of so many familiar signposts.

8. Debates and Policies

Britain at War: the Strategy of 'Hanging-On'

The coming of war in 1939 inevitably transformed the nature of British external policy. The assumptions and habits of peacetime, wherein different groups debated and wrangled about the country's proper aims in the world, were overlain by a common determination that the first aim of all was victory – a determination which hardened as the war went on. In 1914, the government had persuaded the public to follow it into war; in 1939, public opinion itself pushed the government forward. This meant that there was a far greater degree of political unanimity now than in that earlier conflict. German aggressions had discredited the proto-fascists within Britain, and even those who favoured a compromise peace in 1939–40 dared not openly propose it; while the Nazi-Soviet Pact dealt a further heavy blow to any lingering sympathies for Soviet communism. Perhaps serious internal fissures would have developed had Chamberlain remained in power longer than he did, for there was certainly a strong mutual dislike between him and the Labour movement. But Churchill was a genuinely popular leader of a national coalition and, with no real rivals, was able to ride out even the discontent provoked by the loss of Tobruk and Singapore. There was no 'Lansdowne letter' in the Second World War, no significant peace movement, and no growth of a body akin to the Union of Democratic Control. Above all, there was little repetition of that domestic working-class ferment which had so alarmed the British establishment in

1917–19. The voting masses were marching towards long-hoped-for economic and social reforms, no doubt; but they were doing that with dignity and moderation, and without affecting the national unity and pursuit of unconditional victory. This all meant that there was little in the way of domestic *constraint* upon the government's external policy.

Diplomacy also was enormously simplified by the coming of war. The pre-1939 debate upon which of the 'revisionist' powers to appease – or to oppose – was obviously ended by the Anglo-German conflict, which of necessity determined that London's policy towards all neutral powers should be conciliatory. In some instances, this was grudging and enforced: for example, while it would be advantageous to keep Italy out of the war, this could not be achieved at the expense of either British or French interests in the Mediterranean. The Japanese threat in the Far East was far more formidable and caused correspondingly greater concern; but it soon became evident that Tokyo had been shocked by the signing of the Nazi-Soviet Pact and was not going to embark upon further expansion until it was clear which course the European war would take. If the West's dependence upon Japanese goodwill was uncertain and tenuous – in mid-1940, for example, London was forced to agree to a temporary closure of the Burma Road (the supply route to the Chinese Nationalists) – this was the inevitable consequence of needing to face threats nearer home.

In Europe itself, the Allies competed with German diplomacy to secure the benevolent neutrality of third powers, or at the very least to keep them from entering the war on the other side. In this respect, the maintenance of formal relations with Spain must be regarded as a significant gain, and the more so after the fall of France and Italy's entry into the war, at which time a Spanish move against Gibraltar would have paralysed Britain's Mediterranean strategy; despite the wooing of Hitler and Mussolini, Franco chose a cautious neutrality. The same course was followed by

Turkey – in marked contrast to the previous war – and by Greece and Yugoslavia, at least until they were attacked by the Axis. Switzerland, Portugal, the Netherlands and the Scandinavian states all kept to a policy of neutrality, which could only please London and Paris: for, although those countries furnished raw materials to Germany which weakened the impact of the Allied naval blockade, the greater danger was that any un-neutral acts by them might provoke the Nazi war machine to strike – as, indeed, it did against Denmark, Norway and the Netherlands in April–May 1940. Being ill-equipped to resist *Blitzkrieg* tactics, and unable to supply small allies with the munitions they would doubtless demand, it behoved Britain and France to preserve as wide a zone of neutrality as possible.

The really big fish to hook were, of course, the USA and Russia. The respective positions of the Allies and the Axis to the former were the reverse of those they occupied towards the latter. Hitler had no chance of getting the Americans on to his side, but he could hope to ensure its continued neutrality by, for example, restrictions upon U-boat warfare. His greatest ally was the still-dominant isolationism of the American people; his enemy, Roosevelt and a group of advisers and officials in Washington who feared the consequences of a German victory in the West. To the British, and especially to Churchill, the United States represented the key to eventual success; and even if it was too early yet to expect direct American intervention, it was vital to secure access to that country's supplies of munitions and to persuade Roosevelt also to stand firm in the Far East. To achieve this greater end, it was worthwhile making concessions over Caribbean bases. From the American viewpoint, it was important to give the British sufficient moral encouragement and material support to stand up to the Axis – but without subordinating United States interests to those of its older imperial cousin, and without provoking those domestic critics who clung to isolationism. This period was interesting for the growing contact and exchange of ideas between Roosevelt and Churchill; but it was already characterized, in one scholar's words, 'by cautious accommodation and constant manoeuvring for advantage rather than selfless co-operation . . .'[1]

The West, in its turn, had little prospect of bringing Russia on to its side. Britain's willingness to exclude Russia from the Munich Conference, and the dilatory way in which the alliance talks were conducted in the early summer of 1939, had obviously increased Stalin's morbid suspiciousness. The Nazi-Soviet Pact may not have represented his long-term wishes, but he clearly had a more immediate need to keep on formally good terms with Germany than to dispute its claims in central Europe. Furthermore, his relations with Britain and France worsened considerably after November 1939, when he sought to impose military controls upon Finland, as he was just then doing upon the three Baltic states of Latvia, Estonia and Lithuania. Indignant at this transgression, eager for *some* action, and apparently keen to embark upon an anti-Bolshevik crusade, the Western Allies prepared to involve themselves in a war against Russia while already at war with Germany;* but political confusion and military unpreparedness and the sheer physical difficulty of reaching Finland all delayed an actual move until March 1940 when, embarrassingly, the Finns made peace with Russia. None of this, of course, warmed Stalin's feelings for the West even if the Russian dictator was not anxious to give any excuse for a compromise peace between Britain, France and Germany, which might then form a new anti-communist *bloc*. He therefore kept the British at arms' length, even when Cripps was sent as ambassador to Moscow with the special aim of improving Anglo-Russian relations. Like all other European neutrals, Russia operated at this time out of a fear of

---

* Taylor, *English History 1914–1945*, p. 469, fn.1, discusses some of the motives for the Anglo-French policy over the Finnish issue; and closes by remarking that 'At present, the only charitable conclusion is to assume that the British and French governments had taken leave of their senses.'

Germany – especially after the fall of France – rather than any amiability towards Britain.

This diplomatic wooing of the neutrals reflected each side's natural wish to create a more powerful coalition against the enemy; and also the strategic stalemate which attended the first eight months of the war. Poland, the cause of the Allies' entry, was overrun without the West being able to do a thing. No one wished to be the first to instigate massive aerial assaults, even if the aircraft and plans had been available. Nor was there the prospect of capturing German colonies, as in 1914. The naval war was, at this stage, very much a repetition of that in the early part of the First World War: the German surface fleet was not strong enough to risk a full-scale engagement with the Royal Navy, and its U-boats were not yet numerous enough to pose a severe challenge to Allied shipping routes. A few raiders, like the *Graf Spee*, were cleared off the seas in the traditional manner. On land, the opposing armies appeared content to await behind their respective defensive lines. In such a situation, it was not surprising that diplomtic attempts to seduce the neutrals were being made by each side.

The illusion of strategic similarity between the two wars against Germany was rudely shattered in the early summer of 1940. By the successful invasions of Denmark and Norway, the *Wehrmacht* had broken through that North Sea 'gate' to the Atlantic; and by the stunning victories in the west, it not only upset the military balance but it tumbled the British out of the continent and posed a greater danger to the United Kingdom than at any time since Napoleon's army was encamped around Boulogne. Moreover, Mussolini, with a jackal's sense of timing, finally threw in his lot with Hitler, thus opening up a Mediterranean theatre of war and threatening Egypt. All this made it more urgent than ever for the British to find friends in the world, and thus increased the need for the diplomatic pursuit of powerful neutrals and the continued placating of potential foes. Yet non-belligerents were hardly likely to aid Britain until it was clear that it would survive the German onslaught, and this in turn meant that diplomacy depended upon military gains, or at the least, upon the avoidance of defeat. In particular, anxious American planners were divided about whether or not they should send aid to a country which might soon succumb to Nazi expansionism.

Churchill's accession as Prime Minister in May 1940, and his determination to wage war with greater zeal than hitherto, were thus of extreme significance. The successful retirement of most of the BEF from Dunkirk; the rousing of national morale by radio broadcasts; the beating-off of the *Luftwaffe*'s repeated attacks; the establishment of 'Force H' at Gibraltar to seal off the Mediterranean; the ruthless strokes against the French fleet at Oran and Dakar; the beginnings of the military campaigns against Italian possessions in North and East Africa; the intensification of strategic bombing against Germany; and the massive increase in purchasing orders to American industry, were all indications that the war would go on.

Yet if the British were showing that they would be difficult to defeat by military means, it was also true that they had little prospect of *winning* the war by themselves. It would take far greater resources than they and their Empire possessed to undermine the German domination of Europe. Their strategical role was a critical one, but it was also essentially negative – to prevent further Axis expansion in the Channel and North Africa, and to hold open the sea-lanes. Only if the enemy overstretched himself in other directions, or Britain gained a powerful ally, would it be possible to abandon this policy of 'hanging-on' and begin to plan for the downfall of the dictators.

The Peripheral Approach, and its Meaning

The main features of the grand strategy which the British adopted in the months following Dunkirk had been formulated by the Chiefs of Staff as early as February 1939. They did not reckon then, of course, upon France being knocked out of the war, but it was assumed that the Allies would have to be on the defensive during its early stages. Provided the Axis assault was held in the west and at sea, it was hoped to begin an offensive from Egypt, against the Italian Empire. Subsequently, they should turn 'to weakening Germany and Italy by the exercise of economic pressure and by intensive propaganda, while at the same time building up our major strength until we can adopt an offensive strategy. Command of the sea would then confer freedom of choice in striking at the enemy's most vulnerable points.'[2]

The events of summer 1940 removed from the realm of possibility the chief military theatre of operations against Germany – land battles on its Western Front. Yet there is little sign that many Britons were distressed by this new strategic situation; indeed, individuals from George VI downwards expressed their relief that they were no longer harnessed to continental allies. Freed from the political encumbrances of an *entente cordiale*, the British did not need to repeat that 1914-18 debate between 'Westerners' and 'Easterners': all were 'Easterners' now.

This preference for the so-called 'British way in warfare' was based partly upon sentiment, and partly upon realism: in the mind of Winston Churchill, it was often difficult to detect where one factor ended and the other began. The 'freedom of choice' which the Chiefs of Staff believed was conferred by 'command of the sea' was an echo of those traditional forms of peripheral and maritime warfare, represented now in more modern guise by naval patrols of the Greenland Strait and commando raids upon the coasts of Norway and France. There was still an exaggerated belief in the efficacy of naval blockade – British estimates of dwindling German stocks of raw materials in 1940 contrasted sharply with the reality – but this was now accompanied by the perception that aerial blockade would complement, and perhaps even replace, the traditional forms of economic pressure. The danger in this respect, indeed, was soon to be an equally exaggerated belief in the efficacy of strategic bombing, which to 'Bomber' Harris possessed all the advantages that Mahan had ascribed to sea power a half-century earlier. In part, because of Churchill's keen desire to hit the enemy with *something*, and in part because it was still reckoned that a bombing campaign would be inherently cheaper than continental land warfare, the RAF remained the favoured child of the three services. The subsequent controversy upon the role of that force, and in particular its gradual turn towards the morally dubious strategy of area bombing (as compared with the USAAF's preference for more selective targets), has been too heated to permit an historical consensus to emerge; but it seems doubtful in retrospect whether the British got good value for their colossal investment.

The desert war was another aspect of this readily identifiable strategy of indirect approach. On the one hand, it was clearly important to protect the British position in the eastern Mediterranean and Near East, and the more particularly because of the Empire's dependence upon oil supplies. On the other, a campaign against Italy offered a further opportunity of waging *offensive* warfare without enormous manpower losses and of knocking out the weaker of the Axis powers – although even this became much more difficult when the Italian forces were stiffened by Rommel's *Afrika Korps*. To a considerable extent, then, the North African campaign – and the later assault upon Sicily and

Italy – was a rerun of Allenby's offensives in the First World War; and, going even further back in time, played a role similar to that of Wellington's campaign in the Peninsula. It engaged the enemy's troops, but not too many of them, on grounds preferred by the British: it possessed an imperial as much as a continental balance-of-power justification; it seemed relatively cheap, and was a magnificent morale booster; and – an important point – it was the last theatre in which an Imperial Army under British commanders could win victories and thus have a say in the post-war territorial order.[3]

While this overall strategy had been implanted in the British consciousness before the fall of France, it was not altered by the global revolution of June-December 1941, which saw first Russia and then Japan and the United States brought into the war. The first extension of the conflict produced a characteristic offer of support to Russia from Churchill, whose own anti-Soviet suspicions had never (since the early 1930s) matched his opposition to Nazi imperialism. This was probably just as well, for the great bulk of the British Labour movement quickly warmed to the heroic Russian defence and pressed for all forms of aid, from munitions to the opening of a 'second' front. Quite apart from this factor of sentiment – which was arguably the only significant domestic pressure upon the government's strategic conduct of the war – Churchill and his advisers (like Roosevelt and his) desperately hoped that the Russians might hold off the *Wehrmacht*'s onslaught and successfully absorb much of its strength. Where Whitehall differed from Stalin and from the 'Second Front Now' agitation at home was in its wish to avoid an early confrontation with Germany on the mainland of Europe. Until this difference was finally resolved by the D-Day landings some two-and-a-half years later. Anglo-Soviet strategic harmonization could only occur at a secondary level – in Persia, or in the Murmansk convoys.

If Anglo-American relations were altogether more harmonious, this could not conceal a rather similar strategical 'split'. The extensive Japanese gains early in 1942 dealt a devastating blow to the European Empires in the east, and Singapore's loss especially shocked Churchill; yet in terms of grand strategy, it altered little. British eggs had been concentrated in the European and, increasingly, the Middle-eastern baskets, and would not be redistributed now. Provided the defences of India held and Australia was not in dire danger, it was hoped that Japan would be properly dealt with *after* the defeat of Italy and Germany: and within a fortnight of Pearl Harbor, Churchill was scurrying across the Atlantic to persuade the Americans to confirm the 'Europe first' strategy which had tentatively been agreed upon in the secret pre-war planning. This order of priority was accepted by Washington, despite the 'pull' exerted by the US Navy and outraged American opinion for the swift defeat of Japan: both the army and the air force were attracted by the greater scope for their services which the European theatre offered, and Roosevelt himself felt bound to his pledge and was genuinely eager to eradicate the Nazi system. In any case, the Germans were, technologically as well as militarily, too formidable and inventive a foe to leave alone for several years while Japan was being defeated.

Yet it was precisely this strategical logic which made the Americans, too, favour a direct assault upon the European continent and dislike the British suggestions for an indirect approach via North Africa, Italy and perhaps the Balkans. Washington's suspicions of London's ulterior motives in the latter region were largely unfounded and merely reflected the American belief that, despite the common alliance with Britain, they were also still dealing with the old imperial Adam. In fact, there were genuine logistical reasons (especially in the supply of landing-craft) which made impossible a full-scale invasion of France during 1942 or 1943, quite apart from the need to establish an un-challengeable aerial supremacy; and, in the meantime, the deployment of limited Anglo-American forces could turn the balance in the Mediterranean. Yet this disagreement, which occasionally provoked the Americans to threaten to divert more of their resources to the Pacific, reflected more than a quarrel between strategical experts; and more even than the natural geopolitical attraction the British had for their imperial route to India and the Americans for their trans-Pacific interests. It also unmistakably reflected the disparity in sheer military size and potential between the two allies or, for that matter, between the two rising superpowers of the United States and Russia and the declining world power of Britain.

To the Russians, anything less than military action by the West which would divert a substantial number of German troops from the Eastern Front had little appeal. How could the desert war, pinning down a couple of German divisions, be of much use to a country which was fighting off the advances of around 200 German and satellite divisions? Anglo-American munitions were not to be disdained, but the blunt fact was that the *real* war against Germany was being fought in Russia, where the German Army suffered over four-fifths of its total casualties and where Russian population losses were greater than those of *all* combatants in the First World War. In this military holocaust, and in Stalin's eyes also, manpower losses were relatively cheap when measured against the lands reconquered and the casualties inflicted upon the foe. American leaders certainly did not subscribe to that doctrine, but they were advocates of a frontal assault against Germany because they assumed that their own great resources and superiority in military hardware would carry the day. There was no need to waste time on subsidiary theatres, and this was felt the more especially since Washington wished not only to turn its own forces to the Pacific following Germany's defeat but also hoped by that time to persuade Russia to attack Japan as well. For a certain while, Churchill was able to resist this pressure: Stalin had no hold over him, and Roosevelt and his own Chiefs of Staff were aware that a long period would elapse before American forces in Europe were as large as the British. By the time massive US Army reinforcements were being trained in England, and USAAF squadrons were complementing RAF Bomber Command with 'round-the-clock' raids upon German factories and cities, London was quite willing to agree to open up a 'second front' in France. The risks were now far less than before, and any further delay after early 1944 would not have been understood either by the British public or the Allies. Between 1942 and D-Day, however, it was this British preference for an indirect strategy which more than anything else led to dissensions within the 'Big Three'.

Above all else, this disagreement revealed that the British government, although committed to victory, could neither afford the manpower losses of the Russians nor the *materiel* losses of the Americans. Of course, a better point of comparison might be with the German and Japanese attitudes: neither of those states flinched from a quite awful expenditure of human life, but the British were no longer willing to pay that price to remain a great power. Psychologically as well as politically, they had become conservative and prudent. Churchill was, in effect, like a poker player who wished to stay in the game but felt he had few funds left to commit. The fear of trench warfare on the 1914–18 scale was always there – which was why Montgomery, with his penchant for carefully planned, set-piece attacks with assured numerical superiority (from Alamein to Sicily to Caen), was the favourite general. Equally pressing was the apprehension that Britain's productive strength had peaked, and was now gently declining. By 1943, the services' fresh demands for manpower could only be met by taking men away from the vital munitions industries: this, in the main, explains the vast increase in Britain's dependence upon American supplies. Even so, the armed forces could in no way secure the numbers which would give them parity with the Americans, let alone with the Russians. Eisenhower's appointment as Supreme Commander of the Allied Expeditionary Force was due to the fact that American land and air strength in Europe was greater than Britain's, and this disproportion would tilt further as time went on. It could also be seen in the way Britain's early lead in the development of a nuclear bomb was surrendered to the Americans, who alone had the resources to produce one. In one way, all this increased London's desire to see the war in Europe ended quickly, before the balances shifted even more; in another, it intensified the British wish to husband their scarce resources – the more especially since some of them would later need to be deployed in the Pacific war, where (outside Burma and New Guinea) the Americans were doing all the fighting and likely to reap all the consequent benefits.

Although the war against Japan was the one theatre where the British had deliberately abstained from a large-scale military effort, they could not be unaware of the deleterious political results of this 'Europe first' decision; and Churchill, as both a child of the late-Victorian Empire *and* as the man who had kept the imperial possessions in the Orient relatively denuded in 1940–1, symbolized in so many ways this ambivalence – and dilemma. To ignore that region completely was impossible: Malaya's raw materials, and the Singapore base, had to be held; pledges to Australia and New Zealand had to be fulfilled; and could anyone doubt that if Japanese forces were allowed to penetrate the borders of India, the Raj would be finished? Yet the reinforcements, hastily rushed eastwards when Churchill's gamble failed in December 1941, were unsuitable or, at least, inadequate: Hurricane fighters equipped for desert conditions, the *Prince of Wales* and *Repulse* without aircraft-carrier cover, then a fleet of slow battleships from the days of 'Jacky' Fisher, and a motley assortment of British, Indian and Australian divisions. With defeat following defeat, it was hardly surprising that by February 1942 the Australian Prime Minister, John Curtin, looked to America as his country's only saviour, 'free from any pangs as to our traditional links with the United Kingdom';[4] and it was also unsurprising that Indian and Burmese nationalists thought that their day had come.

In the short term, the British could be grateful that this Japanese onslaught was eventually halted. The Australians, with increasing American help, checked the enemy in Papua. The Americans alone, by the clever use of their carriers, blunted the Japanese drive at the Coral Sea and Midway battles, and then launched their counter-offensive. Even the Japanese push towards India was slowed down, and later (at Kohima and Imphal) decisively repulsed by Slim's 'forgotten army'. But what would happen in the longer term, when the post-war order in Asia was to be settled, perhaps to the detriment of British interests? It was in this region, scholars have shown, 'that there occurred the greatest degree of strain between the two Western Allies . . . regarding their proclaimed, implicit and perceived war aims';[5] and, certainly, the alliance did not function there to anything like the degree of intimacy which pertained over European issues. The American pressure about Indian independence provoked Churchill to fury on occasions. In addition, he was never able to take seriously Washington's high regard for the Chinese nationalists and suspected ulterior motives, perhaps relating to Hong Kong. Taken together with the controls which the Americans exercised through lend-lease, the demands for access to tropical raw materials and for the ending of imperial preference and controls upon sterling, it appeared to some Britons that a *Pax Americana* might be created out of the carcase of the dissolved European empires. If the United States was alone responsible for recapturing Malaya and the Dutch East Indies, Churchill warned, Washington might demand 'a dominating say in their future'.[6] These suspicions paled by comparison with those held against Britain by anti-imperialist Americans, and by egoists like General MacArthur or Admiral King, who were not keen upon London's participation – with its own Pacific fleet – in the defeat of Japan. Since, by and large, the

Americans were unchallenged in this theatre, they also had their way; but this provided Churchill and his colleagues with another reminder that the military defeat of the Axis should not be allowed to obscure the need to provide for British interests in the post-war world.

A Carthaginian Peace?

By 1944, the future of Europe was giving Churchill his greatest grounds for anxiety. The collapse of German power was by that time no longer in doubt, and this caused the Prime Minister's older apprehensions about Russia gradually to replace his concern about defeating the Nazis, the more especially since the Red Army was most likely to be in possession of much of east-central Europe by the end of the war. This in turn might not have mattered so much had Churchill managed to be on the same friendly terms with Stalin as he was with Roosevelt; but that presumed an ideological and political identity of views which was quite impossible. Nothing touched the British conscience as much as Russia's attitude towards the future of Poland, over which they had originally declared war and about which its government-in-exile (living in London) constantly pressed for assurances. By extension, this problem inevitably involved consideration about the future of Germany, whose eastern boundaries Russia wished to push as far westwards as possible; and Churchill, Eden and their advisers could not ignore the parallel questions of how Bulgaria, Hungary, Greece and other smaller states should be treated. Here, as elsewhere, the British government perceived that the more time passed, the less likely Britain was to achieve its original hopes. Time was on Stalin's side and, most frustrating of all, the Americans could not at first be persuaded to take these issues very seriously -- chiefly, it was suspected, because

Roosevelt believed that time was on *his* side, although it was also the case that Russia's entry into the Far Eastern war was still desired by Washington. As the war in Europe drew to a close, therefore, the British regarded the future territorial settlement with concern, a feeling increased by the failure to settle the Polish question at the Yalta Conference.

These same developments intensified London's desire to see a resurrection of France. This again, no doubt, was influenced by Churchill's own regard for that country as one of the 'civilized' world states (a view he could never hold of, say, Japan or China), and by his past encouragement of the Free French. On this matter, he gained little support from Roosevelt, who did not conceal his dislike for what he felt to be the arrogant and preposterous claims of their exiled leader, de Gaulle. Churchill's stance, however, was affected as much by *Realpolitik* as by sentiment. Given the very real possibility (as it seemed then) of an American troop withdrawal from Europe soon after the end of the war, London was eager to see the revival of a nation which could, at least to some degree, join it in balancing the Russian predominance: hence Britain's insistence that the control arrangements for the conquered Germany should be altered to provide for a French zone.

Little of this was known by the British public, or, if it was, did not concern it – although there was a minor right-wing revolt in the Commons over Poland following the Yalta Conference. Russia's wartime role was still widely admired by most of the British population and even by the cultural and social establishment, as, for example, George Orwell discovered when he tried to interest publishers in the manuscript of *Animal Farm*. Admiration for Russia was now altogether more widespread and significant than the Russophilia of the left in the 1930s had been, and in any case few Britons would have thought it credible that they were about to finish a world war simply to have it replaced by a Cold War. Few, assuredly, would have been as concerned as Churchill about the disposal of Hong Kong or the Dutch

East Indies. On the other hand, they would also not have anticipated or welcomed the rapid demise of the British Empire. The spontaneous happiness on VE-day (more so than on VJ-day, with its atomic overtones) manifested that sincere satisfaction at having fought the good fight, and finished the race – and that as a unified people, without more than a few Quislings or boundary problems or population transfers to worry about, but instead an improved social future to anticipate.

It was in such circumstances, obviously enough, that Attlee's Labour Party could come into its own. The aura of victory obscured the future uncertainties. Swords could be turned into ploughshares without much apparent risk. The existing strength of the British armed services belied the country's real collapse as a great power. Victory parades obscured the truly frightening economic prospects. Decorations bestowed to Slim's army, or to the Gurkhas, concealed the fact that control over the Indian sub-continent was beginning to disintegrate. Churchill's (and Attlee's) presence at Potsdam suggested that Britain was still the equal of the United States and Russia. Long-awaited letters from loved-ones in garrisons stretching from Hamburg to Saigon confirmed that its world-power status survived unchanged, perhaps enhanced. And, as one student of this whole episode has pointed out, the average Briton's adherence to his own distinctive national institutions and customs had not been affected by this most destructive of wars: 'Parliament, the political parties, the Civil Service, local government, the press, the law, trade unions – all emerged from the war with slightly different surface features, but basically unaltered . . .' which indicated 'that somehow or other, things in their own country were arranged much better than elsewhere in the world . . .'[7]

That said, it becomes clear from such widespread satisfaction that this was *not* really a Carthaginian peace. Victory, well deserved and well enjoyed, was better than a Vichy-like compromise with Nazi Germany, and obviously better than defeat and conquest. Yet it was, nonetheless, achieved at great cost. Such a cost was not, relative to its age, *quantitatively* different from that paid in 1914–18 or even in 1793–1815; but it was *qualitatively* different. Britain had entered the Second World War as an independent great power, but she no longer possessed that status when she emerged from it. How many of the cheering populace around Buckingham Palace or Piccadilly Circus on 8 May 1945 realized that, one wonders? How many cared? How difficult would it be for the nation as a whole to turn from savouring victory to confront the challenges of the post-war world? These were questions for the future; but they were not allowed to interfere with the present enjoyment.

Adjusting to Reality, 1945–51

The years 1945–51 were among the most successful in the history of British external policy. For much of the period, Attlee's administration, with Bevin as its Foreign Secretary, faced a horrific concatenation of problems: Europe in ruins, Palestine in turmoil, India on the brink of civil war, seething discontents in Egypt and other parts of the Arab world, insurrection in Malaya, an alarming decline in relations with Russia, communist pressure from Berlin to Hong Kong, American indifference and then, as it seemed, excessive American belligerency, and all this at a time when the economic pressures upon sterling were both ominous and persistent. Yet when the Conservative government of 1951 entered office, a great number of these problems had been solved, Britain had extricated itself from many untenable positions, threats had been contained, and new structures of security and prosperity had been devised. Much of this was due to good fortune, and much to the constructive action of others, especially the United States; but it is nonetheless true that Bevin adroitly used the materials at hand to produce satisfactory solutions. As such, his period as Foreign Secretary compares well with Salisbury's post-1885 recovery of Britain's diplomatic position, or with Lansdowne's post-1900 adjustment by a policy of *ententes*.

Yet all three periods, it is not unfair to claim, were successful because British external policy more judiciously accorded with reality, that is, with the reality of rising challenges and reduced resources. To say that post-1945 Britain achieved diplomatic successes, therefore, would puzzle those who thought in terms of Palmerstonian triumph and Disraelian pomp, and would certainly be contested – and was *hotly* contested – by those attached to an Empire on which, so they believed, the sun should never set. Similarly, to praise Bevin's role in withstanding Russian pressures, persuading the Americans to assume an ever greater share in West-European defence, and in helping to fashion NATO and other forms of European security and recovery would not be appreciated by his many left-wing critics who urged conciliation with Stalin and independence from the United States before the Cold War worsened. Applauding Whitehall's clever adjustment to reality, in other words, reveals an unspoken assumption about what 'reality' meant for Britain after 1945. Here it is taken to imply that Britain was a medium-sized state within the North-Atlantic and democratic-capitalist world, needing to divest itself of its overstretched imperial possessions, needing also to pay more attention to its European circumstance, and always concerned to secure peaceful change and to prevent – without surrender – an international crisis escalating into a great-power war. Thus defined, British interests were certainly well looked after in these six years.

The key to the solution of most of Britain's external problems, both in Europe and in many overseas regions, lay in the successful influencing of the United States. In the immediate aftermath of the war, this seemed a formidable task indeed. Lend-lease had been cut off, and Keynes and others feared that London's request for some new form of financial assistance would meet with, if not a refusal, then stiff demands on Washington's part. Military co-operation through the Combined Chiefs of Staff had also ended, although the British had proposed its continuance. Truman and Attlee knew little of each other, and there was a considerable American mistrust of the 'socialist experiment' now being undertaken by the Labour government, the more especially if it could be shown to be funded in part by United States financial aid. The Jewish lobby in America vociferously attacked British attempts to halt the flood of European refugees into Palestine. Critics of British imperialism felt that Whitehall was making unnecessary excuses to delay the granting of Indian independence. In another sphere, some Americans dismissed British fears of Russian aims; Churchill's 'iron curtain' speech at Fulton, Missouri, in 1946 was felt to be exaggerated and the call was still to be heard for the withdrawal of American troops from Germany. Although in fact many other Americans were arguing for a 'tougher' stance towards Russia, the isolationist voices were enough to worry the British government for a while.

The loan which Keynes secured during his 1945 Washington visit provided a temporary relief for the British economy; and, if it enabled Attlee's colleagues to concentrate upon their plans to create a welfare state, it also freed Bevin, Alexander (Minister of Defence) and those concerned with external affairs to be able to deal with some of their more pressing problems. The first steps were frequently unsure and wrong-footed, like the tentative decision to create a large British military base in Palestine – in part, so as to extricate amicably the enormous garrison of 100,000 men from Egypt. By 1947, however, it was evident that the chaos and bloodshed in Palestine was far worse than anything the Egyptian nationalists could offer; and Bevin found it more and more intolerable to be criticized as anti-Jewish by American opinion and a considerable part of the Labour Party on the one hand, and as a cunning supporter of

Zionism by most of the Arab world on the other. After reference to an Anglo-American committee had produced only a stalemate, and with the worsening violence in Palestine coinciding with the onset of a sterling crisis early in 1947, Bevin handed the problem over to the United Nations and announced that British troops would leave the region in May 1948. Both steps were criticized by each side and for various reasons; but there is no doubt that the continuance of the British mandate in Palestine under the existing conditions was a farce – and an expensive farce at that.

There were fewer misgivings in Whitehall about the parallel retreat from the Indian sub-continent: that policy was, after all, the long-proclaimed and genuine aim of the Labour Party and, more practically, it was even harder to maintain control over that vast region than over Palestine. The Second World War had in many ways checked the activities of the Congress Party, whereas the Muslim League, which had supported the British and whose followers had enlisted heavily into the Indian Army, grew in strength and influence. Since it violently objected to inclusion within a Hindu-dominated unitary state, there was no prospect of the British being able to reach a tidy solution in the short space of time which they had set: if the peoples of the Indian sub-continent could not agree among themselves, they would have to agree to differ. At any rate, their differences would no longer be held in check by the Raj, articulating Curzonian notions of good government before self-government. On 14 August 1947, to the joy of the Muslims and the muted dismay of the Congress Party, and accompanied by a horrific loss of life in border areas, British India was transformed into two quite independent states, India and Pakistan. Both decided, like Ceylon but unlike Burma in the year following, to remain in the Commonwealth, thus giving sustenance to those who hoped for a metamorphosized imperial link. But no one could doubt that it marked a real watershed in Britain's global position and presumptions. Over a century earlier, Macaulay had predicted that when the time came to grant European institutions and liberty to the Indians 'it will be the proudest day in English history', yet it hardly seemed like that. Attlee and his colleagues received various congratulations from politically conscious Labour followers when the date of withdrawal was announced early in 1947, but most Britons were then concerned with the more prosaic issue of coal shortages, the severe winter, and the continued rationing of food. When the actual day of transfer came, Britain was in the midst of a sterling crisis and the government was preparing a series of austerity measures.

Compared with the Palestine and Indian issues, other aspects of British policy outside Europe in the late 1940s were much less epic. A communist-led insurrection in Malaya was being checked by successful 'counter-insurgency' methods, which permitted some Britons to congratulate themselves upon how much better they were performing than the French in Indo-China – without, perhaps, reflecting that the Malay majority, disliking the Chinese, still supported the British presence. Much less adroit was Whitehall's treatment of Egypt, where, having pulled out of Palestine, the British decided to stay a while (at least in the Canal Zone), thus arousing further nationalist resentment. In better times, this might have been settled to the satisfaction of both sides, for the differences were essentially those of timing. But the new frontiers of insecurity which now existed from Greece to Malaya predictably aroused that atavistic regard for the imperial line of communications through Suez. If the Egyptians were forced to wait until Britain felt its global interests were unthreatened, however, they would clearly need to be patient for much longer, perhaps for ever. Further south, there had been general strikes in Nigeria (1945) and the Sudan (1947), and the riots in the Gold Coast (1948), which showed that nationalistic ferment was spreading; but there was no sign that they caused the British government to revise its plans for a long period of continued 'trusteeship' over its dependent empire.

The real frontier of insecurity to British eyes, however, lay much closer to home – in Europe. The Soviet policy over Poland, the tight controls exercised over its zone in Germany, the pressures upon Greece and Turkey, the quarrel over Trieste, the demand for a share of the Italian colonies and, above all, perhaps, its massive military presence in central Europe, suggested to the Foreign Office a pattern of expansionism rather than the simple quest for security on Russia's part. These unpleasant developments in East-West relations, combined with the received historical wisdom about the folly of 'appeasement', meant that there was now no prospect of any repetition of that post-1919 withdrawal from a continental commitment. Substantial British forces of occupation were, of course, already in Germany and it seemed likely that they would stay there indefinitely. In 1946 Montgomery, the new Chief of Imperial General Staff, argued for a firm British pledge to fight 'on the mainland of Europe', and it was undoubtedly this factor which influenced the retention of conscription in peacetime. In its very early stages, this sort of thinking had anticipated some future revival of German militarism, and the Dunkirk Treaty of Alliance signed with France in March 1947 could easily be seen as another chapter in the twentieth-century history of the *entente cordiale*; but within a very short while it was the Russian threat which was seen to be greater than the German (rather as in 1919); and it was not to be too many years before the West was looking to the Federal Republic of Germany to enter, and to provide troops for, a new West-European bloc.

In 1947, however, the Federal Republic of Germany did not exist and Bevin's chief aim was to bind the United States more closely to the defence of Europe. This was done by a series of announcements and actions which were partly premeditated, but partly forced upon the government by the worsening economic crisis of February-March 1947. The deadline for the independence of India was brought forward. The Palestine issue was handed over to the United Nations.

Notice was given that British assistance to Greece and Turkey had to cease. All three could be seen as indicating a certain loss of imperial will or, alternatively, of imperial muscle and money – this latter interpretation being reinforced by British hints that an economically ruined Europe would never be able to resist communism. The American response is equally well known: the proclamation of the Truman Doctrine, pledging support to friendly states under threat, and the assumption of British responsibilities towards Greece and Turkey by the Americans, were soon followed by the announcement of the Marshall Aid scheme for economic reconstruction. By this, more than anything else, there was created a powerful trans-Atlantic bond in the post-war years.

Russia's refusal to join the Marshall Aid venture, its pressure upon its satellites to do the same, and the continued deadlock over German reparations, simply confirmed London in its suspicion of Stalin's intentions. Ignoring the criticisms of a considerable body of left-wing Labour MPs – for, like Grey, Bevin could always rely upon the Conservatives to support him against proposals from the radicals – the Foreign Secretary pressed ahead with his scheme for further West-European defence, consummated in the Treaty of Brussels of March 1948. By that time, it was escalation all the way. The leaders of the non-communist parties in Rumania, Bulgaria and Hungary had already been eliminated in the previous summer; Mikolajczyk and his London associates were being pushed out of power in Poland; and in February 1948 Czechoslovakia fell to a communist *coup*. Disagreements over Germany led to the Russian closure of the road routes to Berlin, and that in turn to the 'Berlin airlift'. In 1948, the first of the American B29 Superfortress squadrons arrived in East Anglia, the vanguard of a force which steadily expanded as the Cold War intensified, allowing Orwell, just then writing his novel *Nineteen Eighty-Four*, to refer to Britain as 'Airstrip One'. The insurrection in Malaya, and the advance of Mao Tse-

Tung's forces in China, suggested that the communist challenge was now world-wide. And the whole atmosphere darkened further with the realization that Russia, too, possessed the knowledge to manufacture atomic bombs.

The final period of the Labour government witnessed a steep rise in armaments expenditure in response to the Korean War, a conflict in which British and Commonwealth forces, under the auspices of the United Nations, supported the American counteraction against North Korea. But much more important in the long run was Britain's commitment to the NATO Alliance, signed in Washington on 4 April 1949. With it, 'splendid isolation' in the Salisburian or even the Baldwinian manner was gone for ever. Instead, Britain and the other signatories were mutually pledged to each other's defence in an alliance which had no fixed duration. Of even greater significance, however, was the adhesion of the United States to its first formal military alliance in peacetime. This reflected a seismic shift in Washington's attitude towards foreign entanglements and soon the British were to begin to wonder whether a policy of restraint, rather than encouragement, should not be adopted towards the wave of anti-communist sentiment sweeping Congress and much of the American press. Attlee's hurried visit to Truman in December 1950 (when it was feared that the United States might use the atomic bomb against China), and a marked difference in British and American policies over the recognition of the communist regime in Peking, suggest that London felt by this time that some degree of co-existence was to be preferred to mutual antagonism and possible annihilation.

The Defence of Imperial Frontiers, and the Suez Débâcle

The advent of Churchill's administration in October 1951, despite the electoral rhetoric, offered little change in British external policy. Defence spending was still rising, and over-heating the economy, and in 1952 the first British atomic bomb was exploded. Commitment to European security was reinforced, but accompanied by the retention rather than the liquidation of imperial defence obligations; and the relation-ship with the United States was characterized by an underlying recognition of common interests and ultimate British dependence, but also by a divergence over how to respond to the communist world and to indigenous nationalisms. It was in the latter, non-European arena that Anglo-American differences were most marked, since many of the wartime attitudes of rivalry – in particular, the American dislike of British colonialism and of its divergent policy towards China – still survived alongside their mutual commitment to Western Europe.

This British identification with Europe remained, how-ever, ambivalent and conditional. Commonwealth opinion was guarded, and pro-Empire Tories were very cool indeed, to the notions of supra-nationality. The Beaverbrook press criticized any British involvement in a West-European union – the characteristic stance of an 'Empire Free Trader'. Other patriots feared the revival of German militarism, or the contagious effects of being too closely tied to France and Italy, where the communist parties were very strong. The Labour Left, on the other hand, not only disapproved of any firm connection with the Catholic and Conservative ele-ments in Europe, but also disliked being part of an anti-Russian *bloc* and was further opposed to Britain joining in a

Franco-German scheme (the Schuman Plan of May 1950) for the joint administration of their iron and steel industries – Aneurin Bevan roundly declaring this to be only to the benefit of international capitalists. Neither wing need have worried. The Labour government, and its Conservative successor, both supported moves for European co-operation; but both equally assumed that Britain was *not* directly part of that movement. The Tories could not admit that their country was a mere European power; and Labour, explained Dalton, could never permit its great social gains of the 1945–51 period to be put 'in peril through allowing vital decisions on great issues of national economic policy to be transferred from the British Parliament at Westminster to some supra-national European assembly...'⁸ Bevin declined to participate in the Iron and Steel Union; and, more significantly, neither Labour nor Conservatives would agree to merging British forces in a joint European army during the early 1950s, which was the price the French demanded for their acceptance of German rearmament. Although London was willing to sign various declarations favouring the European Defence Community in 1952 and to promise aid on the event of a Russian attack, these were always *supplementary* gestures.

By 1954, however, French and American pressure compelled Eden to make a formal declaration that Britain would 'continue to maintain on the mainland of Europe, including Germany', its present effective strength, which represented a hardening of its NATO commitment. At the same time, it agreed to join the Western European Union, with its proclaimed (though very distant) aim of 'encouraging the progressive integration of Europe'. How distant it was in British eyes was to be seen a few years later when London declined to participate in the moves being made for the formation of the European Economic Community. The *continental commitment* meant, as it had since Elizabeth I's day, a strategic obligation, not a form of political or economic union.

The obverse of this unwillingness to join in the moves towards European political integration was the continued interest in playing a global role – something which the Conservatives under the ageing Churchill took for granted. In their Global Strategy Paper of 1952 (itself a significant title), they accepted wholeheartedly the doctrine of nuclear deterrence and gave 'super-priority' to the production of V-bombers, which was the sign that Britain was still a great power, qualitatively superior to the other medium-size states, and did not wish to be absolutely dependent upon the American nuclear umbrella. Yet this declaration of armaments priorities did not lead to any diminution in conventional weaponry or troop deployment or obligations in the overseas world. A whole string of treaties and interests exercised British diplomacy across the Middle East, from the quarrel with Mussaddiq over the nationalization of oil interests in Iran to the deterioration of relations with Egypt; and the Foreign Office also devoted much of its energies to the future of French Indo-China, which was eventually resolved (under Eden's joint chairmanship) at the Geneva Conference of 1954. If London's role as a mediator on that issue displeased Dulles, then the American Secretary of State was put in better humour by British involvement in the creation of SEATO (South-east Asia Treaty Organization) in that same year, with its pledge to act in concert to resist aggression in that region. A year later, Britain did the same again in the Middle East by entering CENTO (Central Treaty Organization) with Turkey, Iraq, Iran and Pakistan, supported by the United States. Here were obligations, albeit jointly shared, which would have bemused Palmerston, and they brought with them renewed attempts to find a secure *place d'armes* for British forces in the Near East/North-east Africa region – say, in Cyprus, Aden, or even Kenya – in the event of Egypt becoming untenable. While this might all be described in retrospect as 'the search . . . for handholds' by a country sliding downhill,[9] it nevertheless remains remarkable that there was no attempt at any long-term assessment of where and when the slide might properly be halted. It was not only in the earlier acquisition of their Empire that the British appear to have acted, *qua* Seeley, in a fit of absence of mind.

Given such tendencies, it is not surprising that the psychological as well as the political consequences of the Suez *débâcle* of 1956 were correspondingly severe. Since that unsuccessful use of British and French troops to try to prevent Colonel Nasser's seizure of the Suez Canal divided and excited the nation more than any other incident in foreign policy since Munich, and has already bred a formidable bibliography,[10] a repetition of the historical event is not called for here. What it demonstrated, beyond question, was that the older assumptions about how Britain and France could operate by military means to protect 'national interests' were held by fewer circles than ever. There was little use in Eden talking of 'megalomaniacal dictators' and making references to the lessons of the 'appeasement' policy of the 1930s: it was now two decades later, and few foreigners saw much similarity with Nazi imperialism in Nasser's policies. The actual power of the Anglo-French forces to seize the Suez Canal was not in question; but the background elements of national will, public support, economic strength and international opinion were. Soviet opposition and threats were predictable but, coinciding as they did with the crushing of the Hungarian uprising, they were rather cool even for the Kremlin. Much more embarrassing to London was the disfavour shown by Dulles, and when this American opposition extended to the refusal of support for sterling, Eden and his colleagues had little option but to retreat – in turn, alienating the French. Even before then, however, the Suez issue had split the Commonwealth, with India (under Nehru, already 'non-aligned') and most other members bitterly critical of this return to 'gunboat diplomacy', and only Australia offering support. Within Britain itself, the majority of the Labour Party (although not, perhaps, its leader, Gaitskell) were angered by the government's policies and they were joined in their attacks by a significant number of dissident Conservatives who threatened to vote against the leadership.

Suez provided a shock to the system so great as to enable Eden's adroit successor as Prime Minister, Harold Macmillan, to reorientate much of British external policy over the following five years. It is always tempting in retrospect to point to an obvious 'watershed' in political practices when it was in reality far less detectable to contemporaries struggling to understand the normal confusion of daily events and when the changes were, arguably, not always consciously planned by people whose intention in this case was primarily to restore the electoral fortunes of the Conservative Party. Nevertheless, in easing the country out of its imperial obligations, in turning attention towards Europe, in restructuring defence policy, and in concentrating upon domestic prosperity, Macmillan and his colleagues successfully grappled with various problems of Britain's post-war decline which earlier administrations had refused to face – or had not even seen.

Arriving at the Present

Perhaps the least clear aspect of the gradual alteration in British external policy lay in the realm of defence matters. It was true that in 1957 the Minister of Defence, Duncan Sandys, announced a major shift in military procurement and in strategic assumptions: there was to be an even greater reliance upon the nuclear deterrent and in consequence much less upon conventional forces. Conscription was to be ended – the size of the army was more than halved between 1956 and 1962 – and withdrawals of various units were to be made from Germany and from imperial outposts, the idea being to despatch reinforcements by air from Britain to any trouble-spot in a matter of days. Defence spending was cut in absolute terms, and as a proportion of the Gross National Product it fell steadily from 7.8 per cent in 1956 to 6.4 per cent in 1962, which may have been a not insignificant factor in the 'You've never had it so good' years of Macmillan-supervised boom.

Many of these new defence plans had soon to be altered: for example, the East German building of the Berlin Wall in 1961, and pressure from NATO partners, stopped further troop withdrawals from Germany; and the nuclear deterrent policy was thrown into disarray by the technological failure of the Blue Streak missile and the American cancellation of Skybolt, while the later acquisition of a Polaris system, although technologically superior, raised the question of how 'independent' the British deterrent really was when the weapon was supplied and its use controlled in part by the United States. But perhaps the untidiest feature related to extra-European defence, for the notion of using an airborne 'strategic reserve' allowed politicians to reduce overseas deployment of troops *without* cutting overseas commitments – to CENTO, SEATO, Malaya and so on, each of these helping to justify the retention of a string of bases and this whole policy now, curiously, receiving encouragement from a Kennedy administration in Washington which desired stability in the Indian Ocean without an American presence there. Of course, much of this could be explained by the continued tensions with Russia, and by the 'peace-keeping' actions in East Africa, Aden, Kuweit and Borneo; but it all seemed to confirm the assertion of European politicians such as de Gaulle that Britain had interests and ties which made it different from its continental neighbours.

Only in the mid-to-late 1960s was this lingering pretension to an imperial role finally exposed, although not so much by a change of sentiment as by the harsh reality of repeated economic crises. The new Labour government, in its first few years, showed no wish to retreat: in November 1964 Harold Wilson publicly declared, 'We are a world power and a world influence, or we are nothing.'[11] During the 'Six Days War' of 1967 between Israel and its Arab neighbours, he and George Brown were still keen to have British aircraft-carriers alongside their American counterparts in the Eastern Mediterranean and the Red Sea, as if nothing had changed since the days of Disraeli. Yet, over the two preceding years, defence reviews by Denis Healey had already led to a cut in projected expenditures, a reduction in the Territorial Army, a withdrawal of one-third of British forces overseas and the decision to build no further aircraft-carriers; and, a few months after that Arab-Israeli War, the run upon sterling forced Wilson's government to devalue the pound and simultaneously to plan for further cuts in defence expenditure – in part to persuade the Labour left to accept reductions in allocation to the social services. By pulling out of Aden, announcing the future withdrawal from the Persian Gulf and Malaya/Singapore, and cancelling the F-111, the British government was for the first time since 1945 trying to ensure that its commitments were reduced *in line with* cuts in the armed forces. By February 1969 Healey could claim that the seal had been set on 'Britain's transformation from a world power to a European power'. This was not a statement pleasing to the Conservative government of 1970–4, nor to that of 1979; but the tides of change could not be turned back. If there has been a marked emphasis in the priority attached to defence by the Labour and Conservative parties in recent years, this has essentially been about the *amount* of the national budget to be devoted to the armed services and not about the strategic *direction,* which is more or less exclusively centred upon Europe. Eventually, untidily and not a little reluctantly, Whitehall accepted that its military aims and capabilities could no longer be global in scope.

The political and diplomatic corollary of this strategic contraction was the withdrawal from the remaining major colonies and the decision to enter the European Economic Community. If both of those processes appeared almost as untidy and drawn-out as British defence policy itself in the post-Suez era, then that was partly to be explained by factors other than the reluctance of successive British governments to abandon past habits: for there were often practical difficulties which slowed down the pace of 'unscrambling an empire'; and the move towards Europe was considerably delayed by the opposition of de Gaulle, against whom neither Conservative nor Labour administrations could prevail.

Nevertheless, it is also clear that both processes were firmly begun under Macmillan's direction; this in all probability made the alteration in external policy that much less contentious an issue in British politics than if it had been carried out by a Labour administration in the face of a united Conservative stand against 'betrayals' and 'surrenders'. Instead, Macmillan – who had ironically obtained the succession to Eden because he had seemed firmer over Suez – was to imitate Peel, Disraeli and Baldwin in reshaping the party to accord with contemporary realities at the expense of anachronistic doctrines. Of course, even Macmillan assumed that Britain had a particular role to play in world politics and devoted an excessive amount of time towards arranging 'summit' meetings to defuse East-West relations; but under the facade of Edwardian self-assurance, the British government was on the move. The clearest indication that it would avoid what Salisbury had once described as 'the commonest error in politics . . . sticking to the carcases of dead policies', came in Macmillan's famous 'wind of change' speech at Cape Town in 1960. The Afrikaners obviously did not agree with this judicious tacking to new forces in world affairs, and right-wing Tories at home were also upset; but in any event the Colonial Office under the resourceful Iain Macleod was already supervising the dissolution of the Empire. Ghana, the Sudan and Malaya had achieved independence before Macmillan's speech, Cyprus and Nigeria's turn came in that year, and then the trickle turned into a flood. In 1955, there had been only eight members of the Commonwealth; by 1967, there were twenty-eight, and several others had decided not to acquire membership upon gaining their independence. Most of the newer Commonwealth members followed India's example and became republics, thereby cutting any direct link with the British Crown. By the 1970s and 1980s, with lands as small as Tonga, the Bahamas and Grenada becoming full members, only those territories with particular internal problems or external threats – Gibraltar, Hong Kong, the Falkland Islands etc. – remained under British control. Even the lengthy saga of Rhodesian 'UDI' was brought to a close, early in 1980, by the elections leading to a black-dominated government of Zimbabwe under Robert Mugabe. By that time also, the Commonwealth had so changed its nature that it could no longer be regarded as a source of military, economic or political strength, or even as a symbol of Britain's global influence. At the 1971 Commonwealth Prime Ministers' Conference, it had described itself as 'a voluntary association of independent sovereign states'. Three years earlier, as a bureaucratic reflection of this trend, the Commonwealth Office had been fused into the Foreign Office: relations with the newly independent states of the Commonwealth would be conducted in much the same way as relations with other states.

Once again, however, it needs to be recalled how swiftly that change took place and how few contemporaries saw it as the end of an era. 'England', claimed de Gaulle in January 1963 when placing his veto upon the Conservative government's application to join the European Economic Community, 'is insular, maritime, linked by trade, markets, and food supply to very different and often very distant lands . . .'[12] This was much less true than in the immediate post-war years, but many Britons still felt the same way: Empire free-traders; Atlanticists; the Labour left; arch-Protestant sects, disliking links with a predominantly Catholic European Community; and significant Commonwealth interests. Against these stood the various idealists of European integration: the Liberal Party, 'moderate' Conservatives and 'moderate' Labour; business interests eager not to be excluded from the booming European market; and politicians and economists who pointed to the changing pattern of trade relations even while insisting in the same breath that Britain's entry into the EEC would have little effect upon the Commonwealth. But perhaps the strongest argument, especially as the 1960s turned into the 1970s, was the nagging question, 'Where else could Britain go?'

For about four hundred years, from the first Elizabeth to the second, geopolitical and economic circumstances had enabled the people of Great Britain to occupy a place in world affairs out of all proportion to their country's size and population. But the twentieth century, as Mackinder had correctly forecast sixty years earlier, had witnessed 'a correlation between the larger geographical and larger historical generalizations':[13] the tides had turned, and Britain had shrunk back to being an offshore European state, lacking the power to influence global politics and needing once again to be integrated into the cultural and economic matrix of Europe, as it had been before the oceanic discoveries of the sixteenth century had turned its eyes outwards. From 1945 onwards, it had pursued contradictory policies, to a large extent because its leaders were no longer clear where they were going; in Dean Acheson's cruel phrase of 1962, 'Great Britain had lost an empire and has not yet found a role . . .' Similar American comments made it quite clear that an Anglo-Saxon 'special relationship', although greatly distrusted by de Gaulle, lacked reality when one of the partners was almost ten times as powerful as the other. The short-lived European Free Trade Association (EFTA), although more congenial to those Britons who feared supranationality, was also no solution precisely because it had no political role. The European Economic Community, at least, offered a role and one which accorded with geographical realities even if those who argued for membership overestimated the economic benefits which they expected to result from entry.

The path to full membership, from the first application in 1961 to the final entry at the beginning of 1973, was a long and stony one. It involved, on the one hand, intensive debates within the two main political parties and across the whole spectrum of British politics; and, on the other, lengthy consultations with Commonwealth countries. Not least, it involved repeated negotiations with the EEC states themselves, which (after de Gaulle's demise in 1969) welcomed British accession but not at the price of any fundamental change in the structure and assumptions which had existed when the Treaty of Rome was signed in 1957. It remains to this day essentially an agricultural protectionist cartel in its financial arrangements (although with *potential* to develop other aspects), and this has obvious disadvantages for a country like Britain incapable of producing all its own foodstuffs and still attuned to purchasing such basic items on the world market. In consequence, payments to the collective fund threaten to wipe out the traditional surplus in 'invisible' trade which has sustained the British balance of payments for over a century. Industrially, entry into the EEC failed to effect that hoped-for improvement in British 'visible' trade, although this has obviously been the consequence of the repeated and chronic failures of management and trade unions to compete with their European counterparts rather than of any inherent cause in the Common Market itself. Politically, the organization has not greatly advanced from being a device to cement Franco-German relations: in its distant aim, admittedly, it poses the concept of a supra-national state and thus attracts the odium of arch-patriots on the one hand and those favouring 'socialism in one country' on the other; but, so far, it has nothing like a common currency, nor, of course, any central political decision-making body with powers akin to those of a national sovereign or president. Being unsatisfactory on various counts to forces within British society, membership of the Common Market is bound to remain at, or close to, the centre of political controversy in the future.

To certain observers, particularly in continental Europe, all this is evidence that the British have still not reconciled themselves to a reduced, purely regional role. To other critics, the obsession with economic issues such as agricultural-support prices or with changes in trade-union law betrays an introspection and egocentricity which not only stand in contrast to the country's earlier global role but also ignore those trends which make different parts of this entire planet even more interdependent and integrated.

In a way, both criticisms may seem deserved; but that itself is an indication of the difficulties of achieving a correct balance between the country's domestic and European concerns, and its vaguer but still considerable world interests. Britain is, very definitely, only a European power militarily: its defence commitments are almost exclusively to NATO, its weapons-procurement policy involves more and more joint projects and, like its alliance partners, it regards the aims and armaments of the Russian-led Warsaw Pact with considerable distrust. But this basic strategic constellation can never be confined to the European continent alone. Like the bi-polar rivalry which overshadows NATO, the mutual suspicions are extended into Africa, the Middle East, the Indian Ocean and elsewhere. The security of seaborne oil supplies, for example, must enter into defence calculations even if Britain itself can no longer justify a string of overseas fleet bases.

This outward 'pull', to which Conservative governments in Britain are most susceptible, is reinforced by commercial considerations; for, whatever the value of intra-European trade and the enormous problems which a Britain standing outside the EEC might nowadays confront, it is also true that the country's commerce and investments in the world overseas remain substantial. To those less concerned with business matters, moreover, there exists another dimension to British external policy in the realm of culture and institutions. In such things as the English language, the BBC World Service, parliamentary government, legal processes, sport, university structures, intellectual and literary exchanges, it has been argued, there can be seen not only the residues of the past but also those features of political and social behaviour which are of continued and growing importance. Here, even more than in its cosmopolitan commercial connections, Britain *still* occupies a role in the world out of all proportion to its area and population. Consequently, the country's 'Janus-face', scrutinizing and attempting to influence European developments but simultaneously peering with concern at events in Africa or North America, will preserve the ambivalences which have long existed in British attitudes towards external policy.

But there is, one suspects, more to the present British indecisiveness in external policy than this. Most other powers, too, have their problems and ambivalences, but appear in recent years to have been handling them with a greater degree of success than Britain has. Since Macmillan's own adjustments to reality in the early 1960s, the country has seemed to many observers, internal and external, to be floundering. This may to a large extent be attributed to the continual struggle with economic difficulties, and to the many effects of economic decline. In certain ways, in fact, it has become one of the weakest and least successful of the second-rate powers, with only half the economic muscle of West Germany or France; and all that the pretensions and rhetoric of successive British governments in recent years have done is to suggest an enormous – and widening – gap between assumptions and reality. This in turn has not only lowered Britain's position in the eyes of the USA, Russia and many of its EEC partners, but it has also contributed to the widespread domestic disillusionment, with politicians, with trades unions and bureaucracies, and with the Common Market in particular. In turn, this state of public disillusionment has produced further signs of national introspection and a general unwillingness to assume new roles and to think positively. Businessmen in general concentrate upon preserving profits and not (like the Japanese) upon enhancing their share of the world market; trades unions devote themselves to the defence of nineteenth-century practices, rather than pushing for job flexibility and creation; governments, both at national and local level, react to events rather than forge imaginative policies. Although it is impossible to prove that society is an organism, there *is* often a similarity between the life-cycle of an individual and a community; and, in Britain's case, too many commentators have pointed to evidence of national 'tiredness' and 'decay' for one to be able to dismiss the analogy completely.

All this makes it even more difficult for a British external policy to be evolved which would deal with the urgent and confusing developments in world affairs. The need for a common West-European policy is more pressing than ever before, but unlikely to be realized while British politicians and public concern themselves merely with the financial balances within the EEC. The 'North-South' divide, portrayed in the Brandt Report (1980) as the most critical cluster of global problems of all, appears scarcely to bother the Conservative or the Labour leadership, both of which suspect that 'aid for the Third World' is no election-winner. Very few, if any, of the nation's leaders seem to have perceived the long-term significance of such processes as the disintegration of the monolithic communist *bloc*, the American economic crises of the 1970s and the general weakening of the 'imperial' presidency, the even more severe (if usually better concealed) economic weaknesses of the Soviet Union, the revolutionary rise of the economic power of the OPEC cartel, and the rapid transfer of technology to specific Third-World countries: namely, that a decomposition may be beginning in that bi-polar world order which has existed since about 1943 and which, despite its many disadvantages for Britain's power position then, produced a crude stability in international affairs. The politics of the planet Earth are now altogether more fluid and precarious than they were in the days of Eisenhower and Macmillan – which is not an encouraging prospect to a country in Britain's present state.

There is no point in making this study a sermon, or ruminating like some latter-day Gibbon, gazing across the ruins of a lost Roman civilization. But since Britain did occupy for so long such a pre-eminent role in world affairs, it is important to emphasize how swiftly and how completely that position has vanished, and how uncertain and problematic its future remains. Since every historian writes 'in the stream of time', it is of course impossible to devise and to define conclusively the correct external policy for the British people, or for any other people, that would always be valid. Such a policy may in part be suggested by broad geographical and climatic factors which do not change; but it is also determined by economic and technological developments, by changing social and political moods, and by cultural and philosophical traditions. None of the latter, almost by definition, stays still. Alteration and adjustment are inevitable. And the future is, except in its very broad outline, unpredictable. All that one can reasonably do is to point at recent trends, at the dissolution or retention of traditional habits, and at the formative influences upon international politics. Having indicated what these have been in recent years, the historian of British external policy can only close his narrative, not on a conclusive note, but with all the uncertainties and loose ends remaining, as they do in political life.

APPENDIX: British Prime Ministers and Foreign Secretaries, 1865–1980

		PRIME MINISTER	FOREIGN SECRETARY
Liberal	1865– June 1866	Lord John Russell	Earl of Clarendon
Conservative	June 1866– Feb. 1868	14th Earl of Derby	Lord Edward Stanley
Conservative	Feb. 1868– Dec. 1868	Benjamin Disraeli	Lord Edward Stanley
Liberal	Dec. 1868– Feb. 1874	W. E. Gladstone	Earl of Clarendon (until July 1870) then Earl Granville
Conservative	Feb. 1874– Apr. 1880	Benjamin Disraeli	15th Earl of Derby (until April 1878) then Marquess of Salisbury
Liberal	Apr. 1880– June 1885	W. E. Gladstone	Earl Granville
Conservative	June 1885– Feb. 1886	Marquess of Salisbury	Marquess of Salisbury
Liberal	Feb. 1886– Aug. 1886	W. E. Gladstone	Earl of Rosebery
Conservative	Aug. 1886– Aug. 1892	Marquess of Salisbury	Earl of Iddesleigh (until Feb. 1887) then Marquess of Salisbury
Liberal	Aug. 1892– Mar. 1894	W. E. Gladstone	Earl of Rosebery
Liberal	Mar. 1894– June 1895	Earl of Rosebery	Earl of Kimberley
Conservative	June 1895– July 1902	Marquess of Salisbury	Marquess of Salisbury (until Oct. 1900) then Marquess of Lansdowne
Conservative	July 1902– Dec. 1905	A. J. Balfour	Marquess of Lansdowne

Liberal	Dec. 1905–Apr. 1908	Sir Henry Campbell-Bannerman	Sir Edward Grey
Liberal	Apr. 1908–May 1915	H. H. Asquith	Sir Edward Grey
Coalition	May 1915–Dec. 1916	H. H. Asquith	Sir Edward Grey
War Cabinet	Dec. 1916–Jan. 1919	D. Lloyd George	A. J. Balfour
Coalition	Jan. 1919–Oct. 1922	D. Lloyd George	A. J. Balfour (until Oct. 1919) then Earl Curzon
Conservative	Oct. 1922–May 1923	A. Bonar Law	Marquess of Curzon
Conservative	May 1923–Jan. 1924	Stanley Baldwin	Marquess of Curzon
Labour	Jan. 1924–Nov. 1924	Ramsay MacDonald	Ramsay MacDonald
Conservative	Nov. 1924–June 1929	Stanley Baldwin	Austen Chamberlain
Labour	June 1929–Aug. 1931	Ramsay MacDonald	Arthur Henderson
National	Aug. 1931–June 1935	Ramsay MacDonald	Marquess of Reading (until Nov. 1931) then Sir John Simon
National (Conservative)	June 1935–May 1937	Stanley Baldwin	Sir Samuel Hoare (until Dec. 1935) then Anthony Eden
National (Conservative)	May 1937–May 1940	Neville Chamberlain	Anthony Eden (until Mar. 1938) then Viscount Halifax
War Cabinet	May 1940–Aug. 1945	W. S. Churchill	Viscount Halifax (until Dec. 1940) then Anthony Eden

Labour	Aug. 1945–Oct. 1951	Clement Attlee	Ernest Bevin (until Mar. 1951) then Herbert Morrison
Conservative	Oct. 1951–Apr. 1955	W. S. Churchill	Anthony Eden
Conservative	Apr. 1955–Jan. 1957	Sir Anthony Eden	Harold Macmillan (until Dec. 1955) then J. Selwyn Lloyd
Conservative	Jan. 1957–Oct. 1963	Harold Macmillan	J. Selwyn Lloyd (until July 1960) then Earl of Home
Conservative	Oct. 1963–Oct. 1964	Sir Alec Douglas-Home	R. A. Butler
Labour	Oct. 1964–June 1970	Harold Wilson	P. Gordon Walker (until Jan. 1965) then Michael Stewart (until Aug. 1967) then George Brown (until Apr. 1968) then Michael Stewart
Conservative	June 1970–Mar. 1974	Edward Heath	Sir Alec Douglas-Home
Labour	Mar. 1974–Apr. 1976	Harold Wilson	James Callaghan
Labour	Apr. 1976–May 1979	James Callaghan	Anthony Crosland (until Feb. 1977) then David Owen
Conservative	May 1979–	Margaret Thatcher	Lord Carrington

Notes

Chapter 1

1. P. Padfield, *Tide of Empires: Decisive Naval Campaigns in the Rise of the West*, vol. 1, *1481–1654* (London, 1979); P. M. Kennedy, *The Rise and Fall of British Naval Mastery* (London, 1976), chs. 1–3; J. R. Jones, *Britain and the World, 1649–1815* (London, 1980).
2. J. Needham, *Science and Civilisation in China,* vol. iv, part 3, *Civil Engineering and Nautics* (Cambridge, 1971), pp. 379–587.
3. J. H. Plumb, *The Growth of Political Stability in England, 1675–1725* (London, 1967), p. xviii and *passim*.
4. E. J. Hobsbawm, *Industry and Empire* (Harmondsworth, 1969), pp. 49–50. See also the acute remarks in M. Balfour, *The Kaiser and His Times* (London, 1964), pp. 39ff.
5. P. Mathias, *The First Industrial Nation* (London, 1969), p. 250; Hobsbawm, *op. cit.,* p. 134.
6. Quoted in R. Hyam, *Britain's Imperial Century* (London, 1976), p. 48.
7. Apart from the coverage in the books by Mathias and Hobsbawm cited above, see the succinct survey in P. Mathias and M. M. Postan, *The Cambridge Economic History of Europe,* vol. vii, part 1 (Cambridge, 1978), pp. 201–11.
8. Mathias, *op. cit.,* p. 255.
9. W. L. Burn, *The Age of Equipoise* (London, 1964), p. 299.
10. J. L. Garvin, 'The Maintenance of Empire: a Study of the Economic Basis of Political Power', in C. S. Goldman (ed.), *The Empire and the Century* (London, 1905), pp. 69ff.
11. *Hansard* (Parliamentary Debates), 3rd series, clxxvi, 744–6, for Disraeli's speech; British Museum, Add. Mss. 49683 (Balfour Papers), Balfour to Edward VII, 28 December 1903.

12. W. G. Hynes, *The Economics of Empire* (London, 1979), *passim*.

13. B. Porter, *The Lion's Share. A Short History of British Imperialism, 1850–1970* (London, 1975), pp. 353–4.

14. Marquess of Crewe, *Lord Rosebery* (New York, 1931), p. 254.

15. Statistics from A. J. P. Taylor, *The Struggle for Mastery in Europe, 1848–1918* (Oxford, 1954), pp. xxvii–xxviii.

16. Kennedy, 'Mahan versus Mackinder', Chapter 7 of *British Naval Mastery*.

17. Quoted in R. Postgate and A. Vallance, *Those Foreigners. The English People's Opinion on Foreign Affairs as Reflected in their Newspapers since Waterloo* (London, 1937), p. 80.

18. J. Morley, *The Life of William Ewart Gladstone*, 3 vols. (London, 1903), iii, p. 535.

19. Cited in R. B. McDowell, *British Conservatism, 1832–1914* (London, 1959), p. 94.

20. Cited in W. D. Gruner, 'Europäische Friede als nationales Interesse. Die Rolle des deutschen Bundes in der britischen Politik 1814–1832', *Bohemia*, vol. 18 (1977), pp. 120–1.

21. J. D. Vincent, *The Formation of the Liberal Party, 1857–1868* (London, 1966), pp. 257–8 and *passim*.

22. P. Adelman, *Gladstone, Disraeli and Later Victorian Politics* (London, 1970), Chapter 2, offers a brief survey.

23. *Ibid.*, p. 19.

24. H. V. Emy, 'The Impact of Financial Policy on English Politics before 1914', *Historical Journal*, vol. xv (1972), p. 104.

25. The best sources here are B. Mallett, *British Budgets, 1887–88 to 1912–13* (London, 1913); and A. T. Peacock and J. Wiseman, *The Growth of Public Expenditure in the United Kingdom* (London, 1967 edn).

26. Bodleian Library, Oxford, Clarendon Mss., dep. c 747, Clarendon to Loftus (copy), 10 February 1869.

27. Cited in A. J. Lee, *The Origins of the Popular Press, 1855–1914* (London, 1976), p. 21.

28. Bodleian Library, Oxford, Bryce Mss., 17, f.185, Bryce to Goldwin Smith (copy), 23 January 1900.

29. M. J. Allison, *The National Service Issue, 1899–1914* (Ph.D. thesis, University of London, 1975). p. 27.

30. J. Joll, 'War Guilt 1914: A Continuing Controversy', in P. Kluke and P. Alter, *Aspects of Anglo-German Relations through the Centuries* (Stuttgart, 1978), p. 73

31. Hyam, *op. cit.*, p. 49.

32. R. Robinson and J. Gallagher, with Alice Denny, *Africa and the Victorians* (London, 1961), pp. 19–20.

33. D. McLean, 'Finance and "Informal Empire" before the First World War', *Economic History Review*, 2nd series, vol. xxix (1976), pp. 291–305.

34. Z. S. Steiner, *The Foreign Office and Foreign Policy, 1898–1914* (Cambridge, 1969), *passim*.

35. Robinson and Gallagher, *op. cit.*, p. 20.

36. G. W. Monger, *The End of Isolation: British Foreign Policy, 1900–1907* (London, 1963), pp. 262–3.

37. Cited in A. J. Marder, *From the Dreadnought to Scapa Flow*, 5 vols. (London, 1961–70), i, p. 322.

38. On whom, see A. J. P. Taylor, *The Trouble Makers: Dissent over Foreign Policy, 1792–1939* (London, 1969 edn).

39. See C. Howard, *Britain and the Casus Belli, 1822–1902* (London, 1974), for a discussion of these points.

Chapter 2

1 O. Anderson, *A Liberal State at War. English Politics and Economics during the Crimean War* (London, 1967), *passim*.

2 Cited in R. Millman, *British Foreign Policy and the Coming of the Franco-Russian War* (Oxford, 1965), p. 20, fn. 8.

3. Cited in K. Bourne, *The Foreign Policy of Victorian England, 1830–1902* (Oxford, 1970), pp. 388–9.

4. Cited in Millman, *op. cit.*, p. 36.

5. Apart from Millman's book, see also W. E. Mosse, *The European Powers and the German Question, 1848–71* (Cambridge, 1958).

6. Liverpool Record Office, Derby Papers, 17/1/6, Derby to Odo Russell (copy), 3 March 1874.

7. See W. D. McIntyre, *The Imperial Frontier in the Tropics, 1865–1875* (London, 1967).

8. R. Shannon, *The Crisis of Imperialism 1865–1915* (London, 1974), pp. 124–5.

9. W. N. Medlicott, *Bismarck, Gladstone and the Concert of Europe* (London, 1956).

10. Robinson and Gallagher, *Africa and the Victorians*, Chapter V.

11. On which, see G. N. Sanderson, 'The European Partition of Africa: Coincidence or Conjuncture?', in E. F. Penrose (ed.), *European Imperialism and the Partition of Africa* (London, 1975), pp. 20ff.

12. Cited in W. O. Aydelotte, *Bismarck and British Colonial Policy* (Philadelphia, 1937), p. 166.

13. *Hansard*, 3rd series, vol. ccxciv, 1079–1100.

14. *The Letters of Queen Victoria*, 3rd series. 3 vols., edited by G. E. Buckle (London, 1930–2), i, p. 263.

15. Taylor, *The Struggle for Mastery in Europe*, p. 321.

16. P. Kluke, 'Bismarck and Salisbury: ein diplomatisches Duell,' *Historische Zeitschrift*, 175 (1953), pp. 285–306.

17. National Library of Scotland, Edinburgh, Ms. 10243, Rosebery to Kimberley, 28 April 1895.

18. It is best covered in P. Winzen, *Bülows Weltmachtkonzept* (Boppard, 1977).

19. C. J. Lowe, *The Reluctant Imperialists: British Foreign Policy, 1878–1902*, 2 vols. (London, 1967), i, p. 249.

20. Cited in Monger, *The End of Isolation*, p. 133.

21. British Museum, Additional Mss. 49711 (Balfour Papers), f.64, report on the 'Formation of a Permanent Sub-Committee . . .', p. 4.

22. Cited in Monger, *op. cit.*, pp. 281–2.

23. W. S. Churchill, *The World Crisis 1911–1918*, 2-volume edition (London, 1938), i, p. 33.

24. S. R. Williamson, *The Politics of Grand Strategy: Britain and France Prepare for War, 1904–1914* (Cambridge, Mass., 1969), is best on this topic.

25. The most detailed narrative is in L. Albertini, *The Origins of the War of 1914*, 3 vols. (Oxford, 1952–7). For the German side, see V. R. Berghahn, *Germany and the Approach of War in 1914* (London, 1973).

26. K. Wilson, 'The British Cabinet's Decision for War, 2 August 1914', *British Journal of International Studies*, vol. 1 (1975), pp. 148–59. See also the excellent coverage in Z. S. Steiner, *Britain and the Origins of the First World War* (London, 1977), especially Chapter 9.

Chapter 3

1. PRO, Cab. 16/18a, 'Trading with the Enemy'.
2. Peacock and Wiseman, *The Growth of Public Expenditure in the United Kingdom*, pp. 184–6.
3. S. Pollard, *The Development of the British Economy, 1914–1967* (London, 1969 edn), p. 75.
4. B. R. Tomlinson, 'India and the British Empire, 1880–1935', *The Indian Economic and Social History Review*, vol. xii (1975), pp. 349ff.
5. Pollard, *op. cit.*, p. 54.
6. Apart from the good survey in Pollard, *op. cit.*, ch. II, see also the more theoretical reflections in A. S. Milward, *The Economic Effects of the World Wars on Britain* (London, 1970), *passim;* and A. Marwick, *The Deluge* (Harmondsworth, 1967 edn).
7. Marwick, *op. cit.*, pp. 112ff.
8. C. Barnett, *The Collapse of British Power* (London/New York, 1972), p. 430. See also, P. Fussell, *The Great War and Modern Memory* (Oxford, 1975).
9. A. Marwick, *Britain in the Century of Total War* (Harmondsworth, 1970), p. 111.
10. Compare G. Dangerfield, *The Strange Death of Liberal England* (London, 1970 edn), with T. Wilson, *The Downfall of the Liberal Party, 1914–1935* (London, 1966), as key statements of these opposing views.
11. F. S. Oliver, *Ordeal by Battle* (London, 1915), pp. xi–xiii, and *passim* – the classic 'radical right' critique of pre-1914 Liberal external (and internal) policy.
12. See again, Taylor, *The Trouble Makers, passim.*
13. M. Swartz, *The Union of Democratic Control in British Politics during the First World War* (Oxford, 1971). p. 176.
14. Quoted in *ibid.*, p. 134.
15. M. Beloff, *Imperial Sunset*, vol. 1, *Britain's Liberal Empire 1897–1921* (London, 1969), p. 235.
16. Quoted in Swartz, *op. cit.*, p.175. Also very important in this connection is A. J. Mayer, *Political Origins of the New Diplomacy, 1917–1918* (New Haven, Conn., 1959), *passim.*

17. PRO, Cab. 24/67, G.T. 6091 (24 October 1917).
18. These figures come respectively from G. St J. Barclay, *The Empire is Marching* (London, 1976), p. 80; and G. Hardach, *The First World War, 1914–1918* (London, 1977), p. 153. Beloff, *Imperial Sunset*, i, ch. V, is very important on this theme.
19. N. Mansergh, *The Commonwealth Experience* (London, 1969), p. 171.
20. W. K. Hancock, *Smuts: the Sanguine Years, 1870–1919* (Cambridge, 1962), pp. 429ff.
21. W. R. Louis, *Great Britain and Germany's Lost Colonies, 1914–1919* (Oxford, 1967), *passim*.
22. Quoted in Porter, *The Lion's Share*, p. 242.
23 A. J. P. Taylor, *English History, 1914–1945* (Oxford, 1965), pp. 89fn., 105.
24. See P. Guinn, *British Strategy and Politics, 1914 to 1918* (Oxford, 1965), pp. 113–14.
25. Z. Steiner, 'The Foreign Office and the War', in F. H. Hinsley (ed.), *British Foreign Policy under Sir Edward Grey* (Cambridge, 1977), pp. 516–31; R. M. Warman, 'The Erosion of Foreign Office Influence in the Making of Foreign Policy, 1916–1918', *Historical Journal*, vol. xv (1972), pp. 133–9.
26. F. Oppenheimer, *Stranger Within* (London, 1960), pp. 227ff.

Chapter 4

1. See L. L. Farrar, *The Short-War Illusion* (Santa Barbara Oxford, 1973); P. M. Kennedy (ed.), *The War Plans of the Great Powers, 1880–1914* (London, 1979), *passim*.
2. M. Howard, 'The British Way in Warfare' (The Neale Lecture, London, 1975); and see also Guinn, *British Strategy and Politics, 1914 to 1918*, pp. 1–27.
3. For an elaboration of this argument, see my *The Rise and Fall of British Naval Mastery*, chs. 7–9.
4. *Ibid.*, ch. 9. It is pleasing to note that this argument, to which several German critics took exception when reviewing the German-language edition of *British Naval Mastery*, is now confirmed by a German economic historian: see Hardach, *The First World War*, especially Chapter 2.

5. Quoted in Marder, *From the Dreadnought to Scapa Flow*, ii, p. 175.
6. R. R. James, *Gallipoli* (London, 1965); A. Moorehead, *Gallipoli* (London, 1959 edn); Guinn, *British Strategy and Politics 1914 to 1918*, chs. II–III, are probably the best studies.
7. Taylor, *English History*, pp. 22–3.
8. Beloff, *Imperial Sunset*, vol. i, p. 190.
9. Guinn, *op. cit.*, p. 190.
10. *Ibid.*, p. 210.
11. L. S. Amery, *My Political Life*, 3 vols. (London, 1953), ii, pp. 160–1.
12. Guinn, *op. cit.*, pp. 177–8.
13. Hardach, *op. cit.*, p. 147.
14. Beloff, *op. cit.*, i, p. 182. Also important on this topic are Louis, *Great Britain and Germany's Lost Colonies, passim*; and V. H. Rothwell, *British War Aims and Peace Diplomacy 1914–1918* (Oxford, 1971), *passim*.
15. Cited in Guinn, *op. cit.*, p. 283, fn. 4.
16. Taylor, *The Struggle for Mastery in Europe*, p. 530.
17. Quoted in Beloff, *op. cit.*, p. 207.
18. *Ibid.*, p. 184.
19. For the above remarks, see W. Fest, *Peace or Partition: The Habsburg Monarchy and British Policy, 1914–1918* (London, 1978); and K. J. Calder, *Britain and the Origins of the New Europe, 1914–1918* (Cambridge, 1976).
20. A. J. Mayer, *Politics and Diplomacy of Peacemaking: Containment and Counterrevolution at Versailles, 1918–1919* (London, 1968), especially Chapters 5 and 18.
21. PRO, Cab. 23/43, IWC 31, Smuts on 14 August 1918.
22. Quoted in Guinn, *op. cit.*, p. 321. The remark is Henry Wilson's.
23. Lord Hankey, *The Supreme Control at the Paris Peace Conference, 1919* (London, 1963), p. 97.
24. PRO, Cab. 27/24, Eastern Committee minutes, 2 December 1918.
25. G. Schmidt, 'Wozu noch "politische Geschichte"?', *Aus Politik und Zeitgeschichte*, B 17/75 (April 1975), pp. 32ff.
26. Quoted in F. S. Northedge, *The Troubled Giant: Britain among the Great Powers, 1916–1939* (London, 1966), pp. 113–14.
27. *Ibid.*, p. 120.

Chapter 5

1. Quoted in K. Hildebrand, '"British Interests" und "Pax Britannica". Grundfragen englischer Aussenpolitik im 19. and 20. Jahrhunder', *Historische Zeitschrift*, 221 (1975), pp. 624-5.

2. See, for example, A. W. DePorte, *Europe between the Superpowers*, (New Haven/London, 1979).

3. Cited in M. Schlenke, 'Die Westmächte und das national-sozialistische Deutschland: Motive, Ziele und Illusionen der Appeasementpolitik,' in G. Niedhart (ed.) *Kriegsbeginn 1939* (Darmstadt, 1976), p. 291.

4. G. C. Peden, *British Rearmament and the Treasury. 1932-1939* (Edinburgh, 1979), p. 65. Other studies of the Treasury's position are in R. P. Shay, Jr, *British Rearmament in the Thirties. Politics and Profits* (Princeton, 1977); R. A. C. Parker, 'Economics, Rearmament and Foreign Policy: the United Kingdom before 1939 – A Preliminary Study', *Journal of Contemporary History*, vol. 10, no. 4 (1975), pp. 637-47; B. J. Wendt, *Economic Appeasement. Handel und Finanz in der britischen Deutschlandpolitik, 1933-1939* (Düsseldorf, 1971).

5. Quoted in K. Feiling, *Life of Neville Chamberlain* (London, 1946), p. 336.

6. Cited in M. Howard, *The Continental Commitment: the Dilemma of British Defence Policy in the Era of Two World Wars* (London, 1972), p. 79.

7. Cited in K. Middlemas and J. Barnes, *Baldwin: a Biography* (London, 1969), p. 327.

8. Peacock and Wiseman, *The Growth of Public Expenditure in the United Kingdom*, pp. 184-7. Full explanations of the manner of calculating these figures are given in this book.

9. Quoted in Barnett, *The Collapse of British Power*, pp. 434-5.

10. Quoted in C. L. Mowat, *Britain between the Wars 1918-1940* (London, 1969 edn), p. 553.

11. Barnett, *The Collapse of British Power*, p. 60.

12. C. E. Callwell, *Field Marshall Sir Henry Wilson*, 2 vols. (London, 1927), ii. pp. 240-1.

13 See M. Cowling, *The Impact of Labour* (Cambridge, 1971), especially pp. 1–11; idem. *The Impact of Hitler* (Cambridge. 1975), *passim*.

14 Barnett, *The Collapse of British Power*, *passim*.

15 *Documents on British Foreign Policy 1919–1939*, edited by E. L. Woodward, R. d'O. Butler *et al.* (London, 1947 ff.), series 1A, vol. 1, pp. 846ff.

Chapter 6

1. See the coverage in Kennedy, *British Naval Mastery*, pp. 274ff.; W. R. Louis, *British Strategy in the Far East 1919–1939* (Oxford, 1971), pp. 52ff.; S. W. Roskill, *Naval Policy between the Wars*, vol. 1 (London. 1968), chs. v and viii.

2. See especially, W. N. Medlicott. *British Foreign Policy since Versailles, 1919–1963* (London, 1968), pp. 11ff.; A. Orde. *Great Britain and International Security, 1920–1926* (London, 1978), *passim*; and, for a general overview, S. Marks, *The Illusion of Peace: International Relations in Europe, 1918–1933* (London, 1976).

3. Quoted in E. W. Bennett, *German Rearmament and the West. 1932–1933* (Princeton, N.J., 1979), p. 446, fn. 88.

4. N. H. Gibbs, *Grand Strategy*, vol. 1 (London, 1976), pp. 287–8.

5. Howard, *The Continental Commitment*, p. 105.

6. See Kennedy, *British Naval Mastery*, ch. 10; and Roskill, *Naval Policy between the Wars*, 2 vols., *passim*.

7. Cited in Howard, *The Continental Commitment*, p. 81; and see also H. Montgomery Hyde. *British Air Policy between the Wars, 1918–1939* (London, 1976), *passim*.

8. Quoted in C. Thorne, *The Limits of Foreign Policy: the West. the League and the Far Eastern Crisis of 1931–1933* (London. 1973 edn), p. 90.

9. *Ibid.*, *passim;* Kennedy, *British Naval Mastery*. p. 284; Barnett, *The Collapse of British Power*, pp. 296ff.

10. Barnett, *op. cit.*, p. 345; Gibbs. *Grand Strategy*, i, ch. iv.

11. Howard, *The Continental Commitment*, p. 99.

12. A. J. Marder, 'The Royal Navy and the Ethiopian Crisis of 1935–36', *American Historical Review*, vol. lxxv (1970), pp.

1327–56; F. Hardie, *The Abyssinian Crisis* (London, 1974), ch. 15.

13. J. T. Emmerson, *The Rhineland Crisis* (London, 1977), *passim*; R. Meyers, 'Sicherheit und Gleichgewicht: Das britische Kabinett und die Remilitarisierung des Rheinlandes 1936', *Rheinische Vierteljahrsblätter*, Jg. 38 (1974), pp. 406–49.

14. For example, Gruner, 'Frieden, Krieg and politisch-soziales System,' *passim*; but the same comment may to some extent be made of my own article, 'The Tradition of Appeasement in British Foreign Policy', *British Journal of International Studies*, vol. 2 (1976), pp. 195–215.

15. There is a vast amount of literature upon British public and party opinion on appeasement. A short list would include M. Gilbert and R. Gott, *The Appeasers* (London, 1963); N. Thompson, *The Anti-Appeasers* (London, 1971); Cowling, *The Impact of Hitler*; J. F. Naylor, *Labour's International Policy* (Boston, 1969); W. R. Rock, *Appeasement on Trial* (Hamden, Conn., 1966).

16. Cited in Howard, *The Continental Commitment*, pp. 120–1.

17. Medlicott, *British Foreign Policy since Versailles*, p. 176.

18. Should one offer a list of books on the Czech crisis of 1938? The most useful coverages (to me) seem to be in: Barnett, *The Collapse of British Power*, pp. 505ff.; A. J. P. Taylor, *The Origins of the Second World War* (Harmondsworth, 1964 edn), ch. 8; C. Thorne, *The Approach of War 1938–39* (London, 1968), ch. 3; K. Middlemas, *Diplomacy of Illusion: The British Government and Germany, 1937–39* (London, 1972), pp. 181ff.; K. Robbins, *Munich, 1938* (London, 1968) – to which one may add the recent 'blockbuster' by T. Taylor, *Munich: The Price of Peace* (London, 1979), *passim*.

19. Cited in Howard, *The Continental Commitment*, p. 124. See also the impressive study by R. Meyers, *Britische Sicherheitspolitik 1934–1938* (Düsseldorf, 1976), especially pp. 468ff.

20. See the new analyses by M. Hauner, 'Czechoslovakia as a Military Factor in British Considerations of 1938', *Journal of Strategic Studies*, vol. 1, no. 2 (1978), pp. 194–222; and W. Murray, 'Munich, 1938: The Military Confrontation', *ibid.*, vol. 2 (1979), pp. 282–302; and the coverage in Barnett, *The Collapse of British Power*, pp. 505ff.

21. *Ibid.*, p. 519.

22. Howard, *The Continental Commitment*, p. 103.
23. *Ibid.*, p. 124.
24. Cited in G. Niedhart, 'Appeasement: Die Britische Antwort auf die Krise des Weltreichs und des internationalen Systems vor dem Zweiten Weltkrieg', *Historische Zeitschrift*, 226 (1978), p. 81.
25. Gilbert and Gott, *The Appeasers*, p. 118.
26. A. J. P. Taylor, *Beaverbrook* (London, 1972), p. 384.
27. Cited in D. C. Watt, *Personalities and Policies* (London, 1965), p. 165. This topic, too, has its host of historians these days: for the fullest treatment to date, see R. Ovendale, *'Appeasement' and the English Speaking World* (Cardiff, 1975).
28. See the details in the studies by Rock, Barnett, Gilbert and Gott, and Cowling.
29. N. Nicolson (ed.), *Harold Nicolson: Diaries and Letters, 1930–39* (London, 1969 edn), p. 353.
30. Shay, *British Rearmament in the Thirties*, p. 227.
31. D. N. Lammers, *Explaining Munich: the Search for Motive in British Policy* (Stanford, Ca., 1966), p. 20.
32. Cowling, *The Impact of Hitler*, pp. 271ff.
33 P. W. Schroeder, 'Munich and the British Tradition', *Historical Journal*, vol. 19 (1976), p. 242.
34. Shay, *British Rearmament in the Thirties*, p. 243.
35. C. A. MacDonald, 'Economic Appeasement and the German "Moderates" 1937–1939. An Introductory Essay', *Past and Present*, no. 56 (1972), p. 121.
36. Howard, *The Continental Commitment*, p. 129.
37. S. Woodburn Kirby, *The War against Japan*, 5 vols. (London, 1957–69), i, pp. 17–20.
38. Cited in Thompson, *The Anti-Appeasers*, p. 203.
39. Taylor, *Origins of the Second World War*, p. 253.
40. Gilbert and Gott, *The Appeasers*, p. 322. See also the new and very useful summary by L. Kettenacker, 'Die Diplomatie der Ohnmacht', in W. Benz and H. Graml (eds.), *Sommer 1939: Die Grossmächte und der Europäische Krieg* (Stuttgart, 1979), pp. 223–79.

Chapter 7

1. Quoted in Barnett, *The Collapse of British Power*, p. 587.
2. G. Kolko, *The Politics of War: Allied Diplomacy and the World Crisis of 1943-1945* (London, 1969), pp. 242-313 and *passim*.
3. I quote directly from the original Cabinet print in PRO, Cab. 129/1/04971, CP (45) 112.
4. *The Collected Essays, Journalism and Letters of George Orwell*, 4 vols., edited by S. Orwell and I. Angus (Harmondsworth, 1970 edn), ii, p. 117. See also the remarks made by Eden and others, in P. Addison, *The Road to 1945* (London. 1977 edn), p. 72.
5. Porter, *The Lion's Share*, p. 312.
6. A. F. Havighurst, *Britain in Transition* (Chicago/London, 1979), p. 502. See also the essay by D. Capitanchik, 'Public Opinion and Popular Attitudes towards Defence', in J. Baylis (ed.), *British Defence Policy in a Changing World* (London, 1977).
7. Peacock and Wiseman, *The Growth of Public Expenditure in the United Kingdom*, pp. 185-7.
8. I used the 1962 and 1972 figures in my *British Naval Mastery*, p. 342; the 1978 figures have been taken from the 1979 edition of *National Income and Expenditure* (London, 1979).
9. See, for example, *Sense about Defence: The Report of the Labour Party Defence Study Group* (London, 1977).
10. H. Pelling, *Britain and the Second World War* (London, 1970), p. 284.
11. Quoted in C. Thorne, *Allies of a Kind: The United States, Britain, and the War against Japan, 1941-1945* (Oxford/New York, 1979 edn), p. 105. Another very important book on this theme is W. R. Louis, *Imperialism at Bay: The United States and the Decolonization of the British Empire, 1941-1945* (New York/Oxford, 1978).
12. Quoted in Pelling, *op. cit.*, p. 285.
13. Cited in P. Darby, *British Defence Policy East of Suez, 1947-1968* (London, 1972), p. 1.
14. Quoted in Mansergh, *The Commonwealth Experience*, p. 353.

15. Beloff, *Imperial Sunset*, i, p. 7.

16. Kennedy, *British Naval Mastery*, p. 309.

17. *Ibid.*

18. J. Lukacs, *The Last European War* (New York, 1976), pp. 230ff.

19. Cited in M. Matloff, *Strategic Planning for Coalition Warfare, 1943–1944* (Washington, DC, 1959), pp. 523–4.

20. The 1952–72 figures are taken from *The Military Balance, 1973–1974* (London, 1973); for 1977 from *The Military Balance 1978–1979* (London, 1978). The problem of measuring real Soviet defence expenditure, or even the Soviet GNP, is one which Western analysts have wrestled with for decades, and their figures can only be understood as *approximations*.

21. *Statistical Abstract of the United States, 1978* (Washington, DC, 1978), p. 924. Both the Russian and the Chinese figures here are estimates.

Chapter 8

1. J. R. Leutze, *Bargaining for Supremacy: Anglo-American Naval Collaboration, 1937–1941* (Chapel Hill, NC, 1977), p. 252.

2. Quoted in Howard, *The Continental Commitment*, p. 135.

3. Idem., *The Mediterranean Strategy in the Second World War* (London, 1968), *passim*.

4. Cited in Pelling, *Britain and the Second World War*, p. 143.

5. Thorne, *Allies of a Kind*, p. 719.

6. J. Ehrman, *Grand Strategy*, vol. v (London, 1956), p. 442.

7. Pelling, *op. cit.*, p. 326.

8. Quoted in F. S. Northedge, *Descent from Power: British Foreign Policy, 1945–1973* (London, 1974), p. 70.

9. Porter, *The Lion's Share*, p. 328.

10. Apart from the accounts by Eden, Macmillan and Selwyn Lloyd themselves, see H. Thomas, *The Suez Affair* (Harmondsworth, Mddsx., 1970); A. Nutting, *No End of a Lesson* (London, 1967); L. Epstein, *British Politics in the Suez Crisis* (London, 1964).

11. Cited in Northedge, *Descent from Power*, p. 297.

12. Cited in Havighurst, *Britain in Transition*, p. 487.

13. Kennedy, *British Naval Mastery*, p. 183.

Bibliographical Guide

The following is not intended as a comprehensive bibliography, but merely as a guide to further general reading. It therefore excludes specialized monographs and articles, and omits studies which are not in the English language.

The student is now well served with histories of modern Europe. Apart from D. Thomson, *Europe since Napoleon* (Harmondsworth, 1966) and J. Joll, *Europe since 1870* (London, 1973), there is also G. Lichtheim, *Europe in the Twentieth Century* (London, 1972). R. Albrecht-Carrié, *A Diplomatic History of Europe since the Congress of Vienna* (London, 1965 edn) is precisely what its title suggests. A. J. P. Taylor, *The Struggle for Mastery in Europe, 1848–1918* (Oxford, 1954) is a stimulating account of a shorter period. G. Barraclough, *An Introduction to Contemporary History* (Harmondsworth, 1967), analyses the larger historical processes since 1890.

The Oxford History of England provides two standard accounts: R. C. K. Ensor, *England 1870–1914* (Oxford, 1936), now rather dated, and A. J. P. Taylor, *English History, 1914–1945* (Oxford, 1965), slightly irreverent, and always thought-provoking. R. Shannon, *The Crisis of Imperialism 1865–1915* (London, 1974) is an exceedingly sophisticated treatment of the earlier decades. C. L. Mowat, *Britain between the Wars 1918–1940* (London, 1968 edn) is impressively thorough. A. F. Havighurst, *Britain in Transition* (Chicago/London, 1979) – an expansion of his earlier *Twentieth-Century Britain* – is an admirable student textbook. R. Rhodes James, *The British Revolution: British Politics, 1880–1939*, 2 vols. (London, 1976–7) is a nice account of high politics but has little on the 'revolution'. A. Marwick, *Britain in the Century of Total War* (Harmondsworth, 1976 edn) provides some clues.

A number of general works upon British external policy – by Bourne, Lowe and Dockrill, Hayes, and Medlicott – were mentioned in the Foreword. To that list one should add Z. Steiner, *Britain and the Origins of the First World War*

(London, 1977), which is much wider than the title suggests; F. S. Northedge, *The Troubled Giant: Britain among the Great Powers, 1916–1939* (London, 1966); and F. S. Northedge, *Descent from Power: British Foreign Policy, 1945–1973* (London, 1974). A. J. P. Taylor's *The Origins of the Second World War* (Harmondsworth, 1963 edn) is controversial; the same author's *The Trouble Makers: Dissent over Foreign Policy, 1792–1939* (London, 1969 edn) is delightful.

There is no overall survey of British defence policy over the past century. C. Barnett, *Britain and Her Army 1509–1970* (London, 1970) is a good summary of that service's history; his later book, *The Collapse of British Power* (London, 1972), digs deeper and is more provoking. A. J. Marder, *The Anatomy of British Sea Power: British Naval Power, 1880–1905* (Hamden, Conn., reprint, 1964); the same author's *From the Dreadnought to Scapa Flow, 1904–1919*, 5 vols. (Oxford, 1961–70); and S. W. Roskill, *British Naval Policy between the Wars, 1919–1939*, 2 vols. (London, 1968–76), pretty well say all that is necessary about British naval policy. P. M. Kennedy, *The Rise and Fall of British Naval Mastery* (London/New York, 1976) is more interpretive – and speculative. M. Howard, *The Continental Commitment: the Dilemma of British Defence Policy in the Era of Two World Wars* (London, 1972) is a brilliant little book. C. J. Bartlett, *The Long Retreat: a Short History of British Defence policy, 1945–1970* (London, 1972) covers the post-1945 years.

R. Hyam, *Britain's Imperial Century, 1815–1914* (London, 1976) is a thorough survey of nineteenth-century imperial policy; B. Porter, *The Lion's Share: a Short History of British Imperialism 1850–1970* (London, 1975) is full of telling remarks; and N. Mansergh, *The Commonwealth Experience* (London, 1969) is the best book on the development of the Commonwealth. R. Robinson and J. A. Gallagher, with A. Denny, *Africa and the Victorians* (London, 1961) is a major reinterpretation of British imperialism. A. P. Thornton, *The Imperial Idea and its Enemies* (London, 1966) is an authoritative survey of the arguments for and against empire. M. Beloff, *Imperial Sunset*, vol. 1, *Britain's Liberal Empire 1897–1921* (London, 1969) is so full of insights and well-expressed summaries of complex events that this author, for one, had difficulty in maintaining a proper distance from it.

There are four good surveys of British economic history which have been repeatedly consulted for the present work: E. J. Hobsbawm, *Industry and Empire* (Harmondsworth, 1969); P. Mathias, *The First Industrial Nation: An Economic History of Britain, 1760–1914* (London, 1969); J. H. Clapham, *An Economic History of Modern Britain*, vols. 2 and 3, *1850–1914* (Cambridge, 1968 reprint); and S. Pollard, *The Development of the British Economy, 1914–1967* (London, 1969 edn). The basic statistical source is B. R. Mitchell and P. Deane, *Abstract of British Historical Statistics* (Cambridge, 1962). It can be supplemented by B. R. Mitchell, *European Historical Statistics, 1750–1970* (London, 1975); and A. T. Peacock and J. Wiseman, *The Growth of Public Expenditure in the United Kingdom* (London, 1967 edn).

Copyright Note

There are few quotations from original sources in a work of this nature, but I have cited from documents in the Public Record Office several times; those extracts appear by permission of Her Majesty's Stationery Office.

In the early chapters of this book I have also quoted directly from several private letters in the Balfour Papers (British Library), Bryce Papers (Bodleian Library), Clarendon Papers (Bodleian Library), Derby Papers (Liverpool Record Office), and Rosebery Papers (National Library of Scotland). These extracts also appear in my forthcoming study *The Rise of the Anglo-German Antagonism 1860–1914*, which at this moment of writing is at the printers; and I am pleased to repeat my thanks to the respective copyright-owners for permission to quote from those sources.

Index

(Note: the major themes of this book, such as the role of economic factors or of party politics, are detailed in the Contents, pages 7–9. What follows here is an index of places, people, events and institutions.)